DO
THE MEDIA
GOVERN?

DO THE MEDIA GOVERN?

Politicians, Voters, and Reporters in America

Shanto Iyengar
Richard Reeves
Editors

SAGE Publications
International Educational and Professional Publisher
Thousand Oaks London New Delhi

For information address:

 SAGE Publications, Inc.
2455 Teller Road
Thousand Oaks, California 91320
e-mail: order@sagepub.com

SAGE Publications Ltd.
6 Bonhill Street
London EC2A 4PU
United Kingdom

SAGE Publications India Pvt. Ltd.
M-32 Market
Greater Kailash I
New Delhi 110 048 India

Printed in the United States of America

Library of Congress Cataloging-in-Publication Data

Main entry under title:

Do the media govern?: Politicians, voters, and reporters in America /
    editors: Shanto Iyengar and Richard Reeves.
      p. cm.
    Includes bibliographical references and index.
    ISBN 0-8039-5605-3 (cloth: acid-free paper). — ISBN
  0-8039-5606-1 (pbk.: acid-free paper)
      1. Mass media—Political aspects—United States.   2. Press and
  politics—United States.   3. Journalism—Political aspects—United
  States.   I. Iyengar, Shanto.   II. Reeves, Richard.
  P95.82.U6D64 1997
  302.23'-0973—dc20   96-25362

This book is printed on acid-free paper.

97 98 99 00 01 10 9 8 7 6 5 4 3 2 1

Acquiring Editor:	Margaret Seawell
Editorial Assistant	Renée Piernot
Production Editor:	Astrid Virding
Production Assistant	Karen Wiley
Typesetter/Designer	Rebecca Evans
Cover Designer:	Candice Harman
Print Buyer:	Anna Chin

Contents

The Brave New World of Media Politics

RICHARD REEVES

Once upon a time in a land called Hollywood, in a movie titled *Dave*, I played the White House correspondent of the *New York Times*. With John Yang of the *Washington Post*, I stood for a couple of hours in the hot California sun waiting for the "president" and his "wife" (played by Kevin Klein and Sigourney Weaver) outside a full-scale replica of the White House.

The director of the film, Ivan Reitman, apparently feeling some sympathy for amateurs like us, came around to apologize for leaving us out here. Without looking at each other, Yang and I said, in concert, "Don't be ridiculous. This is what we do for a living."

Neither movies nor journalism are as glamorous as they seem. In my business, more often than not, we are captives of who and what we cover. When the president goes to Omaha, we go to Omaha. When the senator says something, we write it down. On the other hand, if no one in the press went, the president or the senator may decide it is not worth the trip without coverage. John F. Kennedy, a president who had worked as a reporter for the Hearst newspapers, understood that and much more about who uses who in the marriage between press and politics and governance. He was the first president who did not call reporters "the boys," in the manner of Franklin D. Roosevelt, who when he had something he wanted in the papers would tell an assistant to "Bring in the boys!"

The press, said Kennedy once, "is a valuable arm of the Presidency." We don't like that kind of talk—because it is usually true. He told his men that they should always remember that no matter how well they all got along with reporters, a time would come when all would go their separate ways. Kennedy played the press, with engaged and determined enthusiasm, as if it were a great theater organ, a mighty Wurlitzer. Writing of the White House in the early 1960s, Hugh Sidey, the designated "insider" of *Time* and *Life* magazines, said: "The White House doors were open. . . . A reporter could tour the offices of the intimates—Salinger, Sorensen, O'Donnell, O'Brien, Dungan, Goodwin, Feldman—and get precisely the same viewpoint from each man."

Many things have changed since then. Reporters are better educated, better paid, and, because of television, often more famous than the people they cover. The biggest changes, however, have been technological. Kennedy took office in a time of typewriters and carbon paper and flashbulbs. Television was a new medium and it was not very mobile. Politicians had to come to television studios if they wanted to be on the tube—and Kennedy would ignore the giant television cameras early on, still believing that the most important single medium in the country was *Time* magazine.

In fact, Kennedy's technological breakthrough in his 1960 campaign for the White House was to routinely use stenographers and banks of typists to provide transcripts of speeches and press conferences almost as soon as they ended—technically tempting reporters to stick to his words rather than their own. He was shameless in exploiting his family and children, using them to take over the slots newspapers usually reserved for photos of local kids and their puppies. That was all within the context of the bottom line, however: If reporters were good to him, he was good to them—if they were not, he sometimes tried to get them fired or at least reassigned. The following is a memo Kennedy dictated on September 5, 1961:

> Tell Fred Dutton to compose a letter to a fellow called Daniels at *Reader's Digest* (copy to the president of *Reader's Digest*) challenging his statistics in the September *Digest* on unemployment, that the program presented this year would cost the taxpayer 18 billion dollars annually in a few years. It is wholly untrue and we ought to make him eat it.

That was the way the game was played then. Carbon paper has been replaced by television satellites, however, changing what people know and when they know it. In fact, in the past two decades, presidents have lost their greatest power—the power to control the flow of information to the nation. Today, pretty much everybody finds out everything at the same time and in the same way—on Cable News Network (CNN) or some other channel out there in information world. At best, a modern president must function as the first explainer of events—and even then he must compete with any other American who can get in front of a camera. Whatever else it is, television is a great equalizer. Everyone is the same size on television—the president, the correspondent, or any citizen who seems at that moment to be making more sense than the man in the White House.

It is, in short, a brave new world. A symbol of the changeover is a story, probably apocryphal, that reporters like to tell about Bernard Kaib's first story as a CBS News correspondent after he left the *New York Times*. With camera and crew, he was waiting outside a closed door—just like in *Dave*—when Senator J. William Fulbright, then chairman of the Senate Foreign Affairs Committee, came out and said something or other about the war in Vietnam. "Wow!, that's a big story," Kalb is purported to have said, putting the microphone under his armpit and grabbing a notebook to write down what the senator was saying.

Moving ahead 30 years, I asked Vice President Albert Gore Jr., who was brought up in Washington, the son of a senator, what was the difference in the capital city he came back to (after working as a reporter in Nashville) as a congressman in 1977 and the one he came to with President Bill Clinton 15 years later. "The whole country is different," said Gore, "All these body blows to the sense of national well-being. The economic transformations. . . . The disorienting effect of all this electronic information."

I must have looked blank. "Do you know Prigogine's work?" he asked.

Ilya Prigogine is a Belgian scientist (Russian born) who won a Nobel Prize in 1977 for his work in thermodynamics. "If you look at a system with more and more energy and matter coming in, it will spontaneously reorganize itself into a more complicated system. Something different will come out, but what it is can't be predicted beforehand."

He drew a diagram, a pipeline leading into and out of an empty chamber. Washington is the chamber: more molecules, more matter, more energy, more heat, more information, new news cycles, new action-reaction-reaction-action—just more stuff, faster and faster. Pow! Something happens inside—Gore scrawls a new world in the chamber—and then something different comes out the other end, which in this case is America beyond the beltway. New men, new women, new media, new money, new information, new relationships, new sounds, new smells, and new laws.

Pow! A Money-Information Complex instead of the old Military-Industrial Complex. Public opinion rules. Polls on the hour. On the half-hour. Numbers make news. Money makes numbers. Three trillion dollars. Forty-eight percent. Polls are the new constituencies. Fame is money. Reporters get more of both than the people they cover. One man plus a fax becomes a majority. The city is separated from the nation by the electronic beltway.

Life speeded up and heated up in Prigogine's Washington in Gore's 20 years. The capital is information-driven now—and, luckily for reporters, that is our business. Decision making is high speed and interactive; analysis and adjustment is reactive and continuous. "News cycles," which not so long ago meant information produced to meet the needs of afternoon and morning newspapers and the evening news, exploded into approximately a million car radios stuck on "Scan."

"These changes," said Gore, "are not friendly to the linear debate envisioned by the Founding Fathers."

The checks and balances and cumbersome process devised in the 18th century to slow down governance are now like flags snapping under an out-of-control skier. It may sometimes seem to citizens that nothing is happening in Washington, but to the players there, too much is happening too quickly to be seen much less understood. For example, the old newspaper staple, the story behind the story, has been overtaken by the story before the story. When a couple of *Los Angeles Times* reporters, Bill Rempel and Doug Frantz, were in Little Rock in the fall of 1993 checking out a new round of rumors about Governor Clinton's sex life, a Republican congressman from California, Robert Dornan, went on Rush Limbaugh's program announcing that the paper was about to publish a story on the new allegations.

It is, simply, a great time to be a reporter—if you are at the top. In the middle ranges, however, journalists are losing freedom—the freedom to roam. There was a time at most newspapers and stations when reporters sitting around in the middle of the day would be asked why they were not out scaring up some news. Now, if they are not at their desks scanning the screen, they are asked where they have been and why. Why do you have to go out and talk to people, including senators and presidential advisers, when it is all on C-Span and the Internet?

Anthony Lake, Clinton's national security adviser, who began his advising in the Nixon White House, added the following: "When I first came here, if you wanted to know what a reporter really thought about the people and issues he covered you had to get drunk with him. Maybe a couple of times. Now I just turn on television to find out what they think."

When Lake was last in town, working for President Jimmy Carter in the 1970s, *New York Times* reporters were generally prohibited from appearing on television. Now the good, gray lady has a public relations agent trying to get her reporters on television shows, partly because the exposure makes those reporters more desirable as leaking partners for the chatterers on Lake's own staff and the information entrepreneurs at the other end of Pennsylvania Avenue.

I asked Lake's assistant, Sandy Berger, a question about the old days and the new. I brought up two names: Peter Peterson, the Wall Street wise man and former cabinet officer who is president of the Council on Foreign Relations in New York, and Thomas Friedman, the young *New York Times* reporter who had recently returned from overseas assignments to write about diplomatic and economic affairs in Washington. I asked Berger which of them was more important to the White House and to the making of American foreign policy?

Berger just laughed. The question was ridiculous. They have meetings regularly in the White House about what Friedman thinks or what he might do tomorrow. Some of the younger folks at those meetings probably have to be told who Peterson is—or was.

In the Clinton White House, the doors that stayed open in Kennedy's day are all closed, often because someone inside is giving his version of something that just happened to a favored and famous reporter. Imagine that, Mom!—here I am chatting with Bob Woodward or Johnny Apple, or talking to Cokie Roberts about what she said on *Nightline*. In the case of Woodward writing his book, *The Agenda*, on Clinton's economic decision making, the president told his people it was their duty to talk to the reporter, much as they would stand for the national anthem. The rich and famous of the press will be telling Bill and Hillary Clinton stories, laughing with the leakers long after this First Couple has a new address in Washington or Little Rock.

On one day I was in the Clinton White House talking to Tony Lake; he was in despair over the lead story on page 1 of the *New York Times*. "Top U.S. Officials Divided in Debate on Invading Haiti" read the headline over the byline of Elaine Sciolino, the paper's national security correspondent, who wrote,

> This division became evident, officials said, at a meeting of Clinton's top national security advisers on Tuesday at the White House. The meeting had been called to draw up recommendations for the President. Defense Secretary William J. Perry opposed . . . Deputy Secretary of State Strobe Talbott. . . . In a sharp exchange, Mr. Perry countered that Mr. Talbott represented a strange morality. He argued that it would be immoral for the United States not to do whatever it could to avoid the loss of lives of American soldiers and the expenditure of taxpayers' money.

The piece went on for 30 paragraphs, reporting arguments of and between "principals," as the highest officials call each other. There had been only eight people in the room on the ground floor of the White House and Sciolino got what they said exactly right, practically word-for-word—one or more of the eight principals had passed the recommendations on to the *Times* (and the world) before they got to the president.

"How? Why? Who?" Lake said. As the president and vice president searched for leakers in their very transparent White House, dialogue was becoming more and more distorted as the meetings were getting smaller and smaller and less and less was put in writing to try to stop the local information hemorrhages. "You lose expertise, you lose precision," said Lake. "People are afraid to speak their minds, or they say things precisely because they want them to be in tomorrow's *Washington Post*."

Clinton came to Washington persuaded that he could dominate or ignore the capital's gigantic press corps. He had, after all, faced down the national political press corps during his campaign in early 1992 when they had assumed he would quit the race for president in shame after tabloid revelations of his relationship in Little Rock with a woman named Gennifer Flowers— sometimes a television journalist, sometimes a nightclub singer. The boys and girls on the bus, pleased as puppies with themselves and their importance, flocked to New Hampshire to watch him do a Gary Hart, quit with a usable "mea culpa." Bill Clinton stood up there and told them to shove it. He appeared on *60 Minutes* to explain, much preferring public humiliation to private life.

After that appearance, candidate Clinton seemed to think that he could one day govern by appearing on *60 Minutes*, on *Larry King Live*, and on *Oprah*. Those folks, however, do not cover government and the White House: correspondents do—although with their own agenda. On March 24, 1994, President Clinton held a press conference in the evening, only the sixth of his first 14 months in office. "With the Congress beginning its Easter recess tomorrow, this is a good time to assess, the real work we are getting done," he began. It had been the kind of day that defines what it is like to be president. An Air Force transport had crashed at Pope Air Force Base in Texas killing 10 men. The leading candidate for president of Mexico had been assassinated. New statistics showed that 2 million new jobs had been created in the United States in 1993. He reviewed the progress of health care and welfare reform bills, a crime bill, and campaign reform legislation being debated in Congress. He stated,

> America's efforts have helped to bring much needed calm to Sarajevo and led to an important political accord between the Bosnian Muslims and Croats. . . . We'll continue our efforts to stop North Korea's nuclear program and to seek progress on human rights in China. This Friday, a week ahead of schedule, our troops will return home from Somalia.

"Terry?" he said, asking for the first question.

There were 21 questions: one on health care, 1 on American efforts to block the development of nuclear weapons in North Korea, 1 on the assassination of Luis Donaldo Colosio—and 18 on Whitewater, an old Arkansas real estate deal with scandal possibilities, and Clinton family finances.

In the new information world, geography or geographical representation obviously does not matter in the way it once did. Many of the self-created new politicians do not come from any place really. Yale, maybe, or Harvard or celebrity, but not from a town or a city in ever-changing districts—those are just places to pump in the information and to run from. They speak a new political language in which words and names and ideas have been replaced by numbers—poll numbers and dollars. That part of it Clinton got right away: Polls are his constituency. Returning to the White House from France in June 1994 after elaborately staged ceremonies commemorating the 50th anniversary of D day, Clinton looked at the numbers, banged his desk and said, "All that work and my approval rating went up just 1.5 percent. Can you believe it?"

Yes. This is poll-driven Washington, as described by an eminent practitioner, Peter Hart, who collects numbers for the Democratic party, such as it is, and for the president:

> The world of public opinion has come into great collision with the art of governance. In the old Washington there were two or three polls, principally Gallup and Harris, and each one took a couple of weeks to do, going door-to-door. And what private polling there was went to the President or the President's party. . . . Now, with new kinds of telephones and computers for tabulation, in a half-hour you can come back and say, "This is what the public thinks. . . ." And the polling is "spin numbers," that is "advocacy analysis," done by the parties, by associations, by corporations, who can use or release only the questions or answers that suit their narrow purposes, which often comes down to changing a number or a word in complex legislation that means someone or some interest gets a few million dollars or someone else does not. At the same time, the networks and the press are polling, because it is prestigious to have your own poll, like every hospital that wants Medivac helicopters.

"It is," Hart said in deliberate understatement, "difficult to put a long-range plan into effect in a world of short-term impressions."

That is all part of the electronic revolution seizing control of flow of information to the great democracy. The president and Rush Limbaugh, the *New York Times*, the *National Enquirer*, the CIA, the Pharmaceutical Manufacturers Association, Larry King, and you and I find out at the same time these days: All information is created equal. So, it seems, are all "surveys," all "faxes," all crimes, and all faces on television, whether it is the president declaring war or the soldier's wife who follows him saying her children need her husband at home rather than being shot at in Somalia or someplace.

As far as polls are concerned, Clinton stiffens at the word. Although his personal pollster, Stanley Greenberg, was being paid almost $2 million a year by the Democratic National Committee, for the President's eyes only, Clinton said

> I can tell you categorically that I do not use polls to decide what position to take. I have used polling information to try to make sure I understand exactly where the American people are, what they know, what they don't know. It's important to know how you're being perceived and what people think—where they're getting their information. But that can't affect the search for what's right for America.

Funny, there were those, some of them great friends of Bill's, who say that in his White House the polls (and focus groups) are the search for America. "Machines can't think, but they change the way people do," said Sandy Berger. Added Hart, "Clinton is a president who doesn't need new information or more information. He explores it all . . . [and] the effects are dramatic, short-term impulses, which means a constantly changing course."

The president's faith in survey research was such that the leader of Great Britain's Labour Party, Tony Blair, passed on this thought after a meeting in the White House: "I do remember something Clinton said, which is that there is no one more powerful in the world today than a member of a focus group. If you really want to change things and if you want to get listened to, that's where you want to be."

So that is what it has come to. The real shadow cabinet on both sides of the Atlantic are shifting groups of eight to twelve men and women paid to sit around a table responding to the questions and directions of a psychologist or pseudo-psychologist—with politicians and their spin-doctors watching and listening on the other side of a one-way mirror.

Of course, groups polls and all that are many-edged swords, as the president learned on May 27, 1993, when he agreed to appear live on CBS's *This Morning* show. The cameras were set up on the White House lawn with an audience of a few hundred tourists. An electronic town meeting. Rattling off a series of poll numbers, the host, Harry Smith, making $1 million a year—five times the salary of the president of the United States—turned to Clinton and said,

"I know you don't pay attention to this sort of stuff—polls. You never pay attention probably, right?"

The comedy over, Smith, with his straight man, the president, still at his side, turned to the crowd and said,

> The negatives are now higher than the positives in the polls. There's a feeling in the country and I think the people here reflect it. I think people in America want you to succeed, but I just want a raise of hands this morning—and don't be intimidated just because you're in the Rose Garden—do you feel like he could be doing a better job? Raise your hands if you think so. Don't be intimidated. Don't be intimidated. There's a lot of folks who feel that way. Do you feel like there's a gap between the promises of the campaign and the performance thus far? If you think so, raise your hands. A lot of folks feel that way. What went wrong?

On May 16, 1963, President Kennedy's national security adviser, McGeorge Bundy, wrote a memo to his boss, stating

> I hope you'll be in a good mood when you read this. . . . We do have a problem of management; centrally it is a problem of our use of time. We can't get you to sit still. . . . The National Security Council, for example, really cannot work for you unless you authorize work schedules that do not get upset from day to day. Calling three meetings in five days is foolish—and putting them off for six weeks at a time is just as bad. A couple of weeks ago, you asked me to begin to meet you [regularly in the morning]. I have succeeded in catching you on three mornings, for a total of about 8 minutes. Moreover 6 of the 8 minutes were an exercise in who leaked [to the newspapers] and why.

An extraordinary memo, I thought—one that took guts to send—prob-ably unique. In October and November of 1993, however, Secretary of State Warren Christopher, Defense Secretary Les Aspin, and National

Security Adviser Lake got together to send Clinton a series of memos almost pleading with the president to give them 1 hour a week to discuss international affairs. Clinton finally said, "Yes," scrawling at the bottom of the last memo, "When possible."

So, perhaps nothing is totally new at the White House. Franklin D. Roosevelt was there when Will Rogers wrote in his daily column in 1934: "They are just children that's never grown up. . . . Keep off the radio till you've got something to say. Stay off that back lawn with those photographers. Nothing will kill interest in a president quicker."

Bill Clinton told me a sad little story about himself and about being president in these times. I had asked him why he felt he had to be on television so much and he answered,

> The inference there is wrong—that I want to be on television every night. . . . Because President Reagan was shot, the press takes the position that they have an absolute right to be with me wherever I am spending the night, which means they want a picture of me running every day, which I think is wrong and bad and overexposes the President.

"Why can't you stop that?" I asked.

"Ask him," he said, nodding toward Mark Gearan, his communications director.

Clinton continued,

> You have to live in a prison. . . . Let me give you an example. I went to western Pennsylvania recently, and we had ten thousand people in a little town called—what was that called? Anyway, it was wonderful . . . for a health care rally. And I was fascinated because on the way in, it was two whole miles of nothing but auto body shops, muffler shops, auto repair shops, and car dealerships. I've never seen anything like it. And all these guys were out there, you know, not exactly my constituency. At any other time I would have stopped and had a visit with those people. You know, I couldn't stop and have a visit with those people because the entire press corps would have stopped, and if they could have gotten two people to say some-

thing bad, then that might have been the story on television that night instead of my going there to talk to ten thousand people. So I had to sit there like Buddha in chains.

He came back to it again, saying,

I would have really enjoyed talking to those guys at those places, and it would have helped me stay, I mean, in better touch with how they feel, it would have helped me a lot. But if my goal as president is to communicate with the American people, I would have run a very high risk that the message I wanted to send out to the people that night wouldn't get there.

PART I

Reporters, Reporting, and the Business of News

1 Overview

RICHARD REEVES

It was not so long ago that reporters were called "The Boys"—and that was not only because their craft was dominated by males. The name pegged them socially and economically. There were exceptions, of course, but most newspapermen were the same kind of men who became cops. Their lives were more interesting than most, but generally they were not particularly well educated, nor were they paid particularly well. In his first year as mayor of New York City, John V. Lindsay, a liberal Republican of patrician manner and Yale degrees, followed a Christmas tradition of giving reporters a bottle. His, however, were filled with red wine, a beverage many whiskey-generation regulars thought was served only in church.

I was the city hall bureau chief of the *New York Times* in those days. During one Lindsay press conference, I watched other reporters rough up His Honor with detailed questions about one municipal outrage after another. "I wonder what he thinks of this?" I asked the reporter next to me, Maurice C. Carroll—"Mickey" to friends and sources.

"He's thinking what he always thinks," said Carroll, "if you guys are so smart, how come you're not stockbrokers?"

That was the late 1960s and the times were changing, to say nothing of *The Times*. Television was turning correspondents into stars and then Watergate turned them into heroes, beginning with Bob Woodward and Carl Bernstein of the *Washington Post*, who became even better known as Robert Redford and Dustin Hoffman. The pay was getting better, too.

Television has enormously increased the reach—and income!—of Washington correspondents. "We all know how it works," said David Gergen, who certainly does. The counselor to presidents, magazine

3

editor, and television commentator put it this way: "You write something provocative enough to get on television, then you say something even more provocative on television and then you make the big money on lecture dates around the country."

For the "reporters" who are television regulars, the lectures alone can produce more income than a senator's salary. Also, the celebrity journalists among them are more often than not a good deal more famous than the people they cover—and there are no term limits for reporters. For example, Cokie Roberts makes more than $400,000 a year on speeches—tips in addition to her salaries from ABC News and National Public Radio and a syndicated column with her husband, Steven Roberts, of *U.S. News and World Report.*

Flying to a lecture date on USAir, I picked up the magazine in the seat pocket in front of me. *USAir Magazine* is published by a division of *The New York Times* and in that newspaper there was an advertisement promoting a feature called "Coming Home," in which "some of today's best-known personalities" write or are interviewed about where they come from or where they live now. Twelve of the 19 celebrities featured in the ad were journalists. The list was headed, alphabetically, by actors Lauren Bacall and Kenneth Branagh, followed by Art Buchwald, Katie Couric, Michael Kinsley, Jane Pauley, George Plimpton, Anna Quindlen, Cokie Roberts, Tim Russert, Diane Sawyer, Gloria Steinem, Gay Talese, and George Will.

Fame is a formidable weapon for a journalist. It is not hard to imagine the so-called "kids" in the Clinton White House—presidencies have always been driven by the sleepless energy of young overachievers—calling home to tell mom and dad, "You're not going to believe who I talked to today, Cokie Roberts!" When Bob Woodward let it be known that he wanted to write a book on the first year of the Clinton Presidency, the president himself told his assistants that they should give Woodward whatever he wanted—as if that were their patriotic duty.

Some of the rich and famous are entertainers playing at journalism, or journalists imitating entertainers, which creates a whole other set of problems for modern politicians like President Clinton—a modern man, sharing, more candid than truthful, who welcomed any chance to deal with media types other than the White House press corps.

Along with the rise of television, public opinion polls were making public officials and politicians less and less inclined to use the power people gave them. They understood that their business, getting elected, was not about making friends but about avoiding making enemies. If polls showed they were going to get in trouble by being decisive, they decided not to decide. The capital is information driven now—or driven crazy by instant information. Decision making is high speed and interactive; analysis and adjustment are reactive and continuous. For example, President Clinton's first shot in anger was to order a Tomahawk missile strike, from U.S. warships in the Persian Gulf, on the headquarters of Iraq's intelligence agency in Baghdad in retaliation, the president said, for a planned assassination of former President George Bush during a visit to Kuwait. Anxious to announce the strike live on the nightly news, Clinton was frustrated because he could not get information on whether the missiles hit their target. His counselor, David Gergen, finally suggested calling CNN rather than the CIA. At 6:30 p.m., Tom Johnson, the president of CNN, was able to tell the president of the United States that the Tomahawks had indeed hit their target. Then the commander in chief went live on CNN (and the three old networks) to announce the news to the people who had told him.

The president, any president, has lost one of the office's critical powers—control over the flow of information to the people of the United States. What the people know, and when they know it, is the engine of democracy. Once upon a time, the president had his hand near the throttle. No more. With direct satellite television transmission, all news all the time, people and leaders get their information at the same time in the same way. That makes it much tougher for presidents, but much more fun and profitable for people in the information business. No one calls them boys anymore.

The contributors whose views are represented in Part I include some of the most well-known and experienced political journalists and media analysts. We begin with excerpts from Lou Cannon's book, *Reporting: An Inside View*. Cannon, a *Washington Post* reporter (and a Californian) became Ronald Reagan's premier biographer as both governor of the Golden State and president. He began at the beginning, writing about how and why men and women become newspaper reporters and television correspondents. One of his subjects was the coeditor of this book.

Cannon's interviews with journalists provide insights into their career aspirations and decisions. Journalism professors David Weaver and Cleveland Willhoit administered two national surveys of working journalists to monitor changes in the profession. Their conclusions include (a) although women and minorities have made inroads, they are still underrepresented, (b) many journalists are dissatisfied with the career, and (c) adversarial reporting is frowned on by a majority.

The murder trial of football and television star O. J. Simpson may or may not have been "the trial of the century" as it was sometimes called, but it was the media event of the 1990s. Because of this, the *Los Angeles Times* assigned one of its most experienced and distinguished reporters, Bill Boyarsky, to write about the relationship among the press, print and television, and the actors in the real-life courtroom drama. Boyarsky's column ran as often as 5 days a week under the title "The Spin." The excerpts reprinted in this book focus on the media's constant preoccupation with itself, with its own comfort and facilities, with the convenience of easily understood information, and, finally, with the effect of massive media exposure on "ordinary" people elevated to instant celebrity.

Larry King Live on CNN emerged as an important political forum during the 1992 presidential election, so it was natural that when he vacationed, King asked prominent political figures to sit in for him. It was also natural that those politicians would choose to turn the tables on important journalists. In Part I, excerpts are presented from two shows in the spring of 1995, one with former Vice President Dan Quayle, a Republican, and the other with former Texas Governor Ann Richards, a Democrat, questioning Rita Braver, the White House correspondent of CBS News, Tim Russert, the Washington bureau chief of NBC News, syndicated columnist Charles Krauthammer, Dan Rather, the anchorman of CBS News, Cokie Roberts of ABC News, and Jane Pauley, host of NBC's *Dateline.*

The discussion on *Larry King Live,* not surprisingly, gravitated toward allegations of political bias and propaganda in the news. Richard Reeves points out that the alleged liberal bias in the press is often in the eye of the beholder and points to the successes of right-wing commentators and pundits in the 1980s and 1990s. The more pernicious bias, in his view, is one representing cultural and lifestyle values. The country's cultural elite—particularly those in the business of producing mass entertainment—are considerably more "liberal" than most middle-class voters. When members of this elite, such as the movie producer Oliver Stone, turn their attention to history and politics, what follows is often far from the facts.

The most famous examination of the lives and daily activities of political reporters was Timothy Crouse's (1974) book, *The Boys on the Bus*, published after the 1972 presidential campaign. Four of those boys got together at a conference sponsored by the Communications Studies Program at the University of California, Los Angeles, after the 1992 election and, sure enough, the discussion evolved into a relaxed (and biased) examination of the relationship between candidates and the reporters who follow them—or, what one of the participants, Robert Shogan of the *Los Angeles Times*, called "combat stories." The other participants were Thomas Oliphant of the *Boston Globe*, Richard Cohen of the *Washington Post*, and Richard Reeves, who had covered national campaigns for *The New York Times* and *New York Magazine.*

Putting the combat stories of Shogan and his friends in perspective, Professor Dan Hallin documents how reporters have come to be more like active interpreters of political campaigns than passive recorders of candidates' utterances and deeds on the campaign trail. Hallin's research shows that the candidate's typical appearance on network news—the sound bite—has shrunk dramatically in recent years. Rather than meeting the candidates firsthand, the news audience gets plenty of journalistic analysis and interpretation.

Journalism, it goes without saying, is big business. How does the constant drive for profitability shape reporting and news coverage? Ben Bagdikian, former managing editor of the *Washington Post* and former Dean of the school of journalism at the University of California, Berkeley, has some answers. Bagdikian argues that the free market does not guarantee a free flow of information. Far from it. Those with market power—such as large corporations that advertise extensively on network television—are able to silence or suppress views and perspectives contrary to their interests.

The growing corporate involvement in the world of news was also the subject of Ken Auletta's book *Three Blind Mice.* In a few hectic months of 1986, all three television networks were taken over by new owners, larger corporations with diverse interests and profit-driven managements— Capital Cities Communications bought ABC, General Electric bought RCA and its subsidiary, NBC, and Loew's Corporation assumed control of CBS. In his book, Auletta described what happened next, including the drive to turn money-losing news divisions into "profit centers."

As countries have become more and more economically interconnected, the demand for news cuts across national boundaries. Japanese
businessmen need to know about the latest developments in the U.S.
presidential campaign; American investors follow the political developments in China. Ted Turner's CNN was the first truly global news-
gathering organization. In "Raiding the Global Village," Auletta describes how Turner's success and the prospects of a worldwide audience
have lured other entrepreneurs into the news business.

Finally, Jeff Greenfield of ABC News offers his own inimitable perspective on what ails broadcast journalism. It has become fashionable to
blame television and the drive for ratings for virtually every social
problem facing America. Greenfield's analysis points to other more
plausible culprits.

2 The Socialization of Reporters

LOU CANNON

Benjamin C. Bradlee, the editor of the *Washington Post*, is fond of telling a story about the two young reporters who were hired by him on the same day. "They were both WASPs. They were both about twenty-seven years old. They had Ivy League educations. They both had non-newspaper experience between college and their beginning in journalism. Bob Woodward had been in the Navy and this other kid had been in the Peace Corps. They both had beaten *Washington Post* reporters in their beats and their clips were comparable, that's all I can say. And we hired both of them and Woodward went on to become Woodward and this other guy left three months later because he didn't have it. I've forgotten his name."

Bradlee can enumerate with ease the qualities he seeks in a reporter. He looks first for energy and says he is "depressed by the number of bright young people who don't have the desire to work the hard and long hours that I think the business requires." He looks for commitment to the news business and for people who take their work home with them. After that he looks for knowledge, ability, "people who know as much as possible about the fields they have been in," judgment and the quality of putting information in perspective.

This mystery about what makes a good reporter reflects the mystique of a craft which never has been able fully to explain the nature of its own business. We prize exactitude, but we are imprecise and often contradictory when it comes to defining what we do and why we do it. There is no general agreement on the nature of news. There is no agreement on whether reporting is a craft or trade, as I regard it, or a profession. There

EDITORS' NOTE: Reprinted from *Reporting: An Inside View*, published by California Journal, 2101 K Street, Sacramento, CA 95816. Used by permission of the author.

is not even agreement by those who consider newspapering a profession on what the professional requirements are or by those who consider it a trade on what would make it a profession. The requirements of reporting remain essentially as vague and mysterious as they were in 1922 when Walter Lippmann described the press as being "like the beam of a searchlight, bringing one episode and then another out of the darkness into vision."

Why are droves of people attracted to this craft with its long hours and (until recently) slender financial rewards? The number of aspiring journalists has vastly increased since Watergate, but there always have been more candidates for newspaper and broadcast jobs than there are jobs to fill. A plurality of the people whom I interviewed seem to have been impelled toward the news business by some parental influence. The father of one reporter was a salesman who wanted to write and won poetry contests sponsored by the *Cleveland Plain Dealer.* The father of another reporter was a Baltimore newspaperman before taking a government job which offered better pay and more security. The mother of another reporter is a Minnesota newspaperwoman. Haynes Johnson, a Pulitzer Prize winning reporter on the *Washington Post,* is the son of a Pulitzer Prize winning reporter.

But people also become reporters because they seek to have some social impact on the world. The desire to promote change was a motivation for reporters long before modern "advocacy journalism." I remember an editor nearly twenty years ago defending the excesses of a young reporter with the phrase, "Scratch a reporter and you'll find a reformer." This is one reason that the "crusading" reporter of the past and the "investigative" reporter of the present always have been treated warily by those who favor things as they are. "Reporters are frustrated reformers as television people are frustrated actors," says Jules Duscha. "They look upon themselves almost with reverence, like they are protecting the world against the forces of evil." Duscha, the son of a St. Paul salesman, became a reporter and worked in Minnesota, Illinois, and Washington. His boyhood heroes were William Allen White, editor of the *Emporia Gazette,* and George Seldes, the press critic.

The reforming impulse often combines with what Duscha calls "the attractions of the byline and of being in on things." Margot Hornblower, a metro cityside reporter on the Washington Post is the daughter of Edith Kermit Roosevelt, a newspaperwoman and conservative columnist.

Hornblower started her career at twenty on the *Charlottesville Daily Progress* where she wrote a story about citizen objections to the location of a country club which the publisher recently had joined. In the publisher's view the story gave too much emphasis to the opinions of the objectors. Hornblower was fired, but the publisher relented and hired her back. She has no apologies for the story which led to her temporary firing, but she looks on her break-in period at the *Daily Progress* with insight into her own motivations. Hornblower was covering Albermarle County at the time, and her chief reportorial targets were a county supervisor and a county executive who had a preference for doing public business in private. "I think it's good to start out on a small paper because as an aggressive young kid you get all the bile out of you. You work off all your prejudices," she says in retrospect. "Now, I wouldn't be as wound up in what I was reporting. Then, it got to be a personal crusade with me. It's a fine line. You should report things without getting emotionally involved. I think I felt myself to be in opposition to the supervisor and county executive who wanted to close everything. They felt I was on a vendetta." Hornblower's desire to reform the governing practices of Albermarle County combined with a reporter's customary delight at being able to see her work in print. She is married to an attorney and has observed that he must wait years to see the results of his own work. "On a newspaper there's the instant fix—your byline," she says. "You have the daily satisfaction of seeing something with your name on it. It's one of the reasons I'm a newspaper reporter rather than a book or magazine writer. We all change." Hornblower became a national correspondent for *Time* magazine.

Curiosity also is an impelling motivation for reporters. Perhaps it is the most important one. Bob Woodward of the *Washington Post* grew up in Wheaton, Illinois, where his father is a judge. "I was raised in a very small town and I think I learned there that everybody always has a secret," Woodward recalls. "The secrets would either come out in gossip or conversation or some cataclysmic event. I always found the secret life much more interesting than the public life people had and that's what I thought of investigative reporting as being. What are people's secrets? It was challenging to find out that there was much more conflict and turmoil than what was on the surface. I was attracted to that." Woodward graduated from Yale in 1965 with the avowed intention of going to law school. But he joined the Naval Reserve Training Corps, and his service was extended because of the Vietnam War. "I used to call it an eighteen-month Gulf of Tonkin resolution on me," says Woodward. "And I was very unhappy, restless, felt my brain might dry up and roll out my ear almost. It's a very stultified existence. I got out of the Navy in August of 1970 and planned on going to Harvard Law School that fall. But I'd always wanted to be a newspaper reporter, or at least try it. It seemed that all of the stereotypes were exciting. You make momentary entries into people's lives when they're interesting, and then you get out of their lives when they're not interesting, so you're doing interesting things. And I liked the upward mobility. It was easy to get to the top, or easier than the law. If you became a lawyer, you almost had to go through a period of indentured servitude."

Woodward had college classmates who were clerking for the Supreme Court or doing other important work, and he wanted to catch up with them. His attraction to reporting was heightened by the My Lai stories of Seymour Hersh, who then was operating as a free-lancer. "I thought, 'here's nobody and he can go in and do these stories,' " says Woodward. "It showed you would do something very rapidly and psychologically I felt terribly behind because I'd spent five years not doing anything." Woodward had completed his naval duty at the Pentagon, and he decided to apply for a job at the nearby *Washington Post*. As Woodward recalls it, he knocked on the door of Harry Rosenfeld, then the metro editor, and said he wanted to work at the *Post*. Rosenfeld asked him how much experience he had, and Woodward said he didn't have any. "You've got to be kidding, this is the *Washington Post*," was Rosenfeld's first response. But something about Woodward's manner or persistence impressed the editor. He decided to give Woodward a tryout, which he flunked. None of the fifteen stories which Woodward laboriously wrote in two weeks of day and night work made the paper. "I felt crushed, really crushed," says Woodward. "But there was something about the news room, something about working there, about being in the flow of things. I liked it." The *Post* editors helped Woodward find a job at the Montgomery *County Sentinel*, a nearby Maryland suburban paper. He worked there for a year and scooped the *Post* on a number of local government stories. He also was sued for libel. In September 1971 Woodward was hired by the *Washington Post*, where he made a big impression on editors from the beginning. "He was aggressive, skeptical and basically fair-minded, which is what I look for in a reporter," recalls

Barry Sussman, then the city editor. "If a reporter doesn't have all these attributes, he isn't any good. I also would like a person who can write if he has all these other qualities, but writing isn't high on my list. Woodward never could write and can't today. We managed to make his stuff read well enough so that its presentation didn't affect what was being told." When the burglars broke into Democratic headquarters on June 17, 1972, and launched the story that was to end with the fall of a President, Woodward already had several local investigative stories to his credit.

Reporting also satisfies a need in some people of explaining things to their fellow human beings. Fred W. Friendly, the accomplished former producer and news division director at CBS, compares this need with the need of comedians to make people laugh. "Journalists are not great scholars, most of them," he says. "Some are very bright but they don't have scholarly brightness. What they have is some kind of drive to explain. And maybe it comes out of the frustration of not being able to communicate as a young person."

The late Howard Simons, the most intellectual of the *Post* editors, believed that there are recognizable types of people attracted to all professions and crafts, including reporting. "Begin with the premise that lots of people who come into the newspaper business are somewhat hyperactive, somewhat creative and somewhat causists. I don't mean that in the contemporary sense of the word. I mean they have some sense, rooted in their stomach, of injustice which the newspaper gives them an instrument to correct. They also have a high capacity for psychic income, the byline, the being out with the big hitters, the being able to do things that are big for them as opposed to their roots. Lots of people at the *Post* come from the small towns in America. And reporters also have a high capacity for neuroticism, they have a high capacity for skepticism, they have all these things in different measure but they are similar things which bring them into the newspaper industry. I would guess that many of them are inherently pro-underdog, pro-citizen participation and anti-big business. Which leads me to the conclusion that when people talk about objectivity, I don't know what that means because there is no way I can squeeze out of any single editor or reporter at the *Washington Post* the inculcations of twenty to thirty years."

The attraction of journalism for people from small towns cited by Simons is an important one. Journalism in America always has been a pathway to the top for talented people who lacked money or the right connections. Unlike their colleagues in Great Britain, journalists in America are not automatically accorded second-class status. Journalism in the United States is an inter-class calling, and reporters are equally at home in the slum, the drawing room or the Oval Office. At least it looks that way to many young people growing up in the small towns of the South, the Middle West, and the West.

In 1947 Richard L. Harwood was twenty-two years old and a Marine veteran of some of the bloodiest fighting in the South Pacific. He was attending night courses at Peabody College in Nashville, Tennessee, when a reporter from the *Tennesseean* spoke to the class. Reporting struck Harwood as "a helluva life." He applied for a job on the *Tennesseean* and became a general assignment reporter at $27.50 a week. Harwood went to school at the same time and acquired a degree from Vanderbilt. "The *Tennessean* was a very interesting Southern paper at the time," he recalls. "It was a very liberal paper by the standards of the South. It also was an extremely partisan, unfair political paper. Our function in life was to elect to office the people that the publisher wanted elected. His great enemy was Boss Crump of Memphis, and we supported Estes Kefauver in his first campaign and Albert Gore and various candidates for governor that the publisher was interested in. This partisanship and this propaganda function that we served extended all the way down to city council races. At one point I was covering a candidate for the state legislature and I'd write a story about him and I'd write his speech and then I'd write an editorial about his speech. By the time I graduated from Vanderbilt in 1950, I was feeling very uncomfortable about that, and I didn't like the partisanship."

Harwood went job hunting and wound up in 1952 at the *Louisville Times* and quickly became an investigative reporter and the newspaper's top political reporter. "I absolutely loved the paper," he remembers. "It was fair, it was not partisan. We had a sense of integrity working for it. I loved Kentucky, and I loved Southern politics. I liked the oratory and the characters who came along." Harwood went to Washington for the Louisville paper and then to the *Washington Post*, where he became an award-winning reporter, ombudsman and three times the national editor. His early disgust with newspaper partisanship never left him, and he became known at the *Post* for his determination to keep ideology, personal causes, and stereotyped labels out of the news columns.

Some reporters seem attracted to journalism—or journalism to them—as by a magnet despite any preparation or display of conscious interest toward a journalistic career. Richard Reeves' preparation for a journalistic career, by his own account, was mostly negative. "I suppose I became a reporter because I always wanted to be a reporter but I didn't know I wanted to be a reporter," says Reeves. "I was an engineer and a lousy engineer." Reeves grew up in Jersey City and graduated from Stevens Institute of Technology in Hoboken. "I didn't know you could write for a living; nobody ever told me that," remembers Reeves. "I grew up in a poor neighborhood. My father was a struggling lawyer and there were no guidance counselors in the high school. I literally did not know you could go to college and read books, because that's what I would have wanted to do. I thought you had to go to college and learn how to do something like be a doctor or a lawyer."

Reeves had a friend whose uncle wanted to start a newspaper in Phillipsburg, New Jersey. He found the man in a deserted movie theater which the friend's uncle had just bought for $4,000 and they sat there in the empty theater talking about making it into the plant for a weekly paper. Reeves had not been successful as a designer of pumps, and the Ingersoll-Rand company had given him a battery of psychological tests and put him to work in the company's advertising department. Reeves worked days in the advertising department and nights on the newspaper he was helping to create.

The friend's uncle sold the ads. The paper was called the *Phillipsburg Free Press*, and Reeves learned about the newspaper business the hard way, the old way. He liked to do investigative stories that told about the town. One story he did was about a slumlord who owned a section of town with open gas heat and wooden plumbing. The slumlord turned out to be the Reeves family physician, and the Reeves family had to find another doctor. In another case Reeves went after a local politician who owned the garage which did work on the Reeves car. "They wouldn't work on my car any more after that," says Reeves. "Their kids wouldn't talk to my kids." This kind of journalism impressed other newspapers in New Jersey. The *Newark News* offered him a job in its Morristown bureau for $60 a week, a big cut from his salary as an engineer. He went from the *Newark News* to the *New York Herald-Tribune* and made a reputation as a political reporter. On April 23, 1966, the day the *Herald-Tribune* folded, Reeves was hired by the *New York Times*.

Reeves believes that many good reporters are introverts who are attracted to journalism because it gives them an institutional base to fulfill personal needs. "Most of us are terribly curious introverts and we need the institutional cloak," says Reeves. "I could go to a party and never say a word to anyone—I don't know how to begin a conversation. But if I say, 'Excuse me, I'm Dick Reeves of the *Times*,' that breaks the ice for me and I can deal with the situation. I've often wondered if that isn't a lot of what we're about."

Newspapers once were the beacon for the shy, curious small-town kid who wanted to make a name for himself. Now, television performs that function. In Harwood's generation of the 1940s a young man saw newspapers as the path to an exciting and productive life. In Tom Brokaw's generation of the 1960s newspapers seemed a pale alternative to broadcasting. Brokaw grew up in Yankton, South Dakota, a town with 12,000 people and two radio stations. One of the stations was small and poor and it hired Brokaw when he was a 15 year old high-school student. Brokaw played records and read the news. The radio station was in competition with a local newspaper and Brokaw liked the immediacy of radio in comparison with the paper, which carried the news the following afternoon. "More importantly," he remembers, "I didn't have any good newspaper models when I was growing up. The newspapers back there are mediocre to bad, whereas I could sit at home at night and watch Edward R. Murrow, Cronkite, Huntley-Brinkley. And they provided very good models for me. You'd pick up the newspaper and it was full of pretty pedestrian writing."

By the time Brokaw reached college he had accumulated enough experience to get a summer job at a commercial television station in Sioux City, Iowa, writing the news and doing booth announcing and commercials. It financed his last two years of college and gave him exposure to television. After obtaining a degree in political science at the University of South Dakota, Brokaw went to Omaha as the morning news editor with KMTV. He went from there to WSV in Atlanta where he became the night news editor and covered civil rights stories for NBC on a holding basis until the network could get a correspondent to the scene. NBC hired him full-time in 1966 and sent him to Los Angeles, where Brokaw became known as a bright and well-prepared interviewer, particularly on political subjects.

Television's record at providing job opportunities for women, and for various minorities, is better than that of most newspapers. Ann Compton, now an ABC White House correspondent, was a drama major who became interested in television as a college senior and interned for WDBJ in Roanoke, Virginia. "It was helpful to be a girl," she recalls. "I was riding the crest of the women's wave and I've made the most out of it. I had a voice that was all right, willingness to work, energy. And there weren't that many women around. Still, the whole business of getting into television was haphazard and becoming a political correspondent was more haphazard still. I lived closest to the airport and I was the junior member of the staff, so overtime costs for me were least. There was a candidate for governor that year (Democrat Bill Battle) who had a penchant for holding morning press conferences at the airport. They sent me. Then, to balance it, they sent me to (Republican candidate) Lin Holton's press conferences, too. The whole haphazard business was typical of too much of television reporting. We learned on the job. Eric Sevareid said we learned at the expense of the audience."

And so have we all, whether we are reporters for newspapers or reporters for radio and television stations. The reasons we became reporters are many and diverse, although I would agree with Howard Simons that the news business is populated with certain recognizable personality types. Perhaps what we all share in common is the characteristic identified by my friend and colleague at the *Washington Post*, David S. Broder, who has developed a stock response when young people ask him why he became a reporter. "It is a somewhat facetious answer but only somewhat," Broder says. "We like to watch, and we like to watch close-up and see what people are doing. I think the essential lure is that we're voyeurs."

3 The American Journalist in the 1990s

DAVID H. WEAVER
G. CLEVELAND WILHOIT

The professionalism of American journalism continues to be debated in these times of great change in the world. In the past decade, as never before, the news and the journalists who produce it increasingly have become center stage in American life. The "professional spirit" of journalists detected in Frank Luther Mott's classic history of American journalism, and in the ideas of Pulitzer and the founders of the first schools of journalism, has not been forgotten but has never been fully developed, as documented in the 1971 national study of U.S. journalists by Johnstone and colleagues, and by our 1982-1983 follow-up study.

More than a decade has passed since the data were collected for our study of U.S. journalists in 1982-1983, which resulted in *The American Journalist*—a book that has been widely cited and used. During this time, great changes have occurred in journalism and in the larger society. Even more dramatic changes have occurred since the 1971 benchmark study. These changes include the wholesale adoption of new technologies that have changed not only the speed of transmission of news but also its nature.

What of American journalists? Have they, too, changed dramatically in the past decade? As the following findings from our new book, *The American Journalist in the 1990s*, will suggest, the answer is both yes and no but mostly no. The past decade has been one of some change, and some progress, among mainstream American journalists, but it has also been a period of little growth in overall numbers and limited change in the representation of women and minorities.

The findings that we report here come from 45-minute telephone interviews with 1,410 U.S. journalists working for a wide variety of daily and weekly newspapers, radio and television stations, and news services and magazines throughout the United States. These interviews were conducted by telephone from June 12 to September 12, 1992, by trained interviewers at the Center for Survey Research at Indiana University's Bloomington campus. Journalists in the main probability sample of 1,156 were chosen randomly from news organizations that were also selected at random from listings in various directories.

General Characteristics of Journalists

Our first finding was that there has been very little growth in the number of full-time journalists in the past decade compared with the previous one. In fact, slightly less than 10,000 more full-time journalists worked for mainstream news media in the United States in 1992 compared with 1982, a growth rate of just under 9%—compared with a growth of 42,572 full-time journalists between 1971 and 1982, or a 61% increase. In terms of overall growth, then, the past decade has been one of very little change for American journalists.

Who are these journalists in 1992? As in 1982, it is difficult to talk in general terms about the "typical" U.S. journalist because there are more than 122,000 of them. It may be derived from our 1992 national survey that the typical U.S. journalist is a white Protestant male who has a bachelor's degree from a public college, is married, 36 years old, earns about $31,000 a year, has worked in journalism about 12 years, does not belong to a journalism association, and works for a medium-sized (42 journalists) group-owned daily newspaper. Such a picture, however, is inadequate because there are substantial numbers of women, non-whites, non-Protestants, single, young and old, and relatively rich and poor journalists working in this country for a wide variety of small and large news media, both group and singly owned.

Many of these journalists differ from this profile of the typical journalist. For example, black and Asian journalists are more likely to be women than men, not to be married, to have higher incomes ($37,000-$42,000) than the typical journalist, to have worked in journalism 10 or 11 years, to be members of at least one journalism association, and to work for larger (100-150 journalists) daily newspapers.

Hispanic journalists are more likely to be Catholic than Protestant and to be more similar to blacks and Asians than to the "typical" U.S. journalist with regard to other characteristics. Native American journalists are more likely to be of some other religion besides Protestant or Catholic, to make much less than the other groups (median income of $22,000), and to work for very small newspapers or television stations (three or four journalists).

Women journalists in general are likely to have worked in journalism 3 years less than men, to have somewhat lower incomes (about $27,000 a year), to be about a year younger than men, not to be married, and to be much more likely to identify with the Democratic Party than men.

How do the journalists of today compare with those of 10 or 20 years ago? To begin, the median, or middle, age of U.S. journalists is examined. It has risen to 36 years old, about where it was in 1971, from a drop to almost 32 in 1982. In general, then, American journalists are getting older on the average, or they are returning to where they were 20 years ago, before the massive hiring of young people during the 1970s. This is especially true for print journalists, whose median age is 37, compared to broadcast journalists, whose median age is only 32.

This aging of American journalists is more dramatically illustrated by looking at some proportions in each age group. Those under 24 years old have shrunk to only about 4% of all journalists, down dramatically from nearly 12% in both 1971 and 1982 mainly because of the small growth in number of new jobs during the 1980s. The 55- to 64-year-old group has continued to decline since 1971, suggesting relatively fewer "elders" in American journalism today compared with the early 1970s. Whether that will change much in the next decade as many of those in the large 35- to 54-year-old group exceed age 55 depends on how many stay in journalism. We do know from our survey that 21% of all journalists say they would like to be working outside the news media in 5 years compared to 11% in 1982-1983 and only 7% in 1971.

One thing that has not changed much in American journalism, to our surprise, is the percentage of women working for all different news media combined. Despite rapidly increasing enrollments of women in U.S. journalism schools during the 1980s, and the emphasis on hiring women since the late 1970s, the overall percentage of women has remained virtually unchanged at 34%. When those journalists with less than 5 years experience are considered, it is clear that the percentage of women is much higher (about 45%). Because the growth rate in American journalism has been so small during the past decade and because there are far fewer women than men with 15 years or more experience, however, these increased percentages of women hired during the past decade have not changed the overall percentage of women in American journalism from 1982 to 1992. It appears that women have been successful in rising within the ranks of their organizations because 42% of them say they have some supervisory responsibility for news and editorial staff, a figure that is identical to that for their male colleagues. We think these findings show that editors and news directors have been successful in hiring and promoting more women during the 1980s, but this success has not been reflected in the overall proportions of women.

Of course, the percentage of women journalists varies tremendously by medium, from about one fourth in the wire services and television to nearly one half in weekly newspapers and news magazines. Obviously, some news media have done better than others in hiring women. The proportion of women journalists also varies considerably by race, with all minority groups (especially Asians, blacks, and Hispanics) represented by more women than the white majority group. This suggests that increased emphasis on hiring minority journalists is likely to increase the representation of women at the same time.

Although minority journalists can boast significantly higher percentages of women journalists than their white counterparts, it is clear that the proportion of minorities in American journalism is still not equal to their proportion in the overall population. There has been some increase during the past decade, but the 8.2% for 1992 still lags far behind the 24% estimated by the 1990 U.S. census.

As with women, some media have done better than others in recruiting full-time minority journalists, most notably radio and television, and some have done much worse. It is fairly certain that the very low percentage of minorities working on weekly newspapers reflects the fact that most minorities live in larger urban areas, but the same cannot be said for news magazines and wire services.

In 1992, black Americans were the most numerous minority journalists, whereas Native Americans were the least common. When these percentages are projected to the total population of full-time mainstream news media, we estimate about 4,500 black journalists, 2,700 Hispanic journalists, 1,200 Asians, and only 730 Native Americans. It should be remembered that because these projections do not include special interest or ethnic media or any non-news magazines, they are very conservative numbers.

There has been a notable change in the political party preference of journalists, with more of them identifying themselves as Democrats and slightly fewer saying they are Republicans. The proportion calling themselves independents has also dropped slightly. When compared to the overall U.S. population, journalists are 5 to 10 percentage points more likely to say they are Democrats and 10 to 15 percentage points less likely to say they are Republicans. The percentage of journalists claiming to be independents is very close to the overall population percentage.

The increase in journalists identifying with the Democratic Party comes partially from the increase in minorities in U.S. journalism. In general, minorities, especially blacks (70%), Asians (63%), and Hispanics (59%), are much more likely to call themselves Democrats than are white journalists. There is also a wide gender gap for political party identification, with women journalists (58%) being much more likely than men (38%) to prefer the Democratic Party. Men are the most likely (40%) of all groups to say they are independents.

Educational Backgrounds of Journalists

The percentage of U.S. journalists with at least a college bachelor's degree continues to increase, especially among journalists working for news magazines and wire services. It is clear that the bachelor's degree has become the minimum qualification necessary for practicing journalism in all media, even radio, which has about the same percentage of college graduates now as existed in U.S. journalism overall in 1971.

The college degree with a major in journalism, however, is still not held by a majority of U.S. full-time journalists despite the large numbers of journalism school students graduating in the 1980s. In fact, there has been no change overall in the percentage of college graduates who majored in journalism during the past decade probably because of the very slow growth in the number of mainstream journalism jobs and the aging of journalists. When those who majored, minored, or took college classes in journalism are summed, however, the percentage rises from

39.4 to 62.3—nearly two thirds who have been exposed to journalism education in college.

Only in daily newspapers is the journalism degree becoming almost the norm. Wire services and weekly newspapers are not far behind. Radio, television, and news magazine journalists, however, are far less likely to hold journalism degrees, which may partly account for why they often seem to be the most critical of journalism education.

Working Conditions of Journalists

One of the most important working conditions is, of course, salary. Our findings indicate that the median income of full-time journalists has increased from $19,000 in 1981 (the year just before our 1982-1983 study) to $31,297 in 1991. This is less than income estimates for other somewhat comparable occupational groups such as internal auditors and accountants. A decline in the rate of inflation during the past decade enabled the increase in journalists' incomes to exceed the rise in the Consumer Price Index. This progress in salary, however, did not restore journalists' relative buying power to its level in the late 1960s.

One of the encouraging findings in our 1982-1983 study was that the salary gap between men and women had decreased somewhat since 1970. From 1981 to 1991, that gap decreased even more than in the previous decade. Overall median salaries for women are now 81% of those for men compared to 64% in 1970.

When years of experience in journalism is considered, the gender gap in income nearly disappears. There is a notable gap among journalists of 10 to 14 years experience. Although we have no ready explanation for that difference, it is true that women with 4 years or less experience tend to work for slightly smaller news organizations than do men, helping to explain the small salary gap for the most recently hired journalists.

Considerable differences in salary are found in the various news media. Journalists at news magazines and the wire services earn the most, and those at radio stations and weekly newspapers earn the least. Not surprisingly, those at the largest organizations and those with the most experience tend to make the highest salaries.

Traditionally, journalists—despite considerable concern about pay scales—have ranked high on job satisfaction. That appears to be changing. Only 27% say they are very satisfied with their job compared to almost half saying that 20 years ago. A majority in 1991 are at least fairly satisfied, but the overall decline in job happiness is considerable, with black and Asian journalists being the least likely to say they are very satisfied. The profile is somewhat less favorable than the picture of job attitudes for some other professions, such as college professors.

One of the most significant predictors of job satisfaction is the extent to which journalists see their organization as informing their audience. There is a slight change in that estimate, with fewer journalists saying now that their newsroom is doing an outstanding job of informing the public, especially blacks and Asians. The reasons for this range from low quality of staff (being complacent or not aggressive enough) to limited resources.

The general picture, however, suggests most journalists do rate their organization as good or very good on informing the public. Those who are most positive are journalists for wire services, who cite high quality of editors and staff and speed of news coverage. The least favorable ratings on informing the public are from television journalists, who mention small size of staff and limited resources.

A majority (68%) of journalists now say the editorial policies of their organization are very important in how they rate their job, an increase of 10 percentage points from the previous decade. Journalists in the print media are more likely to say editorial policies are important than are their colleagues in the broadcast media, and Native Americans are much more likely to say that editorial policies are very important.

The chance to help people remains a very important aspect of news work for a majority (61%), but altruism is somewhat more apt to be cited by journalists, especially by minority journalists, in broadcasting and on weekly newspapers than in other media. Job security (61%) and the extent of their autonomy (52%) also are very important in how journalists rate their jobs. As in the past, however, fringe benefits and pay are much less likely than other factors to be cited as very important to rating a job in journalism.

Our previous study suggested that the number of journalists who planned to leave the field had increased, and that disgruntlement tended to be most visible among the more experienced and altruistic persons. The trend continues in the 1990s because 21% of the sample—almost double that of the 1981-1982 sample—say they plan to leave the field during the next 5 years mainly because of limited pay and the need for a change or a new challenge. Asian journalists are least likely (11%) to say they plan to leave journalism, and Native Americans are most likely (29%) to say they plan to leave.

The journalists in our sample were asked various questions about the importance of various possible roles of the news media. For the most part, the perceptions of journalistic role are broadly similar to those a decade ago. Journalists tend to see their responsibilities as pluralistic, with wide majorities agreeing that there is at least some importance for roles as disparate as surveillance and entertainment. Here, we focus on assessing which roles are seen as most important.

Two journalistic responsibilities are seen as extremely important by a majority: getting information to the public quickly (69%) and investigating government claims (67%). There is no significant difference by race or gender on these journalistic roles, except that Native Americans are much less concerned about getting information to the public quickly.

Compared to a decade ago, journalists are somewhat more likely to rank their role in providing information quickly as extremely important. Television and wire service journalists are much more likely to rank the information function higher than are persons in other media. Investigating the claims of government, which dropped in salience in the early 1980s, is unchanged in relative importance and is ranked about the same by staff in all media except radio. Journalists working for radio stations are much less likely to see this as a responsibility.

The analytical function of news media—providing analysis of complex problems—also remains about the same, with 48% saying it is extremely important. Journalists for the news magazines and daily newspapers are much more likely than news workers in other media to see analysis of complex problems as highly salient. Asian and black journalists are also more likely to rate this role as extremely important.

Amidst the post-Watergate climate of our previous study, the question of journalists' perceptions of the importance of an aggressive stance toward government was of particular interest. We found the adversarial role was considered less salient in the minds of journalists in 1982 and 1983 than many critics expected. Similar results were found in the 1992 survey. Only a small minority of journalists see the adversary role—directed at either government or business—as extremely important. Print journalists, in general, are more likely to be adversarial than are their broadcast colleagues.

In the most recent study, a new question attempts to assess journalistic initiative in setting the political agenda, a topic that has received much attention during the past decade. Few journalists see their role in these terms, with only 4% ranking it extremely important and 41% rejecting it entirely. Three of the four minority groups (blacks, Hispanics, and Native Americans), however, were more likely to say this is an extremely important role. Even among these groups, however, only about 10% view setting the political agenda as extremely important.

As some prominent journalists join the critics in claiming that mainstream journalists are sometimes guilty of yielding too easily to the marketing values on the business side, our findings on the perceptions of the importance of entertainment are interesting. Fewer journalists now than a decade ago—especially among those in broadcasting—are willing to admit that entertainment is important to news organizations.

One of the most significant aspects of contemporary public debate about mainstream news media is the questioning of the ethics of various reporting practices. This is an especially troublesome area for survey research because of the difficulty of asking a respondent to evaluate a reporting tactic that is removed from the context of a news story on which it depends. Our study asks journalists to consider nine practices individually and to state whether they may be justified on occasion or whether these practices would not be approved under any circumstance.

The results suggest a slight decline in the number of journalists saying undercover reporting may be justified but show a substantial increase in the tolerance of using unauthorized business and government documents. The change in the willingness of journalists to envision a circumstance for using confidential documents probably reflects a greater awareness of problems of government secrecy and the difficulty of access to computerized databases. There is a similar pattern, however, regarding the use of personal documents and letters without permission. There is a significant decline in the willingness to pay sources for information.

We also queried journalists about some recent reporting practices that have been widely debated. Not surprisingly, it is television journalists who are much more likely to justify using hidden microphones or cameras. The use of re-creations or dramatizations is tolerated by a minority, again with broadcast journalists being more likely to tolerate these techniques.

Conclusions

The substantial growth in numbers of journalists working for the media that characterized the 1970s has stalled. Despite this, media organizations appear to have made some progress in attracting minorities. A minority workforce of 8%, up from 4% in our 1982-1983 study, by no means indicates sufficient diversity in American newsrooms, but it is in the right direction.

Stalled growth in media employment appears to have affected the representation of women, because they constitute the same percentage of the workforce (34%) as they did a decade ago. We suspect the problem is one of retention, as well as very limited growth in new jobs, because there is evidence of greater parity of representation of men and women at the entry levels of journalism.

The median age of journalists, now 36, has risen and is about the same as it was before the rapid influx of large numbers of young, entry-level employees in the 1970s. Professional identity appears to have declined, however, with a smaller minority of the workforce belonging to journalism organizations than in 1982-1983.

A serious problem of retention may be just over the horizon. More than 20% of those surveyed said they plan to leave the field within 5 years, double the figure of 1982-1983. This is tied to a significant decline in job satisfaction, with complaints about pay and the need for a different challenge being the major reasons for plans to leave.

Overall differences in ideas about journalistic roles and reporting practices, although not great overall, seem to be related more strongly to working for a particular medium than was the case a decade ago. In addition, in the 1992 results, gender and racial differences appear to account for many fewer differences than do the types of news media for which journalists work.

Changes in media audiences appear to be reflected in a perception among journalists that reaching the largest number of people in the audience is not as important as it was a decade ago. Speed in getting the news to the public—likely a reflection of new technology's capacity for immediacy—has become more salient. Investigating government claims remains a high value. On the other hand, there is a tendency to downplay entertainment as an important aspect of the news.

Although recognizing the importance of the adversary role, journalists do not see it as their highest responsibility. In fact, there is evidence that journalists display considerable caution about playing an activist role in their news work. The idea of setting the policy agenda of the nation and their communities is not one they see as very salient to their job as journalists. On the other hand, there seems to be recognition that some aggressive reporting practices may be more acceptable in an environment of government secrecy and the ease with which access to information is affected by computerized databases.

4 Covering the O. J. Trial

BILL BOYARSKY

"Media Monster Feeds on One of Its Own" (*Los Angeles Times*, 9/24/1994)

The O. J. Simpson trial media machine turned on one of its own Friday, treating KNBC reporter Tracie Savage as if she were just another celebrity in a jam. Savage had reported that a pair of blood-marked socks from Simpson's bedroom had been subjected to DNA tests at Maryland laboratory. The tests, according to Savage, indicated that Nicole Brown Simpson was the source of the blood.

For the second consecutive day, Superior Court Judge Lance A. Ito assailed the station, saying that even though the story was erroneous, the station ran it again Thursday, and "they embellished it." He threatened to ban KNBC from the courthouse and to limit other television coverage of Simpson's murder trial.

Within moments, Savage had also become the quarry for the cameras.

Then came the questions from reporters polite because she was a colleague but pointed nevertheless.

As the questions kept coming, Savage's phone rang. It was her bosses, who told her to stop talking. "I don't want to be any more of a story than I am," Savage told the reporters, echoing the wishes of countless men and women who have unexpectedly found themselves in the news.

Reporters get tips and leaks all the time, some of them sound so good, and the sources so reliable, that the reporter has a feeling in the gut that this is the real thing.

EDITORS' NOTE: Reprinted with permission of the author.

Sensing the kill, the reporter checks more sources. Editors demand even more checks. Often during this process, often at the very end, the reporter realizes he or she lacks the essential confirmation needed to run the story. In fact, this happens most of the time. Reporters and editors are supposed to err on the side of caution. We're taught that it's better to be beaten by the competition than to be wrong.

Being wrong is the worst thing a journalist can do.

But in the Simpson murder case, this hardy rule is being forgotten. For competition drives the media monster, a mindless drive to be first. Competition makes the media monster constantly hungry for more news, good or bad, true or false. It's like a Pac-Man, gobbling everything in its path.

Friday, the monster, while looking for a fresh meal, came across Tracie Savage, who became a victim of something she helped create.

"The Press Just Has to Take It Sitting Down" (*Los Angeles Times*, 5/8/1995)

There's not a bad seat in Judge Lance A. Ito's little theater of criminal justice. But when the judge shifted reporter's seating around, Friday, you'd think some of them had been consigned to the last row of the Forum.

It was the first time the judge had rearranged press seating since the O. J. Simpson murder trial began three months ago. Some journalists moved forward, and others toward the rear of a courtroom that has only four rows.

Outrage exploded before court began Friday morning when reporters lined up in a dingy Criminal Courts Building hallway. One journalist after another protested the arrangements to Jerrianne Hayslett, Judge Ito's press aide. "Outrageous!" "A slap in the face!" Those were among the milder comments.

The anger had been brewing since the trial began and Judge Ito had relegated the *Los Angeles Times* and the *Daily News* of Los Angeles to back rows while putting book authors Dominick Dunne and Joe McGinnis in the front row. The legal newspaper, the *Daily Journal*, didn't even get a full time seat. Nor did *La Opinion*, which serves the Spanish-speaking community.

In the new arrangements, authors Dunne and McGinnis retained their front row seats. Worse yet, in the mind of the daily reporters, two other book authors, Joe Bosco and Jeffrey Toobin, were moved up to the first row. The daily press was furious.

This was annoying since neither man was around Friday, both having gone home to visit their families, Toobin to New York and Bosco to New Orleans, and their seat was being occupied by a representative of the *National Enquirer.*

The Bosco move was especially rankling to the reporters, since he has written about his press corps pals for *Penthouse* in an article some of the reporters considered a stab in the back.

Even worse, Ito had displaced City News Service and its popular reporter, Shoreen Maghame, to make room for the Bosco-Toobin combine. And the reporters turned up what they said were serious errors in the court's attendance report.

By day's end Friday, Ito had modified his stern decree. He moved CNS's Maghame back to Row 1. Toobin and Bosco are in the second row.

If the press doesn't like the arrangements, Ito said, he'll switch to a first-come, first-served basis. Or a lottery, with the press competing for seats with the public.

From this account, you can see it's not easy to get along with the press.

We can't help this behavior. It's part of the compulsiveness that makes for a good reporter.

We go crazy at anything we think interferes with getting the story out. That's why the worst job on a presidential campaign is being in charge of media accommodations. Reporters lose their tempers when a phone jack doesn't work, or their hotel room isn't ready the moment the campaign party checks in. No sensible person wants to handle press arrangements, judge. Let someone else do the job. It's a quagmire.

"For Some 15 Minutes of Fame Is Agony"
(*Los Angeles Times*, 4/27/1995)

Andrea Mazzola probably would not have been called to the witness stand in the usual murder trial.

She's a rookie criminologist, a Los Angeles Police Department crime lab employee for just over a year. In a normal case, even the most relentless defense attorneys don't dig that deep for errors. It's the boss, not the assistant, who gets grilled.

But because this is the O. J. Simpson trial, defense attorney Peter Neufield has subjected Mazzola to a painfully brutal cross-examination, trying to turn up a mistake that would help prove Simpson not guilty.

Watching the grilling, I was reminded of all the obscure people who have faced high-pressure media scrutiny in the Simpson trial.

Mazzola, of course, lets herself in for this punishment when she went to work for the Police Department. Still, I know this could happen to anyone, anytime. I can't count the times I've interviewed men and women unwillingly thrust into the spotlight through no fault, or wish, of their own.

The thought of such an experience terrifies most people. It certainly was a nervous time for the reserved 34-year-old who studied forensic science in the comparative calm of the California State Sacramento campus and ended up in the merciless limelight of the Simpson trial.

For journalists and analysts, examining the performance of someone unused to public scrutiny is a difficult challenge, especially if the judgments are based on television. For the TV camera may give an inaccurate or incomplete picture of someone who hasn't learned to perform.

I discussed this with a veteran television anchor and reporter, Warren Olney.

"When you cover some event where people find themselves suddenly and by surprise required to perform on television, you get this very odd mixture of artificial effort to do what they think is right, and at the same time behave in the way they normally would," he said. "There is a sort of dissonance. They are pulled in two directions at the same time."

You can't say the camera never lies, Olney said. "Everyone in television knows that the picture that goes out on the tube is really a distorted image of what the situation was. You use different angles. In the courtroom, you don't see the rest of the room, you don't see the jury. You don't see the lawyers sometimes. You are looking through this little slot. It is like peeping through a peephole and you don't really have an idea of the whole context."

Mazzola survived.

But other novice celebrities may not do as well. They may look nervous. Their eyes may shift and their voiced quaver. Just remember, nerves may mean nothing more than nerves. As Olney said, "It's presumptuous to think that when people are under this kind of stress that you can determine much about them except that they are under stress."

5 Show and Tell

Reporters Meet Politicians on Larry King Live

RITA BRAVER

Former Texas Governor Ann Richards with Jane Pauley of NBC News, Cokie Roberts of ABC News, and Dan Rather of CBS News

Ann Richards: All of you guys collectively represent about 85 years of reporting what's going on. What I want to know is, have things really changed? And don't fudge with me.

Jane Pauley: We used to do poetry readings on the *Today* show—a lot of that, and string quartets. That's certainly changed.

Ann Richards: I want to know if your whole slant has changed in covering stories? I have a feeling, in the newspapers, for example, the headlines will always be much more salacious or exciting than the story actually is. Does the same thing happen to you in television? Do you have to hype it up? And who tells you what to cover? Who makes that decision?

Jane Pauley: If I think of my own stories, then I'm less likely to be assigned something I don't want, or have something imposed upon me. So that doing a profile of, oh, Governor Ann Richards before an election was not a difficult sell, either. But after we've gotten it ready, how is it promoted? That's a different department in the news organization, and I might not be consulted with regard to the language we use, to entice America to watch this profile of Governor Richards. I'm always surprised, if I'm home watching television, and it's on NBC, and there's a promo for *Dateline*, and something I've done is promoted with this

EDITORS' NOTE: This interview was aired March 28, 1995 and is used by permission.

33

breathless, urgent voice, using adjectives that I personally wouldn't have used, like "shocked," everything is shocking. The promotion factor, which is very critical in prime-time, does give you the wrong impression.

Ann Richards: Cokie, I know that there are institutions or foundations or think tanks in Washington that really don't represent any thinking, or very few people across the country. And yet, you all quote statistics and stuff like that from them, like they were some legitimate organization.

Cokie Roberts: First of all, Governor, I would venture to say that you have done well with the pithy quote yourself—that's something you have excelled in. But the fact is that some of the kinds of people that establishment media wrote off as crackpots have become very powerful people. So you have to be careful in saying, "Gee, those people don't count, therefore we don't pay any attention to them." A lot of the upset about the media, in the sense that we were liberal and elite and out of touch and all those things, was the fact that we weren't paying enough attention to voices other than the ones that we knew well.

Dan Rather: Some of those crackpots are now running the country.

Jane Pauley: But those very "crackpots" who then have come to power are keeping their eye on the media. One change in the institution since I've been in it is that it is now much more nervous about being accused of not being balanced.

Ann Richards: Let me ask you something about affirmative action. Where would you be today (without it), Jane Pauley?

Jane Pauley: I would probably be teaching high school English somewhere. And I would not be a good English teacher. Instead of something that I'm fairly good at. I used to say my motto was, "Praise be to the FCC!" because, when I got my job at WISH-TV in Indianapolis, the news director interviewed 30, 50, 100, whatever, women, because he had to find a woman. It was FCC license renewal time in that newsroom, and there were no women in the newsroom, there were none. Supposedly there was someone with a Polish surname was identified as a minority. I don't know whether it was a quota, but that's why they were looking for a girl. They had to get a girl in the newsroom and I was really cheap.

Ann Richards: Cokie, I want to know the same thing from your perspective, the effect of affirmative action and what it had on your career, and what difference do you think it's made in the Washington scene?

Cokie Roberts: Well, pre-affirmative action, when I was looking for jobs early on, people said, out loud and without any hesitation, "We don't hire women to do that. We will not hire women to deliver the news."

Their voices are not authoritative. We don't hire women as writers. Men would have to work for them, and we can't have that." It was overt, and nobody was even embarrassed about it. For the women of my age, it is interesting to us that we now have an accusation that we are only where we are because we are women. For a long time we were told we couldn't be anywhere because we were women.

Ann Richards: Dan, a news story might say the White House tried to influence the Housing Department or the Transportation Department. So-and-so on the president's staff made a call to somebody else, to try to get them to. . . . I thought that's why you ran for president. I thought that's why you became president, so you could affect the actions that government took.

Dan Rather: It has to be done openly in a way that is accountable to the people. Going back to your core question about what has changed: The influence of polls and polling on candidates and on news organizations is one big change. A lot of the coverage is poll-driven. Another is the amount of money. I don't know who the Republican candidate for president is going to be next year, but I can tell you that it will be somebody who has at least $20 million, and probably will need $30 million. The influence of money has increased—both in terms of money committed by news organizations that cover campaigns and the amount spent in campaigns. The third change is competition. When it comes to news coverage, the competition is a lot fiercer now. And one of the reasons we've had a sleazing of the news, a dumbing-down of the news, including campaign coverage, is the fierceness of competition and the increased influence of ratings. No one is immune to that.

Jane Pauley: I read an item in a magazine about Benjamin Franklin, saying that, as he grew older, he learned he had the ability to change his mind. Information, age, experience. We in the media don't allow politicians to change their mind. We call that flip-flopping, or expedience.

Cokie Roberts: That is really a good point, Jane, and it's one of the things that we've been talking about a lot in this town lately, that if somebody makes compromises in order to get something done, that's considered evil, by us in the media—instead of saying that that's what the system requires. That's how you govern: flip-flopping. Poor Bob Dole, you know, every time he tries to run for president, he gets accused of flip-flopping, because he's an effective congressional leader. He is able to move legislation through, which means moving slightly in order to get it done. This notion that compromise is evil, or that learning and maturing is something that we should denigrate, is the strangest thing.

Former Vice President Dan Quayle with Rita Braver of CBS News, Tim Russert of NBC News, and Syndicated Columnist Charles Krauthammer

Dan Quayle: There is this basic liberal bias. Take the networks, the *Washington Post*, the *New York Times*. I'll exclude the editorial page of the *Wall Street Journal*, but the news pages of the *Wall Street Journal*, the media here in Washington. Can we admit that there is bias?

Rita Braver: I think that perhaps for some time there was. I think it's moving away from that. And I think that perhaps because people have been making more of an issue of it, that every news organization is making a bigger effort to try to be fair, and taking a look at what you're doing to say, every day, you know, "Are we being fair?" I think it's happening more.

Dan Quayle: I'm not saying that it's not fair, but it's fair through the liberal prism.

Tim Russert: I think there's more of a cultural bias than a political bias. And by that I mean that the people who are by and large covering the news come from the same background, they went to the same schools. You mentioned the *Washington Post* earlier. There was a demonstration in favor of abortion, it was on the front page and covered extensively. When there was the right-to-life march, it was ignored. And I asked Len Downey, who is the editor of the *Washington Post*, about that. He said, "You know, we didn't even know the story was going on. No one in our newsroom knew anyone who was marching." And he said, "And that's the difficulty we have." I do think that more and more, with George Will and John McLaughlin and William Safire, we see a lot of prominent conservative voices on television. I don't think that's the problem. I think day-in and day-out of the coverage we have to be very careful that we are not bringing a cultural bias to the news that we are covering.

Charles Krauthammer: It goes beyond culture. And it's not just that they've gone to the same schools. It's true that there are conservative columnists. But it's undeniable that the major, the elite media, newspapers, the networks, are heavily liberal. Any time anybody has ever done a poll of leading people in these instructions, they're heavily Democratic. And it does color how things and what kinds of things are covered. I find it amusing that the one outlet in the media, which is clearly in the other camp, which is talk radio, is so heavily attacked. You know, the liberals dominate in the newspapers and the networks, in the universities, even in the museums, in all of the great instruments of culture and society. The one institution which has eluded its grasp is talk radio. And the assault on talk radio is incessant.

Dan Quayle: Let me just ask this question, do you think that a person, a journalist, who had impeccable journalistic credentials, tough, inquisitive, skeptical, fair, everything, but he had these following political beliefs, he was pro-life, pro-gun, conservative on gays and conservative on affirmative action. Do you think that he could ever be, or she, could be Washington chief bureau of NBC News, or be the managing editor of the *Washington Post*? Could that happen with somebody with views like that?

Rita Braver: Sure. The answer is that I don't even know what my editor's personal beliefs are on these issues. I have no idea. I mean, it's not something that you ever talk about.

Dan Quayle: So you think that there is somebody of that belief in a serious position of power?

Tim Russert: Oh, absolutely. Well, I don't know the specifics. We don't have a checklist of where you stand on different issues. I know Brit Hume, I watch his coverage on ABC, he contributes regularly to *American Spectator, National Review*. Or Diane Sawyer, who worked with President Nixon.

Dan Quayle: OK, we'll get off the liberal media. Will you accept the cynical media? This is a cynical town. Are the media, are they too cynical? Are they too negative? Is everything sort of, you know, twisted?

Rita Braver: I think that part of that has to do with age. This is a generation that was raised during the Vietnam era, when a lot of the things that people said turned out not to be true. And a lot of people came to Washington at the time of Watergate, when a lot of things that people heard were not true. I hope we're not cynical. But I think every fiber in my being tells me every day to be skeptical. And the reason is that the times that I haven't asked questions, or that things have seemed too impossible to believe, have turned out to be true. The first time someone told me that there was a guy who was running an operation supplying Contras from the White House, sending down bags of money, I said, you know, this can't be true. This would be against the law.

Dan Quayle: Now, this is strictly my opinion, and maybe it's biased. Four things that make news are attacks, flip-flops, gaffes, and polls. If I'm right that those are the four things that make news, does that breed cynicism?

Charles Krauthammer: Let me add one more. Sex. You talk about cynicism in the press, I think a lot of it is prurience. The way that the politicians and any public figure is covered now is simply astonishing compared to, say, the way that JFK or FDR or Lyndon Johnson were covered. We want to know every detail about the private life of our politicians to an extraordinarily excessive extent. And we rationalize it by saying, "Well, if you know about the private life of a man, it will help you in deciding about his public decisions." Had we excluded in the past leaders who had these unsavory things in their past, we would have lost some of the great leaders of American history. So I think it's beyond cynicism, a lot of it is prurience.

Tim Russert: I think your description of what makes news is pretty close to accurate. And TV, particularly, likes contrast and combat. I've been watching this Medicare debate we're having in Washington, Republicans saying, "We have to save the system," Democrats saying, "They're trying to throw old people on the street."

Dan Quayle: Some of the politicians have said that, and I think it's probably true, that people sitting around this table have a lot more influence about what goes on in America than most members of Congress. That is a fact. And, since you have influence and power, and given the public's right to know about what all of the politicians have done in the past, is there a public's right to know about people that are going to be in the media in a very high-profile, influential, powerful position? Should we know that? Does the public deserve to know that?

Charles Krauthammer: I don't think so in the case of the politicians, and I certainly don't think so in the case of the press. I mean, I think the public stance of public figures is what's important. And private lives ought to be kept in private as much as we can.

Dan Quayle: Your producers there at CBS, or more importantly, the peers at the White House, now do they sit around and say, "Well gosh, you know, we're being a little hard on Clinton. Let's soften up a little bit?"

Rita Braver: Are you serious?

Dan Quayle: Yeah, I am

Rita Braver: Do you think reporters sit around and say that to each other? No.

Charles Krauthammer: There has always been an element of gotcha journalism. I mean, after all, how do you win a Pulitzer? You expose a scandal in some state mental hospital, which is a good thing to do, it's public service, and you win a Pulitzer. And that's how things work. You know, when a plane lands safely it's not news, and when it crashes it is. So, it's in the nature of the news to look for what's unusual or wrong or askew. And that's the basis of adversarial journalism. I don't think there's anything wrong with that. I think, to some extent, it can get pushed. I think in the Nixon era, sometimes in the Reagan era, sometimes with Clinton, there has been an element of deep hatred and resentment of the president as a person, and it shows in the press. And it may also happen with House Speaker Newt Gingrich, I think, for example.

Dan Quayle: Is that the balance? Is that what we're looking for, adversarial reporting?

Charles Krauthammer: Well, you want that in a healthy democracy.

Dan Quayle: Or skepticism?

Charles Krauthammer: Well, look, at the Soviet Union where you didn't have either skepticism or adversarialism. Got to have it.

Tim Russert: Larry Spivak, the founder of *Meet the Press,* with whom I had lunch before he died, God bless him, and I said, "Larry, how do you go about preparing to be a moderator on 'Meet the Press'?" He said, "It's simple. Understand your guest's position and take the other side." And that's what he did for 40-some years. And it's very good advice except if you try to get too aggressive and you become uncivil or rude. Then I think you cross the line. But I think Rita has a point, you can be skeptical, and the way to demonstrate skepticism is by being a bit adversarial to elicit a response to make sure the viewers know that your guest understands what he or she is talking about.

6   The Question of Media Bias

RICHARD REEVES

A great deal is made of the so-called "liberal press," but the liberalism of the elite press is more cultural than political. The royalty of journalism pretty much shares the social attitudes of other well-educated and high-earning Americans, beginning with an aversion to progressive income taxes.

Cokie Roberts of ABC News, it is true, is the daughter of two Democratic members of Congress, Hale Boggs, the late majority leader of the House, and his widow, former Representative Lindy Boggs. Tim Russert, the Washington bureau chief of NBC News and moderator of *Meet the Press*, served on the staffs of two prominent New York Democrats, Senator Daniel Patrick Moynihan and Governor Mario Cuomo. But William Safire of *The New York Times*, John McLaughlin, the television ringmaster, Diane Sawyer of ABC, and David Gergen of *U.S. News & World Report*, all served together on President Richard Nixon's staff—and, at the time, Nixon was trying to hire Robert Bartley, a young editorial writer on *The Wall Street Journal* who became a Pulitzer-Prize winning voice of the right. Sam Donaldson of ABC, energetic defender of the little guy, gets more than $100,000 a year in federal agricultural subsidies for a sheep ranch he owns in New Mexico.

Are they biased? Of course—who isn't?

That bias of the ladies and gentlemen of the press, however, is less than politicians and millions of Americans seem to think. Journalists, like politicians, are anxious to preserve their own popularity and credibility. Both reporters and pundits generally have to deal with both sides of an issue or all sides of ongoing political struggles and they are usually even more anxious to keep the respect of their peers. "Objectivity" is both a cloak and a goal for journalists—most cannot make a living if they are not seen by sources, readers, viewers, and bosses as trying to be fair. That is at least the way it has been for most of the people most of the time. In the late 1960s, young liberals stormed the business, arguing that there was no "other side" on issues like war and poverty and race relations. Most of them soon faded into moderation or obscurity. Then, in the 1980s a wave of conservative thinkers, writers, and "journalists" emerged, many of them complaining that they were being ignored or suppressed by liberal elites.

They were right, in a sense. They were being shunned, not politically but culturally.

All celebrity is created equal in the electronic zoo, so it has become perfectly natural to see things like former Vice President Dan Quayle substituting for Larry King on CNN. The journalists being interviewed were quick to say that "the media" takes great pains to be fair. "I'm not saying that it's not fair," said Quayle, "but it's fair through the liberal prism."

Most liberals, me among them, agree we may have a prism but they, the conservatives, seem to have bigger megaphones. Rush Limbaugh alone gets more electronic exposure than all the lefties on the continent. Anybody with a dollar can find out what Safire or George Will, a former Republican congressional staffer, or the editorial writers of *The Wall Street Journal* think most every day of the year. The nonfiction best-seller list of the 1990s was generally dominated by provocative conservative authors. Even public television was projecting more and more faces of the right, people like William F. Buckley and Peggy Noonan, replaced the liberals who found a home there years ago. A "Christian conservative," Pat Robertson, has his own channel.

Conservatives, in obvious fact, have done a tremendous job in getting their ideas across in the mainstream media. Much of the credit for that should go to William E. Simon, the Wall Streeter who was secretary of the treasury to two Republican presidents. His 1978 book, a best-seller titled *A Time for Truth*, ended with a strategy that worked: "I know of nothing more crucial than to come to the aid of the intellectuals and writers who are fighting on my side. . . . A powerful counterintelligentsia can be organized to challenge our ruling [liberal] opinion makers . . . an audience awaits its [conservative] views."

So it did. Simon urged corporate America to use its "public affairs" contributions to support intellectuals of the right—in journalism, universities and think tanks. To show the way, he used a foundation he controlled, the John M. Olin Foundation, to create university chairs and such for conservative thinkers, such as Irving Kristol and Allan Bloom, and to encourage the creation and financing of independent right-wing college newspapers to recruit and train a new generation of bright conservative writers.

It worked brilliantly. The new conservative generation, however—the winners in ideological wars—whined that liberals still run the world of ideas. Quayle got the beginning of the answer on the King show from Tim Russert. "I think there's more of a cultural bias than a political bias," said NBC News's main man in Washington. That is it exactly. Like Rodney Dangerfield, conservative thinkers don't get no respect. They may be admired for their political impact or envied for their corporate and foundation support, but they are not respected or affirmed intellectually by a cultural elite more "liberal" than most middle-class voters.

In addition, no matter how smart or literate or successful they are, the new conservative intelligentsia—or counterintelligentsia—do not deserve cultural affirmation. They are political activists, not political chroniclers or commentators. You can learn from them, but you cannot trust them. At their best, which can be very good indeed, *Wall Street Journal* editorials, the *American Spectator* "exposes," the books of Charles Murray, and the asides of P. J. O'Rourke compile only information that "works" for their side. They are pamphleteers, not essayists.

In the 1990s, they have not been able to have it both ways. The cultural bias that bothers conservative thinkers (and Quayle) is real—it is the perverse bent of thinkers and writers who inevitably sell out their friends when they are wrong or foolish. The scorned "liberals" could seem pathetic when they beat up on Bill Clinton or any other ideological companion who actually has power. That is the point, however: Cultural respect and affirmation come from choosing argument over power—and so far the new conservative intelligentsia seems incapable of biting the hands that feed them so well.

7 Oliver Stone and History

RICHARD REEVES

A month or so after the assassination of President Kennedy in the third year of his presidency, a young White House assistant named Richard Goodwin tried to console Robert Kennedy by saying: "Julius Caesar is an immortal, but he was only Emperor of Rome for a little more than three years."

"Yes," Bobby said, "but it helps if you have Shakespeare to write about you."

That is certainly true, but, taking no chances on the future, Caesar wrote about himself first. John F. Kennedy intended to do the same after his presidency, emulating his hero, Winston Churchill. The 35th president never got the chance, but his memory and memories of him were well served by two talented assistants, Arthur Schlesinger and Theodore Sorensen, who did their best to immortalize their fallen leader.

It was not the historian, Schlesinger, nor the alter ego Sorensen, however, who cast the image of Kennedy that still thrills the world. It was his widow, Jacqueline Kennedy, telling a friendly writer, Theodore H. White,

> At night before we'd go to sleep, Jack liked to play some records. The lines he loved to hear were: "Don't let it be forgot, that there once was a spot, for one brief shining moment that was known as Camelot." There'll be great presidents again, but there'll never be another Camelot again.

Kennedy's competitor and successor, the 37th president, Richard M. Nixon, did get the chance to make the Churchillian effort to define himself and his deeds in six books after his resignation in 1974. Both presidents tape-recorded White House days as material for their memoirs, knowing that one day they would be competing in the marketplaces of history with both friends and enemies. Historians, playwrights, and assorted charlatans would be out there building statues of word and images or tearing them down. Even a filmmaker, quite an extraordinary one, Oliver Stone, joined the competition, grossly distorting the death and life of Kennedy in *JFK* and then offering *Nixon,* his version of the rise and agony of that strange man.

Years later, which would ordinarily be considered a very long time in the movie business, the controversy continues over the intent and accuracy of *JFK.* Chances are that right or wrong or silly, the film will play in the minds of a generation or two because the commercial and emotional reach of popular movies is so great. More than 50 million people around the world have seen that film to date—and many of them seem to have believed every frame.

In 1995, Stone and I appeared together before the American Society of Newspaper Editors to discuss that movie—or debate its merits and faults—under the program title "When Journalism, History and Art Collide, Where Is Truth?" The most dramatic touch that day came when John Seigenthaler, an assistant to Robert Kennedy before he went on to become the editor and publisher of the Nashville *Tennessean,* stood to ask or declare:

> I appeared before a class of high school students who asked me about what I thought about the assassination. I would say half of them had seen your movie and were convinced that Lyndon Johnson was guilty of conspiracy to murder the president of the United States. Is there any regret on your part for what I consider to be a blood libel on Lyndon Johnson for that accusation of murder? Whatever you admit and whatever doubt you have, there are no doubts in the minds of those children.

Stone responded with his "Hey, it's only a movie" defense saying, "I am not responsible for the interpretation that the audience takes away. Sometimes it is misinterpreted."

Please! My contribution, at that point, was to say to Stone that if this is all entertainment, just another movie, why did Warner Brothers send out cartons of the "JFK Classroom Study Guide," based on the film, to

13,000 school districts around the country—as Disney, the studio behind
Nixon was doing for the new film.

The marketing is the message. Stone's obvious brilliance as a director
is that he knows better than most exactly what audiences are likely to
think and feel when they see his work. That is why *Nixon* opens with a
disclaimer, white words on a black screen:

> This film is an attempt to understand the truth of Richard Nixon,
> thirty-seventh President of the United States. It is based on
> numerous public sources and on an incomplete historical re-
> cord. In consideration of length, events and characters have been
> condensed, and some scenes among protagonists have been
> conjectured.

What Oliver Stone, scarred by the *JFK* attacks, is saying in other words
is this: We are serious people. We read all the books, talked to some of
the people, used what we could from the sources—and then made up
the rest, whatever we needed to make the picture work.

"To govern is to choose," said the real President Kennedy. That is the
critical power, too, of the director—or the journalist or historian. We all
create our own truth. Journalists and historians, however, generally
cannot use the wonderful and malleable tools of entertainment. We do
not make it up. If we do and we are caught, we rarely get a second chance.
The movie business is more flexible than that, at least if the grosses are
good.

Stone would dispute that all up and down the line. In debate, he
argued,

> I think the work of the historian involves great gulps of imagi-
> nation and speculation, the resurrection of dialogues that fre-
> quently were never recorded. I am not trying to denigrate the
> work of the historian, but rather to say that the good historian
> must know well how elusive this thing is referred to all too
> cavalierly by journalists as the truth, the truth, the truth.

Some choosers, truth tellers in their own minds, are more elusive than
others. In *JFK*, Stone wanted to make a case based on the credibility of
an assassination investigation by New Orleans District Attorney Jim

Garrison. He chose not to mention that the jury in the month-long case against the alleged conspirators returned with a "not guilty" verdict after only 50 minutes of deliberation. In the script of that film, the summation of the fictional Garrison (Kevin Costner) covered 106 lines. Those lines included only six phrases from the real summation and there was only one complete sentence among them. That one true sentence from the real Garrison was a quote from Kennedy: "Ask not what your country can do for you, but what you can do for your country."

To boost the credibility of *Nixon*, Stone published an annotated screenplay with 168 research footnotes. (He did the same for *JFK*, but only after the claimed accuracy of his work was widely challenged.) It is pretty shabby stuff. One of the Nixon footnotes reads, "The version contained in this script is not intended to reflect the actual contents of that program." More often than not, the notes refer to marginal books and tracts. There are no notes at all for six or seven pages at a time, particularly when Nixon and his wife are talking.

In several key scenes, notes refer to biographies that, in fact, are retelling stories from Nixon's own writings. The best example of this—and of how the film was put together—is Stone's version of the president's postmidnight visit to the Lincoln Memorial on May 9, 1970, as students from around the country gathered in Washington for a massive antiwar rally. In 1978, Nixon published his notes of the encounter with protestors camping out and his words become the film's dialogue—up to a point.

The end of the scene in the script is fictional. I have condensed that end of the scene here, as set up by Nixon insisting that he is trying to end the war in Vietnam, and that he has withdrawn more than half the troops there. Then:

> **Young woman:** You don't want the war. We don't want the war. The Vietnamese don't want the war. So why does it go on?

(Nixon hesitates, out of answers.)

> **Young woman:** Someone wants it. . . . [a realization] You can't stop it, can you. . . . Even if you wanted to. Because it's not you. It's the system. And the system won't let you stop it.

(The girl transfixes him with her eyes.)

> **Nixon (stumbling):** No, no. I'm not powerless. Because . . . because I un-
> derstand the system. I believe I can control it. Maybe not control it
> totally . . . but tame it enough to do some good.
> **Young woman:** It sounds like you're talking about a wild animal.
> **Nixon:** Maybe I am.

As Nixon is led down the stairs to the limousine by H. R. "Bob" Haldeman:

> **Nixon:** She got it Bob. A nineteen year-old college kid. . . . She understood
> something it's taken me twenty-five fucking years in politics to under-
> stand. The CIA, the Mafia, the Wall Street bastards.

"The System." The conspiracy. That is Oliver Stone speaking.

The Richard Nixon created by Stone and played by Anthony Hopkins is not a totally unsympathetic character—at least to Stone, who sometimes seems downright sentimental about his protagonist. Stone's Nixon— a gifted and productive man, almost consumed by anger, self-pity, and paranoia—sounds a great deal like an older Oliver Stone ranting on about the cruel savagery of The System.

Nixon, real and cinematic, imagined his life as a struggle against "the eastern elite," the Ivy Leaguers who run everything, beginning with Wall Street and its old Washington branch, the Central Intelligence Agency. Oliver Stone is the son of a man (Louis Stone, to whom the film is dedicated) who went broke on Wall Street. When the money was gone, the son had to leave prep school, a leaving he now celebrates because it allowed him to "break out of the mold [shaping me] as an East Coast socioeconomic product." The road away from Wall Street (the subject of another of his films, also dedicated to his father) took him to combat in Vietnam and then back home, in his own words, "very mixed-up, very alienated, very paranoid." Making films, he says now, was the way he tried "to channel my rage."

Stone and his Nixon (and the real Nixon, too) seem to be intent on getting even with America—for what, I do not know. They forget little and seem to forgive nothing, particularly when it comes to the press. When we debated before the newspaper editors, Stone described himself this way: "I am one of those who was sent to that war in Vietnam based on (a) journalist-endorsed lie." In fact, looking at the research cited by Stone in both *JFK* and *Nixon*, the artist who wants us to believe the essential truth of his skilled prestidigitation has adopted the worst of journalism, embodied in a line most editors have heard (or used): "What does it matter whether it's true or not, he said it."

However angry he is about reporters kicking him around, Stone owes much to two of them, Bob Woodward and Carl Bernstein of the *Washington Post*. The Nixon played by Hopkins and constructed by Stone is the one Woodward and Bernstein left for dead in the final pages of their 1974 book *The Final Days*—a kneeling-down drunk. Whatever Richard Nixon was before and after those last days in the White House becomes, in this film, prologue or epilogue to this clumsy and babbling lush confined to darkly lit rooms. The man who made the movie seemed to have tunnel vision and there is no light at the end of this one, which opens with a view of the White House as Dracula's castle.

Perhaps we should get used to this new posthumous "new Nixon" because it seems to be the one that works best on film and television. In the TNT television movie, *Kissinger and Nixon* (shown for the first time in December 1995), the awkward drunk in the Oval Office is played by Beau Bridges. In both entertainments, Nixon seems to have a glass glued to his hand. There are creative differences, however. On the big screen, Nixon drinks scotch, Johnny Walker Black, but on TNT his line is, "Let's have a drink. Bourbon, all around?"

It may be that no presidents are heroes to their many valets, but stumblebum Nixon seems ludicrous to me. He was certainly not a graceful or comfortable man—he once walked me into a stationery closet as he showed me out of his New York office in the late 1970s—but no one in their right mind ever took him as the demented clown being portrayed now.

Beyond watching a great actor portraying someone we knew too long and perhaps too well, *Nixon* does not make much sense on its own. You almost have to have been there to understand resonant conceits such as Maureen Dean's hairdo, a flashed photograph of J. Robert Oppenheimer, or Nixon working in a room in front of a blazing fireplace with the air-conditioning on full blast. With numerous teases hinting at a single Nixon secret, Stone promises us a "Rosebud," something having to do with an assassination of somebody. Kennedy? Castro? We never know. The story line is dropped and Nixon has another scotch.

Sitting through *Nixon* made me think that too much of a fuss may have been made of Stone's dangerous cinematic brilliance in *JFK*. Watching *Nixon*, the use of quickcutting, grainy film, and deliberately misleading pseudodocumentary techniques seem flatter and flatter because the film has more point of view than point. In retrospect, what caused a national shouting match over *JFK* was separate from Oliver Stone's mastery of the mysterious powers of cinema. It is clear now, at least to me, that it was not how Stone said it in *JFK*, but what he said. He said and marketed the idea that there was a conspiracy at the highest levels of American government to murder a president. This time, with *Nixon*, it is clear that all the Shakespearian pretensions and cinematic pyrotechnics in the world have very little impact if you have nothing much to say.

8   Combat Stories

RICHARD COHEN
THOMAS OLIPHANT
RICHARD REEVES
ROBERT SHOGAN

Richard Cohen: I have been listening to journalists now ever since the end of the 1992 election, even before the end of the election, talk about what a great job we have done this year compared to 4 years ago. And by and large I agree, that every year we do a little better than we did 4 years before. Overall, the mediums tend to change on us a bit, the politicians always stay a little bit ahead of us, figure out how to manipulate us, we catch on a little late, all these things are true.

Starting up in New Hampshire, the one thing we kept getting struck with over and over again was the intensity of the feeling about this election. People were closely following what was going on. And the questions people were asking over and over again were detailed and they were about the economy. What you didn't see was a repeat of the Bush-Dukakis kind of election where it was over before it began. There weren't really a lot of issues in that election. There was the Pledge of Allegiance, and the flag salute, and all kinds of other nonsensical, symbolic stuff.

This year people kept saying over and over again "we're hurting" and we want to know what you are going to do about it. So it was an entirely different election and I think that we tended to respond pretty quickly to what we saw was grave seriousness on the part of the electorate. I remember right before the election I was debating Fred Barnes in Redlands at the university there and somebody brought up the issue of Gennifer Flowers and what did that mean. Fred and I started debating it, thinking that this is what people would be interested in since it is about sex. Somebody got up and said "you don't get it, we don't care about Gennifer Flowers, we want to know about the economy, we want to know about our tuition fees, we want to know about student grants, we want to know about loans." So we were forced to talk about issues, which we muddled through for the rest of the evening. It was that intensity and the seriousness of the economy that focused everyone on real issues as opposed to symbolic or silly issues.

Bill Clinton early on realized by looking at the numbers that the average American was worse off than they had been. If you go back to 1973 the trend from the end of the war to 1973 was that each year the average American worker made more money. Earned more money in real dollars. In 1973, that stopped and the trend started going the other way. By 1990, there was a 19% loss in average annual wages in real terms. A lot of things disguised that. One was inflation itself. Every year the average American took home a bigger paycheck. It was bringing him less but it looked better. Going into debt is another way of maintaining your standard of living. And third and not least was the tendency toward more working wives. So instead of one income you had one and a half incomes or two incomes and you could maintain your standard of living that way.

By 1989, there was a ceiling on those things and people began to feel hurt. Then you had a recession which focused a lot of attention on the economy. Recessions come, recessions go, this one happened at the worst time. The issue of the national debt became salient thanks to Ross Perot. Perot got people to understand that this is a real thing, a real problem and not just theoretical. The economy is in trouble, the government is in trouble, the books are not in balance. The deficit came to signify that something was dreadfully wrong in Washington and needed to be fixed.

So in my opinion, the reason why the press did a better job in 1992 than in 1988 was that the people of this country paid more attention to issues. Given the audience, we rose to the occasion.

Tom Oliphant: If I were teaching a course about the press and presidential politics I'd list a few things that I think it is our job to do. The press in a way sets the stage for the campaign. How are we doing as a country, what's going on in the world? What's the condition of America? The press does biography. It also does stenography. Make sure your tape recorder is running when the candidates are speaking so their words can get in the paper the next day. We serve the role of correction. Mistakes about the record, personal or official, are made as a function of investigation when that is called for or even when that is not called for. The role of description. What does a candidate look like? Sound like? What are the crowds like? That's the media baseline, but as always, there were new jobs and new phenomena this time.

Take the talk shows. Direct access between voters and candidates on a scale never before seen. Years ago it was candidates on local television news programs. This time the interview programs resulted in an explosion of access for ordinary Americans. Same for the debates. We argue in our business for months about what is the right way to do it and what's the wrong way to do it. Should the moderator stand here and wear a tie or stand there and wear a tank top? But four debates were held and something like 75 to 90 million people a pop watched them. And they worked like a dream.

Two networks came into the forefront this time. Both emphasizing direct access to candidates talking on the part of people. One, CNN, using news coverage, the other, C-SPAN, largely just using a camera. They provided people who cared an opportunity to see presidential politics in action in a way they could never have seen before.

I believe that we reporters showed less proficiency and lower standards in dealing with matters concerning candidates' personal and private lives than we did in 1988. I think it is much easier in this day and age to get junk into the mainstream of the media than it ever was.

What do the pluses and minuses have in common? Things that went the best this time involved candidates and peoples' access to what they had or didn't have to say. I think the things that didn't go well involved the press in an unusually self-inflated role. We get in the way of the process rather than help it along. My hope is that the trends that are under way now are going to be favorable toward the direct access candidates and unfavorable toward the kind of "We'll tell you what you need to know" attitude that I think has polluted much of the press's work in the last decade.

Robert Shogan: I'd like to start with a combat story. Fairly early in the campaign there was an opportunity for me to ask Governor Bill Clinton about Mario Cuomo and he certainly didn't want to talk about this. What he said to me was, "That's a question that the press asks, real people don't ask that. I have never been in a campaign where there is such a difference between the questions people ask and the questions reporters ask." That is very interesting governor, I said, "Why do you suppose that is? Are the real people getting worse?" Then he said "I'm not gonna answer that either, because you'd make something out of that too."

So the press is part of this process. Although we like to think of ourselves standing apart, that's a little unrealistic. We are used and manipulated. Although we do things on our own, the things we do are predictable. Because most of them are reactive. And in a way that maybe is the way it should be. I don't think we should create or forge the system. I think by doing our job right we help keep the wheels going. The question is was it right and what should we cover? Should we cover substance or should we cover the horse race? Should we write about this or write about that? I think each question has to be answered each day of each edition.

Consider two examples which I thought were very large factors in the last campaign. One is Republican and the other is Democrat. I thought by and large we did not do a good job in explaining the relationship between the triumph in the Gulf War and Bush's presidency. When the stuff hit the sand out there in the Middle East people said Bush now has a chance to define his presidency. This is after the guy had been in the White House for more than 5 years and the pattern of his presidency had been clearly set. I think if you look back at the criticisms that were made of Bush and the ones that eventually brought about his downfall, they were pretty apparent in the summer of 1990. Bush had indicated he would be forced to break his promise on taxes. The S & L scandal and the activities of Neil Bush were already embarrassments. Now the Gulf War came along and it froze political debate, but did not change it. The Gulf War and the success Bush could have achieved there would have meant something only if Bush had used that to drive some domestic agenda. And lo and behold, 6 months after he was at the top of the polls he was in deep trouble. All of which I think was foreseeable. And I think that's because we lost the connection between governing and what expectations there would be of the political campaign.

The Democratic example has to do with the character issue. There are generational divisions, believe it or not, within journalism. And it struck me that some of the reporters, people who are younger than I, seemed almost squeamish about the idea of dealing with this sort of personal stuff concerning his marriage and his draft status during the Vietnam War—two pretty important components of his life.

Clinton was the candidate who stood before the Democratic convention and said I accept your nomination in the name of all the hard working people in America who played by the rules. And no one even tittered. No one raised the question the next day or the next week and said wait a minute, what's going on here. What sort of rules is he talking about?

Is this a contradiction? The idea was not to embarrass Clinton, who embarrassed himself. The idea should have been to give people the opportunity to judge Clinton's answer. There are two things we can do about this so-called character issue. One big thing and then two little things.

The big thing is to tie character to governing. This is something we have learned about a guy, but does this matter? And there are two ways to raise that question. One is to look at a guy's record so far. The other way is to look back at the presidency and guys like Nixon and Lyndon Johnson and go back to their presidencies and to the decisions they made. If we do that there is no way we can tell people that character does not matter. Of course it matters. Everybody has good and bad characters. What we need to tell people is the difference it might make. No, you're not going to get a perfect person. But at least you won't be surprised out of your life. That's what I think we should do is keep people from having unpleasant surprises.

Richard Cohen: I was in the newsroom of the *Washington Post* when we got word that the *Star* was going to print this story about Gennifer Flowers and she was getting paid for it. We got a fax in the newsroom and I read it and said to myself, "This is some story." And it was gripping. There was some filthy, great stuff. You wanted to read it. But then I turned on the TV and watched Peter Jennings; they didn't use it. No mention of it on CBS. NBC broke it, sort of in passing. The next day's *New York Times* and *Washington Post*, not having any idea what to do with the story, placed it inside and rather small. At eleven o'clock, or ten o'clock where I was in New York, it was the lead story. Enormous story on local TV. The next morning's *New York Times, New York Daily News, New York Post,* and *New York Newsday* carried front page headlines. Every talk show in New York was talking about it. So we are sitting there, the established press, saying, "Wait a minute we want to check this out."

Who is Gennifer Flowers? Did she get paid? We don't like paying for news. If she got paid did she embellish the story? What newspaper is this, one that does stories about Martians. They took the story away from us. It simply got taken away from us. And the reason it got taken away from us is because it was a hell of a story. Now it may not have been the type of story I wanted journalism to cover. But it was an engrossing story about a man that the American people still did not know.

We in the big-time press, the people at this table, had said early on that Bill Clinton was a front runner. And we said that Bill Clinton, for years, had come into Washington and secretly eaten dinners with everybody who counted, or thought they did. He had this network of friends, who have been calling me for years saying I ought to meet Bill Clinton. He also raised more money than anyone else. So he was the presumptive front runner even though he hadn't won a single election. So the press and Bill Clinton went to dinner and he acknowledged that yes he and Hillary had not had a perfect marriage. And after that there was an attempt to cover up—now you guys are sort of in on the secret and you will protect us. And in fact it almost worked. But the reason it didn't work is that Gennifer Flowers went to this ratty newspaper in Florida and blew the story wide open.

I don't think the American people knew anything about Bill Clinton at the time and they wanted to know more. They looked at the Flowers story and they wondered and they said, is this relevant? Can we make a connection between this and the way he governs? Does this mean you have to revise your estimation of the Kennedy administration based on what we know now about his womanizing? What does it mean about Lyndon Johnson? Richard Nixon? Nixon never cheated on his wife, just the country. It's a very tough thing. And the other question is are you entitled to the information. And who are we to say that it is not germane? The Constitution doesn't say you have to vote on the issues. You don't like the guy? He's too tall, too short—vote that way. You don't like a guy who cheats on his wife? Vote that way. Maybe you ought to get that information.

Robert Shogan: The reaction to the *Star* story was heavily colored and influenced as I think it should be by what nearly every political reporter had been told about Bill Clinton. Dick talks about him coming to Washington wanting to go to little dinners to meet with Policywatch. But let me tell you, we heard about other little affairs he had that weren't necessarily good policy. We weren't hanging around back alleys to hear this. A party chair of a southern state asked me, "What do you think is going to happen to Clinton?" I said what do you mean? She said, "I was at a meeting a few months ago and there were ten women and I looked around and knew he had three of them. And not me included." Within that context it was like a whole series of high heeled shoes getting ready to drop. This wasn't just something that came out of the blue.

Tom Oliphant: I don't see Gennifer Flowers as one incident but as a continuum. And as you go down that continuum my contention is that the standards of the media have gone down rather than stayed the same. What's interesting to me about these episodes is that they teach us that the ethical distinctions at the editorial level, as opposed to the journalistic level, between, say, the *Los Angeles Times* and the *National Star* are not as clear as they once were. These episodes show how easy it is to get stuff into play in the media compared to other periods.

Richard Reeves: I was taken by the audience's favorable reaction to Tom's point about "the press getting out of the way." My reaction to that is also favorable. I watched the 1986 French presidential campaign in which there was a single debate between Francois Mitterand and Jacques Chirac. And it was the first time the French had ever seen anything like it. There was great excitement. We, my wife and I, watched the debate—it was called "Le Duel"—at a friend's house and for those 2 hours not a single car passed on the boulevard. One of France's most popular anchor women was the moderator, and midway in the debate she tried to interrupt an argument. Mitterand, the president, told her to be quiet and she pushed her chair back and that was it for the moderator's role in that debate. I compare that to what I considered the low point of the 1992 campaign here. The NBC debate moderated by Tom Brokaw in which about seven Democratic candidates were seated behind a long, low desk and the camera angles were such that they had to look up at Tom who was roaming a'la Donahue on a high platform. It demeaned the candidates and the process. Tom was presented as the authority figure, very assertive and very professional, cutting people off at will. It served only the purposes of NBC. The debate was about promoting NBC.

I thought why do these people sit there and take this? It was an extraordinary event and I think that coverage did improve after that. It had to improve, at least in my mind.

9 Sound Bite News

Television Coverage of Elections

DANIEL C. HALLIN

Since 1968 television has become increasingly central to the conduct of presidential campaigns. At the same time the nature and style of television news has changed dramatically. The change is complex. But one simple index provides an excellent way to begin understanding it: the length of the average sound bite. The term comes originally from radio (where it is also known as an "actuality"), and refers to a film or tape segment, within a news story, showing someone speaking.

The length of the average sound bite has been shrinking from more than 40 seconds in 1968 to less than 10 seconds in the 1980s. It has become common in recent years, as political commentators have discovered the sound bite, to hear people decry the 20-second bite. In fact, in 1988 only 4% of sound bites in the sample were that long. Twenty years before, nearly a quarter of all sound bites were a minute or longer, and it was not unusual to hear a major political figure speak for more than two minutes.

A couple of examples will help to illustrate the significance of this change: partial transcripts of two sets of TV news stories, one from 1968 and one from 1988, each reasonably representative of the campaign journalism of its era. The first is from the CBS Evening News, October 8, 1968.

> **Walter Cronkite:** Hubert Humphrey said today that the nuclear age calls for new forms of diplomacy, and he suggested regular summit meetings with the Soviet Union. He made his proposal to a meeting of the nation's newspaper editors and publishers in Washington.

EDITORS' NOTE: Reprinted from *Journal of Communication, 42,* 5-24. Used by permission of Oxford University Press.

Humphrey (speaks for 1 minute, 26 seconds.)

Cronkite (over video of press conference): Humphrey was asked about the battered state of the Democratic party.

Humphrey (speaks for 49 seconds.)

Cronkite: Last Thursday, when he became George Wallace's running mate, retired General Curtis LeMay characterized nuclear weapons as, quote, "just another weapon in the arsenal." He made clear he did not advocate their use in Vietnam. But in his words, "I think there are many occasions when it would be most efficient to use nuclear weapons." Today at a news conference in Los Angeles the subject came up again.

LeMay (speaks for 1 minute, 29 seconds, including an exchange with a reporter at his press conference.)

Cronkite: Campaigning in Connecticut today, George Wallace appealed at one stop for, quote, "the support of people of all races and colors." And at another stop he attacked the 1968 open housing law. In Wallace's words, "when both parties joined together to destroy the adage that your home is your castle, they're not fit to run this country."

Cronkite (following commercial break): Sources close to Richard Nixon say he believes that George Wallace reached his peak last week and will decline in strength. Today Nixon stepped up his attacks on the third party candidate. Bill Plante has that story in Michigan.

Plante (over video of Nixon striding through crowd to the podium): In Flint Nixon made the same appeal as he did last week in the South, because the threat is the same: George Wallace. Several local unions here have endorsed Wallace. He divides the state enough so that Nixon and Humphrey are running almost even. Therefore Nixon's tactic is to convince the voters that a vote for him is the only real vote for change.

Nixon (speaks for 32 seconds.)

Plante (over video of Nixon shaking hands with exuberant children): Earlier Nixon brought his motorcade to a sort of scheduled unscheduled stop at the Michigan State School for the Deaf where he told the youngsters of his Aunt Olive, a missionary though afflicted by deafness, and encouraged them. The Dean interpreted his remarks.

Nixon (44 seconds): When a person may not be able to hear, then he develops other qualities. Qualities of the heart. Qualities of understanding that people who may be able to hear do not develop to the same extent. It shows you that in the world in which you will be living that your country needs you, and that what you learn here in this school will give each of you a chance to render wonderful service to this country.

Here the report ended, and Cronkite went on to a story from Capitol Hill. Now let's jump forward 20 years. Here is ABC's election coverage for October 4, 1988.

Peter Jennings: Ever since the first presidential debate turned out to be pretty much of a draw, Dukakis's campaign staff has been seeking new ways to get at Vice President Bush. Here's ABC's Sam Donaldson.

Donaldson (over video of Dukakis rally): The Dukakis game plan has three parts. First an increasingly strident stump attack on George Bush's record by the candidate himself. Here's today's version.

Dukakis: He was asked to head up a task force on international terrorism. What happened? Mission failed. When he was asked to lead the war on drugs, we all know what happened. The mission has failed.

Donaldson: To be sure, Dukakis still talks about his own solutions to national problems.

Dukakis (talking to workers in a factory): I wanna make sure that every working family in this nation has basic health insurance. You have it here—it's terrific.

Donaldson: But more and more his stump speech is aimed at cutting Bush down.

Dukakis (in factory): They asked Bush about it; he said, "Well we're going to help the unemployed buy into Medicaid." Tell me what that means. You're unemployed you haven't got any money, George can't buy into anything.

Donaldson (over video from Dukakis TV ad): Part two of the strategy is to run television ads aimed at undercutting Bush's own attacks on Dukakis. Actors play the part of cynical Bush advisers who try to hoodwink the voters.

Cynical Bush adviser: How long do you expect to get away with this furlough thing?

Second adviser: Hey Bernie, how long till the election? (Laughter.)

Announcer (over graphics): They'd like to sell you a package. Wouldn't you rather choose a president?

Donaldson (over video of Bush-Dukakis debate, then Quayle, then Bentsen): Part three of the strategy is to show up better in the televised debates. In this Wednesday's Bentsen versus Quayle, the Dukakis camp is counting on Bentsen to look like the heavyweight.

Campaign Chairman Paul Brountas: He knows the issue and I expect he will do a very good job.

Donaldson: This strategy, they believe, will produce a winner.

Advisor Francis O'Brien: We are making steady progress, and again, it's all the pieces fitting together.

Donaldson: The themes of this campaign have turned out to be more negative than positive. But the Dukakis people believe they can still win that way. If they can't help you like their man more, they believe they can help you like his opponent less. Sam Donaldson, ABC News, Toledo.

A report on the Bush campaign followed. Here are a few excerpts:

Barry Serafin: Under criticism even from some Republican party elders not talking enough about issues, and seeking to blunt Democratic charges of callousness, Bush unveiled a new proposal called YES, Youth Engaged in Service, aimed at enlisting wealthy kids to help poor ones.

Bush: The end result, I hope, is that citizen service will become a real and living part of every young American's life.

Serafin: But by the second stop of the day . . . the vice president was back to the tried and true, the one-liners that in California, for example, have helped him erase a double-digit deficit on crime.

Bush: I support our law enforcement community.

Serafin: On education:

Bush: I will be the education president.

Serafin: And another familiar refrain:

Bush: Read my tips: No new taxes!

Sound Bites and Mediation

The average sound bite in the 1968 report was 60 seconds; in the 1988 report (counting the excerpt from the Dukakis ad as one sound bite), it was 8.5 seconds. But this merely reflects a more fundamental change in the structure of the news story and the role of the journalist in putting it together: modern TV news is much more mediated than the TV news of the 1960s and 1970s. During the earlier period the journalist's role as a communicator was relatively passive. Most television journalism, like the CBS report quoted above, was dominated more by the words of candidates and officials than by those of journalists. One should notice that Cronkite not only introduced long, uninterrupted sound bites from speeches and press conferences but also spent much of his time quoting the candidates. This too was typical of the journalism of these years, which was replete with phrases like, "in Wallace's words," and "the President said."

Today's television journalist displays a sharply different attitude toward the words of candidates and other newsmakers. Today those words, rather than simply being reproduced and transmitted to the audience, are treated as raw material to be taken apart, combined with other sounds and images, and reintegrated into a new narrative. Not only are speeches and other statements chopped into brief sound bites, but visuals, including both film and graphics, are used much more extensively. Journalists use outside material, information brought in at the initiative of the journalist rather than offered by the candidates, to put the statements and actions of the latter into perspective. Using experts to comment on the campaign, for example, is a very recent development.

Material from different settings is also combined more frequently. One striking example of this and in general of the mediated form of modern TV news is a CBS story on Bush's vice presidential campaign (September 28, 1984) in which correspondent David Dow illustrated a point about Bush's strategy by having the Vice President say a single sentence made up of five one-second sound bites taken from speeches in different cities. This shifts the focus from what Bush is saying, to what the journalist is saying about the Bush campaign.

Finally, the journalist in a modern television story generally imposes on all these elements the unity of a clear story line. The difference between Donaldson's 1988 Dukakis story and Plante's Nixon story illustrates this well. Donaldson's report has a single organizing theme that runs from beginning to end: Dukakis's three-part "game plan." Plante does some interpretation of Nixon's strategy, but his report does not have a consistent unifying theme. Notice that it simply ends with Nixon speaking: the correspondent doesn't "wrap" the story up. About 12% of filing reports in 1968 ended without closing lines by the correspondent; no such story appeared in the sample after 1976. These numbers only hint at the change, though, since closing lines in the earlier years didn't always sum the story up the way they usually do today. Some, for instance, simply told where the candidate would appear next. The metaphor of wrapping up a story is quite apt: a modern television news story is tightly "packaged" in a way that its predecessors normally were not.

This packaging means that the modern news story is much more journalist-centered than its predecessor: the journalist, not the candidate or other "news-maker" (a term that seems increasingly inadequate as the making of news has become more interactive), is the primary communicator.

Why the Change?

Three kinds of explanations for this change are plausible. The first has to do with technical evolution of the television medium—not only technology in the narrow sense, but the evolution of technical culture more broadly, of television "know-how" and a television aesthetic. There were, of course, many new machines developed that made it easier to produce highly complex modern news stories, including graphics generators, electronic editing units, and telecommunications technologies that made it easy and cheap to transport video images. Beyond this, it simply took television people—who, after all, in the early days were trained in radio and in print—considerable time to develop a sense of how to communicate through this new medium. Looking back at the television news of the 1960s and early 1970s, a period increasingly lionized today as the golden age of the medium, much of it seems not only more "primitive" in the sense that it is technically simpler than modern TV news, but really less competent—dull, disorganized, and difficult to follow. Television journalists are better at using the medium today than they were in 1968.

But technological explanations for political and cultural changes rarely can stand by themselves. A second factor was the weakening of political consensus and authority in the years of Vietnam and Watergate, which pushed all of American journalism in the direction of more active reporting. At the beginning of the 1960s, American journalism in general, print or broadcast, was relatively "unmediated," in the sense that statements of government officials and other major political actors were for the most part reported at face value, with relatively little questioning or interpretation by the journalist. As political divisions widened in the 1960s and 1970s, however, and as the "credibility gap" over Vietnam was followed by Watergate, the old forms of reporting no longer seemed adequate.

Elections were important in their own right to the change in journalism. NBC's John Chancellor, who heard some of the results of this study at a 1990 conference, responded by saying, "I think that the politicians started it," that is, the sound bites and the packaging. And there is much truth to this. The journalists were responding to election campaigns increasingly packaged for television, with a heavy reliance on pacing and visual imagery. The Nixon campaigns of 1968 and 1972 were especially significant. In 1968, for example, the Nixon campaign hired Roger Ailes, formerly a producer of the *Mike Douglas Show,* to create a series of one-hour television shows directed at the voters of particular states. These shows were built around television "production values" of a sort that television journalists had barely begun to consider, including considerable concern with the length of Nixon's answers to questions posed by the selected panels of voters, which Ailes carefully measured (McGinniss, 1969). Journalists were excluded from the "set" during these shows, and this sort of adversary relation between campaigns and the press was often characteristic of the new, television-oriented form of campaigning, as it was of television-oriented politics in general (Kernell, 1986). Television made it possible for candidates to reach the voters without the mediation of journalists.

Following the 1968 and 1972 campaigns, journalists often sounded alarms about the danger that the media would be manipulated by image-making candidates. This anxiety was particularly strong among television journalists, who were correctly perceived as the main "targets" of modern image-making. Sig Mickelson, an executive of CBS news, wrote following the 1972 campaign:

Television news has acquired skills experience, remarkable electronic machinery, and sophistication. But there seems to be no place or way to use them. The political managers seem to have learned more. They discovered the methods required to bend news reports to their own ends and to take the leadership themselves. They have the momentum. It now remains to be seen whether the broadcasters can recover the initiative (Mickelson, 1973, p. 168; see also Mickelson, 1989).

The manipulation of television and the need for journalists to be less passive was also a major theme of Timothy Crouse's (1974) influential book on the 1972 campaign, *The Boys on the Bus.*

As television journalists became increasingly wary of being manipulated, they responded by taking a more adversarial stance toward the candidates, dissecting their statements, as Donaldson and Serafin do in the 1988 stories quoted above, and debunking their image-making strategies. The more interpretive reporting of 1980s campaign coverage is largely preoccupied with this debunking enterprise.

One result is that election coverage has become increasingly negative in tone. In a study of CBS coverage of the 1980 campaign, Robinson and Sheehan (1983) found that stories negative toward the candidates were about twice as common as positive ones. Following their analysis, we coded stories as positive, negative, ambiguous (or mixed), or neutral in the predominant tone of their commentary. The results show that the negative tone developed simultaneously with the 10-second sound bite: in 1968 positive and negative stories were about equally frequent; from 1980 on, however, negative stories clearly predominated.

The Political Meaning of Sound-Bite News

In many ways modern TV news is much better journalism than it was 20 years ago. It is, first of all, often more interesting to watch; there is certainly nothing wrong with television people learning to use the medium more effectively. It is also more serious journalism in several ways. Media critics pressed the networks to be less passive, to tell the public more about the candidates' image-making strategies. The networks have done so, and this is surely an advance. Modern campaigning is based on refined, often manipulative techniques of image-making and news management, and the public needs to know how these techniques work.

And yet there is a great deal that is disturbing in the mediated style of modern campaign reporting. First and simplest, it is disturbing that the public never has a chance to hear a candidate—or anyone else—speak for more than about 20 seconds. Showing humans speaking is something television does very effectively. Some of the long sound bites in early television news were very dull, to be sure; many could have been cut in half with little loss, and many no doubt could have been eliminated altogether. It's hard to see what viewers gain by hearing Richard Nixon ramble for 43 seconds about his Aunt Olive. But often it was extremely interesting, or so it seems to me looking back from 20 years later, to hear a politician, or even once in a while a community leader or ordinary voter, speak an entire paragraph. One had a feeling of understanding something of the person's character and the logic of his or her argument that a 10-second sound bite can never provide. One also had a feeling of being able to judge for oneself, a feeling that the modern "wrap-up" denies. That feeling may have been false for the average viewer, given the limited background information the old style of journalism provided. But analysis and background information can be provided without shortening sound bites to 10 seconds and less.

Finally, the rise of mediated TV news is connected with an increasing preoccupation with campaign technique and a kind of "inside dopester" perspective that puts the image-making at the center of politics and pushes real political debate to the margins. Even when a modern campaign report devotes significant time to issues, the main story line typically focuses on strategy and tactics, often on the question of whether the candidate has made a "good move" in focusing on a particular issue (Boot, 1989).

The dominant tone that results from all this, as Todd Gitlin (1990) has pointed out, is a kind of knowing, "postmodern" cynicism that debunks the image and the image-maker, yet in the end seems to accept them as the only reality we have left. It is hard to be nostalgic either for the politics of 1968 or for the passive television journalism of that era. But it must be said that in 1968 one did have a feeling that the campaign, as it appeared on television, was at its core important, that it was essentially a debate about the future of the nation. As sophisticated as it is, modern television news no longer conveys that sense of seriousness.

10 The U.S. Media

Supermarket or Assembly Line?

BEN H. BAGDIKIAN

The proper measure of a country's mass media is whether, by thorough examination and reporting, they increase understanding of important realities and whether, through presentation of the widest possible spectrum of thought and analysis, they create an adequate reservoir of insights into the social process. The media may produce entertainment and sell merchandise, but if, in addition, they do not create a rich marketplace of ideas and serious information, they fail a prime function. Diversity and richness in the media are not ornaments of a democracy but essential elements for its survival.

Typical assertions of the vitality of the media marketplace have, I believe, two basic flaws. One is the equating of the quality of media outlets, the volume of their output, and their impressive revenues with diversity and richness of content. This is done, I think, because that equation is quantifiable and, in our national reverence for numbers, is accepted as unassailable proof. There is a tendency to avoid social analysis of media content because it is only partially quantifiable, is highly subjective, and involves politics and ideologies.

The other common flaw is to ignore one of the two basic processes by which the mass media relate to their society. One process involves the distribution of media content to the public, and in this the United States is among the most successful in the world: Almost the entire population has access to an extraordinary volume of media output in print, broadcasting, and recordings. The other crucial process determines who and

EDITORS' NOTE: Reprinted from *Journal of Communication, 35,* 97-109. Used by permission of Oxford University Press.

what can become part of the media message. How many voices, how many subgroups of society, how many creators of ideas and analyses have entry to the mass media? It is this process that receives inadequate attention in the more optimistic views of the marketplace of ideas. The U.S. media are becoming more homogenized in content and structure at the same time that the population is becoming larger and more diverse and confronted with rapidly changing circumstances. There is a growing gap between the number of voices in society and the number heard in the media.

The only reliable source of diversity and richness in U.S. mass media content is diversity of ownership of the media and a public attitude that accepts the legitimacy of a rich marketplace of ideas including unconventional and anti-establishment ideas.

Unfortunately, the first condition—diverse ownership—is necessary before the second—public tolerance of diversity—can be achieved. Public acceptance of a full range of public ideas does not emerge solely from exhortations for tolerance. It comes from experiencing diversity. A public used to a narrow range of ideas will come to regard this narrowness as the only acceptable condition.

Media operators often claim that their media properties are open to all ideas, but they are not. Diversity cannot come from noblesse oblige in those who control the media. True pursuit of ideas comes from those who personally believe in them. A wide collection of diverse knowledge and ideas in the media comes from a widely diverse set of individuals among whom there are significant differences in sincerely held ideas and values.

The United States has more media outlets than any other society, but the reason is too often ignored. In most other democracies, all major social policies and programs are decided and implemented by the national government. The news and analysis of governmental decisions are presented by national newspapers and broadcasters. A cluster of national papers, all distributed throughout the nation, compete with each other in social-political outlook as well as commercially. Local media outlets in such countries are called "provincial" not just because of their outlying locations, but because they do not carry serious governmental and commercial news. The United States is radically different. Some central policies—education, property taxes, police, land use, etc.—are decided by local governments. As a result, a national press has been slow to develop: only in the last twenty years the *Wall Street Journal* and, more recently, *USA Today* and the *New York Times*. At best, all New York and Washington centered papers have only seven percent of national circulation. Instead, there is a local press that combines not only serious national and international news but also the crucial local news that is not available in any national medium.

For the same reason, all licenses for radio and television are made on a local basis, with the broadcasters obligated to maintain local studios and, theoretically, to originate a significant quantity of strictly local programs. If local politics and economics were not crucial in the United States, modern technology could duplicate here what exists in other countries—all serious newspapers created centrally and distributed nationwide, and a few broadcast studios in a central place and easily relayed to each city and town.

In recent decades two basic changes have altered the nature of these media: the growth of control in a relatively small number of corporate hands, and a rapid homogenization of content that increasingly makes most newspapers and broadcast programs uniform in basic content, tone, and social and political values.

For reasons that will be described later, the content of different media has become increasingly uniform despite the vast number of individual outlets. The great majority of newspapers have the same content in nonlocal serious news and in their specialized sections, and they share the same political and social values. Magazines differ in their specialization, but in most major categories the content is similar, as, for example, among all popular women's and news magazines.

Broadcasting is the most uniform of all. In radio, despite 8,000 different commercial stations, a dozen formats—certain types of music or talk shows—fill most of the hours of transmission, most of it recorded centrally and played identically in every station using that format.

In television, three networks provide most of the content for the 1,000 local commercial stations; what remains is filled almost entirely with prerecorded syndicated programs that not only have nothing to do with a particular locality but are similar in content even among competing programs. There are, for example, no serious differences in the content or basic approach to programs among the three networks.

There continue to be small operators in most of the media, and they continue to play an important role. Small papers, journals, and book publishers periodically produce important and useful work. Historically, it has been the small voices that created the germinal and most brilliant new knowledge and insights. That continues. But, with few exceptions, the small voices, when they are important, have a quiet, long-term impact; they cannot compete with the major media in distribution or in influence over public opinion and government policy.

It is natural to look for explicit proof that monopoly and concentrated control change the nature of public information and popular culture. One piece of evidence is the "smoking gun" proof that an owner has intervened in a self-serving way in the selection of news, programming, or literature. There is a steady succession of known incidents of owners suppressing or distorting journalistically legitimate stories, of books killed at the corporate level out of corporate prejudices, or of producers, editors, and reporters fired or demoted for offending owners with accurate stories, articles, and programs. Any media organization requires only one publicized incident of this kind to have a widespread and lasting effect on all. Not only is self-censorship likely but also, as a result, professional practices may become established, under the label of conventions, that last after the originating incident has faded.

Systematic studies show that, even without observable owner intervention, monopoly and cross-ownership by themselves reduce public information. Results of these studies have differed over the years. A 1956 study by Nixon and Jones in *Journalism Quarterly* found no significant differences between competitive and monopoly newspapers. Writing in the same journal ten years later, Rarick and Hartman found more serious news in competing papers. Eleven years later, Thrift found reduced editorial vigor in chain papers. In a 1978 Berkeley master's thesis, Keller found more live local and national news in independent papers compared with chain papers. A narrow range of news in cities where the local newspaper and television station are owned by the same corporation was found by Gormley in a 1976 study. The weight of these studies is that monopoly and concentrated ownership do reduce breadth of information.

The principal impact of concentrated corporate control of media content is not, unfortunately, easily studied or measured, nor as visible as the publicized punishment of professionals who offend owners' political sensibilities.

There is a larger influence that is far more subtle and pervasive. Suggestions that owning corporations influence the nature of news, entertainment, and literature because they are large monopolies or oligopolies often evoke the image of cartoon media barons—the swashbuckling publisher ripping unwanted stories daily from his newspaper, the magazine or book house executive screening each article and book to make certain that it promotes a single-minded favorite idea, or masters of the media meeting in secret to plot a unified propaganda for the country. There are individuals who try to run their media corporations this way, but they are the exception.

Major media owners differ among themselves, as do their corporations, in personality, style, and outlook, but these differences are minor on any realistic scale of the total values of society. They have a narrow, common outlook not because of a conspiracy but because corporations of this size and power by their nature have common goals and outlooks, particularly in economics, in politics, and in sustaining the status quo. They have self-interest, as does every individual and institution, but they have more power to pursue that self-interest, and they control access to the public mind.

Concern with narrow control of the media does not require a belief that corporately owned media are totally devoted to their owners' personal propaganda. Modern media are complex, and the need to capture and keep large audiences inhibits propaganda that is too obviously propaganda. The major media carry much that their owners personally disagree with. But this does not prevent propagandistic use by emphasizing certain issues and de-emphasizing others, by pursuing some subjects relentlessly and quickly abandoning others. This was done in the late nineteenth century by many prominent newspapers, right and left, and it is done today in more subtle ways (except for unsubtle operators like Rupert Murdoch).

Finally, the concern with concentrated control and a narrow marketplace of ideas does not require a belief that professional reporters, writers, editors, and producers within the major media are corrupt or without professional standards. Journalistic performance standards are higher in the United States than in any other democracy, if that judgment is based on the average U.S. journalist compared to the average elsewhere and if it defines this American excellence as accuracy of observation of visible events and clear presentation of factual material. What is weak in U.S. journalism, compared to the best journalism in other democracies, is systematic political and social analysis that indicates the sources, relationships, and consequences of individual events.

Owner influence in the media is exercised primarily at second hand, in ways that are effective, necessary, and natural: Owners hire and fire those who make the everyday decisions on content. It is a rare corporation that hires an influential executive known to be inimical to the owner's heartfelt social values.

Entire organizations, whether automobile assembly lines or ballet companies, are easily socialized to conform to a leader's wishes. Individuals make their hourly and daily work decisions in conformity to observed conventions without receiving explicit written or spoken orders on how to treat their work. The same is true in news organizations, as any observation makes clear and as the studies of others have shown.

Consequently, narrowing of political and social content in the media comes not from killing existing content but from a more subtle process before the content is ever created. Most reporters and writers insist that they are never told what to write, by which they usually mean that they are not told to write something they believe to be false. But most are told every day what to write, in the sense that it is a necessary function in the media to decide which of the infinite number of possible subjects to pursue, assign, and publicize and which to ignore. It is a normal and necessary function in all the media to pursue some subjects and ignore others, to emphasize some material and de-emphasize other. It is within this necessary professional decision making that corporate values and the central aims of owners are embedded.

The narrow range of ideas in the mass media is not the result solely of narrow and uniform ownership of the media; it comes, perhaps in even more basic and intractable ways, from the economics of the media.

Concentrated ownership has at least a theoretical remedy—divestiture through antitrust action—although this is unlikely given the political power of present owners. But the profit motive is essential as an alternative to government-operated media, and while it has produced pathologies and limitations in the media it has also been indispensable. The reliance on advertising by newspapers, magazines, radio, and television is not inevitable, but it, too, has altered media content in negative ways.

Profits and advertising are affected through media ownership by large national and multinational corporations that compete in world markets for profitability and therefore escalate media profit margins by, among other things, intensifying advertising revenues. But even if all the media were owned by small entrepreneurs, money making and advertising would narrow the range of ideas.

There is no practical alternative to free enterprise for the majority of the media in the United States. Many of the world's more distinguished newspapers are owned by nonprofit foundations, but the U.S. media are too numerous and have too different a history to make this plausible except for a few exceptions. The same is true of broadcasting, magazines, and book houses.

Furthermore, the profit motive has basic advantages. It is an efficient way to create new ventures that have a perceived future. It inhibits, but does not prevent, too obvious a narrow use. If there is competition, it forces efficient operation and represents some measure of public acceptance.

Unfortunately, the advantages of the profit motive in the media have been used to obscure some of its disadvantages. At the least, major media have not been generous in informing their audiences about these disadvantages, including the development of monopoly, oligopoly, excessive profits, and overly uniform content.

In the simple village trade in turnips of Adam Smith's marketplace, farmers may have been tempted to sell poor quality turnips at exorbitant prices. But if they did, other farmers would seize the opportunity to win away housewives with better quality and lower prices. The housewives were experts on turnips, which they could feel, smell, taste, and, if necessary, grow themselves. In this way, profit making was a self-righting mechanism against monopoly and unscrupulous manipulation of the product. But most of the U.S. media are monopolies or oligopolies. Ninety-eight percent of cities with newspapers have a monopoly paper. Three networks with largely similar content control most of the television audience. The magazine and book field is rapidly becoming concentrated in ownership and imitativeness. The individual consumer of news and entertainment, unlike Adam Smith's housewives with turnips, cannot create a substitute product. If there is a monopoly or oligopoly making very high profits, which most do, the entry costs for newcomers in such large enterprises are so high that few can become new competitors, and these are limited to large corporations with the same characteristics as those already entrenched.

Existing operators in the media have another advantage over the turnip farmer. Turnips are turnips, and most users have absolute measures of taste and ability to grow their own. But media operators to a large extent create the public's standard of judgment: What the U.S. public has seen on television for decades becomes the standard of what is expected from television.

Furthermore, the "product" of the mass media, including light entertainment, unlike turnips, is complex and filled with social, political, and economic meaning. Dominant media corporations operate at the highest levels of national and international power and have political and social goals crucial to their power. Overwhelmingly they favor lower corporate taxes, lower levels of social services for the general public, and governmental and market advantages for large corporations rather than for small entrepreneurs; they resist antipollution and other public health measures that might reduce their profits; and they demand governmental, tax-supported protection for their overseas investments. That is natural for them. But it is hardly the best basis for control of the media marketplace of ideas.

The politics of media owners have affected media content and public opinion on major issues. The media were notoriously slow to report seriously on post-World War II phenomena like the existence of structural poverty, the depredations of McCarthyism during the Cold War, and resistance to racial segregation. It took dramatic public outbreaks or governmental and judicial action before journalistic attention was directed at these profound developments. Most of the major media for years resisted overwhelming evidence of U.S. policy failures in Vietnam or the early evidence of the Watergate scandal in the Nixon administration.

Thus, when media operators say that, if they used their properties in manipulative ways, "the public would not stand for it," this justification has only limited validity. The public cannot react to what it does not know. In entertainment and literature, as with news, the public cannot make a choice unless it is presented with clear alternatives.

Moreover, media content is sufficiently complex so that one segment can offer positive or neutral material for the consumers while elsewhere the owner can press personal or corporate goals. This was done by Hearst, Pulitzer, Scripps, and Dana in the nineteenth century and in the twentieth century by, among others, Frank Gannett, Colonel McCormick, and Henry

Luce, who stridently pressed their own political aims while collecting large audiences and high profits. The elder Hearst even demonstrated the maximum possible manipulation of a large mass medium by using his newspapers in the nineteenth century to push one end of the political spectrum, socialism, and in the twentieth reversing himself and pushing ultraconservatism. Henry Luce influenced a whole generation of public attitudes toward China. Stressing the U.S. fear of communism and support for Christianity—strong values that already existed in the population— he de-emphasized the Chinese Communists' popular support and rejection of Stalinist doctrine and similarly de-emphasized the opposition of the Nationalists' corruption, ineffectiveness, and lack of popular support. He did this while making *Time* magazine so profitable that it became the basis for the present formidable media empire of Time, Inc.

The existence of high profits in the newspaper business, for example, does not mean that the politics of a newspaper are supported by its readers. Daily newspaper presidential endorsements since 1948 have averaged 78 percent for the Republican candidate, while the average for voters for those candidates was 51 percent. The heavy pro-Republican editorials may or may not have influenced votes: That is a matter of dispute, though the effect on news coverage is less in doubt. But it is clear that the values of media owners are substantially different from those of the public at large. The need, of course, is not to eliminate the profit motive or owners' opinions, but to prevent monopoly and oligopoly in the mass media through sheer economic power.

The other business influence on homogeneity, in addition to monopoly and oligopoly, is advertising. Advertising is the major source of profits for newspapers, magazines, radio, and television. The conventional fear of advertising is that advertisers may have the power to censor editorials and programming in their favor. The public exaggerates that danger as it applies to day-by-day operations, but it is not a misplaced fear when it comes to larger issues over a long period of time. The most dramatic example of the media's thematic self-censorship in order to protect a major advertiser has been the media's extraordinary silence and de-emphasis for the last sixty years in handling scientific evidence about a major killer of Americans: heart-lung disease as linked to tobacco use. For decades, newspapers, magazines, and broadcasters were silent about the medical evidence. Later, overwhelming evidence and public concern led to the other de-emphasis technique: the hesitant use of medical evidence and its constant equating with heavy use of the nonscientific denials of the tobacco industry. This was done while at the same time dramatizing other, far less prevalent diseases—diseases whose cause had no commercial sponsor. Reporting has improved in recent years, but the worst damage has been done.

The impact of advertising on broadcasting has been even more dramatic. With few exceptions, programs are designed primarily to make their commercials more effective. There are documented instances of specific accommodation of advertised products within programs. When cigarettes were advertised on television, villains in dramas were not permitted to smoke the advertised brand; all smoking was required to be shown in a positive manner. There is a similar tenderness toward major advertisers in most national programs. Children's programming on U.S. commercial television has resisted years of medical evidence of damage and of public appeals to end the persistent violence, aggression, and other antisocial programs used to fix attention of infants and children and thus promote advertised goods and increase network profits.

But the most important impact has been on the general nature of programs. In the 1950s, the largest audiences were for serious, original dramas on television. But after the spot commercial became the biggest moneymaker, possible to be dropped into any kind of program, television programs were consciously redesigned to be lighter, superficial, pervaded with fantasy, and not too involving in a continuous way, in order to create a buying mood in support of the commercials. The occasional serious program in prime time has large audiences, but it is not the best attraction for high-priced commercials.

Another major impact of advertising has been to narrow the desired audience for newspapers, magazines, radio, and television. The major advertisers wish to reach affluent individuals and families who are in their maximum buying years of family formation, ages 18 to 49.

Broadcasters cannot control who receives their programs and, because of the intense competition for audience size, this unrestricted reception serves a useful purpose for ratings. But broadcasters are similarly under pressure to show that, within the total audience for their programs, there is a higher proportion of affluent individuals than for competing programs.

Second, all advertising-supported media control the nature of their audiences by controlling the nature of their content. They publish and broadcast what will attract the affluent consumers between the ages of

18 and 49—the most desirable audience for advertisers. Thus, without being deliberately racist or class-prejudiced, newspapers, magazines, and broadcasters de-emphasize the content that will be relevant or interesting to the less affluent and the older population. These unwanted categories of people represent a large part of the American people. The unwanted subject matter represents some of the more important issues before the body politic.

Advertising has homogenized all nonadvertising content. Advertising-supported media aim for the same carefully defined audience, not a cross-section of the whole society. And they are designed to stimulate buying of merchandise, since that is the measure by which advertisers will support the media. So it is not surprising that, though the United States has huge numbers of media outlets, and the major media differ markedly from each other in their production and methods of transmission, they have ever-increasing uniformity of social and political content.

It might be argued that it is understandable for media owners to pursue this strategy to maximize their profits. But it does not result in an adequate marketplace of ideas.

The media marketplace of ideas cannot be measured by its size and technological virtuosity. Blandness and noise do not constitute ideas and information. When instruments of narrow ideas and triviality have sufficient power, they drown out lesser voices and discourage thought. The existence of lesser voices does not, by itself, relieve responsibility of the media. Today the smaller voices have less access than ever to the media: The usual saving remnant of small voices is less audible than ever.

History will not judge the U.S. mass media harshly simply because they provided light entertainment, fantasy, and salesmanship. Those are normal elements in any society. But a strong and creative society has needs beyond that. The question that will be asked is whether, in their insatiable pursuit of commercial values and the narrowness of their ideas, the operators of this most powerful communications system in history have lacked a proper regard for the richness and breadth of their society and for the realities of an all-too-real world.

11 Three Blind Mice

KEN AULETTA

"Shit!" shouted Jack Welch, the chairman of General Electric, after his company bought NBC in 1986. Welch pounded the table. "Ted Turner puts on CNN for twenty-four hours a day for only $100 million! Ted Turner makes $50 to $100 million. We do three hours of news. We spend $275 million and lose $100 million." To Welch, Larry Grossman, the president of NBC News, was behaving like a typical bureaucrat. "I have yet to find," Welch said, "a functional organization in twenty-seven years of running a business that ever had enough money." He said he expected Grossman to comply with his request for a 5 percent cut in the news division's budget.

Rupert Murdoch's Twentieth Century Fox was among the first to transfer to television the sex and violence that sold copies of Murdoch's *National Star* and *New York Post*. Fox was a ratings winner with *A Current Affair*, which featured lurid accounts of true crimes and other sensational material. In addition to *A Current Affair*, Fox introduced *America's Most Wanted*, a popular series about actual fugitives, some of whom were apprehended as a result of the show. Tabloid TV, as it is called, was hot. Audiences flocked to syndicated talk shows hosted by Oprah Winfrey, Phil Donahue, and Geraldo Rivera, which tantalized viewers by offering witches, bigamists, bigots, male strippers, and child molesters—what critics dubbed the Freaks of the Week.

Everywhere there was evidence of relaxed sexual standards. Calvin Klein and other advertisers flaunted sex to sell jeans. Men no longer wore shirts on daytime soap operas, and beds became a favorite prop. The dimple displayed by the *Cosmopolitan* girl was no longer on her chin. And

EDITORS' NOTE: Reprinted with permission of the author.

even family-oriented sitcoms featured dialogue that just a few years before would have been scrubbed clean. "Do you use any protection?" asked the teenage girl from under the sheets of NBC's *Valerie*, whose 8:30 p.m. time slot meant it was targeted at kids.

NBC News joined the parade when it presented a one-hour primetime special, "Scared Sexless," on December 30, 1987. Hosted by correspondent Connie Chung, "Scared Sexless" did something no network news documentary on defense or race relations or any other serious topic had done in a long time—it magnetized an audience. Nearly a third of the viewing public watched it, as the special achieved an astonishing 30 share and a 17.5 rating. On her quick tour of the subject, Chung peeked in on singles bars, on gay sex and AIDS, and on unwanted pregnancies; she listened in on sex education classes and interviewed such "experts" on sex as actors Alan Alda and Goldie Hawn, as well as Los Angeles Raiders running back Marcus Allen.

Many within NBC News sensed a line had been crossed. Network news, like newspapers themselves, had always flirted with entertainment as opposed to news values. Network news flaunted graphics and music and too rarely permitted people to complete a sentence. They cluttered the morning news shows with celebrity interviews, and when the network did a cutaway at a ball game or a supermarket counter they tried to linger on a pretty face. Newspapers also offered screaming headlines and conflict and gossip. But at heart, a network newscast, like most newspapers, took its news obligations seriously.

But "Scared Sexless" supplied the ratings now demanded from the News. Within a week of the "Scared Sexless" telecast, Larry Grossman announced that NBC News would soon offer specials on such eye-popping subjects as "Women Behind Bars," "American Men in the 80s," and "Stress." The specials, the NBC News press release emphasized, would highlight the lifestyles of various individuals. Sandwiched between were some sober documentaries on the homeless and on Islam, to be hosted by Tom Brokaw, but these were not to be the thrust of NBC News's documentaries. Over the next three years, the traditional barriers between news and entertainment would continue to collapse.

Behind "Scared Sexless," and behind tabloid TV's syndicated "Titanic" specials, crouched a dirty little secret: Viewers were bored. They craved excitement. Their attention span had shrunk. Increasingly, programmers assumed the only way to keep their attention was with surprise or shock.

Just as ABC's *Roseanne* or Fox's *The Simpson's* would offer ever more oddball families than the *Honeymooners* or *All in the Family*. Just as sending the *Today* show, *Good Morning America*, or the three anchors on the road might electrify viewers with a sense of immediacy, of something different. Novel news specials would, it was hoped, liberate the news divisions from corporate pressure to reduce losses.

By jumping aboard the tabloid TV bandwagon, NBC News was sliding down the slope Neil Postman, in his book *The Disappearance of Childhood*, ascribed not to the malevolence of TV executives, but to something more banal. TV, Postman wrote, "requires a continuous supply of novel and interesting information to engage and hold" an audience. Television has a constant need for material. "The bias and therefore the business of television is to move information, not collect it." Unlike print, television "cannot dwell" on a subject: "There may, for example, be fifty books on the history of Argentina, five hundred on childhood, five thousand on the Civil War. If television has anything to do with these subjects, it will do it once, and then move on."

Increasingly the networks pressured their local stations to promote network entertainment shows and stars on its newscasts, thus tarnishing the independence a newscast needs to retain the trust of viewers—the "big shill factor," Verne Gay of *Newsday* called it. News re-creations knocked down the walls, as did most docudramas, including ABC's version of Bob Woodward and Carl Bernstein's *The Final Day*, complete with invented dialogue. The new owners speeded the trend to hold news to the same ratings standard as entertainment shows. If a news documentary or special couldn't approximate the desired Nielsen numbers, it usually got the hook. Slowly but perceptibly, the center of gravity—the value system—shifted within much of network news. Which probably helps explain why NBC's newest magazine entry—*Expose*— in April 1991 aired a sensationalist eleven-minute report on Senator Charles S. Robb's alleged extracurricular escapades, why NBC *Nightly News* closed a newscast earlier that month with an exclusive interview with a man who claimed he had been Merv Griffin's lover, or why ABC News dabbled in re-creations of news events. Each lowered the wall between network news and such tabloid TV fare as *A Current Affair*.

Network sales scaled some walls of its own by conniving with advertisers to camouflage commercials. Increasingly the networks, like the
movie studios, accommodated advertisers by letting products be plugged
within a program or film. For example, Coca-Cola induced CBS and
Grant Tinker to let an actor on Tinker's *TV 101* ostentatiously gulp from
a can of Coke. As profit pressures mount and mass markets splinter into
hundreds of distinct market segments, advertisers will holler to knock
down more walls. "A network is not in the program business. It's not in
the news business or the sports business. It's in the business of selling
advertising," said Roy J. Bostock, president of the world's ninth-largest
ad agency, D'Arcy Masius Benton & Bowles. To sell more advertising, he
said the networks had to be more willing to hide ads within shows. Or
to name sporting events after products. Or to allow advertisers a say in
programming or to own entire shows, as they often do in daytime soap
operas and as they once did in prime time. Or to enter joint ventures with
the network. Perhaps the networks and local stations can let popular
weathermen talk about, say, Anacin, in the middle of a weather report.

Working from a twenty-page budget packet distributed to everyone
in the room, Grossman went through his budget plan in great detail. The
News budget, he said, would dip from $257.8 million in 1987 to $245.9
million this year, and down to $237 million by 1990, when they would,
he was happy to report, break even. News would have to do three things:
boost revenues; make sharp cost reductions; and exclude from the ac-
counting the $40 million the network charged to News as its share of
corporate expenses. Since personnel costs represented three quarters of
the News budget, the staff would be hardest hit. Employment in News
would drop from a high of 1,362 in 1936 to 1,000 in 1990. News would
eliminate all twenty-four National Association of Broadcast Employees
and Technicians (NABET) desk assistants, shrink the pool of correspondents from 79 to 59, cut producers from 312 to 219, slice nearly a third of
its 143-person foreign bureaus, and rely more on foreign news services
like Great Britain's Visnews.

"This is very good," the usually impatient Jack Welch would say more
than once. Welch couldn't believe what he was hearing. Larry Grossman
sounded like a convert! He even heard Grossman say the protective wall
between News and other divisions should be lowered. News hoped,
Grossman said, to co-produce with Entertainment and Sports a ninety-
minute magazine show. And to those who said news programs should

be held to a much lower Nielsen rating standard, Grossman dissented: "We would never tolerate a *West 57th* or *48 Hours*. We would never tolerate anything less than an 18 share!" Nor would News shirk new business opportunities in programming for cable, in selling programs overseas, in packaging news programs for the syndication market, in making and selling news video cassettes.

"This is a terrific job," Welch announced when Grossman had finished, "You've got a lot to be proud of. You're on your way."

As Welch rose to leave, Grossman interrupted. "One last thing, Jack," he said. "There's not a person in the place who believes GE cares about News. And since we bought into your priorities, it's important you buy into ours." He wanted some recognition of the good job NBC News had done in snaring the Gorbachev interview and the debate among the presidential contenders. He wanted Welch to make a statement extolling NBC News.

"I have no problem with that," Welch responded. "I'll be honest, I did until I saw this. . . . I know what you guys accomplished—the debate, Gorbachev. But without this [he tapped the 20-page document] Gorbachev is hogwash!"

12 Raiding the Global Village

KEN AULETTA

"Unless American soldiers are there, American television is not there," the Cable News Network correspondent Christiane Amanpour observed recently about network coverage of foreign stories. Amanpour says that in the world's various trouble spots she occasionally encounters a competitor from ABC, the American network that offers the most determined coverage of overseas news. Rarely, however, does she find herself competing with CBS or NBC, each of which saves money by having a correspondent in Washington or London do an authoritative sounding voice-over with pictures from a video service. She more often notices reporters from the BBC or Reuters, or, sometimes, a team from Rupert Murdoch's British Sky Broadcasting, or the cameras of national broadcasters from France, Australia, Canada, or Spain. But Amanpour does not generally feel the heat of competition from other television-news outlets. "Everywhere I go, foreign news equals CNN," she says.

CNN has come to dominate the world-news stage. Its ascendancy was confirmed in 1989 with its blanket coverage of the Tiananmen Square massacre. That coverage was followed by coverage of the collapse of the Berlin Wall; of the first coup attempt on live television, in the Soviet Union; and of the first live war, in the Persian Gulf. Only CNN could dedicate its twenty-four-hour news channel to these events. Only CNN reaches two hundred countries and more than sixteen percent of the world's eight hundred million TV homes.

When President Bill Clinton ordered the bombing of Iraq's intelligence center, in June, and the armed services had yet to confirm a hit, David Gergen, who had just been appointed counselor to the president, phoned

EDITORS' NOTE: Reprinted with permission of the author.

CNN's president Tom Johnson, and got a confirmation. Only then did Clinton announce the mission.

Using the latest satellite technology, CNN, which was launched by Ted Turner in 1980, has captivated decisionmakers and the public alike. It proclaims itself to be the creator of Marshall McLuhan's electronic "global village" and "the world's only twenty-four-hour global television news network." But Turner is now being challenged by competitors in the same way that he and cable TV challenged the dominance of the big three American television networks. The most prominent challenger is the BBC, which in early last year [1992] announced the launching of BBC World Service Television, a twenty-four-hour global-news channel. Just this March [1993] the BBC forged a still vague alliance with ABC, saying that it would swap footage and pool foreign bureaus with ABC, the most diversified of the big three networks. This electronic alliance, the BBC proclaimed, would strengthen its hand against CNN—which the BBC dismisses as an American news service rather than an international one.

ABC itself was also challenging Turner. The network had shrunk, but still had more foreign bureaus or offices (a dozen) than either CBS or NBC, and its nightly newscast used more stories from overseas than either of the other two. ABC/Capital Cities owned eighty percent of a third player, Worldwide Television News (WTN), a video service that often competed with the BBC. "The announcement that ABC is linking with the BBC is one we are tracking carefully," Tom Johnson said.

A fourth challenger is Reuters Television, which includes what used to be known as Visnews and now serves a hundred and fifty broadcasters in eighty nations. Like WTN and the Associated Press, Reuters has concentrated on being a wholesale supplier rather than a retail distributor of news over a dedicated channel. But this may be changing. Telemundo, the Spanish-language television network, after deciding not to renew a five-year alliance with CNN, teamed up with Reuters and the BBC to create a twenty-four-hour Spanish language news service to be disseminated throughout South America, Spain, and parts of North America. In contrast to CNN, whose international news is packaged out of Atlanta, London, and Washington, Reuters is decentralized, and is delivered in fifteen languages. Since Reuters provides customers like CNN with its video wire service, it does not want to antagonize them, but its executive director and editor-in-chief, Mark Wood, makes it clear that Reuters is open to other alliances. "If other opportunities come along in other languages, we'd look at them," he says.

The Associated Press is also looking at the possibility of using its bureaus (ninety of them outside the United States) to provide video as well as print and radio reports. "The board has authorized us to return with a plan for an international video service," A.P.'s president, Louis D. Boccardi, says, adding that he hopes to reach a decision on this matter by the end of the year. Though Boccardi stresses the point that "we don't see ourselves in the retail business" (and thus as a direct competitor of A.P. clients), an A.P. video service could strengthen the hand of CNN rivals.

Then, there is also Murdoch's Sky News. Sky has teamed with twelve state-owned broadcasters to form Euronews, which broadcasts by satellite throughout the continent, as well as in Britain, in five languages. And Murdoch is also trying to expand into Asia, the world's most populous continent.

Although the two less active American networks seem to have pulled back from the international arena—NBC sold its stake in Visnews to Reuters last year, and CBS can no longer claim to be the world's premier television-news outlet—there are signs that they, too, are stirring. NBC has kicked off a twenty-four-hour Spanish news service and is talking to Reuters and an Italian-owned superstation as it searches for partners. "Gartner did nothing overseas," the NBC News president, Andrew Lack, says of his predecessor, Michael Gartner. Lack goes on to say that the president of NBC, Robert C. Wright, who appointed him, is "so concerned that we are walking around with our pants around our ankles" that he appointed a committee to explore new relationships overseas. CNBC, the twenty-four-hour cable channel owned by NBC, which now broadcasts most business news, has become a chip in the negotiations. "It's a component, because for foreign partners it's another outlet for them," Lack says. "They're trying to crack the North American market." None of the big three networks will let them on their channels, but CNBC would. "CNN won't be there by itself anymore," Robert Wright says.

CBS has been the most cautious of the big three American networks. Until recently, CBS has been content to maintain, like the other networks, a video-exchange program with various foreign broadcasters. But CBS is now talking to potential overseas partners, including CLT, the European media conglomerate in Luxembourg, which has a powerful satellite signal throughout Europe. "We're talking to people. We're looking for opportunities right now," said Jay L. Kriegel, a CBS senior vice president.

Each of these real or potential competitors was coming at CNN frontally. Coming at CNN from other directions are local broadcast and cable outlets and national and regional news operations, all of which have blossomed as television has been privatized overseas and as satellite, cable, and fiber-optic technology has enhanced their reach. They were riding the wave of government deregulation and technology in the 1990s just as Ted Turner did in the 1980s.

CNN has a nice head start in the race to be the dominant force in international news. Its global reach has multiplied seventy fold since Turner launched it. When it first appeared, in 1980, it had a million seven hundred thousand household subscribers and in its first six months it had seven hundred million dollars in revenue. In its first five years, it lost money. In 1992, it reached a hundred and thirty-six million viewers, brought in five hundred and thirty-six million dollars in revenue, and earned a profit of a hundred and fifty-five million dollars. In 1985, to expand overseas, Turner created a new channel—CNN International. He then worked out cooperative agreements with a hundred and forty-three nations, rotating their news reports regularly on CNNI, and built solid relationships. CNN's credibility with the Iraqi government helped make it the only outside network broadcasting live from Iraq during the Gulf War.

Like soft-drink and cigarette manufacturers, who have looked to other markets as their domestic business leveled off, CNN is targeting its future growth outside the United States. Its broadcasts can now be seen in twenty-three Asian countries, and it plans to open a production center in Asia next year. In Europe, CNN is expanding its studio production facilities in London, and Turner has recently got over a long-standing aversion to being involved in any business he could not put his brand name on. In one year, Turner acquired a quarter of the shares of NTV, a twenty-four-hour German language news service, and became an equal partner with a group of former Soviet television executives in Russia's first independent TV channel, Moscow 6 TV. CNN also announced an agreement to distribute its programs to households in 5 African countries—Nigeria, Ghana, Kenya, Zambia, and Uganda. Meanwhile, in Latin America, Turner amended CNN's de-facto policy that its news will be transmitted only in English; CNN now produces four daily half-hour news programs that are broadcast in Spanish to nineteen countries in Central and South America.

Perhaps the biggest advantage CNN has against upstart competitors is that it is a franchise with instant name recognition. The level of recognition was demonstrated in Somalia in June [1993]: While American and United Nations troops were unable to find the fugitive warlord Muhammad Farah Aidid, he did let reporters find him, and he declared that to keep abreast of events he had been hiding only in homes that received CNN. On being asked to describe CNN's strength, Turner says, "We're welcomed everywhere in the world. What's the reason to have another one?" Still, he knows that CNN is open to attack from competitors on at least three fronts: It is not yet truly international; it is not local; it has so few overseas partners that its distribution system is stretched thin.

CNN presents news packaged from an American viewpoint. And news from an American viewpoint does not have mass appeal overseas as the big three networks can attest, since they have never had much success selling their nightly newscasts elsewhere. Parochialism is an issue that the BBC and other competitors regularly use to club CNN with. It becomes a delicate point in a world in which nationalism is resurgent and many nations are already alarmed about American "cultural imperialism."

In describing CNN as "a global English-language service" Peter C. Vesey, who runs CNN International, identifies both CNN's niche and its frailty. From the outset, CNN has spoken in one language, and Turner has decreed that most newscasts be assembled in Atlanta. CNN has nineteen overseas bureaus; CNN International has a staff of a hundred in Atlanta and just three in London. While CNN is working to improve these numbers, at present forty percent of the twenty-four-hour newscast on CNN International from Monday through Friday is recycled from CNN's domestic news; on weekends, eighty percent is recycled. The international news is delivered from anchor desks in Atlanta, London, and Washington and is produced in Atlanta, where Vesey is based. In March [1993], responding to the BBC's World Service Television's linkup with Star TV, the most powerful satellite-distribution system in Asia, CNN launched a week of live programming from Asia. But instead of using a local news staff CNN sent three American anchors—Bernard Shaw, Larry King, and Lou Dobbs—to Hong Kong and Tokyo.

John C. Malone, who is the chief executive officer of Tele-Communications Inc., the nation's largest cable operator, and is one of the part owners and board members of CNN's parent company, Turner Broadcasting, worries that CNN has too strong an American identity. "This is a debate I've had with Ted Turner for years," he said recently, "Ted's going to have to have some local partners. Ted hates partners." Indeed, before the BBC linked up with Star TV, whose parent company is partly owned by the Chinese government, Turner rejected an alliance with Star. "They took a deal we turned down," Turner says of the BBC. "They're working for the Chinese."

Tom Johnson says CNN is shoring up its defenses and broadening both its language and its anchor-correspondent base. "We will also serve the world in other languages," he says. "How many of those languages, I don't know." But surely, he goes on, CNN will one day replace the two hours a day of subtitled translations now shown in places like Japan, and, in addition to Spanish and Russian, will probably broadcast at least some news in Japanese, Chinese, and French. CNN is in a push to hire more non-American journalists. It recently recruited Riz Khan, who was born in South Yemen; Sonia Ruessler, who has dual Argentine and Dutch citizenship; and Linden J. Soles, a Canadian who anchors CNN's newscasts from Atlanta. "We're not all American-looking and sounding," says Amanpour, who herself was born in Britain, and whose parents are British and Iranian.

CNN's strong American identity reflects a deeper vulnerability: By pursuing its stated goal of being "the world's only twenty-four-hour global television-news network," CNN is obviously determined not to be local. It does not provide abundant local, or even national, weather, sports, and community news in the countries it sends its newscasts to. It does not promote local personalities. "That's where he's truly vulnerable," Herb Granath, the president of ABC/Capital Cities' Video Enterprises, which has many partnerships all over the world, says of Ted Turner. By presenting international news in English, Granath says, Turner bumps into the reality that more nations want news in their own language. "I do believe there will be a national news service in most European countries with twenty-four hours of news in the local language," Granath goes on. Such local services are or will soon be operating in France, Hong Kong, England, Germany, and parts of southern China. In this sense,

CNN suffers from the same threat that the new video democracy poses to any channel that offers a uniform program at a single, prescheduled hour: Viewers want, and increasingly enjoy, the freedom to customize what they watch and to make their own schedules.

But overseas partnering does seem to be the vogue as communications companies seek to share risks and costs and to lower local political barriers. Right now, CNN's stiffest competition is not any single international competitor but many competitors. They change from continent to continent. In Europe, it comes from, among others, Sky News and Euronews, whose programming includes news from the BBC. In Africa and the Middle East, the Middle East Broadcasting Company, which owns United Press International, is now a CNN rival, and so is the BBC. In South America, the Reuters/Telemundo alliance looms, and so do NBC and Grupo Televisa S.A., the world's largest Spanish-language broadcast company, which now owns half of PanAmSat L.P. and plans to launch three private satellites that will distribute Spanish news and programming. In Asia, the BBC has more viewers than CNN, and there are burgeoning news services in Japan, China, Indonesia, and India. In Australia, where Murdoch's News Corporation continues to be a dominant player, the national network has joined with the Canadian Broadcast Company to share technical facilities and crews. And, as the boundaries between the television set and the computer and the telephone converge, telephone companies may continue to join with one another or with giant communications companies, as they have begun to do both here and abroad.

This suggests that there are at least two competing future models for world news. One is Ted Turner's. "Nationalism is not growing," he says. "Internationalism is growing. Look at the growth of the United Nations. In Somalia, the United States is part of the United Nations force." The Cold War is over, nations are no longer forced to choose sides, and CNN can be a single, common international carriers of news, Turner says. In the next breath, however, he says "Localism is strong. I know that." Nevertheless, he thinks he has certain advantages. "The networks have closed down their international operations," he says, somewhat hyperbolically. Murdoch's Fox network, which a year ago threatened to start a news service, has recently scaled back its domestic plans. "We're the only distribution system that goes out to the whole world." And his will remain low-cost.

In many ways, the development of global news parallels the development of an interconnected world economy. The world's elites—travelers, government leaders, diplomats, and corporate and communications officials—want a common database, which CNN supplies. They also want to know that a news standard is upheld—that the news strives for fairness and balance. For this niche CNN is now rivaled only by the BBC.

But there is a chasm between the elites and the mass of viewers, whose vision is primarily local. To reach this larger mass of viewers, CNN would have to dramatically change its vision of a single, English-speaking global network. But to effect that change Turner would need to seek partners and would need to localize. "We don't want to alienate the American traveler who wants to know how his ball team did last night," Turner maintains. "But we are evolving. We will have editions in different countries."

Perhaps Turner will continue to change. Or perhaps he is now as self-satisfied as the networks once were. He claims to be unfazed by the competition. "If I were going to worry, I'd worry about the one-fifth of humanity that doesn't have decent drinking water," he said. "I'd worry about an area the size of Michigan that becomes desert every year. I don't worry too much about CNN. CNN is doing a pretty good job. And each passing day we get stronger."

13 The Business of Television News

JEFF GREENFIELD

As many of you know, there is a long tradition in this industry, and at gatherings such as these, which I have come to think of as the ritual mortification of the spirit at the hands of an angry prophet.

Year after year at gatherings of news directors and at convocations of publishers, editors, advertisers, reporters, correspondents, and other worthies, a speaker is invited to stand before a group such as this and decry the sure, steady descent to hell in a hand basket in which we—and you—are willing, eager passengers. I hope you will forgive me if that is an honor that, in one sense, I have chosen to decline.

Such a speaker notes the technological wonder of modern communications, invokes the potential glories of an enlightened civilization which communications once promised, deplores the current state of grubby commerce and shameless pandering to the public appetite, and hurls the lightning bolts down at the offending miscreants with the zeal of Reverend Jonathan Edwards calling down the wrath of heaven on sinners in the hands of an angry God. The speech ends, the speaker feels himself a cleansing agent, the audience feels purified. The speaker goes home, you go to lunch, end of assignation.

The tradition is so deeply rooted I suspect that some centuries ago a guest writer at the Fifth Annual Company Dinner of Gutenberg Printers decried the tawdry commercial ventures of moveable type. In 1958, Edward R. Murrow told a convention of radio and TV news directors that the networks were offering entirely too much of "decadence, escapism, and insulation from the realities of the world in which we live. And without courage and vision, television is nothing more than lights, and wires in a box." Three years after that, FCC Chairman Newt Minow, invited members of the National Association of Broadcasters to sit down in front of their TV sets and told them that "you will observe a vast wasteland." It was in this spirit that Lee DeForest, inventor of the electron tube and one of the fathers of the television industry, said "you have debased my child. . . . You have made him a laughingstock of intelligence, a stench in the nostrils of the gods of the ionosphere."

So it is long since past time that those of us who toil in the Elysian Fields of network news stop the pretense that we somehow are above the tawdry compromises with commercialism, sensationalism, and pandering that afflict the lesser journalistic breeds. Somewhere between the cross-country chase for Tonya Harding, and Camp O. J., our virginal white has acquired more than a few hints of tattle-tale gray. Too often we sound like Claude Rains as the inspector in *Casablanca*, who was "shocked—shocked" to learn of gambling in Rick's establishment before the waiter rushed over to hand him his winnings.

If the networks are truly the last bastion of civilized restraint, then why are so many of these deplorable programs on the local stations that the networks themselves own and operate? If a sober, responsible network newscast ends at 6:58 p.m. and the latest slam-bang tabloid program begins two minutes later on the same network owned-and-operated station, then how much standing do we really have to proclaim that we are not part of that world?

Television executives should, at this point be asked a question—one wrapped not in the mantle of moral superiority, but in the more modest trappings of hard-nosed, practical, enlightened self-interest—why does the industry want to hand its critics a 12 pound lead cudgel with which to beat us over the head at a time when television is once again being attacked for things that are manifestly not the medium's fault? Why are we so anxious to provide supporting evidence for the most extreme, outlandish criticisms of television?

Let me be clear about what I mean: Long before I ever imagined that I would ever work on television, I was writing about it, its programs, and about its alleged impact on the political and social life of the nation. I slowly but surely became convinced that much of the attacks on television—attacks almost as old as television itself—were fundamentally misplaced; that the medium was being blamed for social changes that were rooted in forces far, far more powerful than the most ardent television salesman would ever dare claim.

In the early 1950s, the first congressional hearings were held that indicted TV for its alleged impact on the then-shocking emergence of juvenile delinquency. That kind of inquiry became a tradition, continued in the U.S. Senate by Senator Paul Simon of Illinois who considered proposing or imposing a variety of restrictions on TV, in the interests of curbing the epidemic of violence in the United States. And yet for all of the attacks on TV, all of the academic studies that counted every set of aggression from dramatized slaughter to the misadventures of Bugs Bunny and Daffy Duck, few ever bothered to look at what had happened in the United States not because of TV but coincident with and independent of TV.

This country uprooted itself after World War II. By the tens of millions we left the neighborhoods, the towns, the cities where we had been for generations. We left for better jobs, freedom, opportunity, excitement, for a new life. But with uprooting came upheaval; we were liberated not just from limited opportunity but from restraint, social contract, the guard rails of the extended family and neighborhood. And so crime and disorder rose, families fractured and the familiar faded, and our culture became not just more free but more uncertain.

Television did not do this to us.

Or consider: In the early 1960s television was very much a world where married couples slept in separate beds with enough night clothing to ward off an Arctic chill. As far as an alien viewer would be able to tell from the tube, human beings reproduced by parthenogenesis. At that time a pill came on the market that uncoupled sex from pregnancy for the first time in human history. And this at a time when the explosion in American prosperity had already given us more opportunity for young people by the millions were going off to college on their own, no longer under parental control. That prosperity and mobility gave many women their first chance to think about whether a lifetime in marriage was their only possibility. And so the whole idea that sex must be confined to marriage weakened and premarital and extra-marital sex, always a reality, now became far more widespread and increasingly acceptable.

Television did not do this to us.

Or consider the changing nature of work combined with increasing opportunity for Americans once doomed to privation because of racial bigotry, which delivered a deadly one-two punch to our least well-off neighborhoods. Those with the education and the talent left for greener pastures. Those who remained found work harder and harder to find. And with that, as has happened in every afflicted community within memory, men without work found little to tie them to the whole concept of family, and with that disconnect came the whirlwind of children having children and epidemic violence that afflicts us today.

Television did not do this to us.

So why do so many blame television for so much? Why do voices that agree with each other on almost nothing else unite to declare that television is not simply the messenger, but the carrier of so many social ills? Why do Senator Jesse Helms of North Carolina and Senator Paul Simon, who would not agree on what day of the week it is, unite in their belief that television has helped bring us to our sorry state?

Part of the explanation is simple: timing. Television came into our homes just when the post war upheaval was beginning. So why not assume that, since television arrived with our growing national nervousness, television must have caused it?

Television was, is, and always has been an incredibly subversive medium. Subversive not in the sense that the late Senator Joseph McCarthy would have used the phrase, but in the fact that every new medium of communication is subversive because it undermines established ways of looking at things. If you were a traditional white Southerner in the 1950s, TV showed you a reality about black and white you never had to see before, and therefore never had to think about. If you were an American who knew only good things about our boys in uniform and our foreign adventures, television showed you a face of war you had never seen before. If you were a good-hearted liberal convinced that a government program could cure the ills of society, television showed you a heart of darkness and a harsh reality about the enduring nature of evil that no one liked.

And more generally, television was far more intrusive than other media because it poured out of the tube into your home in front of your family. As a viewer, you had little real control over what was coming at you. Industry voices pointed to the "on-off" switch, but this has always been a ludicrously weak argument—if something shocking or upsetting to you pops out of the tube—then it is too late for the "on-off" switch.

And consider: Conservatives get to dislike it because it comes out of Hollywood and New York, the two most despised communities for conservatives now that Moscow is no longer Communist. And it is sustained by big corporations in pursuit of profit, which means liberals get to hate it too. But there is another reason why the medium is blamed so eagerly for consequences it did not produce and lurking here is a real danger for our common enterprises. One of the reasons people believe that television is responsible for so many ills of our society is that we make it so easy for them to believe it with what we are willing to put on the air.

Why shouldn't people believe in television's capacity to contribute to societal breakdown when we prove every day that we can be supremely indifferent to the way we treat vulnerable and helpless human beings? Why shouldn't our critics believe that we don't care about the consequences of turning the pain and grief and rage of weak and hurting human beings into the modern-day equivalent of freak shows? The case grows even stronger when you consider the way we defend such programs. It would be one thing to say simply, "people watch them eagerly; they're cheap to produce; they get ratings; they make money." That would at least have the virtue of being honest.

But instead, we hear these arguments: "Oh, but people want to see these programs. It's the marketplace in action." Well of course they want to see them. If they didn't, there wouldn't be any argument at all, unless some demented programmer insisted that he was putting such programs on as a public service.

Back in the early days of television there was a popular program called *You Asked For It*. It was a program that answered viewer's requests for stunts of one kind or another. And do you know what the most requested segment—by far—was? It was for a televised execution. Television was a more elitist medium then, and the request was never honored. Sometimes, late at night, I conjure up a syndicator offering a new, updated version of *You Asked For It* in today's marketplace. It is not a pleasant thought.

Well, says the host of one of these popular syndicated offerings, it is a free speech issue; who are we to deny these people a chance to air their stories in public? Listening to such an argument makes it easier to understand how this particular host's former career as a politician ended when he had the bad judgment to employ the services of a prostitute and pay her with a check.

The question isn't whether there is a constitutional right for people to produce and participate in such programs. The question is—what are television executives doing producing such programs, airing them, and what are other corporations doing by sponsoring them? Given the legal right that television executives have to air such shows, the public has a right to draw their logical conclusions about TV's sense of restraint and common ordinary decency. What conclusion should the public draw regarding television's sincerity in its claim of serving the public interest?

Well, the argument goes, nobody is dragging these people in front of the camera; they are there because they want to be.

I want to give credit to the producers of these programs. They are skilled in finding people for whom the prospect of a free airplane ticket, a ride in a limo, a hotel suite with room service, and their first and last chance to be on television is a prize well worth the sacrifice of any shred of dignity and privacy. They are also skilled in convincing their "guests"— let's consider for a moment the irony of that term—to earn their free trip by hurling angry words and by sitting still for that surprise confrontation that audiences love so much. But now let me pose a different scenario for these shows, one that came to me when I became the target of one of the third-tier tabloid shows now sadly dispatched to that great curing-room in the sky.

My sin was to decline, politely, an interview request by the show's anchor—a request delivered with the camera rolling about six inches from my face. My punishment was to be pursued by a young man with a hand-held video camera, screaming at me, demanding to know why I was "afraid" to talk to this show. Across the street, another camera was rolling, in case I had the bad judgment to physically assault my interrogator.

After the airing of this episode, I began to play with a revenge fantasy. It would do no good to go after the anchor or the producers, that would just make better television for them. Instead I imagined going to the offices and to the homes of the top officers and directors of the Chris-Craft Company—for it was their show. I thought of surrounding these people with two video cameras, jamming one of them in the face of the board chairman and demanding to know why he was willing to profit from the debasing of the American TV industry. If he refused to answer? Follow him for as long as I could demanding to know why he was afraid to talk to the American people.

From there the fantasy blossomed. I learned that many of the most noxious of these programs actually are produced and aired by some of our most well-respected, prominent organizations—huge media conglomerates run by people who spend half their evenings getting Humanitarian of the Year awards. Why not invite several of them on a show like *Nightline*, allegedly to talk about serious matters of telecommunications policy, or the social responsibility of business. Then, after careful research, we would stash backstage people from their past that they would really, really rather never see again.

People who knew something profoundly embarrassing about their lives. Odds are, they all have such a person in their past; God knows I do.

As we go on the air live we would bring out these guests and let them denounce our major corporate and communications leaders for whatever, preferably for sins of the most intimate, private sort. And we wouldn't even have to check their stories out all that carefully. After all, we have a First Amendment, don't we?

Or maybe we'd try a different kind of approach. Take a hidden camera and follow these important industry people everywhere they went. Maybe we'd catch one of them visiting someone that he wasn't supposed to be visiting. Could we catch another in a magazine store, thumbing through the wrong sort of magazine? Maybe we'd see them knocking back one too many scotches and sodas. Inevitably we'd find him or her out with their spouse or their kids, getting into one of those delightfully frank and open exchanges every spouse and every parent has gone through at the supermarket or a restaurant. And there it would all be—caught on tape!

When the fever subsided I realized how weak this revenge fantasy was. In the first place, many of these folks have security guards, chauffeurs, assistants to assistants—you probably couldn't get to them. Second, we'd never put that material on the air, because ABC has important business relationships with these people. We'd be jeopardizing tens of millions, maybe hundreds of millions of dollars with such tactics—not to mention the fact that I'd be in line for food stamps the next day.

But the real reason we wouldn't air such material is because we know these people. We know them—or at least most of them—to be good, decent people, with friends, families, and reputations. We could not imagine treating anyone we know with such contempt, without even a shred of decency. The Sermon on the Mount got it exactly right. "Do unto others."

So it doesn't help television's cause one bit that lots of people love to watch these shows. We all know that television people do not always reach for the highest shelf in the library of good taste. As one viewer put it, "I see better things and approve them; I go for the worst." Actually, it was the Roman poet Ovid who wrote that. They may watch this stuff, but I'll bet that a lot of viewers aren't very happy with themselves for watching, and they sure as hell aren't happy with us for letting them feed such appetites.

These shows undercut everything else that I and everyone else involved in television tries to say about what it is we are doing. There is so much worth praising about what is on the air today: There is so much genuinely funny comedy, moving drama, real public service, important news. I've been blessed to spend my work days first at *Sunday Morning* on CBS and now at *Nightline* on ABC, and to have been with these programs is a source of enormous satisfaction. And when you combine broadcasting with cable what we have is more choices than ever before in the history of this medium.

Nor is it required that we only talk about the most uplifting or earnest efforts. TV is a mass medium, an entertainment medium. If David Letterman's inspired foolishness makes a long day end with a smile, if Regis and Kathy Lee give viewers an hour of cotton candy in between a rushed morning and a long day, if a daytime drama gives a weary domestic worker some diversion along with a cup of coffee, that's a public service as well.

And yet after one day spent watching the parade of dysfunctional horrors, leering hosts, and audiences who were last seen crowding around the guillotine in Paris 200 years ago, I start to think about TV in the words of an old joke: "Apart from that, Mrs. Lincoln, how was the play?" Apart from the nine hours a day of human degradation and exploitation, how was today's TV?

We should not pretend to be confused about why so much of the public feels, despite all of our after-school programming and all of our community outreach programs, that we are part of the problem of a steadily coarsened public conversation and not part of the solution. Let us not pretend that we are puzzled by the misplaced sense of so many citizens that television has made us worse off, not better off.

I would finally say this to television executives: Just sit back one afternoon and turn on the television set. What you are seeing is a result of deliberate, conscious decisions of some of the most powerful, respected people in this business. This is what we choose to put out over the public airwaves. It would not be there if we did not want it to be.

References

Boot, W. (1989). Campaign '88: TV overdoses on the inside dope. *Columbia Journalism Review, 27*, 23-29.

Cannon, L. (1977). *Reporting: An inside view*. Sacramento: California Journal.

Crouse, T. (1974). *The boys on the bus*. New York: Ballantine.

For some 15 minutes of fame is agony. (1995, April 27). *Los Angeles Times*, p. A19.

Gitlin, T. (1990). Blips, bites and savvy talk. *Dissent, 37*, 18-26.

Gormley, W. (1980). An evaluation of the FCC's cross-ownership policy. *Policy Analysis, 6*, 61-83.

Hallin, D. C. (1985). The American news media: A critical theory perspective. In J. Forester (Ed.), *Critical theory, and public life*. Cambridge: MIT Press.

Kernell, S. (1986). *Going public. New strategies of presidential leadership*. Washington, DC: Congressional Quarterly Press.

Lippmann, W. (1922). *Public opinion*. New York: Free Press.

Media monster feeds on one of its own. (1994, September 24). *Los Angeles Times*, p. A17.

McGinniss, J. (1969). *The selling of the president*. New York: Trident.

Mickelson, S. (1973). Blurred image in the electric mirror. In M. Barrett (Ed.), *The politics of broadcasting*. New York: Crowell.

Mickelson, S. (1989). *From whistle stop to sound bite*. New York: Praeger.

Postman, N. (1982). *The disappearance of childhood*. New York: Delacorte Press.

Rarick, G., & Hartman, B. (1966). The effects of competition on one daily newspaper's content. *Journalism Quarterly, 43*, 459-463.

Robinson, M. J., & Sheehan, M. (1983). *Over the wire and on TV: CBS and UPI in Campaign '80*. New York: Russell Sage.

Simon, W. E. (1978). *A time for truth*. New York: Reader's Digest Press.

The press just has to take it sitting down. (1995, May 8). *Los Angeles Times*, p. A16.

Weaver, D. H., & Wilhoit, G. C. (1986). *The American journalist: A portrait of U.S. news people and their work*. Bloomington: Indiana University Press.

Woodward, B., & Bernstein, C. (1976). *The final days*. New York: Simon & Schuster.

PART II

Reporters and Public Officials
Who Uses Whom?

14 Overview

RICHARD REEVES

President John F. Kennedy, who genuinely liked some of the reporters who covered him, used to tell his men to remember that no matter how friendly reporters were or what good company they were, that in the end their interests were different than his. He knew what he was talking about—having been a reporter himself between military service and his entrance into politics. His men knew, too. What interests reporters, above all, is conflict—confrontation and challenge. They are there to record change—the rise and fall of powerful men and women.

Reporters like comebacks too. Clinton had a friend, a very successful television producer named Harry Thomason, who told him, accurately I think, "You have to know this about reporters. They kick you into the gutter, but then they feel bad and think, 'He wasn't really a bad guy was he, he was trying?'—and they reach down and help you up."

As public officials have become more accessible to the press, they have also learned how to better use the press to serve their own ends. We present four different perspectives on the relationship between the press and elected officials. Two of our experts are scholars who have written extensively on the efforts and counterefforts by journalists and politicians to influence each other—Professors Lance Bennett and William Dorman. Contrary to the stereotype of the reporter as the aggressive adversary of those who hold public office, their work shows that major news organizations routinely accept the assumptions and assertions of policymakers, and these assumptions indelibly color news reports. Bennett points out that journalists are trained to index the news to what is being said in high places and Dorman shows that the crisis in the Persian Gulf was but a further instance of such "official journalism."

101

Although Bennett and Dorman suggest that journalists' assumptions about what is important shape their work product, the influence wielded by public officials is often less subtle, at least according to Benjamin Bradlee, the former editor of the *Washington Post*, and Daniel Schorr of National Public Radio (formerly with CBS News). Bradlee chose "lying" as the topic of a lecture at Harvard University. He went right to the top, cataloging the lies and consequences of lying in The White House—and in the process shed some light on the cynicism of both politicians and reporters. For his part, Schorr (also lecturing at Harvard) focused on a more subtle form of deception in which officials "leak" information to reporters so as to serve their political needs.

15 Cracking the News Code

Some Rules That Journalists Live By

W. LANCE BENNETT

When we read the newspaper or watch television, we encounter a world of images and symbols. No matter how realistic they may seem, however, news accounts are representations—that is, symbolic constructions—of distant political realities that the vast majority of people never experience firsthand. The importance of recognizing news as a symbolic construction dates to the writings of journalist Walter Lippmann at the dawning of the media age early in the 20th century. Lippmann's (1922) classic work on public opinion made the enduring point that opinion is not shaped by direct experiences of politics but through the images planted in our minds by news accounts. An important and still largely unanswered question is how journalists and news organizations, acting in intense competition with one another, manage to represent the political world with images that are both standardized and believable enough to become the basis for our public political debates and for individual participation in political life.

Benedict Anderson (1983) has argued that the very existence of these things we call nations depends on the construction of imagined communities through the media. National identities are forged with the symbols that tell people who they are in relation to each other and to the rules of the political game. The symbols of society and nation are expressed in many ways but perhaps most commonly through the public institutions and officials who dominate the news. Images from flags and party labels to ethnic stereotypes appear in both news and entertainment programming along with references to myths, legendary events, and popular

103

heroes. The news also provides a daily refresher course on the grand rule systems of constitutions, legal codes, elections, and legislative procedures that set the boundaries of the imagined—or at least the legitimate— political universe. The symbolic makeup of this finely constructed world allows complete strangers to identify each other and to decide which side they are on in dramatic struggles over abortion, civil rights, taxes, health care, and the dozens of other national issues brought home in the news. As indicated by the culture wars that have torn American politics in recent years, the news can also become a divisive battleground in which the symbols of society and government are hotly contested and redefined.

Iyengar (1991) has noted that the news generally comes at us in isolated and highly dramatized episodes that lack the thematic coherence to really explain much about the larger situations from which the stories are drawn. The fragmented and highly dramatized properties of news may reinforce the popular impression that the political world is a confusing and chaotic place (Bennett, 1996). For all its chaos, however, the news also displays some surprising patterns of political content that may shape popular perceptions of power and the citizen's sense of personal involvement in politics. The following section reviews some of these symbolic patterns in the news and introduces some of the rules and practices that guide journalists in producing these familiar representations of American politics.

Symbolic Patterns in the News

News content is highly patterned. For example, government officials and authorities are more likely than other political actors to be given voice by reporters (Blumler & Gurevitch, 1981; Brown, Bybee, Weardon, & Murdock, 1987; Hallin, Manoff, & Weddle, 1990; Sigal, 1973). By contrast, grass roots groups, social movements, and protesters with causes that are not on the government agenda are not only less likely to get their messages reported, but they are far more likely to be portrayed as disruptive, lawless elements than more established political groups (Entman & Rojecki, 1993; Gitlin, 1980). Even when grassroots groups are allowed to tell their stories, their messages tend to fade out of news coverage sooner than those of better organized interest groups with the resources to sustain media campaigns (Goldenberg, 1975).

Discovering the implicit journalistic rules for opening the media gates to some voices and closing them to others is the central preoccupation of a burgeoning public relations industry. Important elements of the journalistic code have been cracked by communication experts and technologies dedicated to getting clients' messages into the news. For example, Manheim (1994) analyzed the successful strategic communication efforts of Hill and Knowlton, the public relations firm hired by the Kuwaiti royal family to drum up political support in the United States for a military intervention following the Iraqi invasion of 1990. The centerpiece of the media campaign involved the use of congressional hearings to get a carefully designed political message into the nation's newscasts—all for a bargain price of less than $12 million.

In deciding what stories to tell, journalists necessarily adopt simplifying assumptions about the nature of politics in different kinds of settings. For example, the range of viewpoints in coverage of most national policy debates is tied or "indexed" to the public pronouncements of, and the degree of public opposition among, key public officials who can affect decisions about the issues. This means that if a prominent politician such as the president takes a strong position on an issue, it will be covered widely. Moreover, if there is opposition—for example, from key members of Congress or from visible interest organizations with access to key members of Congress—and those opponents have the potential to block the presidential initiative, then the news gates are likely to open to views other than those of the administration. The indexing rule explains why some issues receive little coverage at all, whereas others are covered from one dominant point of view, and still others are reported from the diverse viewpoints of many social groups, opinion polls, experts, and critical editorializing from the prestige press (Alexseev & Bennett, 1995; Bennett, 1990; Zaller, Chiu, & Hunt, 1994).

Indexing explains some patterns in the news, but it is just one rule in the journalistic rule book. Our goal is to find other rules that explain how different political situations are reported. Consider, for example, one obvious area of politics that cannot be explained at all by the indexing norm—patterns of election campaign coverage. The familiar horse race plot that dominates election reporting places more emphasis on candidate surges and positions in voter polls than on issue positions or the disagreements and conflicts among the contestants (Zaller, 1994). Adding to the contrast between election versus nonelection news patterns is that the way in which opinion polls are reported differs depending on whether they appear in the context of an election story or during a national policy debate (on the same issue) that falls outside of an election period (Bennett, 1989).

Implicit journalistic assumptions about how the political world works are built into the very bureaucratic routines used to gather news. For example, the basic institutional structure of government in the United States is reflected—albeit crudely—in the system of beats used by news organizations to post their reporters. These beats reflect common sense (if not always accurate) perceptions of where power in the American political system lies. This journalistic map of power in government is exaggerated further by business considerations such as where the best— simple, dramatic, easily reported, and audience pleasing—stories about politics are likely to be found on a regular basis. Thus, more reporters are stationed at the White House than anywhere else, whereas a much smaller press pack stalks the Supreme Court. No large news organization even has a beat called "lobbyists, PACs, and political finance," much less one that covers the activities of Wall Street lawyers and corporate executives after they receive government appointments. The beat system, in short, is laid out on a journalistic map of power in the United States based loosely on the blueprint sketched in the Constitution more than 200 years ago and adjusted according to economic calculations affecting the news business. The news reports that emerge in this system are fashioned as narratives that gain as much credibility from their standing as cultural truths as from any claim that they represent the most complete, documentary accounts of situations (Gans, 1979).

By contrast, journalists in many other democracies gather news less by staking out decision-making institutions than by covering the political parties—an efficient means of monitoring government in parliamentary systems in which decisions are often made inside parties before they move through the formal institutions of government. In his analysis of Gulf War news coverage, Cook (1994) noted that the American news beat system produced characteristic kinds of information. First, quite different political messages came from the different beats making up the so-called Golden Triangle of executive branch foreign policy coverage: The White House was primarily a source of strategic political spin on policy goals and activities, whereas the State Department produced descriptions and

status reports on administration policies and the Pentagon mainly supplied topical information about capabilities, preparedness, and deploy-
ments. When combined with relative silence along the congressional
beats, this news system helped the Bush administration domesticate a
foreign policy crisis in the dual sense that (a) its views were magnified
well above those of its critics, and (b) the story maintained a U.S. focus
despite an extraordinary volume of available international perspectives.
In comparison, Cook's analysis of the early days of French news about
the Gulf crisis revealed a journalistic orientation toward political parties
and international actors that quickly opened up representations of the
situation to a wide range of voices and viewpoints. On an even larger
scale, a multination comparison by David Swanson and colleagues
(Swanson & Carrier, 1994; Swanson & Smith, 1993) shows that the reality
of the Gulf War depended largely on which national news system was
representing it.

When we combine norms such as indexing and news-gathering practices such as working from the beat system, some even more surprising
patterns in news content begin to come into focus. For example, a study
by Donovan (1995) of *New York Times* coverage of the acquired immunodeficiency syndrome (AIDS) activist group ACT UP shows that stories
coming from political beats tended to portray the group as a disruptive
protest organization with an unclear message. The same group, however,
was accorded considerably greater respectability and message coverage
in stories on AIDS that came from medical and science beats. Could it be
just an isolated occurrence that the same group and the same story received
markedly different coverage from different beats inside the same news
organization? A variation on this pattern was found in an analysis of
George Bush's ill-fated trip to Japan in 1992 (Dahl & Bennett, 1995). The
president's untimely illness during a state dinner (he threw up on the
lap of the Japanese prime minister) unleashed numerous political stories
in the prestige American press suggesting that the United States had lost
its position of global economic supremacy to Japan. At the same time,
however, American business reporters were revealing symptoms of
serious economic ills in Japan that gave little support to the mythic
stories of Japanese strength and American weakness on the front pages.

To summarize the discussion thus far, the news displays a number of
clear but curious patterns in political content. These patterns suggest an

underlying set of common-sense journalistic understandings about politics, power, and society—understandings that are often tempered by business considerations and filtered through cultural narratives. The result is a national information system that links journalists, politicians, and publics in mutual, if not always mutually agreeable, communication. These rules for representing politics do not produce accounts that are necessarily true or analytically useful (nor do they specifically prevent such accounts). Rather, they constitute a pragmatic basis on which information is produced within a complex ecology of relations among politicians, publics, and the press (Ettema et al., 1991). The news, in short, is a daily negotiation among various actors occupying different niches in the information ecosystem: political actors seeking to control news content, journalists who operate simultaneously within a profession dedicated to informing citizens and a business that sells a product to audiences, and those citizens and audiences who are also members of a culture for whom the news must ring true with what they believe about themselves as a people.

Journalism as Profession, Business, and Culture

Journalists somehow operate routinely in this complex news world. Given the pressures and pitfalls of life in the political conflict zones, how do they go out every day and come back with a large volume of plausible material that is recognizable by critics and supporters alike as news? Moreover, how is it that this news matter looks much the same—with some obvious variation in length and informational detail—whether viewed on ABC or CNN, read in the *Des Moines Register* or the *New York Times*, or supplied by an on-line service via the Internet? In short, what norms guide journalists in the daily construction of those symbolic representations that we call news?

With regard to reporting politics, journalists can draw on a long-standing professional obligation to cover what matters most in ways that inform people about the activities of their elected representatives. This is called the "professional ideal" of news reporting about politics. As journalism students are taught about the history of the free press and the heroics of journalists from Peter Zenger to Bob Woodward, however, they are also reminded—if, indeed they need reminding—that the news is also a big business.

As small news organizations are consumed at an alarming rate by larger national and international media conglomerates, the news is pressed to become more commercial and more spiced with the drama and entertainment values that draw audiences (Bagdikian, 1992). This is called the "economic reality" of journalism. The economic pressures on journalists may run against the professional ideal by encouraging political coverage that is easier and cheaper to report as well as easier and less challenging for consumers to digest. As these twin gods of professionalism and economics become increasingly hard to reconcile, the news becomes transformed into a hybrid of information and entertainment—called "infotainment" by scholars and media critics.

The efforts of journalists to appease the conflicting pressures of business and profession increase the routinization and standardization of reporting through story formulas and well-worn news-gathering routines. Thus, we witness reporters following politicians around in packs, picking up information handouts, and recording staged media events designed to put one partisan spin or another on the news. What passes for a critical press in this environment is the familiar genre of personal attack journalism in which the press pack turns surly, snarling at press conferences and attacking politicians hapless enough to have poor media handlers or foolish enough not to heed the advice of good ones. News organizations sponsor little investigative or enterprise journalism and shy away from complex political stories. It is not surprising that the spectacle of the feeding frenzy circling the manipulative, media-wary politician has soured the public on both the press and public officials (Sabato, 1992).

The obvious tensions within this odd blend of hand-fed news and attack journalism are often managed and relieved by a third broad foundation of the journalistic guidance system—the storehouse of familiar cultural story plots that allow politicians, press, and publics to build fragile realities within this often confusing information environment. A large cultural vocabulary of symbols and political folktales facilitates efforts to report on politics-as-usual, even as signs of social decay or political corruption threaten to undermine the premise of normalcy. Thus, when personalized attack politics render the news senseless or intolerable, we are reminded that American culture has always been cruel to its politicians. The attacks on Thomas Jefferson and Abraham Lincoln are rolled out as though to offer perspective and relief from the slurs heaped on a modern leader. When politicians fail to inspire people with governing visions, and their communication degenerates into posturing and finger pointing, other familiar cultural themes are sounded in the news. Enter the modern politician, armed with scripts from media consultants, preaching the ills of government itself. These oxymoronic characters spare little effort or expense trying to make the news with time-worn but market-tested cultural messages about how big government threatens the individual and causes the problems of society.

The role of journalists as cultural storytellers becomes even more important when crises erupt, accidents happen, and politicians lose control of political situations. In those moments when events slip the politician's grasp, journalists must interpret their significance without the aid of political scripts or planned press activities; available cultural themes become a safe rendering of reality that can be pointed to as shared experience. Thus, when accidents such as those that plagued nuclear power plants in an earlier era sent politicians into hiding, journalists could write stories around the eternal questions of whether we had created a monster through technology or whether, with typical American ingenuity, we would surmount the obstacles and find solutions for the radioactive threat of our own making.

In the broadest sense, then, journalists answer the call of three broad guidance systems:

The professional ideal of informing citizens in a democracy

The business imperative to make their product entertaining and sellable

The cultural device of telling familiar stories about ourselves

These broad news principles are applied in daily reporting practice through specific rules (such as the indexing norm) that guide journalists in representing specific political events and situations. Figuring out how everyday reality is represented in the news is akin to cracking a complex code. Some of the implicit rules that journalists use in coding the news are noted in the following section.

A Starter Set of Basic Journalism Rules

The following five propositions about how journalists implicitly organize the political world are generalizations from research on news content patterns. Recall when proceeding with this discussion that these are not necessarily the most accurate bases on which to code or represent politics, but they are reasonable guidelines for operating within the ecology of political information outlined previously—that is, for organizing news beats, making daily news assignments, selecting sources for stories, and, ultimately, for deciding what in the world has happened and what it means.

Rule 1: Keep the Political Focus on Representative Democracy. The overwhelming dominance of officials in news accounts suggests a fundamental journalistic assumption: Power in American politics is based on the representative process in which people elect representatives to act on their behalf. If the people do not like what their representatives are doing in the news, this assumption asserts, they can elect different ones. Framing news stories (whenever possible) with this rule makes sense because it draws on common knowledge about government and politics that journalists, along with most other citizens, receive early on (though surely not everyone accepts equally) in the political socialization process: the civics book version of power and citizen accountability in the American democracy.

The self-defined role of the press as an actor within this representative system has been different in different historical periods, with varying degrees of emphasis on a partisan press, a watchdog press, and a press that serves as a passive information channel. Today's press system seems to have settled on the role of passive information channel, with editors and news directors proclaiming that their audiences prefer to make up their own minds based on just the facts (Bennett, 1996). As a result, what substitutes for critical (thematic) reporting in this system largely involves personal attacks on individual politicians and play-by-play coverage of their public approval ratings wars.

An anthropologist attempting to decipher this media culture might suspect that politicians worship—and fear—the god of public approval, whereas the press plays the devilish role of stirring up mischief between publics and politicians. A naive anthropologist might conclude that public approval somehow reflects the soundness of a politician's ideas and the strength of his or her personal political power. A more discriminating observer might point out that politicians go to great lengths to use the news to create the public approval in which they then bask. Personal political power in this view is an elusive, and often illusive, thing (Bennett, 1996).

The latter analysis raises troubling questions about just what a representative democracy really means: where political marketing ends and political substance begins, what the correspondence is between what politicians say in the news and what they do behind the scenes, what public approval really means, and more generally, whether politicians commonly represent independent public input or whether they commonly create public fears and concerns in the first place. Such questions have, of course, been raised by critical observers of politics and communication, most notably, Murray Edelman (1964, 1987).

The difficulties of representing representative democracy in the media age may help to explain why the press probes delicately, if at all, beneath the surface of civics-book images of politics. Even when press attention is devoted to problems with the system, the media light dims when it comes to illuminating what the underlying causes and solutions to those problems might be. In place of such thematic analysis, critical news accounts are dominated with dramatic episodes—officials trying to appease angry citizens, candidates trying to turn voter anger against their opponents, and nearly everyone singing in the chorus that government itself is somehow the cause of the trouble. Thus, news content has settled into the overarching pattern of attacks on individual politicians mixed with largely face-value, civics-book reports on the policy agendas and decisions of legislatures, executives, and courts (institutions that are, of course, populated by individual politicians).

Rule 2: Index Issue Coverage to Institutional Agendas and Conflicts. As proposed previously, the range of viewpoints in mainstream press coverage of most political issues is filtered through (what reporters perceive to be) the status of the issue on the government agenda. In particular, both the social diversity of news sources and the ideological range of their viewpoints expand or contract (i.e., are indexed) according to the degree of consensus or conflict among powerful institutional actors whose power is implicitly understood by reporters as having some role in deciding the outcome of the issue.

When politicians are not being pilloried in the press, the activities of government are reported as though government operated closer to some Madisonian constitutional ideal than to a Madison Avenue caricature. Key institutional locations (i.e., places where news beats are located) are examined for signs of activity and for pronouncements by the officials who preside at those locations. When statements are issued (or reporters are tipped to behind-the-scenes activity) from these presumed sites of government power, issues make the media agenda, and journalists calculate levels of consensus and opposition at other institutional decision points in deciding implicitly which other viewpoints to let pass through the news gates.

Thus, opposition to a president from a few scattered members of Congress is not likely to dilute the dominant news play given to the president's position on a national issue or initiative. Views that compete with the president's, however, are likely to flood the news when opposition emerges from actors capable of blocking or modifying his legislative agenda. For example, the early days of the Clinton national health care initiative were characterized by a high level of favorable coverage of the administration plan. When opposition emerged in the Republican ranks in Congress, dissent against the plan began to filter into the news. As important members of the Democratic party in Congress backed their own plans, the volume of criticism of the administration proposal grew louder, and the news gates opened wide to the views of many interest groups with links to Congress and the political parties. When a huge volume of advertising was added to this already noisy environment, the public became increasingly confused about the issue and finally rejected all the leading proposals in the polls despite remaining committed to the importance of health care reform in general. The ironic result of this wide-open media debate suggests that a free flow of information does not, by itself, guarantee public understanding or the crystallization of policy alternatives.

Rule 3: Follow the Trail of Power. As noted previously, indexing cannot explain news content in coverage of all political situations. There are several other types of political situations in which issues do not pass neatly through government institutions on their way toward resolution. Thus, we must look for other reporting rules.

When a political issue or conflict does not fit easily within (or moves outside of) domestic institutional decision settings, journalists follow the trail of power to the actors, including international actors, deemed most likely to decide or resolve the conflict. The trail of power is not charted by some objective theory of politics but rather, once again, by implicit journalistic assumptions about political actors regarded as having the potential to change the outcome of a situation.

For example, many foreign policy situations are not decided exclusively within U.S. governmental institutions. Decisions, such as the use of force against terrorists, the conduct of peace-keeping operations, and the terms of trade agreements, often involve actors in the United Nations, North Atlantic Treaty Organization, and in other countries. In these situations, particularly when levels of conflict among domestic officials are not pronounced, it is expected that journalists follow the trail of power to decision makers in other nations or international organizations. A case study of the Reagan administration's bombing of Libya (Althaus, Edy, Entman, & Phelan, 1995) found higher levels of foreign voices and more opposition to Reagan administration positions than would have been expected from applying the indexing hypothesis to the domestic debate alone. This finding clearly suggests that journalists followed the trail of power to non-U.S. decision makers who had considerable input into the course of administration action. In this case, foreign governments had the all-important power to decide whether the United States could launch the attack on Libya from their nations or fly over their countries in the course of that mission. Thus, when decisive actors emerge outside of domestic political institutions, journalists can be expected to bring their voices and views into stories.

Rule 4: Observe and Narrate the Rituals and Customs of the Political Culture. Many important political situations unfold almost entirely outside of the decision processes of formal government institutions. To the extent that such political activities are driven by familiar cultural scripts, traditions, or rituals, such cultural frameworks become the basis for journalists' representations.

Elections are the most common case of this type. Zaller (1994) demonstrates convincingly that elections are covered in ways quite different from the comparison case of foreign policy decisions. As grand cultural rituals of popular sovereignty, elections dramatize the power of the people and the subordination of politicians to the popular will. Unlike routine institutional decisions in which the (already elected) representatives of the people dominate the terms of public debate in the news, election coverage tends to elevate the symbolic role of publics. Using the vague cultural script of the horse race, journalists report the often strange dynamics of candidate posturing, the tallies of convention votes needed to secure the nomination, and the approval shifts among the candidates as the election draws near.

Many critics argue that reporting on elections has become impoverished in recent years by the overbearing focus on candidate attacks and glitzy media events. Some contend that the election process itself has become corrupted by the rhetorical pandering of the political candidates who are entrusted with enacting the ritual (Jamieson, 1992). Others blame the media for sacrificing serious coverage at the alter of business pressures for sensationalistic news (Patterson, 1994). Either way, the press becomes an integral part of the cultural change process.

Rule 5: When Politically or Culturally Volatile Material Enters the News, Journalists May Speak in a More Active, Even Analytical Voice, Until Rules 1 Through 4 Produce Stable Frames for the Developing News Story. There are important occasions when the trail of power and the familiar signposts of culture become difficult to follow: politics-as-usual breaks down, crises elude the press management abilities of politicians, or accidents happen. In these moments, the news can become a forum for new ideas and challenging political viewpoints, and journalists may exercise greater interpretive license. During such episodes of relative press autonomy, the news can become a forum for minority voices, for the recognition of simmering social conflicts, or for the mainstreaming of emerging values, beliefs, and new cultural images.

For example, the issue of waste recycling moved from the counterculture margins of the news to a mainstream policy solution for a newly recognized garbage crisis in 1987. The precipitating news event was the sailing of the garbage barge Mobro from Long Island, New York. Requests to unload the trash were rejected at every port of call. The barge became something of a media icon, offering journalists the opportunity to invoke its image in independent reporting about the newly discovered trash crisis and to move recycling into the mainstream of policy options (Bennett & Lawrence, 1995). Officials were, of course, invited into the story (as the indexing norm would predict), but they more often than not embraced recycling as the leading policy option rather than attempting to move it back to the margins of public debate.

Other examples of news icons that have introduced greater journalistic voice into the news include the aforementioned incident in which George Bush became ill on a state visit to Japan (Dahl & Bennett, 1995) and the widely reported beating of Rodney King (Lawrence, 1995). These moments of journalistic license do not imply that journalists are free to make up their own scripts; they are more likely to adjust the weighting of viewpoints already being expressed in society. Thus, the authenticity of the video image of a group of white police officers watching colleagues beating a black victim, when combined with the lack of agreement among officials as to what had happened, allowed journalists to turn up the volume of grassroots charges that racism affects the way in which justice is administered to blacks in America.

Some of the material that slips into the news so strains the bounds of cultural acceptance that journalists quickly abandon their independent plotting of news stories. Stories that become too hot to handle are generally turned over to officials along familiar beats who are, in effect, invited by journalists to perform repair operations on the fabric of cultural understanding. One case of such "news repair" occurred during the Reagan administration when an unemployed person set himself on fire in front of a TV news crew in what he represented as a despairing protest against Reagan administration social and economic policies. This news story, with its highly unconventional form of political action and its equally radical message, was quickly replaced by official pronouncements from local authorities (none of whom were at the scene of the original event) that the man was not in his right mind. The news media then completed the repair operation on the momentary tear in the seamless web of cultural meaning by condemning the decision to report the story in the first place as bad journalism (Bennett, Gressett, & Haltom, 1985).

Conclusion

The quality of a national information system depends directly on how information is packaged and transmitted to the people. The quality of a national information system can also be measured in terms of the information that is either not coded for transmission or that is passed along in ways that are difficult for citizens to access, interpret, and share. Cracking the news code (finding the rules that journalists use to encode political reality) can help to explain

What aspects of our politics are emphasized and de-emphasized

Which images of power are promoted in the press and which ones are not

When the general public is represented as central to making national decisions and when they are excluded from the political picture

Which Americans are represented as worthy and deserving of a voice in their own affairs and which groups are seldom allowed to speak for themselves

Perhaps most important, when wrongdoing or problems in government are brought to public attention and how the seriousness and the roots of those problems are defined

Among the many mysteries that decoding this news system can help resolve is how what is arguably the world's most free and independent press produces news that is so standardized (Patterson, 1992). Another mystery that may yield to this line of investigation is how one of the most technologically advanced and "wired" nations is filled with citizens who seem poorly informed and frequently confused about the politics they encounter in the news. Cracking the implicit journalistic code may also help to explain changes in news representations of politics such as those described previously involving election coverage. In these and other ways, the symbolic representations of politics that we call news have real consequences for the political lives we live.

16 Press Theory and Journalistic Practice

The Case of the Gulf War

WILLIAM A. DORMAN

Deeply rooted in democratic theory is the notion that the American press should play an adversarial role to the state, whether in domestic politics or foreign affairs. If one were to judge from the comments of politicians, mainstream academics, and much popular opinion, the theory has been realized in journalistic practice, particularly throughout the Cold War. I argue, however, that the historical record points in a much different direction, at least in the realm of foreign policy. Far from routinely challenging the assumptions and policies of the state, such major news organizations as elite newspapers, wire services, news magazines, and network news have tended to accept strategic assumptions of policy-makers since World War II, even if they may occasionally come to question the means by which announced goals are pursued (Hallin, 1986).

There is a consistent body of evidence that supports a far more compliant model of journalism than either journalists themselves will admit or policy officials will acknowledge unless they are long removed from the arena of power (McNamara, 1995)—whether it be regarding Iran in 1953, El Salvador in 1982, Guatemala in 1954, Vietnam in the 1960s and 1970s, Africa in the 1960s, or Cuba in the 1980s.

Why there should be such widespread agreement that the press has nipped closely at the heels of the state during the Cold War, despite ample evidence to the contrary, requires a more complicated answer than the scope of this essay provides. Suffice it to say here that one reason is observers fail to pay sufficient attention to the distinction between domestic and foreign affairs—between a highly contentious arena in which there are many competing interests and one in which national interest (and perhaps survival) is believed to overshadow all else. In this regard, imagine how the press and editorial pages would react should the president by executive order outlaw all abortions, for example, or announce the end to tobacco subsidies. Contrast the imagined response with how the press actually did react when Johnson called for the Tonkin Gulf Resolution or when Bush ordered the invasion of Panama or later ordered a deployment of 150,000 troops to Saudi Arabia.

Certainly, as I hope to make clear in this essay, there is little reason to believe the press acted as an authentic adversary during the 1990-1991 confrontation with Iraq in the Persian Gulf. In most of my work on press coverage of the Third World in general and the Middle East in particular I have tried to devise standards for judging journalistic performance that go beyond questions of who is telling the truth or, as the field prefers, questions of objectivity. Instead of the usual question of objectivity, then, I have come to focus on questions of press autonomy from the state.

The questions I have come to ask are the following: Does the press report what is reasonably knowable about a conflict in which U.S. interests are involved and, if things are not knowable at the time, does the press correct the historical record as facts become known? Does the press provide historical context? What sources of authority are dominant in news reporting? What use is made of non-status quo authority, particularly academic authority outside the charmed circle of Washington think tanks? How closely do dominant news frames coincide with those offered by policy elites? What labels are used? How is domestic dissent from foreign policy portrayed? and so on.

In particular, I have been interested in identifying major autonomy shifts in a policy story over a period of time and attempting to discover why they occurred. In the case of the Persian Gulf confrontation, there were at least three journalistic phases. The first period lasted roughly from August 2, 1990—the invasion of Kuwait by Iraqi forces—to November 8, 1990—the president's announcement of a second deployment to the Gulf. Based on my research, at least, this was a low-autonomy phase, as measured by the criteria suggested previously.

The second phase lasted roughly from November 8, 1990, to January 15, 1991, and was characterized by a wider ranging public debate about the Bush administration's policy; I characterize this as a moderately high-autonomy period. The third phase was the war phase that, of course, began January 16, 1991, and lasted until a cease fire. As is the case in any society at war at any time, I argue, this was a low-autonomy phase.

The period that has drawn the most attention from the general public, academics, and policymakers alike and proved to be the most controversial is the war period. As regularly seems to be the case since Vietnam, there was a hue and cry over press performance from all sides of the issue. Assorted jingoes and demagogues ranging from Rush Limbaugh to Reed Irvine, conservative political pundits, and government officials, including Vice President Dan Quayle, suggested the press might be doing the propaganda work of Saddam Hussein with news stories about coalition bomb damage to civilian populations in Iraq.

For their part, journalists and observers concerned about erosion of the First Amendment complained bitterly about stiff military controls over information from the Gulf. The result was a public dispute that journalism quickly found itself losing, at least judging from opinion polls.

Now let me be as clear as I can about criticism of the press from the Jingo Right such as Rush Limbaugh and Senator Allan Simpson. They are to serious media criticism as *Penthouse* magazine is to women's studies. The charge that the press was doing the propaganda work of Baghdad is so removed from sober scrutiny, so removed from even a casual reading of the evidence, that it can only be categorized as clinical paranoia. Indeed, such critics should someday be asked to explain how it is that fully 90% or more of Americans came to support the war if the news media were as unpatriotic and adversarial as they claim.

It is worth noting that for at least the past decade, in an effort to do their own part toward ending the presumed Vietnam Syndrome, the political Right in every significant foreign affairs crisis has launched such preemptive strikes. By focusing attention on the claim that the press is serving the interests of our adversary of the moment, these critics neatly preclude discussion of the possibility that news media may actually be adopting the official Washington's perspective rather than challenging it.

What then was the nature of the media war? During this period, Americans were seemingly transfixed by war news, in large part, probably because this was the first "instant replay war." Television in particular gave it an immediacy that no other war in history has possessed.

In retrospect, Americans never actually saw much action on television. We thought we did, however, and we always expected to see more. What

I mean by this is that we saw very little of importance other than SCUD attacks or footage from the Battle of Khafji, which consisted largely of the same footage played over and over. Nevertheless, Americans tuned in to broadcasting outlets and bought newspapers at such unprecedented rates that one Georgia psychologist suggested some families should be put on a CNN "diet." He said that even mentally healthy people were exhibiting signs of addictive behavior, which he called the "CNN Complex."

In my judgment, what most Americans were getting on television was a sort of "techno-pornography." The emphasis was on the nuts and bolts of a sophisticated war machine, but the consequences were never made plain. In other words, television portrayed the war as a war without victims, just as the usual kind of pornography frequently portrays sexual violence without victims. Indeed, the press as a whole bought into the notion that this was somehow a kinder and gentler war.

The usual observations made about the war phase are the following. First, it was the most closely managed news operation in contemporary memory. Second, the press operation clearly followed the Falkland Islands War model, which the U.S. military perfected during the invasion of Panama in 1989 (Bennett & Paletz, 1994; Fialka, 1991; Gottschalk, 1992; Sharkey, 1991; Taylor, 1992).

In any event, from the reporters' perspective censorship during the war period was not the main problem—restricted access was. If journalists are not allowed near the action, there is no need to censor their work. In this regard, the real problem was the extensive use of pools in which small numbers of journalists working under carefully controlled conditions reported for the great majority confined to the rear echelon. Interestingly, in the context of this discussion, not one major news organization joined in a suit filed against restricted access before the war began.

Issues of military control aside, what must be understood about this period of coverage is that mainstream news media, print and broadcast, supported the Gulf War policy almost without exception. In part, this was because of the unprecedented control exercised over journalists in the war zone and in part because of the inexperience of many of the correspondents. The main reason news coverage favored the official view, however, was simply because the press in any country at any time supports the state during times of war. This is as natural as rain or earthquakes. Journalism, like other institutions, is no match for the

intense feelings of nationalism, pride, and fear and anger that characterize a society at war, particularly during the conflict's early stages
(Knightley, 1975). The American press in the Gulf was no exception.

What was really at issue was the proper degree of journalistic deference. Viewed from this perspective, a press that raises questions about
tactical matters should not be confused with one that has a strategic
disagreement with the state—a distinction that frequently eluded critics
of the press from the jingoistic Right. For instance, although the mainstream press questioned the Pentagon closely about the best time to
launch a ground war, rarely did journalists ask whether it ought to be
launched at all.

Working backward in time, the second period of coverage that I identify
immediately preceded the war phase. This was a moderately high-
autonomy phase, and this second period lasted roughly from November
8, 1990, to when the war actually began in mid-January of 1991. The
period was characterized by a wide-ranging public debate, at least over
the soundness of Bush's stated means for bringing Iraq to heel, and was
the period that most closely met the expectations of democratic theory.

Why this period opened up the question of the president's intentions
and policies can largely be explained by the impact of the influential
elites that began to raise questions. Dissent in high places began in
earnest when President Bush announced, 2 days after the November 6
midterm elections were safely past, that at least 100,000 more troops
would be dispatched to the Gulf, bringing the figure to about 350,000. It
was at this point that the Democratic Party, which had also been hiding
out until after the elections were over, began to raise questions in earnest.
Most important, an astonishing number of prominent Americans, perhaps the longest such list in contemporary history, stepped forward to
argue for giving sanctions a chance and against the war option. This list
included several former secretaries of state, a former chair of the Joint
Chiefs of Staff, assorted former national security advisers, and a continuing stream of prominent Middle East experts.

It is precisely under such conditions—when elites defect from a policy
consensus—that the American press will open up debate on foreign
policy or security issues. The problem is that the press waits for permission, and a policy is usually already deeply in trouble by the time debate
is opened up, rendering the whole matter moot. The Gulf confrontation
was no exception.

This brings me to the phase I think was most significant, which was the first period of press coverage that began August 2, 1990, the day of the invasion, and lasted fully until the November election. It was during this period that the boundaries of public thought and discourse about U.S. policy were formed and a range of acceptable policy alternatives was established. It was during this early period that the press helped lay the foundation in public opinion for the escalation that would follow.

In broad terms, what were the deficiencies of this period? First, there are stories that went unreported or under-reported, chief among them the U.S. role in helping Saddam Hussein throughout the 8-year Iran-Iraq war. For instance, there was scant mention in the major news media of the fact that the Reagan-Bush administration had looked the other way for approximately 6 years when Iraq used chemical weapons in its war against Iran, or that it was the Reagan-Bush administration that had convinced the U.S. Senate not to cut off all aid to Iraq when it used chemical weapons against the Kurds in the spring of 1988. In addition, few stories mentioned that the United States had been supplying Iraq with intelligence information during its war with Iran, or that the Bush administration had reviewed U.S. policy toward Iraq just after taking office and decided there should be no changes. These errors of omission were significant if for no other reason than they might have served to undercut the moral high ground Bush assumed during the early stages of the confrontation.

Similarly, there was widespread journalistic acceptance of the arguable assumption that the United States move had been entirely defensive. Middle East policy experts who seriously doubted whether Saddam had ever intended to invade Saudi Arabia were virtually shut out of the news columns.

Perhaps the greatest success of the Bush administration during this period was to convince Americans that a Third World country with the gross national product of Kentucky was as dangerous to world peace as Hitler's Germany. This could not have occurred without the news media's uncritical acceptance of the president's frames (Dorman & Livingston, 1994). By accepting the frames offered by Bush, the press helped to limit debate at the time when it would have done the most good—before the United States got in so deeply that war became inevitable.

Perhaps the most important question of this discussion has to do with why the press behaves as it does. There are a number of reasons, some more significant than others. First, congress was on vacation when the invasion occurred, and American journalism is indexed closely to structured institutional debate (Bennett, 1990). The press did not know who to turn to for critical reaction to the president's initial policy. In other words, when it comes to foreign policy, if a member of Congress did not say it, it is not as likely to get covered.

In addition, as one veteran correspondent has observed, "Too many reporters pamper their sources, relish their proximity to power, or simply fall unwittingly onto a 'team.' " By team, he means that reporters either begin to identify with the national security apparatus and the military or they find it too difficult to swim against the current. All of this said, perhaps the main thing that undermines contemporary journalism of foreign affairs is the national security state.

Politicians, right wing critics, and much popular opinion aside, a fair-minded reading of the evidence shows that foreign affairs come to us from a system of news gathering that is deeply flawed by the subtle influence of a worldview that favors policymakers. The result is what can be described as a journalism of deference to the national security state. What is meant by journalism of deference is the willingness of the press in most situations most of the time to defer to Washington's perspective on the world scene and policy agenda. In other words, news workers have tended to internalize or psychologize the assumptions of the national security state (Dorman, 1986). The media's deference on national security matters is directly rooted in the establishment in this country of a sense of continuing crisis since World War II that has created a particularly powerful worldview. Such a deference does not mean that journalists deliberately hew to doctrine or that they consciously color their reporting according to individual ideological bias. Rather, what is at work is a nonpartisan, "collective bias" that what is good for the United States is good for the world. In other words, ideology.

It must be understood that widely shared bias or ideology appears to be no bias at all, and no journalistic system of which I am aware has yet been devised to eliminate it. As a journalist who covered the Middle East for the *New York Times* during the 1950s once remarked to me about the subtle effects of Cold War ideology on his work, "Is a fish aware of water."

In conclusion, it seems almost a forlorn task to focus on journalistic derelictions during wartime. Of course, such failures are worth worrying about and ways should be found to keep them to a minimum. That said, however, flawed journalism during wartime is inevitable given the pressures of modern nationalism.

By contrast, it was the early period in the confrontation with Iraq—before war started—that should concern Americans most, just as it is the period before the next conflict, wherever it may be, that should occupy attention in the future. If Americans value debate over policy in an open society, the most important work of the press comes before war starts because once it begins, it is too late. The lesson from the Gulf crisis for journalism, however, seems to be that the deference to national security assumptions, which took root during the Cold War, still seems to have a hold over American journalism whether missiles are flying or not.

17 Lying

The Theodore H. White Lecture at Harvard University

BENJAMIN BRADLEE

Access to politicians, of course, is a mixed blessing. It gives the reporter opportunities to delve deeper and deeper in search of truth, and it gives those who are accessed opportunities to manipulate that truth a little or a lot or beyond all recognition. Theodore H. White [the author of the *Making of the President* books] made reporters feel that they needed this super access to do their job. They needed a seat in the convention hall command center. They needed unlimited time alone with the wife, the children, the close advisers. And politicians got the message. They began to give selected reporters that kind of super access and the great manipulation madness was under way.

None of this is thunderously original. In the sayings of the Jewish fathers, there is this wonderful advice to journalists—love work, hate domination and don't get too close to the ruling class. The great Walter Lippmann gave me the same advice 2,000 years later when he learned of my friendship with Jack Kennedy.

My thesis is not that access breeds manipulation, although it damn well can, my thesis is that the manipulators have one way beyond the granting of access or the withholding of access in their campaign to influence, and thereby distort, reality. And that we in the press have shown remarkably little righteous indignation about it.

I would like to talk tonight about the most primitive of all forms of manipulation, lying. Nothing subtle like a TV spot suggesting that Barry

EDITORS' NOTE: Reprinted with permission of the author.

Goldwater will nuke us all back to the Stone Age or a TV spot suggesting that Mike Dukakis will flood the streets with convicted rapists. I'm not talking about exaggerating, misrepresenting, misspeaking, I'm talking about the real McCoy—lying.

"Lord, Lord. How this world is given to lying!" cries Falstaff in King Henry IV, and things have been going downhill ever since. In fact, lying has become just another tool for making deals, for selling beer or war, soap or candidates.

But it seems to me that lying has reached such epidemic proportions in our culture and among our institutions in recent years, that we've all become immunized to it. What the hell ever happened to righteous indignation, anyway?

Let's concentrate on lying by the executive branch of government, let's concentrate on presidents. If we cannot trust our presidents, who can we trust? If our leaders lie routinely, who should we follow, or even worse, why should we follow?

President Bush ran a little photo opportunity last summer—photo ops are lies in themselves, aren't they?—to announce Judge Clarence Thomas as his nominee for the Supreme Court vacancy created by Thurgood Marshall's resignation. From his lawn at the summer White House in Kennebunkport, the president looked the press and the television camera in the eye and lied: "The fact that he is black and a minority [black and a minority?] has nothing to do with the fact that he is the best qualified at this time."

I don't know anyone in America who believes that statement to be true, either that his color had nothing to do with his appointment or that he was the best qualified.

After the bloody Tiananmen Square massacre in Beijing in June of 1989, President Bush announced that all "exchanges" between the U.S. and China had been banned in protest. Less than a month later, in fact, National Security Advisor Scowcroft and Deputy Secretary of State Eagleburger were in Beijing over the July 4th weekend. No national security argument for that particular lie. Just an exercise in deceiving the American people, who had been told that our outrage over Tiananmen Square made such exchanges impossible.

Of course the president lied. My favorite Reagan lie was his claim that during World War II he had served as a signal corps photographer who had filmed the horrors of the Nazi death camps. President Reagan first told this lie to Israeli Prime Minister Yitzhak Shamir during a White House meeting in November, 1983. The roots of his concern for Israel could be traced to the time he photographed Nazi death camps as a signal corps photographer, Reagan told the Israeli Prime Minister. Afterward, he said, he had saved a copy of the death camp films for himself because he believed that the day would come when people would no longer believe that 6 million Jews had been exterminated. Years later, when a member of Reagan's family asked him if the Holocaust had actually occurred, he showed them the film, according to an article in the Israeli newspaper *Ma'Ariv*, known to be close to Shamir. The accuracy of the *Ma'Ariv* story was confirmed some months later by Dan Meridor, who was Secretary to the Israeli cabinet at the time.

President Reagan repeated this lie in February, 1984 to Nazi hunter Simon Weisenthal and Rabbi Marvin Hier, according to both Weisenthal and Hier, both known for their fluency in English and their attention to detail. Secretary of State James Baker said that the president told him he never left the country in World War II and never told anyone that he did. Of course the president lied.

President James Earl Carter deserves a special place in any discussion of presidential lying, for alone among modern presidents, he made not lying a lynch-pin of his campaign. Who can forget that open good ol' boy face telling the world, "I'll never lie to you." I can find no major lie on the Carter record with the exception of a series of perhaps forgivable statements leading up to the abortive hostage rescue mission in the Iranian desert. But the record is filled with smaller lies that would make Diogenes shake his head.

"If you ever have any questions or advice for me," Carter told audiences throughout his campaign, "please write. Just put Jimmy Carter, Plains, Georgia, on the envelope and I'll get it. I open every letter myself, and read them all." In fact, all mail so addressed was forwarded to Atlanta headquarters, unread by the candidate.

During his campaign, Carter claimed with pride to "have reduced administrative costs by fifty percent." In fact, Carter's spending increased fifty percent during his first three years in office and the total number of state employees increased thirty percent.

Carter often boasted that he left Georgia with $116 million budget surplus. (In his biography, that surplus grew to $200 million.) But according to the State Auditor's Office, Carter inherited a surplus of $90 million and left office with a surplus of $4 million, a net depletion of almost $48 million.

Of course President Carter lied, especially while he was running for office. Once in the White House, his record makes him something of a hero in this melancholy drama.

That brings us backward to President Richard Milhouse Nixon, doesn't it, after a graceful leap over the accidental presidency of Gerry Ford. Where to begin?

For me, the world was never quite the same after President Nixon went on national television to say that he could not tell us about Watergate because "national security" was involved. The toughest lie to rebut, when one is out there on the cutting edge, all alone with a story we all found hard to believe in the first place. I mean, any president knows more about national security than a bunch of reporters or editors, right?

And then who can forget the menu bombing of Cambodia? I bet you've all forgotten it, menu bombing because it consisted of Operation Breakfast, Operation Lunch, Operation Dinner, Operation Snacks, and Operation Dessert, 3,630 B-52 raids on Cambodia, dropping 110,000 tons of bombs for fourteen months. Never happened, said the president of the United States. Although one has to wonder there, too, about the use of national security as justification for lying. The Cambodians and the Viet Cong who were in Cambodia certainly knew about Operation Menu and that meant the Russians and Chinese knew, and in those days, that's who we were trying to keep secrets from. Only the American people had to be kept in the dark.

An embarrassment of riches faces anyone looking for a favorite LBJ anything. The larder is full of stories about this larger-than-life man lying. Did you ever hear the one about his great-great-grandfather dying at the Alamo? Doris Kearns has the definitive version of that lie in the prologue of her wonderful book, *Lyndon Johnson and the American Dream.* Hugh Sidey had written in *Time* about President Johnson talking to American troops in Korea in 1966, alleging that the president had claimed that his great-great granddaddy had fallen at the Alamo. Working on the LBJ book, Kearns had asked him about the incident. Before she even finished retelling the Sidey story, Johnson interrupted: "Goddamn it," he said, "Why must all these journalists be such sticklers for detail? The fact is that my great-great-grandfather died at the Battle of San Jacinto, not the Alamo. Anyway, the point is that the battle of San Jacinto was far more important to Texas history than the Alamo. Why, the men who fought there were as brave as any men who have walked the face of this earth."

Kearns writes how the president went on to describe the battle of San Jacinto for another fifteen minutes. By the end of their conversation, she had heard not only that San Jacinto was the most important event in the history of Texas, but that his great-great-granddaddy had been the hero of that great and courageous moment. All of it lies. All of it lies. Investigation proved that the great-great-grandfather had not been at Alamo, he had not been at San Jacinto, he was a real estate trader who died at home, in bed.

Of course President Johnson lied.

And that brings us to John F. Kennedy. That marvelous man who wrapped up this country in cords of promise, hope, and confidence for a short, short thousand days. Did our friend, the friend of so many of us lie, too?

President Kennedy lied about Addison's disease. He said he didn't have it. The explanation for that lie must be in the description of the disease itself, a disease caused by failure of the adrenal glands, characterized by weakness, low blood pressure, and brownish discoloration of the skin. Not exactly the words of choice for someone trying to be the first president born in the twentieth century, the youngest man to seek the office. Would he have been elected if the voters had known that truth?

Are these all just little lies? Maybe petty exaggerations that slip out in the heat of political discourse and leave no mark on history? Are these molehills in a landscape where men are judged by their ability to move mountains? And what about the poor government servant who gets lied to himself and thus eventually lies to his president and to his country? That happens, too, doesn't it? It sure does.

Maybe Washington is largely indifferent to the truth. Certainly Washington is the seat of pressure applied by experts on experts. Maybe pressure is, by definition, selective about truth. But pressure without truth is not persuasion but deception.

What about these little dishonesties that add up to lying, but are never quite defined as lying by society numbed beyond righteous indignation to all these little lies?

If you were the admissions officer of Harvard College, would you accept a student who boasted that his great-great-granddaddy died a war hero at the Alamo when you knew he died at home in bed? If you were chairman of the search committee looking for a new president of a great university, how would you feel about a man who told you how moved he had been by the sight of Nazi death camps when he was taking pictures of them when you knew he had never left the country during World War II?

The trouble with overlooking little lies is the damage done to reverence for truth. If the truth is not revered, there is no conscience, there is no compass. And without a compass, a man gets lost, a country gets lost.

Just look at Vietnam. The man who couldn't tell the truth about his great-great-granddaddy felt no compunction about lying in January 1964 about how American soldiers were doing in Vietnam. In December 1963, Secretary of Defense Robert McNamara, at the end of his first fact finding trip to Vietnam for the new president, held a press conference at Tonsonhut Airport in Saigon. He told an anxious nation that he was "optimistic as to the progress that had been made and can be made during the coming years" in the fight against the VC. Landing at Andrews Air Force Base the next day, McNamara told another press conference, "We have every reason to believe that U.S. military plans for '64 will be successful." Both statements were lies.

A chopper trip to the Oval Office later, the secretary of defense told the president the truth, a truth the world didn't learn until seven years later again from the oft-cited but tardy read Pentagon Papers. In fact, McNamara told the president he returned from Vietnam "laden with gloom." Viet Cong progress had been "great. My best guess being that the situation has in fact been deteriorating to a far greater extent than we realize. The situation is very disturbing."

Don't tell me that lies are ever little. Think for a minute how history might have changed if these lies had been left untold, and if the secret truth had been publicly stated.

18 Who Uses Whom?

The Theodore H. White Lecture
at Harvard University

DANIEL SCHORR

What is the interface with journalists and the people we interview, and write about, and put on the air? The advancing technology of instantaneous worldwide communication, in a very strange way, is making life unpredictable for both of us, the politician and the reporter. The traditional relationship is symbiotic, although we are reluctant to dwell on how often our successes are really somebody else's successes in using us.

When I was the CBS correspondent in Moscow, a Soviet official called me at the bureau in Moscow and referred to the latest of the letters we wrote every month, in which we asked for a television interview with Premier Nikolai Bulganin. Now the official on the phone wanted to know, were we still interested in an interview with Nikita Khrushchev, head of the Communist Party? "Well, sure," I said, not mentioning that it was Bulganin we had asked for, not Khrushchev.

The result was an hour of Nikita Khrushchev on American TV. President Eisenhower criticized CBS for letting this Communist boss into American's living rooms. How had it happened? Was it my brilliance? Was it my persistence in getting Khrushchev? Was it some great coup of mine?

Well, in fact, Khrushchev was trying very hard to figure out a way to resume relations with the West, torpedoed in 1956 by the bloodbath in Hungary. He wanted American television to help him in his campaign for renewed coexistence, that led two years later to a tour of America and

EDITORS' NOTE: Reprinted with permission of the author.

his parley with President Eisenhower at Camp David. So, the truth about our scoop? Kruschev did it.

Closer to home, in 1976, I obtained a draft for the final report of a House Intelligence Committee, which had been investigating the failures and misdeeds of the CIA. The Ford Administration was trying, and eventually succeeded, in having the report suppressed by the House.

I had a copy of the report and I arranged to have it published. I don't talk about sources. I didn't then and I don't now either. But, let me say that I am fully aware that I served somebody else's purpose by seeing that this report did not sink forever down the memory hole. It is a fact that I took the best I could get. I wanted CBS to publish it. I asked newspapers to publish it. In the end, I ended up with a report in the *Village Voice*.

Now, we are on the oldest established feature of Who Uses Whom. "Leak" is an interesting verb, if you are interested in language. Originally, it was an intransitive verb when used. Something leaked, oozed out, escaped, seeped out, somehow. Then, somehow, in the arrangement between the press and the government, we turned an intransitive verb into a transitive verb.

Now, things are leaked. Somebody leaks. There are "leakers." There are "leaking sessions." Michael Kelly, in the *New York Times* says that former Secretary of State, Jim Baker, spent 35 hours a week leaking at a very high level.

One has to divide leaks into two general categories—the authorized leak and the unauthorized. The conversations of President Nixon and Secretary of State, Henry Kissinger, as revealed in White House files, are full of references to "we will leak this, we will leak that, this should be leaked to this columnist, let's give this one to Evans and Novak, let's give that one, too." What should be leaked to what magazine.

But "unplanned" leaks—that is, leaks unplanned by them—drove Nixon and Kissinger up the wall and into wiretaps of officials and journalists, and into creating a leak-plugging unit aptly named "The Plumbers," which dealt, among other things, with the biggest unplanned leak of all, the Pentagon Papers.

There is also something that might be called a "secondary" leak. In January, 1975, President Ford let slip, at a White House luncheon with the publisher, editors, and columnists of the *New York Times*, that the CIA had been involved in assassination conspiracies. Then, realizing he had made an error, Ford tried to pull it back by saying, "Listen can we consider this off the record?" Later on, Publisher Arthur O. Sulzberger, much to the distress of some of his staff, ordered that this explosive remark not be pursued.

Well, it came to my ears, never mind how. That resulted in an exclusive on the CBS Evening News that precipitated a Senate investigation and, finally, exposure of the CIA's efforts, in league with the Mafia, to try to eliminate Fidel Castro.

Again, without quite discussing my source, I can say that no one in authority in the U.S. government and, certainly, no one in authority in the *New York Times* wanted that leak to occur, and none of them benefited from it. The public, I submit, did benefit and mightily. This exposed one of the darkest chapters in the CIA's history—a secret that the agency had scandalously kept from the Warren Commission investigating the assassination of President Kennedy.

If those plots to assassinate Castro had been known to the Warren Commission back then in 1963 and 1964, they might have better understood the motivations of Lee Harvey Oswald, who knew about the assassination plots because Castro had talked about them publicly and who, chances are, was a self-appointed avenger of Castro against Kennedy.

Is anybody here curious about the identity of the most talked-about and speculated-about "leaker" of modern times, that is, "Deep Throat?" Have you wondered why somebody who was apparently so inside as to know what was going on would be so disloyal to President Nixon, and take such risks? I believe that case has been broken by Jim Mann, who was a reporter and colleague of Bob Woodward at the *Washington Post*, and who now works for the *Los Angeles Times*.

He had it all worked out in an article he wrote for the *Atlantic Monthly* magazine. According to his theory, Deep Throat was one or more of the three top-level FBI officials who were furious because Nixon had picked an outsider, L. Patrick Gray, to succeed J. Edgar Hoover as the head of the FBI. Furious also, that Gray and the White House were obstructing the investigation of Watergate, which would then make the Bureau end up looking bad.

So, was the Watergate conspiracy punctured by G-men, jealous of their turf and jealous of the Bureau's reputation? I think so. So, where does that end up? The *Washington Post* got a Pulitzer Prize, the FBI got Nixon. Who used whom? What was that about?

The leak has become so commonplace as to be totally devalued. It just isn't the way it used to be. Television correspondents now routinely report what the president is going to say in his speech tomorrow. Names of prospective nominees are floated and withdrawn without regard to their reputations. All of these examples are leaks. There is hardly an official report, starting with the federal budget, that you won't find summarized in the papers and on radio and television before it is released.

The "leak" has been absorbed into a much bigger kind of industry. That is called the "spin." Secret-keeping has now fallen prey to the bigger industry of image-making. As a consequence, the massaging of the media, the care and feeding of the media, almost has overshadowed the policy-making process, the decision-making process.

First, you leak something to the press. You feed the press, then you get feedback. If the feedback is negative, you go and make some changes in the thing you were planning to say—that is called "fine tuning." The danger is that communicating will become not only a way of explaining policy, but will dictate the policy and ultimately will become the policy. The policy will be what sounds right, in this strange interaction we have now between policymakers and the media.

So, "spin patrol," "damage control," "message of the day"—the process has become so ingrained as to make governing seem like a form of theater. No one was better at it than President Reagan. President Clinton added still another dimension to governing by theater. He effectively hijacked television from the journalists by talking over their heads at town meetings, talks to MTV, talks to Larry King. Reporters, columnists, and commentators have now become supplicants. They want to be invited to lunch with the president, so they can write something that he hasn't already said on the air.

Now, having said that the press use politicians and politicians use the press in a largely symbiotic relationship, we come to the next stage in this "who is using whom?" business: the stage in which television itself as a technology takes control out of the hands of the press and policymaker alike.

President Reagan saw on television the relatives of hostages in Lebanon who blamed him for not doing enough to bring home their loved ones. He said, "They are killing us with that. We have to do something about the hostages." This was not anything that journalists had done. It was simply a reflection of what happens when he saw something on television. Seeing a political problem, he launched his ransom-by-arms-sales initiative.

President Bush, having decided to get American troops very quickly home from the Gulf in 1991, suddenly became aware that America was looking at frightful scenes of Kurds in flight from Iraqi genocide. Because he saw this on television, and because he knew America was looking at it and reacting to it, he sent the troops back to protect the Kurds. He said, "No one can see the pictures, and not be deeply moved." You know that when Americans are moved, then politicians are moved.

Somalia is a classic case of pictures dictating policy. In Somalia, scenes of starvation pulled America into humanitarian, and then military, intervention. Other scenes—of an American soldier's body being dragged through the streets—drove President Clinton to pull the troops out of Somalia. Going in and coming out—a function of reaction to the pictures that you see today on television. Clinton's National Security Advisor Anthony Lake confessed that "the pictures helped make us recognize that the military situation in Mogadishu had deteriorated in a way that we had frankly not recognized." Think of that. He has got military people there. He's got a couple of generals over there, and he needs pictures on television to tell him that the situation has deteriorated.

Richard Reeves in his book on President Kennedy reports one small incident about how I covered the beginning of the Berlin Wall early on a Sunday morning in August, 1961. He recalls that by the time the film reached New York and got on the air on the next available news program, Kennedy and his staff had time to read the cables from Germany, consult their allies, and decide how to react. It doesn't work that way anymore.

If it happened today, the official and all Americans would see the event on television around the time it was happening. They saw the Wall coming down on television. If we had satellite transmission back then, they would have seen the Wall going up on television and the administration would have had to scramble for a public response before they could consult anybody and know what their response really should be.

However, the picture is far from being the whole reality. Images now tend to replace reality or create their own reality. We end up reacting to pictures that show you what pictures can't show. It is a reality of what is on television.

Print journalists catch up more slowly and much less vividly than TV, and with much less impact on the people who make the policy based on what they see in the television age. That also happens some in domestic policy because when policy is driven by television, it tends to be driven by the reality that television creates. Vivid displays of violence, including juvenile violence, create an impression of pervasive crime all over the country. FBI statistics indicate that violent crime has been decreasing in large cities in recent years. But higher ratings on television are to be found in anecdotes of blood and gore than in statistics or analysis of where crime is or what crime is and why crime is.

So you find a crime bill being fashioned today resulting from the reality of crime but by pictures. If you see kids lying dead in the schoolyard, we want hundred people guarding that schoolyard right away. This is a reaction to the anecdotal part of the message rather than to the real meaning of it. So great is the obsession with reception and spin that spin tends to become policy.

Who uses whom? We journalists have tried so hard to serve as guardians of reality, only to be no longer sure there is a reality or whether our bosses care if there is a reality. Spin doctors are gaining on us, and the technology is gaining on all of us.

Some forty-five years ago E. B. White, that great essayist, saw the coming age of television as a race, "between things that are and things that seem to be." I think that, were he here today, he would say that "seems to be" is running far ahead. I just hope that a younger generation of journalists will run very hard to reclaim "things that are."

References

Alexseev, M. A., & Bennett, W. L. (1995). For whom the gates open: Journalistic norms and political source patterns in the United States, Great Britain, and Russia. *Political Communication, 12,* 395-412.

Althaus, S., Edy, J., Entman, R. M., & Phelan, P. (1995). *Revising the indexing hypothesis: Officials, media, and the Libya Crisis.* Paper presented at the 1994 Annual Meeting of the International Communication Association, Albuquerque, NM.

Anderson, B. (1983). *Imagined communities.* London: Verso.

Bagdikian, B. (1992). *The media monopoly* (4th ed.). Boston: Beacon.

Bennett, W. L. (1989). Marginalizing the majority: Conditioning public opinion to accept managerial democracy. In M. Margolis & G. Mauser (Eds.), *Manipulating public opinion* (pp. 321-362). Belmont, CA: Dorsey.

Bennett, W. L. (1990). Toward a theory of press-state relations in the United States. *Journal of Communication, 40,* 103-125.

Bennett, W. L. (1996). *News: The politics of illusion* (3rd ed.). White Plains, NY: Longman.

Bennett, W. L., Gressett, L. A., & Haltom, W. (1985). Repairing the news: A case study of the news paradigm. *Journal of Communication, 35,* 50-68.

Bennett, W. L., & Lawrence, R. (1995). News icons and the mainstreaming of social change. *Journal of Communication, 45,* 20-39.

Bennett, W. L., & Paletz, D. L. (Eds.). (1994). *Taken by storm: The media, public opinion, and U.S. foreign policy in the Gulf War.* Chicago: University of Chicago Press.

Blumler, J. G., & Gurevitch, M. (1981). Politicians and the press: An essay in role relationships. In D. Nimmo & K. Sanders (Eds.), *Handbook of political communication* (pp. 467-493). Beverly Hills, CA: Sage.

Brown, J. D., Bybee, C. R., Weardon, S. T., & Murdock, D. (1987). Invisible power: Newspaper sources and the limits of diversity. *Journalism Quarterly, 64,* 45-54.

Cook, T. E. (1994). Domesticating a crisis: Washington newsbeats and network news after the Iraqi invasion of Kuwait. In W. L. Bennett & D. L. Paletz (Eds.), *Taken by storm: The media, public opinion, and U.S. foreign policy in the Gulf War* (pp. 105-130). Chicago: University of Chicago Press.

Dahl, M., & Bennett, W. L. (1995). *Icons, indexing, and framing: News representations of George Bush's trade mission to Japan.* Paper presented at the Annual Meeting of the American Political Science Association, Chicago, IL.

Donovan, M. C. (1995). *All the news that's fit to kill? ACTUP, the New York Times, and the processing of AIDS activism.* Paper presented at the Annual Meeting of the Midwestern Political Science Association, Chicago.

Dorman, W. A. (1986). Playing the government's game. In L. Ackland & S. McGuire (Eds.), *Assessing the nuclear age*. Chicago: University of Chicago Press.

Dorman, W. A., & Livingston, S. (1994). News and historical context: The establishing phase of the Persian Gulf policy debate. In W. L. Bennett & D. L. Paletz (Eds.), *Taken by storm: The media, public opinion and U.S. foreign policy in the Gulf War* (pp. 63-81). Chicago: University of Chicago Press.

Edelman, M. (1964). *The symbolic uses of politics*. Urbana: University of Illinois Press.

Edelman, M. (1987). *Constructing the political spectacle*. Chicago: University of Chicago Press.

Entman, R. M., & Rojecki, A. (1993). Freezing out the public: Elite and media framing of the U.S. anti-nuclear movement. *Political Communication, 10*, 155-173.

Ettema, J. S., Protess, D. L., Leff, D. R., Miller, P. V., Doppelt, J., & Cook, F. L. (1991). Agenda-setting as politics: A case study of the press-public-policy connection. *Journal of Communication, 41*, 75-98.

Fialka, J. J. (1991). *Hotel warriors: Covering the Gulf War*. Washington, DC: The Woodrow Wilson Center Press.

Gans, H. J. (1979). *Deciding what's news*. New York: Vintage.

Gitlin, T. (1980). *The whole world is watching*. Berkeley: University of California Press.

Goldenberg, E. (1975). *Making the papers*. Lexington, MA: D. C. Heath.

Gottschalk, M. (1992, Summer). The media and the Gulf War. *World Policy Journal*, 449-486.

Hallin, D. C. (1986). *The uncensored war*. Berkeley: University of California Press.

Hallin, D. C., Manoff, K., & Weddle, J. K. (1990). *Sourcing patterns of national security reporters*. Paper presented at the Annual Meeting of the American Political Science Association, San Francisco.

Iyengar, S. (1991). *Is anyone responsible?* Chicago: University of Chicago Press.

Jamieson, K. H. (1992). *Dirty politics*. New York: Oxford University Press.

Knightley, P. (1975). *The first casualty*. New York: Harcourt Brace.

Lawrence, R. (1995). *Policing brutality: New York Times coverage of police use of force in the aftermath of Rodney King*. Paper presented at the Annual Meeting of the American Political Science Association, Chicago, IL.

Lippmann, W. (1922). *Public opinion*. New York: Free Press.

Manheim, J. (1994). Strategic public diplomacy: Managing Kuwait's image during the Gulf Conflict. In W. L. Bennett & D. L. Paletz (Eds.), *Taken by storm: The media, public opinion and U.S. foreign policy in the Gulf War* (pp. 131-148). Chicago: University of Chicago Press.

McNamara, R. S. (1995). *In retrospect: The tragedy and lessons of Vietnam*. New York: Times Books.

Patterson, T. E. (1992). *Irony of the free press: Professional journalism and news diversity*. Paper presented at the Annual Meeting of the American Political Science Association, Chicago, IL.

Patterson, T. E. (1994). *Out of order*. New York: Knopf.

Sabato, L. (1992). *Feeding frenzy*. New York: Free Press.

Sharkey, J. (1991). *Under fire: Military restrictions on the media from Grenada to the Persian Gulf*. Washington, DC: Center for Public Integrity.

Sigal, L. V. (1973). *Reporters and officials: The organization of news reporting*. Lexington, MA: D. C. Heath.

Swanson, D. L., & Carrier, R. A. (1994). Global pictures, local stories: The beginning of Desert Storm as constructed by television news around the world. In T. A. McCain & L. Shyles (Eds.), *The 1000 hour war: Communication in the Gulf*. New York: Greenwood.

Swanson, D. L., & Smith, L. D. (1993). War in the global village: A seven country comparison of television news coverage of the beginning of the Gulf War. In R. E. Denton, Jr. (Ed.), *The media and the Persian Gulf War.* Westport, CT: Praeger.

Taylor, P. M. (1992). *War and the media: Propaganda and persuasion.* Manchester, UK: Manchester University Press.

Zaller, J. (with Hunt, M.). (1994). The rise and fall of candidate Perot: Unmediated versus mediated politics—Part I. *Political Communication, 11,* 357-390.

Zaller, J., Chiu, D., & Hunt, M. (1994). *Press rules and news content: Two contrasting case studies.* Paper presented at the Annual Meeting of the American Political Science Association, New York.

PART III

Media-Based Political Campaigns

19 Overview

SHANTO IYENGAR

Political campaigns have come a long way in the past 100 years. In the presidential election of 1896, Republican William McKinley defeated Democrat William Jennings Bryan, populism reached its apogee, and the political fault lines set in place by the Civil War were permanently redefined. The campaign that led up to this crucial election was filled with colorful sloganeering and partisan conflict. In other respects, however, it bore little resemblance to today's campaigns. Most important, the voters of 1896 were far more engaged by the candidates and the issues. Bryan criss-crossed the country delivering more than 600 public speeches to a total audience estimated to exceed 5 million people. The Republicans countered Bryan's compelling oratory with a well-financed and centralized campaign masterminded by Marc Hanna, who was the forerunner of the modern political consultant. Both parties attempted to mobilize their supporters, sending out armies of precinct workers to get voters to the polls, and to stimulate public interest through noisy and boisterous partisan displays (brass band-led parades by day and torchlight processions by night).

Political campaigns in 1896, in theory and practice, were supposed to empower citizens by encouraging them to vote and were considered an invaluable component of democratic politics. Twentieth-century scholars have continued to take for granted that campaigns fulfill a civic or "mobilizing" role by direct efforts to get their supporters to the polls, by simply recharging voters' partisan sentiments, or by activating media and interpersonal communication about the election.

Do the campaigns of the 1990s, however, really do all this? Electoral reforms and technological advances have ushered in a new form of campaigning in which the mass media have replaced the political party as the key intermediary between voters and candidates. During the era of party-controlled campaigns, candidates relied primarily on human capital supplied by local party organizations—teams of volunteers who provided crucial services including organizing local appearances for the candidate, canvassing neighborhoods, knocking on doors and distributing campaign literature, and getting people to the polls on election day. Of course, it was more than public spiritedness and devotion to party ideology that made people activists; for many, electoral victory meant employment and a regular paycheck until the next election.

As the postindustrial era has progressed, the role of grass roots political organization and traditional partisan infrastructure has waned, whereas the candidates turned to the electronic media as the chief means of communicating with the electorate. In the process, the role of the ordinary citizen diminished from that of occasional foot soldier and activist to passive spectator. Between 1968 and 1988, the percentage of Americans who reported having done work for a party or candidate fell by half.

In the television era, campaigns typically consist of a series of choreographed events—conventions and debates being the most notable—at which the candidates present themselves to the media and the public in a format that sometimes resembles a mass entertainment spectacle. The "act" of viewing television commercials has replaced the act of attending a political meeting or organizing a campaign rally, while at the same time the steady diet of television has dulled voters' appetite for politics. Fewer and fewer Americans are mobilized by campaigns; turnout in both presidential and off-year elections has declined steadily since 1960.

A second major difference between the campaigns of the 1990s and the campaigns of 100 years ago relates to the content of the issues that formed the public debate. In the election of 1896, the public was galvanized by such policy issues as free trade versus protectionism, the gold standard versus free silver, and the power of large corporate "trusts" and monopolies. During the presidential campaigns of 1988 and 1992, by contrast, the public was been deluged with information concerning the personal character of the candidates. In modern times, the candidates' private lives and bedroom behavior are subjected to ever-increasing scrutiny, and even minor indiscretions can dash electoral prospects. Gary Hart's candidacy was doomed when his extramarital liaisons were brought to light. Bill Clinton's strategists had to struggle to survive the revelations of his efforts to avoid military service during the Vietnam War. In effect, campaigns are waged over the candidates' "good behavior" quotient rather than the substance of their policy proposals or visions for the future.

The public's appetite for politics has been further dulled by the tactics employed by the candidates and the press. The tone of campaign discourse has turned increasingly hostile and ugly (Ansolabehere & Iyengar, 1995). More often than not, candidates use their media opportunities to criticize, discredit, or ridicule their opponents rather than to promote their own ideas and programs. The 1994 midterm elections featured several prominent vituperative campaigns, including the California Senate contest between Michael Huffington (characterized in his opponent's advertisements as "the Texas businessman Californians simply can't trust") and Dianne Feinstein (characterized by Huffington's advertisements as "A career politician who'll say anything to get elected") and the Senate race in Virginia between Lieutenant Colonel Oliver North and incumbent Senator Charles Robb.

In attempting to respond to the new style of campaigning, the press has been forced to repeat, interpret, and analyze the candidates' attacks and charges. Consistent with their professional norms, reporters have assumed the role of independent referees who owe it to the public to scrutinize, judge, and report on the accuracy and fairness of campaign advertising. The result of this trend has been an increasingly adversarial or negative tone in news coverage of campaigns. In 1992, for instance, all three presidential candidates were the subject of more negative than either positive or neutral news reports. The shift in the tone of news reports can be traced directly, it seems, to the content of campaign advertisements. Thus, even when candidates do address the substantive issues, the press is quick to question their accuracy, sincerity, and intentions. Whenever and wherever they look, the public encounters information critical of the candidates. In short, the daily news coverage itself contributes to an atmosphere of extreme negativity.

The spiral of negative campaigning takes its toll on the policy-making process as well. Candidates who get elected by disparaging the motives and credentials of their opponents are not inclined to bury the hatchet— or to cooperate gracefully with members of the opposing party—the day after the election. In the absence of bipartisanship, coalition formation, and the spirit of compromise, it becomes more difficult for governmental institutions to accommodate and manage political conflict. As the partisan sniping, name-calling, and other elements of the "blame game" escalate, voters become even more disenchanted with their institutions and leaders. Where will it all end? Democratic and Republican politicians seem unaware of the consequences of their actions on the political hopes and aspirations of the people. A significant percentage of Americans are now willing to throw their support behind a third party candidate, somebody who is not identified with the stale and shrill partisan rhetoric. A third party candidate, however, is unlikely to produce effective and smooth governance. Democrats and Republicans in Congress are unlikely to roll over and play dead for an independent president. The more promising scenario (from the standpoint of the government's ability to deal with pressing social and economic problems) is the adoption of incentives for candidates to campaign on the basis of substantive and well-reasoned appeals and to avoid the name-calling and sloganeering that has come to dominate campaign communication. The most effective such incentive, of course, is the promise of public support. Only when voters turn against candidates who rely on attack advertising and who refuse to debate the opponent on the issues can we be confident that campaigns will return to their traditional uplifting and mobilizing roles.

The selections that follow shed significant light on the workings of media campaigns. Academic research on campaigns suggests that campaigns are actually relatively unimportant. Political scientists have had reasonable success in forecasting presidential elections (although not in 1992) on the basis of economic conditions (such as the unemployment rate) and the popularity of the incumbent president. These prediction models ignore campaign events altogether!

For years, the conventional wisdom in academic circles was that campaigns did little but reinforce voters' preexisting loyalties. As researchers turned to more powerful methods for assessing the effects of campaign communication, however, this conclusion has been revised and refined. The "revisionist" view of campaigns and their effects is described by Ansolabehere and collaborators. Although early research was based on the idea that candidates attempted to "inject" voters with persuasive messages, today researchers are more apt to view candidates and voters as partners in an ongoing dialogue.

Moving from the general to the particular, we next consider the importance of gender in political campaigns. Elective office in the United States is a male bastion. For decades, fewer than 10% of United States Senators,

Representatives, and state governors have been female. Does media coverage of women candidates and the women's movement contribute to this gender imbalance? According to the research by Kim Kahn and Edie Goldenberg, press coverage of women candidates, by depicting women as "nonstarters," impedes their ability to attract voter support.

The 1992 elections appeared to mark a turning point in the electoral fortunes of women. Following the dramatic Senate confirmation hearings of Justice Clarence Thomas, large numbers of women declared their candidacies resulting in a campaign environment dubbed "the year of the woman." This new political activism resulted in a significant increase in the number of women elected to the United States House of Representatives and Senate. The female headcount increased to 7% in the U.S. Senate and 18% in the House of Representatives. Following the 1992 election, several pollsters, reporters, and academics gathered at UCLA to discuss the newfound success of women candidates. During the conference, two of the country's leading pollsters—both women—offered their views concerning the importance of gender in political campaigns. As part of that same discussion, the coeditor of this volume summarized his research concerning the campaign strategies of women candidates.

One of the most frequently encountered criticisms of media campaigns is that they fail to inform voters about matters of substance—most important, the candidates' positions on the issues. Sam Popkin, one of the few academics with firsthand knowledge of the operational side of campaigns (having been part of the Carter and Clinton campaign teams), argues that the mainstream media continue to fixate on nonsubstantive topics, most notably, sleaze and scandal. In 1992, however, the Clinton campaign was able to change the subject from his character to his economic plan by turning to "alternative" media outlets such as call-in talk shows. Exposure on these programs made it possible for Clinton to explain his policy positions without being interrupted about his draft record or encounters with Gennifer Flowers. As a result, Clinton reconnected with voters and their awareness of his economic proposals allowed them to withstand the Bush campaign's assault on his character.

The previous selections have focused on the media as the prime mover in campaigns. Who sets the media agenda, however? In presidential campaigns, it is clear that "spin control"—being able to shape the daily flow of news—is crucial to electoral success. Popkin's observations of the 1992 campaign suggest that Clinton's advisers, by cultivating talk show hosts, MTV, and similar programs, were able to maximize their control over the media message. Had they ventured into the studios of NBC News or World News Tonight, they might have had less success. More generally, as John Petrocik argues, candidates have a huge interest in getting the media to focus on stories or issues on which they enjoy favorable reputations. Most Americans grow up subscribing to beliefs about the relative prowess of Democrats and Republicans to deal with political problems; Republicans are seen as good budget balancers, tax cutters, and crime fighters. Democrats are seen as caring about the underprivileged and as better creators of jobs and an expanding economy. Petrocik shows that political campaigns invariably veer toward the issues on which candidates exercise "ownership." Democratic candidates campaign on their promises to create jobs and to protect the elderly, the poor, and the sick from economic insecurity. Republicans, on the other hand, trumpet calls for law and order, greater cost cutting in government, and related themes.

The final selection, by Ansolabehere and collaborators, focuses on the role of negative advertising as a precursor of voter involvement. Their evidence suggests that campaigns cannot be counted on to generate voter interest and enthusiasm; candidates can and do use negative appeals to get voters to stay home. In today's media era, candidates are more concerned with maximizing their "market share" than with maximizing total turnout.

20 Shifting Perspectives on the Effects of Campaign Communication

STEPHEN ANSOLABEHERE
SHANTO IYENGAR
ADAM SIMON

Every political campaign is an evolving information environment that begins even before the first candidates announce their intention of seeking public office. The environment consists of three interwoven components—voters' existing beliefs, advertising by the competing candidates, and the filtration of the candidates' words and deeds through the news media. As information environments, campaigns are increasingly interactive and complex. The content and form of "paid" political advertising and "free" news coverage both shift rapidly as the candidates and the media respond to each other and the flow of events.

Research concerning the effects of political campaigns, like campaigns themselves, has evolved from simple to more complex forms. Early work, which focused exclusively on the persuasive effects of campaigns and which relied primarily on surveys, yielded a verdict of "minimal consequences." More recently, as scholars have begun to broaden the search for campaign effects and utilize more powerful methods of research, the pattern of evidence has shifted significantly.

The earliest and still predominant way of thinking about the effects of campaigns has been to assume that candidates win over voters simply by "injecting" them with appropriately designed messages. Assuming that the message is perfected (by carefully crafting the content, timing,

EDITORS' NOTE: Reprinted by permission from *Research in Political Sociology*, 7, 13-31. Used by permission from JAI Press, Inc., Greenwich, CT, and London, UK.

and form of presentation), adequate exposure is all that candidates need; the more people they reach, the more likely they are to win. The all-absorbing task of the campaign consultant is to predict which variety of messages will be most advantageous and to design the campaign accordingly. In effect, campaigns are as good as the resources and talents behind them.

The hypodermic model of campaigns has not fared well in the scholarly literature. Some fifty years of research into the conduct and management of campaigns has yielded only scattered evidence that campaigns reinforce the electorate's partisan preferences. Over the course of the campaign, Democrats become more entrenched in their support for the Democrat while Republicans become more committed to the Republican. Campaigns only allow parties and candidates to "awaken" their supporters and keep them from straying from the fold.

It is paradoxical that political scientists subscribe to the "minimal consequences" verdict in the age of media campaigns and multimillion dollar expenditures for television advertising. There are two explanations for the paradox. First, the initial wave of research was fanned by the singleminded pursuit of one form of campaign effect, namely, political conversion or persuasion. Second, the dominant method of research—the sample survey—proved insufficiently sensitive to record what effects, if any, campaigns might exert on the electorate.

The focus on political persuasion was a natural outgrowth of World War II, as social scientists expressed alarm over the potential impact of mass communication on the stability of the democratic process. The sudden rise to power of Adolf Hitler and Benito Mussolini suggested that ordinary citizens could be easily manipulated into supporting extremist leaders skilled in the art of propaganda. The development of television as a truly national medium only heightened fears that voters would do the bidding of the candidate with the most sophisticated advertising techniques.

Contrary to these expectations, the first wave of post-television research indicated that the public was far from manipulable. Studies of the 1956 presidential campaign—the first to be characterized by widespread broadcast advertising by both candidates—found that voters who were most exposed to campaign messages shifted their preferences little, if at all (Lazarsfeld, Berelson, & Gaudet, 1948; Berelson, Lazarsfeld, & McPhee, 1954). Campaigns merely reinforced or strengthened existing allegiances.

The stability of voter preference over the course of campaigns was attributed to several factors. First, voters have "standing commitments" that make them relatively impervious to campaign messages. Second, the voters most likely to monitor campaigns were those with the strongest sense of partisan loyalty. These attentive voters were likely to absorb the messages of "their" candidate and tune out messages of the opposing campaign. Other voters, who might be more open-minded and hence persuadable (such as those lacking a party identification and with no interest in the issues or candidates), were insufficiently motivated to attend to campaign advertising and other messages, thus precluding their being influenced.

In addition to the single-minded focus on persuasion, the failure to detect significant effects of campaign communication can also be attributed to deficiencies of research design. National polls are not well-equipped to detect short-term swings in political opinions in response to specific stimuli (Hovland, 1959). Moreover, survey-based measures of exposure to campaigns are notoriously unreliable (Price & Zaller, 1993). As researchers began to adopt experimental methods of research in which voters' exposure to campaign messages was physically manipulated, they began to abandon the minimalist view of campaigns.

Beyond the Hypodermic Model

The hypodermic model presumes that an effective campaign will be effective regardless of the type of the office at stake, the political leanings of the electorate, the nature of the opposing candidate, or the circumstances of the moment. In contrast, more recent theorizing about campaigns has emphasized the importance of the "environmental surrounding" of campaigns.

The "resonance" model of campaigning accepts the premise of the hypodermic model that voters can be persuaded by carefully designed messages, but attaches great significance to the overall campaign context. In particular, the resonance model evaluates two sets of electoral forces, "long-term" (dispositional) influences and "short-term" (circumstantial) influences. Dispositional forces are voters' prior beliefs, attitudes, and values—their prevailing political predispositions and loyalties. Most Americans acquire a sense of party identification and related affiliations at an early age, and these psychological anchors remain with them over the entire life cycle.

The relevance of voters' stable predispositions goes beyond the mere fact that self-identified Democrats are more likely to vote Democratic and self-identified Republicans are more likely to vote Republican. The political culture also provides voters with expectations and cues about candidates for public office. Democratic candidates, for instance, are seen as responsive to the interests of the working person, while Republican candidates are expected to exhibit a strong sense of fiscal responsibility, opposition to big government, and a tough posture on crime.

These expectations act as important filters for interpreting and understanding campaigns. The typical voter lacks even the most elementary level of factual knowledge about the candidates and campaign issues. Psychological research shows that messages that confirm rather than contradict existing stereotypes are more easily assimilated and retained. Therefore, campaigns that are designed to take advantage of (or resonate with) voters' expectations are most likely to be effective. A Democrat should be better off using ads that emphasize his intent to reduce unemployment, while a Republican should promote his support for a balanced budget.

Short-term influences as well as long-term voter predispositions play a role in electoral outcomes. Contemporary campaigns resemble elaborate kaleidoscopes with multiple sources and forms of information. Voters have access to news programs, talk shows, prime time sitcoms and dramas, candidate debates, newspapers and magazines, and interpersonal communications, each of which provides a different glimpse of the candidates. Bill Clinton played his saxophone on the *Arsenio Hall Show*; he and his wife discussed the state of their marriage on *60 Minutes*; he debated the issues with George Bush and Ross Perot on prime time television. Issues tend to emerge and fade away with predictable regularity. The rapidly changing flow of information has important consequences for candidates. Campaigns that do not "fit" or mesh well with the current information stream are not likely to receive much attention. Essentially, this is a problem of information "clutter." Political campaigns are much more likely to be effective if they are consonant (in terms of subject matter) with other sources of information, especially television news. For example, during or after a sensationalized murder trial, the news media (and the public as well) are likely to be preoccupied with issues relating to crime; the candidates realize this and typically seize the opportunity to demonstrate their credentials on this issue. Synchronizing advertising with the ebb and flow of current events is key to the resonance model of campaign advertising.

In sum, the resonance model suggests that campaigns work interactively in tandem with both long-term and short-term electoral forces. While the hypodermic model assumes that effects are due entirely to the particular characteristics of each campaign, the resonance model anticipates that effects are contingent upon the degree of fit between the campaigns and the prevailing campaign context.

The "competitive" model is the third and most sophisticated approach to understanding the effects of campaigns. This model assigns particular importance to the strategic interactions between the candidates. In the hypodermic and resonance frameworks, campaigns are studied in isolation from each other. In effect, the candidates are treated as "solo" voices who act to maximize their position vis-à-vis the electorate with little regard for the actions of their opponents. The competitive model, on the other hand, sees the effects of any particular message as conditioned by the effects of competitors' messages. This model recognizes that candidates are interdependent rather than independent actors.

In the world of commercial advertising campaigns, there are few if any situations in which consumers encounter "monopolistic" messages from only one advertiser. The more general scenario is one of competition—Domino's and Pizza Hut vie for the attention of pizza eaters, Ford and Chevrolet for the loyalty of drivers. The recognition that advertising campaigns are reactive is especially important in the political world. Unlike product manufacturers and retailers, candidates for public office feel free to air ads that feature their opponents. Campaigns have increasingly turned to "attack advertising," in which candidates or their surrogates directly attack or seek to discredit their opponents. Although the impact of attack messages is thought to depend upon certain qualities of the sponsoring candidates (such as their popularity), practitioners generally acknowledge that it is the response of the attacked candidate that is more important. Generally, the attacked candidate will suffer if he or she fails to rebut or otherwise discredit the attack. According to Roger Ailes' First Law of political advertising: "once you get punched, you punch back."

The question of advertising tone (i.e., attack vs. self-promotion) is only one element of the strategic equation. Candidates must also choose from any number of advertising themes. A candidate whose opponent is considered especially qualified on a particular issue might prefer to organize his advertising around alternative issues or, instead, attempt to neutralize his opponent's advantage by highlighting his own credentials on the issue in question.

In structuring an advertising campaign, a candidate must anticipate not only his opponent's probable strategy, but also the activities of the news media. In the aftermath of the 1988 presidential campaign, reporters have shown a penchant for examining campaign ads. In 1992, all major news outlets regularly offered "ad watch" reports which scrutinized particular campaign ads for their accuracy and fairness. The intent behind this new genre of campaign journalism is, of course, to deter candidates from using false, distorted, or exaggerated claims. However, this form of news coverage also has the potential to provide the candidates with considerable free exposure by recirculating the campaign message to a vast audience. Some studies of ad watch reports have concluded that they actually have the effect of strengthening the impact of the scrutinized ad. Candidates may therefore make the strategic choice to design ads that are especially likely to attract news coverage. By making their ads newsworthy, candidates obtain additional (and free) exposure on subjects of their choosing. A second layer of strategic interactions thus involves candidates and the press. From the perspective of the candidate, the goal is to design ads that not only counter the opponent's strategy, but succeed in attracting extensive news coverage.

In summary, we can distinguish among three different frameworks for understanding the effects of campaigns. The most simple is the hypodermic model in which the effects of campaigns are autonomous. Elections can be won by well-designed and well-financed campaigns. The resonance model attributes the influence of campaign messages not only to the intrinsic qualities of the messages, but to the match or fit between them and the campaign context. Ads that deal with timely issues and which do not violate voters' intuitive expectations are likely to prove especially persuasive. Finally, the competitive model views candidates as contestants who must take into account the immediate political environment, the particular strengths and weaknesses of their opponent, and the potential risks and rewards which may result from news reports that focus on their advertisements.

The systematic study of campaigns and their effects demands the monitoring of all three components of the information environment—campaign advertising, news coverage, and voters' prior beliefs. Electoral fate is determined by a series of interdependencies within this continually shifting environment. Research that focuses on one of these components to the exclusion of the other two will fail to provide an adequate account of the influence of political campaigns.

21 The Media

Obstacle or Ally of Feminists?

KIM FRIDKIN KAHN
EDIE N. GOLDENBERG

In this article, we investigate how the news media cover women candidates and how coverage patterns may influence public opinion. Women's issues have traditionally received very little attention in the press. Kahn and Goldenberg, in a study of Senate campaign coverage in 1984 and 1986, found that women's issues were rarely discussed in the news coverage of Senate elections. In fact, only 2% of all issue coverage was devoted to women's issues, such as news about the Equal Rights Amendment (Kahn, 1994a). Because the public's issue priorities are largely shaped by the media, the lack of attention to women's issues in the news does little to push these issues to the top of the agenda (see Iyengar & Kinder, 1987).

Even during the rise of the women's movement in the late 1960s and early 1970s, coverage was scant. What coverage did appear was on the women's pages and not in the news section. For many, the movement was not really news, but rather information appropriate only for women.

As the movement developed in the early part of the 1970s, coverage began to increase but serious coverage was still hard to come by. Stories concentrated on the sensational, not the substantive issues of the movement. The women's liberation movement was presented in the press as the "antics of a handful of disgruntled, unattractive bra-burners." Women's

EDITORS' NOTE: From *Annals of the American Academy of Political & Social Science*, Vol. 515, pp. 104-113. Copyright 1991. Reprinted by permission of The Academy of Political and Social Science.

libbers were described as "hostile, aggressive man-haters" who were not serious about politics (Baehr, 1980). Like other protest activities and social movements seeking media attention, what became newsworthy about the women's movement tended to focus on style rather than substance and on features that tend to discourage an expanded membership.

By late 1972, coverage became less hysterical. The stereotype of the "frigid, silly lesbian" was replaced with a more attractive stereotype of the "independent, assertive career women." As coverage became more positive, it became less plentiful and less prominent.

Consistent and positive treatment of the women's movement in the press could have spurred the movement's development. Without it, that route to increasing public support and political strength was blocked. Why was positive press coverage so hard to achieve? Some suggest that the establishment media, in an attempt to maintain the status quo, suppressed information about the women's movement. By keeping information about the movement to a minimum, the public remained largely ignorant of the movement's message, which demanded fundamental social change.

Several more subtle reasons also contributed to poor press during the late 1960s and the early 1970s. The first is the predominance of male gatekeepers. Men, who were making most news-selection decisions at the time, were disinterested in what they perceived as a "women's story" and did not encourage reporting on the movement.

Second, the women's movement was difficult to cover. Activists emphasized the importance of substantive issues. But events, because they have definite actors and occur at a particular time and place, are easier to cover than issues and generally fit better into standard definitions of news used by editors and reporters. By stressing issues more than events, feminists reduced the probability of coverage of the movement.

Coverage was also made difficult by a scarcity of authoritative sources (Molotch, 1978). Reporters and editors rely heavily on standard operating procedures, including the use of authoritative sources, when doing their jobs. In the case of the women's movement, press relationships were rarely routinized and many activists were openly hostile to reporters. The lack of established contacts with the press discouraged coverage of the women's movement in the news.

As women achieved political influence, their concerns made front-page news. Once legitimate leaders voiced concern for the women's agenda, the news media covered it and spread the word further. One aspect had particular importance—the idea that women as a group have different candidate preferences from those of men.

Feminist leaders encouraged news coverage of the gender gap. Many believed that a gender gap would force mainstream politicians to take the women's vote seriously. Early in the evolution of the phenomenon, the National Organization for Women (NOW) established a careful press strategy to attract media coverage of the gender gap. After Evans Witt of Associated Press found that 6% fewer women than men were likely to vote for the GOP in 1980, feminists actively encouraged pollsters to compare vote intentions of men and women (Bonk, 1988). By 1982, the NOW press office was regularly releasing monthly "Gender Gap Updates" to several thousand reporters to keep the issue alive.

Borquez, Goldenberg, and Kahn (1988) conducted a systematic study of gender gap coverage in the press. During the 1980, 1982, and 1984 elections, they examined coverage in the *New York Times* and in four Michigan papers of various sizes: the *Detroit News*, the *Detroit Free Press*, the *Lansing State Journal*, and the *Alpena News*. The amount of gender gap coverage grew steadily from 1980 to 1984.

The story of the gender gap, as reported in the newspapers, evolved over time. Discussions began to consider the possible causes of the gender gap as well as the likely consequences. By 1984, the gender gap and women as a voting bloc had become part of routine campaign reporting in resource-rich papers like the *New York Times* and the *Detroit News*. Leaders of women's organizations had become regular and important sources of gender gap information; they were quoted in 18% of all gender gap stories.

The definition of the gender gap also changed over time. In 1980, the gender gap was discussed as Reagan's or the Republicans' problems with women. By 1984, the press sometimes had characterized the gender gap as Mondale's disadvantage among men. This change in theme reflects both the Republican success in spreading their views of the gender gap and the changing political circumstances. In 1980, there were more potential female voters than male voters and less than a majority of women favored Reagan. But by 1984, although women still held less favorable views toward Reagan than did men, more than 50% of the women had come to prefer Reagan to Mondale.

Women's rights groups, like NOW, were active in securing coverage of the gender gap early in the 1980s and in promoting the view that Republicans had a problem with women. Activists seemed to have learned lessons from the early media treatment of the women's movement and made the proper adjustments. By making themselves and their polling information easily accessible to friendly reporters, activists helped generate and sustain coverage of the gender gap in the press, and the discovery of the gender gap and its prominent play in the press probably helped women in the political arena. By emphasizing the significance of the women's vote, media coverage gave credence to women as a potent force in the electorate.

By establishing the reality of a women's voting bloc, news attention to the gender gap may have encouraged more women to run for political office. Yet, if the news media treat women candidates differently from their male counterparts, then the press may act as a roadblock for women in their quest for elective office. We explored this possibility by systematically comparing press coverage of male and female U.S. Senate candidates from 1982 to 1986 and by exploring the impact of these coverage patterns on evaluations of candidates (Kahn, 1991, 1994b). The results clearly show that male and female candidates are treated differently by the press and these differences may have important effects on how candidates are evaluated.

News coverage of men and women candidates varies along a number of dimensions, all of which have implications for voter information and candidate preference. First, women candidates receive less coverage in the news. Regardless of the status of the candidates—whether an incumbent, a challenger, or a candidate for an open seat—or the closeness of the contest, women consistently receive less attention in the news than do their male counterparts. With less information available, voters may have a more difficult time acquiring rudimentary information about women running for office. This lack of available information may also hurt a woman's chance of election because it inhibits voter recognition of women candidates.

Gender differences in coverage are not limited to differences in the quantity of press attention. There are also systematic differences in the substance of coverage for male and female candidates. First of all, reporters devote more time to the horse race aspect of an election—for example, who is ahead in the polls, who has the strongest campaign organization—when covering female candidates. This preoccupation with the horse race for women candidates persists even if one controls for the competitiveness of the race and the status of the candidates.

Furthermore, reporters spend more time discussing negative horse race information when covering women candidates. Reporters routinely rate women candidates as less viable than their male counterparts and devote more space to discussing negative campaign resources, such as a lack of endorsements or lack of campaign funding, for women candidates. Again, these gender differences occur for both competitive and noncompetitive candidates and for incumbents, challengers, and candidates in open races.

Greater attention to negative horse race information for women candidates probably hurts women's chances of election. The news media's emphasis on horse race issues for women candidates may make their election chances more salient to voters. Moreover, because the content of this horse race coverage is often more negative for women candidates, voters may develop negative evaluations of women candidates, and evaluations influence how votes are cast.

Unlike horse race information, issue coverage is more prevalent for male candidates than for female candidates: 3.7 paragraphs a day are devoted to issues in stories about male candidates for the U.S. Senate while only 2.9 paragraphs a day discuss the female candidates' issue positions. This relative scarcity of issue attention, along with the greater emphasis on the horse race for female candidates, encourages voters to discount issues and emphasize viability when evaluating female candidates. Issues, on the other hand, probably play a more central role in evaluations of male candidates since issues receive more play and horse race less play in the news coverage of their candidacies.

The substance of issue coverage, as well as the amount of issue attention, differs for men and women candidates. Forty percent of the women candidates' issue coverage is devoted to so-called female issues, while only 30% of the men's issue coverage concerns female issues. Male issues, on the other hand, are discussed more often for men candidates than for women candidates. Male issues include those policy areas where men are seen as being more competent, for example, foreign policy, defense, economics, and agriculture, while female issues are those where women are considered more capable, such as minority rights, the environment, abortion, school prayer, drugs, and discussions of social programs.

Furthermore, women reporters are more likely than their male counterparts to discuss female issues in their campaign coverage. This difference in issue emphasis is most pronounced in the coverage of women candidates. In fact, when covering women candidates, women reporters devote 42% of their issue discussion to female issues while male reporters discuss female issues only 19% of the time.

These differences in the substance of issue coverage for men and women candidates can influence voters' evaluations of men and women candidates. Since media coverage affects the salience of issues for the public, voters exposed to races with female candidates may come to believe that female issues are important and these female issues, because they are more salient, may be used when voters evaluate the candidates.

The greater salience of female issues, coupled with the sexual stereotypes held by voters, could lead to more positive evaluations of the female candidates. For example, if education—a female issue—is emphasized in the campaign coverage of a race with a female candidate, voters exposed to the campaign coverage may come to believe that education is an important issue and therefore may evaluate the opposing candidates with regard to how well they can deal with educational problems. Since most voters believe that female candidates are better able to deal with educational issues, the higher salience of education as a campaign issue has the potential to lead voters to develop more positive evaluations of the female Senate candidate.

Since women reporters are more likely than men to discuss female issues when covering female candidates, the presence of female reporters probably encourages more positive evaluations of female candidates. Therefore, the presence of women reporters on the staffs of major metropolitan newspapers may be an important resource for women running for elective office. Unfortunately, women political reporters are still relatively rare—only 24% of all the campaign articles in our sample are written by women.

Why are men and women candidates treated differently by the press? Some of the differences may be based on reporters' and editors' expectations or stereotypes about men and women candidates. For instance, more attention to female issues for women candidates is a likely consequence of newspeople believing that women candidates can deal with female issues better than their male counterparts can. On the other hand, male and female candidates may emphasize different types of issues in their campaign appeals and the press may simply be reporting these differences. Similarly, women candidates may receive less coverage, overall, because newspeople consider women less serious contenders and therefore less newsworthy. Historically, women have been less viable and have had a difficult time securing election to the U.S. Senate. The historical abundance of unsuccessful women candidates probably promotes the emphasis on the horse race that was noted in the content analysis.

Given the systematic differences in news coverage of men and women candidates, it is important to investigate whether these differences influence voters' perceptions of men and women candidates. An experiment was conducted to examine this question. In the experiment, Kahn recreated the differences in press coverage found in the content analysis and examined the influence these gender differences in media presentations have on evaluations of Senate candidates. By controlling for all other factors, the experimental design allows one to examine whether differences in news coverage of men and women candidates influence voters' evaluations of the candidates.

The results suggest that differences in news presentations advantage male candidates. For example, candidates who receive typical male-candidate coverage were considered to be more viable than candidates who received female-candidate coverage. This was true whether the candidate was identified as a man or woman. The advantage that comes with being covered like a typical male candidate has important electoral implications since voters are more likely to vote for a candidate they think will win. Similarly, male-coverage candidates were viewed as stronger leaders and were also seen as better able to deal with military issues as compared to candidates covered like female candidates. Since both trait and issue evaluations can influence vote choice, these gender differences in news coverage appear to advantage male candidates and hurt female candidates.

These results suggest that the media act as a barrier for women striving for electoral office. The press treat men and women candidates differently and this likely encourages voters to develop more negative evaluations of women candidates, which probably influence voter choice.

Conclusions

This review suggests that, under certain circumstances, media treatment of women in politics can serve as an obstacle as women try to achieve their political goals. In other circumstances, the news media can act as an additional resource. It is quite clear that the early media treatment of the women's movement did not help the movement to grow. In fact, the press coverage of the women's movement, when any existed, was unflattering, and the movement grew in spite of the media attention received. Yet, the negative coverage of the women's movement cannot be blamed solely on the media. Activists involved in the movement did not understand the routines of news gathering and, consequently, did not make themselves available even to friendly reporters and editors. By the early 1980s, activists had improved their relationships with the press; the coverage of the gender gap reflects this improved relationship.

The press continues to treat women candidates for political office differently from their male counterparts. These differences seem to be based on the press's conception of the typical woman candidate, which is grounded partly in sexual stereotypes and partly in historical circumstance. Given these current coverage patterns, women candidates may want to make adjustments to their campaign strategies as a way of encouraging more equitable treatment by the press. Female incumbents, who can manipulate the media's agenda because of their status as incumbents, could be well served by emphasizing female issues in their campaign appeals. If female incumbents can make these types of issues more salient to the voters, then they will be advantaged in terms of the voters' evaluations. Because voters' sexual stereotypes produce positive assessments of women candidates' abilities to deal effectively with female issues, if voters believe these are the issues that are most important, then voters will use these salient dimensions when evaluating opposing candidates for office. That will produce favorable evaluations of female senators.

Increasing the number of female reporters on the staff of major metropolitan newspapers could also help women candidates. Women reporters are more likely than men to discuss female issues when covering women candidates. Given the stereotypes held by voters, increasing the number of female reporters will increase the salience of female issues among the electorate, and that would encourage more positive evaluations of women candidates.

Although this strategy is desirable, given the relative scarcity of women incumbents and the small number of female political reporters, it cannot be effective immediately. Instead, it may be more prudent to try to eliminate both voters' sexual stereotypes and gender differences in news coverage. Concerning the former, female incumbents, since they receive prominent coverage in the press, can take a leadership role in discouraging sexual stereotyping by voters. When female incumbents act in an unstereotypical way by demonstrating their competence in dealing with traditional male issues, voters may revise their image of the typical woman candidate. Recent research on the modification of stereotypes suggests that such a strategy can be successful. Using the candidacies of female incumbents to alter sexual stereotypes would ease the way for other female candidates.

Women's electoral chances could also be improved by eliminating gender differences in news coverage. This may be accomplished by educating editors and reporters about current differences in press coverage and encouraging them to alter their news-reporting routines. Eliminating gender differences in coverage could even the political playing field, thereby improving women's access to the electoral arena.

22 Women as Political Candidates

Was 1992 the "Year of the Woman"?

CELINDA LAKE
LINDA DiVALL
SHANTO IYENGAR

Celinda Lake: I think that the so-called "year of the woman" was as much about voters' desire for change and women's representation of change as it was about gender per se. Women candidates embody change in three different ways. The first element that they represent is responsiveness to the people—being in touch with the lives of ordinary Americans. In 1992, voters wanted change because President Bush seemed out of touch to them; voters didn't want to vote for someone who did not recognize a grocery scanner. And voters were disturbed by the Hill-Thomas hearings because the Senate seemed arrogant and out of touch. So one aspect of change that women represent, which was powerful in 1992, was simply being more in touch.

The second element of change that women represent is populism and a willingness to fight for the public good. We saw it clearly in the 1992 Barbara Boxer race, in the Patti Murray race, and in a number of other races: women as fighters for the little guy. While voters are frequently uncomfortable with "aggressive" women as their wives or sisters, they are very comfortable with women who fight for them in Washington.

The third element of change women represented involved the policy agenda. Voters were basically unconcerned with foreign policy and defense in 1992; they wanted action on the domestic front. Voters were happier with candidates who couldn't find Greece or Madagascar on the map, and women were more likely to be perceived that way. On the domestic agenda, there were any number of issues on which voters

165

accorded women the advantage—health care, constituency service, being concerned about children and people. But there were also some domestic issues on which they worried about women candidates. It used to be that most voters felt that male candidates were better than female candidates on handling the economy. Men and women now are seen as equal on the question. However, you still saw many men running against women using economic appeals. A second issue that was used against women was crime. You saw it in California, in Illinois, and even in Montana, which has the lowest percentage of people concerned about crime. Yet they still ran a death penalty ad against Dorothy Bradley in Montana. Crime is the "gender card" which opens up a whole range of criticisms of women candidates—they are too soft and compassionate to crack down on criminals.

The enormous energy that women candidates create around change and not being a typical politician also has a downside. Obviously, Republican male candidates understood that knocking the female candidate off her pedestal was a key way to campaign. And what we have found is that when women candidates begin to teeter, they fall much faster than men. When charges surface about a male candidate, voters say "yeah, that's what I expected all along." But when you have a woman who bounced checks or who failed to pay taxes, it is a much more fundamental violation. It's not what people expected. Because of that, the candidate falls much harder. It is a violation of the essence of the woman's campaign—not more of the same, not politics as usual.

The other aspect of this dynamic is that women tend to be penalized for attacking their opponent. So here's this person teetering on her pedestal and about to go negative, which voters think is very much politics as usual. Even when women who are not being attacked by an opponent put out an attack ad, their negatives go up and more so than men facing similar circumstances. Being an outsider thus does have its costs.

Linda DiVall: As a Republican, I find the whole notion of 1992 being the year of the woman a little bit frustrating. I worked for Lynn Martin and Claudette Schneider in 1990 and both lost by very big margins. We also had two other women—Pat Saiki in Hawaii and Christine Whitman in New Jersey—who lost by much narrower margins. I don't think any of them lost because of their gender; they lost because they were Republican challengers running against Democratic incumbents.

While "change" was running rampant at the top of the ticket in 1992, it was still the year of the incumbent. Ninety-three percent of all incumbents were reelected. Where women won, they did it in open seats where they could compete more effectively. They didn't have to worry about the incumbency factor and the money was spread more evenly.

Having said that, I still think that the 1990s can be considered as sort of the decade of the woman. And I do think that the Hill-Thomas hearings were indeed a galvanizing influence in terms of allowing many women to say "goddamit, I am going to run." It didn't matter who you believed—Clarence Thomas or Anita Hill—the experience mobilized us all. It was the first time that the male-dominated system was really exposed on television. To take one instance, Chairman Joe Biden announced a 5 minute adjournment and everyone came back 95 minutes later. No average person can afford to say, "Okay, I'll take a break for a cup of coffee and come back 95 minutes later." That person would not have a job. The U.S. Senate was exposed as an institution that could not follow its own agenda, could not run on time. I think what that conveyed to people was that there could be a system that runs better. If Nancy Kassebaum had sat on that committee, things might have been different. She was only one person, but as a Republican female she could have reached across parties and demonstrated where changes were needed. So the entire experience was a galvanizing experience for women who ran for office, who volunteered for campaign work, who worked as communications directors, campaign managers, and various other critical roles. Women became involved to an extent we hadn't seen before.

I would also agree with Celinda that women candidates benefitted from the theme of change. Women are not members of the club. And even if they were—as was the case with Boxer and Feinstein here in California— they still enjoyed the perception that they were open-minded, would allow new people in, and the key word, that they would listen. In all the polling and focus groups I have done, people were really outraged not because of gridlock or the power of special interests, but by elected politicians who, once they got to Washington, stopped listening to working people. They were thought to be controlled by some other entity than that which elected them. Women candidates, however, were seen as much more likely to listen to common people, to understand the concerns of working families.

Women are also able to understand the balancing act, in terms of work and family. In the presidential race, I think this was a real plus for Bill Clinton. He understood what women in the workforce were encountering. In my opinion, the Bush campaign couldn't have done more to alienate women from wanting to vote for Bush. They kept saying that we need to build more jet fighters, but we don't have any money for family leave. That's contradictory. But even worse, it says that Republicans really don't care about what women want or what they have to face in the workplace. That cost George Bush dearly. We will have to wait and see if it hurts the Republican Party. I think it will not because we have a lot of Republican governors and senators who understand the importance of the female vote.

Winning at the congressional level is still a difficult battle for women. You have to stand for change, you have to have experience, you have to have a fundraising apparatus, you have to crack the old boy network. It can be done. One of the races we were involved with this year was Tillie Fowler who ran for the House in an open seat in Florida. She was running against a Democratic male who was a circuit court judge. The district was 55% Democratic. Once she decided to run, she told me that she would raise $250,000 in a month. I thought she was crazy. She raised $275,000 in a month. That is the type of woman it takes to win in today's campaign environment. You have to stand for change and you have to raise money. She was able to attract contributions from the business world of Jacksonville that had always supported Charlie Bennett. She was also able to compete on the crime issue. As the first woman president of the Jacksonville city council, she had supported an expanded budget for the sheriff and for building more prisons. She was able to put that issue away on the basis of her own experience.

In conclusion, the biggest challenge that women politicians face is that they are elected as reformers which means that the timetable is very short for change to begin. I don't think we are done with the theme of change. We will see massive change and turnover in 1994 because there are a number of incumbents on both sides who don't want to face a vicious campaign and will retire. Women will thus have greater opportunities to win office.

Shanto Iyengar: The Clarence Thomas-Anita Hill hearings contributed significantly to the "gendering" of political campaigns in 1992. All Americans were riveted to that event. For women, the hearings told them something about their status in American society and the responsiveness of political institutions to their problems. After the hearings, large numbers of women declared their candidacies resulting in a campaign environment dubbed "the year of the woman."

Just as voters are socialized to expect stable policy differences between the political parties and the candidates who run as Democrats or

Republicans, so too are they willing to make gender-based inferences about candidates' credentials. As a result, female candidates will enjoy a "built-in" reputational advantage on issues that call for "feminine" attributes, while male candidates will be preferred on issues that invoke "masculine" traits. Defense and military issues will be especially persuasive as campaign material when the candidate is a male war hero; child care and matters of educational policy will resonate well with voters' stereotypic beliefs about a female candidate.

The UCLA studies show that women candidates who emphasize "female" attributes during election campaigns enjoy significant electoral advantages. We compared the success of U.S. senatorial candidates Barbara Boxer and Dianne Feinstein and presidential candidate Bill Clinton when they broadcast a campaign advertisement that dealt with issues of particular relevance to gender. We found that campaign advertising on gender-related issues was persuasive for Boxer and Feinstein, ineffective for Clinton.

The experimental manipulation was limited to a single 30 second commercial. We used this design to manipulate the gender of the candidate sponsoring the advertisement. Thus, the very same advertisement on the issue of sexual harassment was presented on behalf of Senate candidates Barbara Boxer and Dianne Feinstein, and presidential candidate Bill Clinton. Because the advertisements were replicas of each other (with the exception of the name of the sponsoring candidate), any differences in the effectiveness of the advertisement can be attributed only to the gender of the sponsor.

The results strongly supported the hypothesis that female candidates benefit when the campaign agenda highlights women's issues. When women initiated campaign messages, they fared best with women's issues and worst with crime. The female sponsor's share of the vote increased by 11% when the subject was women's issues. When the same message on sexual harassment was used by Bill Clinton, it increased his vote margin by a mere 3%. For Clinton, an advertisement dealing with women's issues was less effective than an advertisement on the economy. These results suggest that there are inherent differences between male and female candidates in their ability to profit from specific issue appeals. While the use of women's issues as a rallying cry significantly improved the women candidates' prospects, it had little impact on Clinton's level of support.

These results suggest that to be a woman candidate conveys information to voters about the candidate's willingness or ability to deal with issues that closely impinge on gender—such as sexual harassment. When gender-connected issues become central elements of a campaign, women candidates are advantaged. A woman who calls for educational reform or for more stringent enforcement of gender discrimination laws will be taken more seriously than a woman who calls for the death penalty or more aggressive monitoring of terrorist groups.

23 Voter Learning in the 1992 Presidential Campaign

SAMUEL L. POPKIN

Voters learn from campaigns because they know how to read the media and the politicians. Because they can reason about what they see and hear, they can learn about policies and character and competence. Three facts voters learned from the Clinton campaign were critical to his election: that he had an economic plan, that there was more to his character than presented on standard television news shows, and that he had enacted welfare reform in Arkansas.

Read My Plan

In 1990, the largest tax increase in history increased the already stratospheric distrust of Washington, giving momentum to term-limitation campaigns and anti-incumbent voting across the country and providing Democratic presidential hopefuls with their first major campaign issue to use against George Bush. By 1992, the public was increasingly affected by slow but real decline in net wages, an issue that not only boded ill for the incumbent president but accentuated concerns over whether Democrats could address the economy. In short, the loss of faith in Reaganomics did not revive the voters' faith in Democratic liberalism, and the Democratic presidential candidates had to convince primary voters that they were not traditional "tax and spend" liberals from Washington who would raise taxes to start social programs.

Throughout 1992, voters said their greatest fear about a potential Democratic administration was increased taxes. The cue Democratic primary voters used to distinguish traditional liberals from Democrats concerned with economic decline was the candidate's economic plan. The debate in the early primaries was dominated by Paul Tsongas and Bill Clinton, and what distinguished them from the others was their campaigns' ability to focus on concrete steps for dealing with the economy, to the point of publishing actual plans for voters to read. The effect of these plans on voters cannot be overstated: In New Hampshire, for example, these two candidates garnered 61% of the vote, with Tsongas winning by 35% to Clinton's 26%.

The press regarded these plans as gimmicks devoid of substance, but thousands of voters in New Hampshire obtained copies of the Tsongas and Clinton economic plans, and thousands more actually went to public libraries to read them. The Clinton plan was released, along with a television commercial promoting the plan, during the first week of January; in the next week, Clinton moved from 16% and fourth place to 33% and first place in the polls. In the next 6 weeks, 18,000 people in New Hampshire telephoned Clinton headquarters to request a copy of the plan—the equivalent of more than 10% of the primary electorate (Rosenstiel, 1993).

The experience of the 1992 campaign suggests that whenever a candidate makes a clear and confident offer, such as "Read my plan" or "Call my 800 number," it is an important cue for voters. A candidate who is willing to have his or her program examined, and thus expose him- or herself before the electorate, is giving people a chance to see his or her flaws. Furthermore, voters need not personally read the plan to believe in its content; they can assume that its meaning will emerge from public debate as the candidate rebuts attacks on it by the other candidates and their surrogates. If voters reasoned that what they had not read was credible, it was largely because they expected that the flaws in the plan would be attacked by the other candidates.

The content of the plans also mattered; primary voters learned enough about the plans to see the difference between the Clinton and Tsongas plans. Blue-collar, high school-educated voters and white-collar, college-educated voters evaluated these plans differently. Blue-collar workers, who as a group had experienced a decline in wages and jobs during the course of the 1980s, were attracted to an emphasis on investment in human capital; white-collar workers were drawn to an emphasis on making more capital available to businesses. In every primary, Tsongas' support was much stronger among college graduates and professionals, and Clinton's was much stronger among blue-collar, high school-educated voters. In the critical Florida primary, Clinton defeated Tsongas among high school-educated whites by three to one, whereas Tsongas beat Clinton among college graduates. In other words, it was not simply the move to the South that led to Clinton's defeat of Tsongas—it was the Clinton campaign's focus on a clear distinction between the two economic plans that emphasized Tsongas' lack of attention to working families.

From "Slick Willie" to "The Man From Hope"

As the only candidate with an economic plan that spoke to the concerns of the majority of blue-collar and minority Democrats, Bill Clinton won the nomination despite a staggering load of negatives. When Clinton formally clinched his party's nomination, he was such badly damaged goods that Jay Leno, for example, suggested that when he had a call-in show, the number should be "Rescue 911." After charges of marital infidelity and draft dodging and countless stories about prevaricating, less than candid replies, his public image was very much that of "Slick Willie."

What voters learn, and which cues they use to assess politicians and policies, depends on how much knowledge about politics they already have and how well they understand the operations of the federal system. Voters with less knowledge about politics are particularly prone to rely on assessments of personal character as a way of estimating political character or judging the issue positions of the candidates. No matter how much Clinton talked about issues, it was still much easier for many voters to absorb the unflattering stories about his personal character than to learn about his career or issue positions. Also, the more time he spent addressing these personal charges, the more attention he focused on them and the more political he looked. Without the new media and the new media formats that were so prominent in 1992, it would not have been possible for Clinton to give voters information with which they could learn more about him and his record.

On January 26, Super Bowl Sunday, Bill and Hillary Clinton appeared together on the CBS program *60 Minutes* to rebut charges that the Arkansas governor had an affair with a would-be nightclub singer, Gennifer Flowers. Clinton denied any affair with Flowers, but said that his marriage had troubles and that people would "get the drift" of what he meant by that. The next week, a *Wall Street Journal* story said he had avoided serving in Vietnam by promising to join a Reserve Officers Training Corps (ROTC) unit, which he never joined. One week later, a letter he had written in 1969 to Colonel Eugene Holmes, who had been in charge of the ROTC unit he did not join, was released to the press. In the letter, Clinton thanked the colonel for "saving him from the draft" and linked his decision not to openly resist the draft to a desire "to maintain my viability within the system." Later, 2 days before the April 7 New York primary, there were news stories that Clinton had indeed received an induction notice—which contradicted earlier statements he had made about the draft.[1]

The week before the New York primary, Clinton, who had answered previous questions about marijuana use with denials that he had ever broken any state's drug laws, was asked if he had ever tried marijuana in England while he had been at Oxford as a Rhodes Scholar. In his answer he replied: "I never broke a state law . . . but when I was in England I experimented with marijuana a time or two, and I didn't like it. I didn't inhale it, and never tried it again." In addition, there were stories about Clinton's use of corporate jets while he was governor, stories about campaign contributions from companies accused of polluting the state of Arkansas, stories about small business investments with savings and loan owners, and charges that Mrs. Clinton's law firm had profited from work with the state government.

Most voters did not believe that Clinton's all-but-admitted adultery and alleged evasion of the draft disqualified him from the presidency, but the way he handled the charges led a majority of the country to the conclusion that he was insincere and overly political.[2] Phrases such as, "I didn't inhale" and "maintain my political viability" were interpreted as evidence that he was an ambitious politician who would say anything and who could not be trusted personally.[3] When *Washington Post* reporters Dan Balz and David Broder conducted a focus group in Chicago, partici-pants described Clinton with words such as "slick," "slimy," and "cunning." They also compared him to television evangelists Jimmy Swaggart and Jim Bakker (*Washington Post*, 1992; see also Rosenstiel, 1993, p. 143). These assessments of character precluded him from telling many voters about his policies. When shown television commercials of Clinton discussing his programs, potential voters in focus groups reacted derisively and discounted most of what he said as slick propaganda ("How He Won," 1992, p. 41).

Less than 6 weeks after most voters were discounting everything Clinton did and said as "political," Clinton was rising so quickly in the polls that Ross Perot dropped out of the race and attributed his decision, in part, to a revitalized Democratic Party. He came back because of a "campaign within a campaign." In June, after the primaries, Clinton launched a month-long campaign to get voters to give him a second look and many did reassess their initial impressions of him.

Clinton's comeback would have not been possible 10 years earlier because it depended on new television networks, such as MTV, Fox, and CNN, and on specific types of programs and formats, particularly viewer call-in shows, that had only recently risen in prominence. These programs afforded Clinton the opportunity to give longer answers. The campaign's focus groups had shown that short sound bites of Clinton speaking were insufficient to overcome the people's preexisting beliefs about him. Viewers who saw him talking at length, however, as well as those who saw him in situations in which traditional politicians had seldom appeared, often noticed that there was something more to Clinton than they had expected. He was able to give more information and to restore enough credibility to talk about issues.

Immediately after he had secured the nomination, Clinton began to make guest appearances not only on the traditional television programs on which politicians had been seen for decades but also on entertainment outlets. He appeared on the late-night *Arsenio Hall Show* wearing sunglasses and playing the saxophone and he appeared on the NBC *Today* show and *CBS This Morning* answering hours of questions called in by viewers. He appeared on CNN's *Larry King Live* and on an MTV "Rock the Vote" special program answering questions from its youthful host, Tabitha Soren, and an audience of 18 to 25 year olds.

After 2 weeks of talk show appearances, Clinton had made major progress in breaking through the cynicism about him. On May 30, when voters were asked whether each of the candidates was "telling enough about where he stands on the issues for you to judge what he might do if he won the presidential election," 33% thought Bush, who had no plan, was telling enough, 32% thought Clinton, who did have a plan, was telling enough, and 15% thought Perot, who said he would soon present a plan, was telling enough. Over the next 3 weeks, Clinton was ignored by the traditional networks, which devoted most of their coverage to Perot, who had just hired Ed Rollins, Ronald Reagan's 1984 campaign manager, and Hamilton Jordan, Jimmy Carter's campaign manager in 1976 and 1980, and thus became the center of a media firestorm. At the same time, however, using talk shows and alternate settings, Clinton made major strides in informing voters about his plan. In mid-June, whereas 22% thought Perot was telling enough and 32% thought Bush was telling enough, 43% now thought Bill Clinton was telling enough[4]

Wendy Rahn, John Aldrich, and Eugene Borgida (1994) have run ingenious experiments that help explain the importance of the new media and new formats by showing how difficult it is for less knowledgeable citizens to learn about politics and politicians from traditional news shows on American television. Simulating a state legislative campaign, they made 15-minute films for two candidates composed of personal background, policy positions, and discussion of their political party. One group of subjects was exposed to the information as two separate 15-minute presentations. The other group was exposed to the information as a debate; the two films were edited so that the candidates appeared to be answering questions from a moderator. In the debate format, persons with lower political knowledge were not as able to process information about the candidates and integrate it into their ongoing candidate evaluations.

Just as infomercials are more useful ways for less knowledgeable citizens to learn about candidates than are debates, interview shows may be better than the typical news program. Television news, with a staccato style of sound bites, jump cuts, and advertisements, has the kind of "busyness" that makes it harder for less knowledgeable citizens to absorb political information (Rahn & Cramer, 1994). Indeed, Daniel Hallin (1991) has found that the length of the actual quote from a president on the news has gone from 45 seconds in 1968 to 9 seconds today. Instead of a short introduction from a reporter and a long look at the president, now we are given a short introduction from the president and a long look at the reporter. This style of reporting made it hard for Clinton not to look "political" and provided no opportunity for him to change how voters perceived him. Thus, bypassing the network news not only gave Clinton the opportunity to control the content and establish his policy positions, it also allowed him to reestablish his credibility.

For many voters, then, the only stories they could absorb from standard television news were stories about personal character. The inherently cynical style of television also adds to the difficulties of less knowledgeable voters. As Paul Weaver (1972; see also the discussion in the conclusion of Iyengar & Kinder, 1987) has shown, the reporters' analysis downplays the policy stakes involved. In the eyes of a network reporter (Weaver, 1972),

> Politics is essentially a game played by individual politicians for personal advancement. . . . The game takes place against a backdrop of governmental institutions, public problems, policy debates, and the like, but these are noteworthy only insofar as they affect, or are used by, players in pursuit of the game's rewards. (p. 69)

In 1992, it is fair to say that changing the channel was also changing the issue. The supposedly less news-oriented alternate channels and venues could provide more political information for many voters to learn about the candidates. In fact, on the call-in shows, more of the questions were about issues and fewer concerned personal charges than in the more traditional formats! (Rosenstiel, 1993, p. 183).

The second part of the plan to reintroduce Clinton was a decision to use the Democratic convention to give people more of Clinton's personal, as opposed to political, biography. On the evening of July 16 at the Democratic National Convention, the biographical film shown about Clinton, "The Man from Hope," successfully brought forward an important part of Clinton's life story: He had been born poor in the small town of Hope, Arkansas, had an alcoholic stepfather and a brother who later had drug problems, and had attended college on scholarships. This film, and Clinton's subsequent acceptance speech, corrected inferences about him that voters had drawn from the earlier stories that had erroneously led them to conclude that Clinton had led a life of privilege.

After the Democratic convention, 84% of the public said they thought Bill Clinton had worked his way up from humble origins, 62% said they thought he shared the values of most Americans, and approximately half said they thought he was telling them enough about his stands on issues for them to know what he would do in office.[5] This evolution in voters' perceptions of Clinton suggests that the best way to fight charges or problems against a candidate's character during a campaign is to provide additional information about other aspects of his or her character to give voters the fullest possible picture.

Welfare Reform: A New Kind of Democrat

The Bush attack on Clinton borrowed heavily from the recent British election in which the Conservative Prime Minister, John Major, had won an eleventh-hour, come from behind victory over the Labor Party (Blumenthal, 1992).[6] The Bush offensive focused on the argument that Clinton was radical, that the Democratic Party was a party of minorities and losers, and thus that any changes the Democrats made would be the wrong changes for the majority of Americans.

Clinton had an economic plan, and a large part of the electorate knew of it and believed that he had told them what he would do if elected. First, he established the credibility of his plan by running campaign advertisements featuring nine Nobel Laureates in economics as well as hundreds of business executives from prominent corporations who also endorsed the plan. Moreover, these business executives were not "losers" but rather the heads of some of the most successful high-technology firms in the country, such as Apple Computers and Hewlett-Packard. Despite Bush's attacks, the percentage of the population who thought the Clinton plan was worth trying did not decline.

Most important, Clinton's campaign advertising featured the candidate's record on welfare reform. During his tenure as governor of Arkansas, Clinton had developed a training program for mothers on welfare that had succeeded in moving 17,000 women off the welfare roles and into jobs. Compared to millions of unemployed nationally, 17,000 was a minuscule number, but the fact that Clinton had promoted a successful welfare reform provided an important source of reassurance that he was a "new kind of Democrat." In campaign surveys, after pollsters read to respondents the Republican attacks on Clinton as a tax and spend Democrat and then told them about his accomplishments as governor, the welfare reform program was the most reassuring element of his record as rebuttal to Republican charges against him. Welfare reform was even more reassuring than 11 consecutive balanced budgets, an Arkansas growth rate twice the national average, or a rate of creating manufacturing jobs in Arkansas that was 10 times the national average. A successful record on welfare reform and an often-stated philosophy that welfare was a second chance and not a way of life made it difficult for the Bush campaign to assert that Bill Clinton was an old-fashioned liberal who was out of touch with the middle class.

Conclusion

Political campaigns attempt to achieve a common focus—to make one question and one cleavage paramount in voters' minds. In 1992, no candidate could rely on their party's historical record to justify their claims for the next 4 years as they sought to define the critical cleavage or distinction with the other candidates. Internationally, the end of the Cold War meant the Republican record on defense was no longer as relevant as it had been. Domestically, Reaganomics had not meant lower taxes, less government spending, or sustained growth. Democratic candidates, on the other hand, had to convince voters skeptical about government that they were not tax and spend traditional Democrats concerned about social programs, but rather Democrats who would emphasize private-sector job creation and deficit reduction.

The Clinton campaign sought to convince voters that the most telling distinction between Clinton and Bush was "change" versus "more of the same." People felt major change was needed and the Clinton campaign sought to remind voters that George Bush, who failed to make the changes he had promised in 1988, could only offer more of the same. Indeed, the much-cited sign on the wall of the "war room" in Clinton campaign headquarters had "change versus more of the same" as the top line, followed by "the economy, stupid" and "don't forget health care." Much of the campaign thus depended on assuring voters that they would not get a "liberal" change.

The distinction the Bush campaign sought to emphasize was "trust versus taxes." George Bush was a leader who could be trusted, whereas Bill Clinton would only raise taxes. This meant, in effect, that Bush had to convince the public that his second term would be different from his first term when he had broken his "no new taxes pledge" and ignored domestic concerns. In short, he had to convince people that, "This time

I really mean it," and "Now I really care." Given the difficulty of raising his own ratings, a good part of his campaign was devoted to lowering ratings of Clinton and the Democratic Party—a strategy that Clinton countered successfully by publicizing welfare reform and job creation in Arkansas.

Without a credible economic plan, one that neither his primary opponents nor Bush could discredit, and without a record of welfare reform, Bill Clinton could not have convinced voters that he was not a traditional liberal, but rather a growth-oriented Democrat. Without new media and new formats that allowed him to talk at length about himself, however, he would never have had the credibility to sell his plan or his record.

Notes

1. The *Wall Street Journal* story appeared on February 6; the letter to Colonel Holmes was printed in the *New York Times* on February 13, and the stories about his induction notice appeared there on April 5.

2. In ABC polls in New Hampshire, for example, only 11% of the respondents thought the information on Clinton's marriage was relevant, whereas 80% thought the press was wrong to discuss the charges (Rosenstiel, 1993, p. 70). National polls showed similar figures, whereas the number of voters thinking the draft charges were relevant was generally around 20%. Only 24% of respondents in the April CBS-*New York Times* poll, however, said they thought Clinton had more integrity than most people in public life. At the end of the primaries, 62% thought he said "what he thinks voters want to hear," whereas only 28% of registered voters thought he was a person who "says what he believes most of the time" (CBS-*New York Times* poll, June, 1992). These figures had been relatively stable since March.

3. The Clinton campaign's research, including surveys and focus groups, about the "character problem" is described in "How He Won" (1992).

4. CBS-*New York Times* polls May 27-30, 1992, and June 17-20, 1992.

5. The last two questions are from CBS-*New York Times* polls for July and August, 1992. The first question was from a poll conducted for the Clinton campaign by Greenberg-Lake Research.

6. Blumenthal (1992) describes the attempts by the Bush campaign to imitate the successful campaign by the British Conservative Party.

24 Campaigning and the Press

The Influence of the Candidates

JOHN R. PETROCIK

Almost every campaign produces a pivotal event that explains the outcome, at least in the minds of the reporters who tell us about it. Gerald Ford's assertion in the televised press debate that Poland was not a captive of the Soviet Union; Lloyd Bentsen's acid retort to Dan Quayle: "Senator, you're no Jack Kennedy;" and Michael Dukakis' passive reaffirmation of his opposition to the death penalty in response to a hypothetical question about the rape and murder of his wife are memorable examples of such "defining moments." By the conventional wisdom, each was a turning point or a lost last chance to save a campaign. Everything else the candidates said and did over weeks and months, and what the voters thought about it, were considered irrelevant. By this account of campaigns, the substance of a campaign is less important than the media's reporting of electoral momentum, disorganization, gaffes (the horse race), voter predispositions (party identification), and circumstantial variables (such as the state of the economy). The candidates and their campaigns, independent of how the media treat them, are generally regarded (with apologies to Shakespeare) as sound and fury signifying little. Campaigns have not been ignored, but their influence on turnout, candidate images, and election outcomes has been regarded as less important than the predispositional, structural, and media effects of the textbook model. The media is regarded as especially important. Reporters put issues in play and set them aside; their feelings about the candidates, the play between the candidates, and between the candidates and voters color their stories and shape outcomes in the "textbook interpretation" of campaigns.

The textbook model described previously misunderstands and underestimates the influence of campaigns. It needs revision. The media is as influenced by campaigns as they are influences on it. The influence of campaigns is not always observed because the observers are looking for dramatic, discrete events of the sort noted previously. All campaign activity, however, is not dramatic, and not every important influence occurs in a brief moment in time. A campaign is a lengthy process of persuading and mobilizing. In addition, it has a particular character. This chapter describes the candidate activity that shapes the reporting of the media and the choices of voters.

Campaign Influence: An Example

In the same debate in which Dukakis was asked the famous murder-rape question,[1] there was an unnoticed instance of a campaign strategy that had led to another question. The question itself was undramatic, unremarkable, and unremarked on by the press, but it was a clear example of what had confronted Dukakis all year.

One of the panelists pitched a hard question to Bush by noting that although he had been in charge of the government's campaign against drug use during the Reagan administration, the drug problem in America had become worse. He wondered, therefore, what programs and plans Bush was considering that would work better than what had been tried during Reagan's presidency. Bush's response did not offer new programs and initiatives. His answer went down an entirely different path. Drug use, he asserted, is a problem that starts with flawed families and bad values. The solution, he went on, was to strengthen families and return to those traditional values that foreclosed the use of drugs. In short, Bush ignored the question.

Note that Bush did not deny that drugs were a problem. Nor did he deny that the federal government may have to formulate new programs and spend more money. His response, however, did not focus on those possibilities either. Instead, Bush identified the drug problem as a personal moral failure that could be remedied in the long term only by reinvigorated family values. Bush reframed the issue!

What prompted this response? Personal beliefs and tactics. Bush almost certainly believed that drug use reflected a personal deficiency with roots in the failure of a user's family to teach a code of personal behavior that avoided drug use. His solution—to strengthen families— matched his diagnosis. Personal beliefs aside, however, his answer was also rooted in a campaign strategy to force Dukakis and the press to focus on questions and problems that were inherently advantageous to Bush. A winning coalition required Bush to win (a) the votes of Republicans, (b) easily swayed independents, and (c) harder to influence marginal Democrats. His response was tactical because it appealed to these three target groups. Morally traditional voters who are a mainstay of the Republican electorate would be gratified by his answer. It confirmed their beliefs about the source of the problem and it signaled to them that he, George Bush, shared their beliefs and perceptions about it. The appeal to independents and potential Democratic defectors with this answer was more indirect.

George Bush's formulation of the drug problem was based on a recognition that the Democrats are the party of governmental activism in the minds of most Americans. Government-based programs involving drug diversion and preemptive social spending are mainstays of the Democratic approach to social problems. A Democratic solution involving social spending and government programs would certainly be more generous and wide ranging. The details of a Bush proposal that would be palatable to his core Republican constituency would probably seem half-hearted and ineffective to the swing voters needed to win. If Bush presented government-based solutions, therefore, he would have allowed the more government-oriented Democrats to trump his limited-government, Republican approach. Marginal and swing voters would be likely to find the typical Democrat's approach more persuasive. Bush would have put himself in a defensive and half-hearted posture on a problem that he had made more salient. He would have defined the drug problem in a way that produced an unfavorable comparison for him. Therefore, he avoided even talking about the problem along those lines. He interpreted the problem as a result of a breakdown of traditional families and traditional morality. Core Republicans and the targeted swing voters would be inclined toward him and the GOP with this sense of the problem because the Republicans were more likely than the "permissive" Democrats to promote traditional families and morality.

The Bush Rule for Campaigning:
Emphasize Republican Issues

What Bush did with the drug question he had done with most issues that year. Throughout 1988, Bush emphasized excessive government spending, high taxes, crime and social disorder, and a weakening of traditional values because these issues were "owned" by the GOP. Ownership of an issue exists when voters are inclined to believe that one of the parties is likely to handle the problems represented by the issue better than the opposition. Bush and his strategists were convinced that marginal and swing voters could be joined to core Republicans if GOP-owned issues were the most salient. They believed that a majority of voters would never choose Dukakis to resolve the problems of big government, high taxes, crime, and declining traditional morality. Voters, they believed, knew that Dukakis and the Democrats were not inclined to see high taxes or a decline of traditional values as important problems. The Democrats could not be trusted to solve problems they did not perceive. The tactical imperative for Bush and his strategists, therefore, was to make GOP issues the programmatic meaning of the election, make Dukakis address them, or, failing that, make him appear to be avoiding them.

This conscious strategy by the Bush campaign in 1988 is natural to all campaigns. Parties and candidates emphasize some issues and avoid others. They attempt to make owned issues the programmatic centerpiece of the election. If they are successful, either because of their efforts or because of the situation, they are likely to win the election. The press aids this strategy by helping the candidates get their message out to voters. As much as the individual reporters and media might have a particular bias, their major role in campaigns, despite themselves, is to help candidates promote their issues. They report what the candidates talk about, and that helps each candidate make his or her issues salient to voters.

Parties "own" issues because Americans perceive differences between them in their ability to "handle"—to resolve—the problems represented by the issue.[2] The handling differential reflects a history of differences between the parties in their attention toward problems, which, by the dynamics of party conflict, is regularly tested and reinforced.[3] Keep in mind that many, perhaps most, political issues reflect the competing interests of the groups in the society. Tangible economic interests are behind some of the disagreements (managers and employees divide over employment issues), some of the conflicts are quasi-economic (whites often object to policies designed to improve the social and economic conditions of blacks), and others involve group status, cultural beliefs, and ideological concerns (e.g., when the religiously observant attempt to keep expressions of religious commitment in public activities or minorities propose practices that promote recognition of their presence and achievements). Whatever the specific difference, parties reflect them because they are the politically organized face of the religious, economic, ethnic, linguistic, and regional groups that define a party's constituency (the classic statement of this can be found in Lipset and Rokkan, 1967; contemporary data are in Lane and Ersson, 1991). The identification of parties with distinct social groups is not complete, but it is sufficient—even in the United States—for the competing groups to give parties distinctive programs and agendas. Groups support a party because it attempts to use government to alter or protect a social or economic status quo that harms or benefits them; the party promotes such policies because it draws supporters, activists, and candidates from the groups. When President Bush, for example, opposed the 1991 Civil Rights Restoration Act as an inappropriate complication of business decisions, he expressed a judgment that the concerns of blacks were less weighty than those of businessmen. It was a trade-off that might have resulted differently if both blacks and businessmen were equally important GOP constituencies or, with the existing party constituencies, the president had been a Democrat. The general result of such choices is that the parties confirm their reputations for particular concerns.

Not all owned issues are constituency issues that differentiate the parties because of the kinds of voters who support it. Some reflect the record of the incumbent. The incumbent's record confers ownership when one party can be blamed for performing poorly on some matter that is consensual. Both parties hope to be regarded as competent to achieve "good times." But wars, failed international or domestic policies, unemployment and inflation, or official corruption can happen at any time and provide one party with a "lease"—short-term ownership—of a performance issue. The challenger acquires an advantage, a performance-based ownership of the issue, from this irrefutable demonstration that the incumbent party cannot handle the problem.

Both kinds of issues confer advantages on a candidate in any given election. A stable party system makes these issue more predictable, but they are typically long-lived even when the party system is undergoing shifts. Table 24.1 offers an abbreviated (not every class of issues is represented) inventory of the electorate's perception of issue-handling differentials during the past decade. The questions behind the answers reported in Table 24.1 simply asked voters to choose which party would be more likely to "handle" the problem. That is, the question read: "Which party is more likely to handle the problem of social security, the Democrats, Republicans, both equally, or neither?" Few voters see equality between the parties. Democrats are seen as better able to handle welfare problems. The GOP is better able to handle social issues (e.g., crime and protecting moral values). The data also document the GOP's hold on foreign policy and defense through the late 1980s. Opinions were mixed on economic matters but were generally a GOP asset (by an average of about 13 points). Government spending, inflation, and taxation were also Republican issues.

Voters and Issue Ownership

Voters recognize the parties' reputations, but they are not well-informed issue ideologues.[4] The median voter is uncertain about what represents a serious problem, lacks a clear preference about social and policy issues, is normally disinclined to impose thematic or ideological consistency on issues, and is inclined to view elections as choices about collective goods and resolving problems and not about the specifics of the resolution.[5] The key fact for this voter in the polling place is not what polices candidates promise to pursue, but which candidate can be trusted to handle the problems (e.g., medical care needs and high taxes) that need to be resolved.

Ideological voters may have clear ideas about what policies best deal with a problem. Most voters, however, are pragmatic and instrumental, mostly interested in "fixing" problems, and they see (as Table 24.1 indicates) differences in a candidate's ability to fix a problem depending on the candidate's party. If they see Republican-owned problems as the most important, they tend to vote Republican; they tend to vote for the Democrats when Democratic-owned problems are the most important.

TABLE 24.1   Perceived Issue Handling Competence of the Parties

	Problem Is Better Handled by (%)	
	Democrats	Republicans
Social welfare issues		
Developing policies that are fair to all	45	31
Protecting social security	52	27
Better public school education	44	28[a]
Improving education	39	41[b]
Helping the middle class	48	34[b]
Helping the homeless	54	27[b]
Helping the elderly	60	24[b]
Helping the poor	64	22[b]
Improving health care	51	22[a]
Foreign policy and defense issues		
Reaching nuclear arms agreements	28	48
Dealing with the Soviet Union	21	58
Dealing with international terrorism	21	52
Maintaining strong defense	19	61[a]
National defense	17	68[b]
Increasing U.S. influence	26	60[b]
Conducting foreign affairs	23	59[b]
Nuclear war	34	43[b]
Keeping United States out of war	42	37[b]
Economic issues		
Reducing the deficit	35	43[b]
Solving farm problems	48	27
Dealing with foreign imports	34	40
Promoting growth and prosperity	33	43
Promoting growth and prosperity (February 1992)	43	41
Reducing unemployment	45	38[b]
Holding down taxes	30	50
Taxes	35	44[b]
Controlling government spending	33	40
Controlling inflation	27	55
American industry	26	55[b]
Economy	32	49[b]
Inflation	34	49[b]
Social issues and other		
Promoting moral values	33	42
Reducing the drug problem	26	48[b]
Crime	28	46[b]
Environment	40	35[b]

NOTE: Respondents with no opinion and those who saw no difference between the parties are not shown. Data with no superscripts are from various 1988 to 1990 Market Opinion Research surveys.
a. Data from a June 1991 CBS-*New York Times* survey.
b. Data from a March 1991 ABC-*Washington Post* survey.

TABLE 24.2   The Issue Agenda and the Vote, 1988

Type of Problem/Issue	Frequency	% for Bush
Republican issue		
Social issues/traditional values	44	58
Big government/taxes/spending	47	56
Democratic issue		
Race relations	1	43
Domestic social problems	64	44

NOTE: Frequency refers to the proportion of the population that mentioned this as a problem in 1988.

Table 24.2 illustrates this effect for 1988 by comparing the vote with the problem concerns of the voter. Bush received majorities among those concerned with Republican-owned issues (social issues, traditional values, foreign policy, military security, big government concerns, taxes, and spending); Dukakis won a majority among voters concerned with civil rights, social welfare problems, and class or group status. Bush won a majority among those concerned with the economy.

Election outcomes aggregate the behavior of individual voters. Figures 24.1 and 24.2 plot the relationship between the vote and the issue-ownership score of the electorate for each election between 1960 and 1992. The issue-ownership score for both plots is constructed from responses to open-ended questions about problems facing the country. Figure 24.1 plots the Democratic share of the two-candidate vote against the party ownership score. The party issue-ownership score is determined by subtracting the proportion of the public who are more concerned about Republican-owned issues from the proportion who are more concerned about Democratic issues. Positive values indicate the percentage point surplus of Democratic mentions, and negative numbers indicate a surplus of GOP-issue mentions. Figure 24.2 plots the incumbent vote against the incumbent's issue-ownership score using a comparable algorithm. It employs the same algorithm for party-constituency issues, except that it is measuring the issue advantage of the incumbent. The issue advantage score for incumbents also incorporates performance issue concerns by allocating performance issues to the incumbent or challenger depending on the condition of the country. In both figures, the two-party division of the vote follows the issue agenda

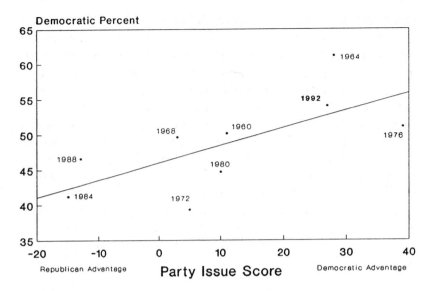

Figure 24.1. Issue Score and the Vote, by Party: 1960 to 1992

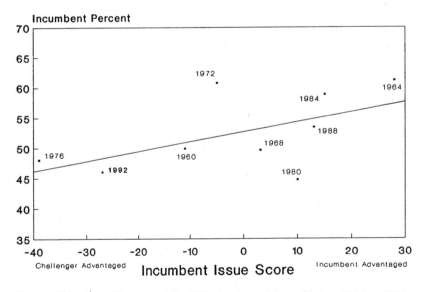

Figure 24.2. Issue Score and the Vote, by Incumbency Status: 1960 to 1992

of the electorate. Democrats do better when the issue agenda favors the Democrats; incumbents do better when the issue agenda of the electorate favors the incumbent candidate's party. A notable quirk in the regression line in Figure 24.1 is that the Democrats require an issue advantage of approximately 10 points before they have a reasonable assurance of defeating the Republicans. This party difference may indicate a "weakness" in Democratic issues. There is some evidence that voters have reacted more strongly to GOP issues in the past three decades. The downward displacement of the intercept certainly seems to reflect the election-specific effects of performance issues, which are not represented in Figure 24.1. When the issue-ownership score for the election is recalculated to take account of each candidates' advantage on leased performance issues (Figure 24.2), the apparent anomalies largely disappear and the dependence of the election outcome on the issue concerns of voters is clear.

The Candidates and the Campaign

With this knowledge of voter choice and election outcomes in the candidate's mind, is it any wonder that campaigns are agenda-setting struggles? The Democrats would like to see the bulk of the voters concerned about Democratic-owned problems. The Republican candidate would like to have them concerned with GOP-owned issues. Each, therefore, makes the campaign a "marketing" effort in which the goal is to achieve a strategic advantage by making problems that reflect owned issues the criteria by which voters make their choice. Each candidate emphasizes the strengths of his or her party and sidestep the opponent's issue assets. Each would prefer to talk about their core concerns, but their formulation of the opponent's issues, if they must deal with them, will reflect an advantageous interpretation of the problem (e.g., Bush's traditional family interpretation of the drug problem). Sincerity and tactical advantage lead each candidate to a preferred issue agenda. A Republican campaign that emphasizes urban unemployment can easily lead to discussions about government initiatives to promote job training. This would violate GOP ideological predispositions, but, more important, it could easily be quickly expanded by a Democratic opponent into a program whose size would run against competing GOP commitments to keep spending and taxes low, leaving the Republican looking less committed than the Democrat. Similarly, a Democrat has no incentive to make crime reduction a central issue. A promise to attack crime can hardly avoid a law enforcement response that would allow GOP enthusiasm for hiring more police, building more prisons, and punishing with longer sentences to trump Democratic proposals (the fate that befell Clinton's 1994 crime bill).

Both candidates, therefore, have a powerful incentive to avoid textbook debates in which each addresses points raised by their opponent. They will not attempt to change opinions on issues. They will, instead, attempt to make issues they own more salient. Issue concerns will, of course, depend on the existing national conditions, but nonideological, instrumental, and sociotropic voters are prepared to believe that almost any problem is important, and they are susceptible to priming and framing (Iyengar & Kinder, 1987; Krosnick & Brannon, 1993; Krosnick & Kinder, 1990) efforts by the candidates. The media, in reporting about campaigns, aid this effort.

The responsiveness of the press to the interests of the candidate is apparent in the issue stories that they write about candidates. Consider the record from presidential elections from 1952 to 1992. Figure 24.3, based on a content analysis of candidate-generated stories about issues and public policy in the *New York Times* during October of each election year from 1952 to 1992 (candidate-generated issue stories are those that report speeches or position papers by the candidates or his or her surrogates—the VP candidate, national party officials, other party candidates and officials, and so on—that identify problems, issues, or policies), illustrates the issue emphases of candidates in recent elections. The content analysis reduced the coded stories into two groups: issues owned by the Democrats and issues owned by the Republicans. The stories can be positive or negative: They are positive when they involve proposals or an assessment and negative when they concentrate on the failures of the other party or candidate; they can also be a combination of the two. Stories identified as Republican refer to campaign stories that predominantly dealt with issues owned by Republicans; Democratic stories are those that dealt with issues owned by Democrats (performance-issue stories are not presented). The numbers in the figure are percentage differences between the proportion of campaign-generated stories that are owned by one's party less the proportion that are owned

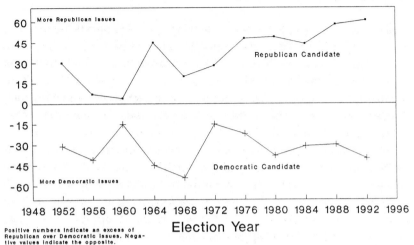

Positive numbers indicate an excess of
Republican over Democratic issues. Negative values indicate the opposite.

Figure 24.3. Candidate Issue Agendas in Presidential Campaigns:
1952 to 1992

by the opposition. The graph represents Republican problem themes with positive values; large negative numbers indicate an excess of Democratic themes.

The pattern is clear: Without exception, *New York Times* stories about the candidates placed greater emphasis on issues owned by that candidate's party. There are election and party differences. The campaigns were the least differentiated in 1960 when Nixon (especially) and Kennedy put more emphasis than normal on performance issues (see Jacobs & Shapiro, 1994, for an account of the 1960 election that confirms the relative failure of Nixon and Kennedy to pursue a straightforward issue-ownership campaign in that year). There is also some evidence that the Republicans are more single-minded in their campaign appeals than Democrats, especially if the Nixon elections are not included. The most impressive feature of the graph, however, is that the press faithfully reports each candidate's expected focus on issues owned by his or her party. The *Times* and other newspapers do not spend a great deal of time on political campaigns. Noncampaign news dominates the content of papers and electronic reporting. They can, by this route, use editorial discretion to focus the electorate's attention on some problems to the exclusion of others. Here too, however, what is happening in the world determines their noncampaign reporting just as much as the content of each candidate's campaign shapes their coverage of them. Also, there is an important difference between campaigns and events of the world: The former are quite purposive. Campaigns are efforts to win a struggle for election. The candidates will do what helps them, and they will avoid issues that are harmful. A campaign may not be able to control every event during an election cycle. They will, however, pursue a consistent strategy over the course of the election to control what a reporter writes or says about them. It is not flashy, but it relentlessly builds an issue environment within which the uncontrolled events of the sort mentioned at the beginning of this chapter are only (they hope) distractions. Campaigns, in short, shape the environment of voter decision making. It seems probable that this pervasive environment affects more voters, more fully, than does the occasional gaffe.

Conclusion

Campaigns may lead voters to the "obvious" decisions (Clinton's campaign against Bush's recession was obvious), but that does not diminish the importance of the campaign. No matter how difficult or easy it was for Clinton to make a poor job performance case against Bush, it was in making it that the campaign shaped the vote. The economy had been limping along since early 1991; Bush was ahead until the summer of 1992. When conditions are less clear than they were in 1992 (and they usually are), the messages of the campaign might be particularly important in shaping the choices of swing voters. Elections preceded by a 90-day campaign may frequently have different results from one held with only 24 hours notice.

A final note: Partisan association is not the only attribute that produces a claim of superior competence with an issue, and issue ownership is not peculiar to partisan elections. Although party is a major source of an issue-handling reputation, any characteristic that distinguishes candidates might establish the differential. It can, for example, operate in primary elections in which a candidate may create an advantageous agenda by emphasizing issues in a way that persuades the more politicized voters who show up in primaries that he is especially committed to the concerns of a "real" Democrat. Alternatively, a personal characteristic can convey ownership of an issue—for example, gender can determine who is the more credible candidate on matters of sex discrimination, and a retired war hero is a particularly credible commentator on military security. Issue-handling competence is the key. The press is a faithful communicator of these candidate efforts.

Notes

1. The questioner was Bernard Shaw of CNN and the question asked Dukakis how he would react were his wife to be raped.

2. I am greatly indebted to Budge and Farlie (1983) who were the first to use this idea systematically in studying elections. I have substantially modified their formulation to accord with my understanding of party systems and how I have found campaigns to be conducted in the United States. There is no way, however, to minimize the importance of their analysis to my thinking on this matter. Related themes underpin Repass's (1971) conceptualization of issues (see also Salmore and Salmore, 1989, pp. 115-143; Trilling, 1976).

3. Issue-handling reputations are not completely invariant. A candidate or a party can lose control of their issues because a dissatisfied electorate will be inclined to deny the party or candidate with whom they are unhappy any "redeeming" qualities. This should be a short-term phenomenon. Perceptions of a party's issue competence probably change very slowly, when they change at all. Most change is confined to a reinforcement of the general perception. That is, a party's advantage is likely to grow in response to campaigning on the issue. There are, however, instances of abrupt shifts in a party's issue competence. There are examples from the first year of Reagan's presidency. A more recent example can be found in 1992: Bush was competent at very little according the NES. Campaign data from 1992 found similar results.

4. The long-standing debate about the level of issue consistency among voters may be resolvable in light of the insights of priming and framing. Voters may not have become more ideological in recent years, but it is entirely possible that levels of issue consistency do vary, as Nie, Verba, and Petrocik (1979) asserted, according to the salience of candidate conflict over issues.

5. A specific example, a 1985 national survey by Market Opinion Research of Detroit asked respondents to rate 18 different issues in terms of their importance as objects of government intention. On a 0 to 10 scale in which 10 indicated the highest priority, the typical issue was rated about 7.8. Only three issues (school prayer, increases in social services, and abortion) produced means below 7 among Republican identifiers; four issues (a balanced budget amendment, Central America, school prayer, and abortion) produced means below 7 among Democratic identifiers. In other words, of the 36 means examined, only 7 fell below 7 on the 10-point scale. This receptivity to various issues agendas explains why agenda-setting activity by the candidates is critical.

25 Does Attack Advertising Demobilize the Electorate?

STEPHEN ANSOLABEHERE
SHANTO IYENGAR
ADAM SIMON
NICHOLAS VALENTINO

It is generally taken for granted that political campaigns boost citizens' involvement—their interest in the election, awareness of and information about current issues, and sense that individual opinions matter. Since Lazarsfeld's pioneering work (Berelson, Lazarsfeld, & Mcphee, 1954; Lazarsfeld, Berelson, & Gaudet, 1948), it has been thought that campaign activity in connection with recurring elections enables parties and candidates to mobilize their likely constituents and "recharge" their partisan sentiments. Voter turnout is thus considered to increase directly with "the level of political stimulation to which the electorate is subjected" (Campbell et al., 1966; Patterson & Caldeira, 1983).

The argument that campaigns are inherently "stimulating" experiences can be questioned on a variety of grounds. American campaigns have changed dramatically since the 1940s and 1950s (see Ansolabehere et al., 1993). It is generally accepted that television has undermined the traditional importance of party organizations, because it permits "direct" communication between candidates and the voters (see Bartels, 1988; Polsby, 1983; Wattenberg, 1984, 1991). All forms of broadcasting, from network newscasts to talk show programs, have become potent tools in the hands of campaign operatives, consultants, and fund-raisers. In

EDITORS' NOTE: Reprinted from *American Political Science Review, 88*. Used by permission from the American Political Science Association.

particular, paid political advertisements have become an essential form of campaign communication. In 1990, for example, candidates spent more on televised advertising than on any other form of campaign communication.

We are now beginning to realize that the advent of television has also radically changed the nature and tone of campaign discourse. Today more than ever, the entire electoral process rewards candidates whose skills are rhetorical, rather than substantive (Jamieson, 1992) and whose private lives and electoral viability, rather than party ties, policy positions, and governmental experience, can withstand media scrutiny (see Brady & Johnston, 1987; Lichter, Amundson, & Noyes, 1988; Sabato, 1991). Campaigns have also turned increasingly hostile and ugly. More often than not, candidates criticize, discredit, or belittle their opponents rather than promote their own ideas and programs. In the 1988 and 1990 campaigns, a survey of campaign advertising carried out by the *National Journal* found that attack advertisements had become the norm rather than the exception (Hagstrom & Guskind, 1988, 1992).

We assert that campaigns can be either mobilizing or demobilizing events, depending upon the nature of the messages they generate. Using an experimental design that manipulates advertising tone while holding all other features of the advertisements constant, we demonstrate that exposure to attack advertising in and of itself significantly decreases voter engagement and participation. We then reproduce this result by demonstrating that turnout in the 1992 Senate campaigns was significantly reduced in states where the tone of the campaign was relatively negative.

Experimental Design

To overcome the limitations of previous research, we developed a rigorous but realistic experimental design for assessing the effects of advertising tone or valence on public opinion and voting. Our studies all took place during ongoing political campaigns (the 1990 California gubernatorial race, the 1992 California Senate races, and the 1993 Los Angeles mayoral race) and featured "real" candidates who were in fact advertising heavily on television and "real" voters (rather than college sophomores) who on election day would have to choose between the candidates whose advertisements they watched. Our experimental manipulations were professionally produced and could not (unless the viewer were a political consultant) be distinguished from the flurry of advertisements confronting the typical voter. In addition, our manipulation was unobtrusive; we embedded the experimental advertisement into a 15-minute local newscast.

The most distinctive feature of our design is its ability to capture the casual effects of a particular feature of campaign advertisement, in this case, advertising tone or valence. The advertisements that we produced were identical in all respects except tone and the candidate sponsoring the advertisement. In the 1992 California Senate primaries, for example, viewers watched a 30-second advertisement that either promoted or attacked the general trait of "integrity." The visuals featured a panoramic view of the Capitol Building, the camera then zooming in to a close-up of an unoccupied desk inside a Senate office. In the "positive" treatments (using the example of candidate Dianne Feinstein), the text read by the announcer was as follows:

> For over 200 years the United States Senate has shaped the future of America and the world. Today, California needs honesty, compassion, and a voice for all the people in the U.S. Senate. As mayor of San Francisco, Dianne Feinstein proposed new government ethics rules. She rejected large campaign contributions from special interests. And Diane Feinstein supported tougher penalties on savings-and-loan crooks.
> California needs Dianne Feinstein in the U.S. Senate.

In the "negative" version of this Feinstein spot, the text was modified as follows:

> For over 200 years the United States Senate has shaped the future of America and the world. Today, California needs honesty, compassion, and a voice for all the people in the U.S. Senate. As state controller, Gray Davis opposed new government ethics rules. He accepted large campaign contributions from special interests. And Gray Davis opposed tougher penalties on savings-and-loan crooks. California can't afford a politician like Gray Davis in the U.S. Senate.

By holding the visual elements constant and by using the same announcer, we were able to limit differences between the conditions to
differences in tone. With appropriate modifications to the wording, the
identical pair of advertisements was also shown on behalf of Feinstein's
primary opponent, Controller Gray Davis, and for the various candidates contesting the other Senate primaries.

In short, our experimental manipulation enabled us to establish a
much tighter degree of control over the tone of campaign advertising
than had been possible in previous research. Since the advertisements
watched by viewers were identical in all other respects and because we
randomly assigned participants to experimental conditions, any differences between conditions may be attributed only to the tone of the
political advertisement (see Rubin, 1974).

Our experiments spanned a variety of campaigns, including the 1990
California gubernatorial election, both of the state's 1992 U.S. Senate
races, and the 1993 mayoral election in Los Angeles. The campaigns we
examined were all characterized by extensive broadcast advertising and,
in most cases, by frequent use of negative or attack advertising. Our
experimental advertisements dealt with a variety of campaigns and
themes. In all cases, however, the advertisements corresponded to the
actual focus of campaigns. In their content, the experimental advertisements closely reflected the advertisements aired by the candidates.

Subjects and Procedure

We recruited subjects by multiple methods including advertisements
placed in local newspapers, flyers distributed in shopping malls and
other public venues, announcements in employer newsletters, and by
calling names from voter registration lists. Subjects were promised payment
of $15 for participation in an hour-long study of "selective perception"
of local news programs.

Although the "sample" was obviously nonrandom, our participants
resembled the composition of the greater Los Angeles area. Across all the
experiments, 56% of the participants were male, 53% were white, 26%
were black, 12% were Hispanic, and 10% were Asian. The median age
was 34. Forty-nine percent of the participants claimed affiliation with the
Democratic party, 24% were Republicans, and 21% were independents.

Forty-four percent were college graduates, with the balance being evenly divided between high school graduates and individuals with some college.

On arrival, subjects were given an instruction sheet informing them that the study concerned selective perception of local newscasts. They then completed a short pretest questionnaire concerning their social background, media activities, and political interest. Following completion of the pretest, participants were taken to a viewing room, where, depending upon the condition to which they had been assigned (at random), they watched a 15-minute (complete with commercials) videotape recording of a recent local newscast (described to participants as having been selected at random).

The experimental or "treatment" advertisement was inserted into the first commercial break midway through the tape. The political spot was shown always in the middle position in a three-advertisement break. As described above, the advertisements in the various conditions were identical in all respects except for the factors of valence and source.

Following completion of the videotape, participants completed a lengthy posttest questionnaire tapping their beliefs and opinions on a wide range of campaign issues. Of course, we also ascertained participants' voting intentions and general level of involvement in the campaign. On completion of the posttest, participants were debriefed and paid.

Analysis and Results

We limit our analyses to the effects of negative advertising on intention to vote. In our posttest questionnaire, we ascertained whether participants were registered to vote. Using registration as a filter, we then asked, "Looking forward to the November election, do you intend to vote?" (In the case of the preliminary election study, the question was worded accordingly.) We identified "likely voters" as those who were both registered and who stated their intention of voting.

After pooling the studies, we compared the percentage of viewers classified as likely voters among participants who watched the positive and negative versions of the experimental advertisements. The demobilization hypothesis predicts that exposure to negative advertising will lower the percentage of likely voters. Among those who watched a positive advertisement, 64% intended to vote. Among participants who saw a product advertisement instead of a political one, 61% intended to vote. Among participants who were exposed to the negative versions of the campaign advertisement, only 58% were likely to vote. A one-way analysis of variance yielded an F statistic of 2.2, significant at the .11 level.

The decision to vote depends upon aspects of the campaign other than advertising valence. To capture these contextual and disposition effects on turnout, we regressed intention to vote on advertising tone and a set of dummy variables corresponding to specific elections, as well as various indicators of individual differences. The individual difference variables included the frequency with which people said they followed public affairs, prior voting history, the "match" between viewer's and the candidates' gender and party identification, age, race, and education. This multivariate analysis, in essence, estimates the independent effects of the campaign advertising stimulus on voting intention above and beyond campaign-specific influences and personal predispositions.

After taking into account these factors, advertising tone significantly (at the .05 level) affected turnout. Those exposed to the negative version of the advertisement were 2.5% less likely to vote than those exposed to no political advertisement. Conversely, the positive version of the advertisement increased voting intention by 2.5 percentage points. In short, the initial estimate of demobilization effect survived the multiple controls.

Overall, the experimental results demonstrate that exposure to negative (as opposed to positive) advertising depresses intention to vote by 5%. Considering the scope of our experimental manipulation (a single 30-second advertisement embedded in a 15-minute newscast) and the variety of campaigns examined, these effects seem remarkable. Despite our best efforts at experiment realism, it is possible that the effect has been magnified by some aspect of the research design. It is important, therefore, to place the experimental findings in the context of the world of actual campaigns.

Replicating the Experimental Results

To reconstruct our experimental framework in the real world, we measured the tone of the campaign in each of the 34 states holding a Senate election in 1992. Senate campaigns are especially appropriate for our purposes because the candidates rely heavily on advertising. Moreover, four of seven experiments focused on Senate campaigns.

Our indicator of campaign tone was based on a systematic content analysis of news coverage of the various Senate races. We searched through the NEXIS and DATATIMES databases for all newspaper and newsmagazine articles bearing on Senate campaigns in general and the candidates' advertisements in particular. This search yielded a total of over 2,500 articles ranging from a high of 1,000 on the Feinstein-Seymour contest in California to a low of 28 in the case of the Idaho race. Based on a reading of the news coverage, campaigns were classified into one of three categories: generally positive in tone (scored 1); mixed (scored 0); and generally negative in tone (scored –1).

As our indicator of turnout, we simply computed the votes cast for U.S. Senate and divided by the state's voting-age population. In addition to turnout, we also examined ballot roll-off in the Senate elections. For each relevant state, we subtracted the total number of votes cast for senator from the total cast for president and divided the latter. The roll-off indicator has two distinct advantages. First, the roll-off indicator is a campaign-specific effect measuring the degree to which people who were sufficiently motivated to vote in the presidential election chose to abstain in the Senate race. Second, because roll-off uses the presidential vote as a baseline, it adjusts for a variety of state-related differences (e.g., demographic factors, political culture, and party competition), which affect the level of voting turnout.

Turnout in senatorial elections depends upon a variety of influences in addition to the tone of the campaign. These include the competitiveness of the race, TV volume (or "decibel level") of the campaign, and the electorate's sense of civic duty. (For a thorough discussion, see Rosenstone & Hansen, 1993). Our measure of the volume of the campaign was the level of campaign spending by incumbents and challengers. Competitiveness or closeness was measured by the squared difference between the Republican and Democratic shares of the total vote. Lastly, to incorporate differences in civic duty and other relevant orientations, we also controlled for per capita income, turnout in the 1988 presidential election, percentage college-educated, region (South, non-South), and the census form mail-back rate.

Having compiled the turnout, roll-off, and campaign tone indicators, we proceeded to replicate the experimental results. For both turnout and roll-off, we found significant effects of campaign tone. Negative campaigns decreased turnout by 2%. (This also means that positive campaigns boosted turnout by 2%, for a total difference of 4%.) Negative campaigns also increased ballot roll-off by 1.2% and vice versa. Since the demobilization hypothesis is directional, we resorted to one-tailed tests (i.e., negative campaigns decrease turnout and increase roll-off, while positive campaigns increase turnout and decrease roll-off). The t-statistics for this hypothesis were 3.64 for turnout and -2.26 for roll-off, both significant at the .05 level.

The use of both experimental and nonexperimental methods to measure the very same naturally occurring phenomena is highly unusual in the social sciences. It is even more unusual if both methods yield equivalent results. In our study, the aggregate-level analysis of turnout and roll-off in the 1992 Senate elections and the experimental studies of negative advertising converge: Negative campaigns tend to demobilize the electorate.

Conclusion

Taken together, our studies demonstrate that attack advertising extracts a toll on electoral participation. In the experiments, voting intention dropped by 5% when participants were shown an attack advertisement in place of a positive advertisement. Our aggregate-level replication of the experimental results suggests that Senate turnout in 1992 was roughly 4% lower when the candidates waged relatively negative campaigns. Since the scope of the experimental manipulations never exceeded a single advertisement, our estimates of the demobilizing effects of campaign attacks may be consecutive. Over the course of two or three weeks of sustained negative advertising, the flight of voters can be more substantial.

The effects of attack advertising on the decision to vote have significant implications for our understanding of the impact of campaigns on electoral outcomes. Voter withdrawal in response to negative advertising also raises questions concerning the legitimate and fair uses of broadcast advertising.

The most important implication of these results is that in the era of media campaigns, both surges and declines in turnout can be generated by high-intensity campaigns. Candidates with sufficient resources can, through the use of negative messages, keep voters away from the polls. Campaigns are not inherently mobilizing forces, and the secular decline in presidential and midterm voter turnout since 1960 (for evidence, see Rosenstone & Hansen, 1993) may be attributed, in part, to the increasingly negative tone of national campaigns.

Finally, this research raises normative questions concerning the trade-off between the right to political expression and the right to vote. Should candidates be free to use advertising techniques that have the effect of reducing levels of voter turnout? In the case of publicly financed presidential campaigns, is it legitimate for candidates to use public funds in ways that are likely to discourage voting? How do we weigh the public interest in free political expression against the competing public interest in widespread public participation? When, if ever, should politicians' expression be restrained or subjected to incentives to modify its form or content?

In other areas of public communication, allegations of "antisocial" effects have prompted extensive analysis and debate. In some areas, the outcome has been governmental regulation. Thus the tobacco companies have been banned from using the airwaves for certain forms of commercial speech and are required to include mandated health warnings in their print advertisements. Direct regulation of political speech, which is at the core of the values protected by the First Amendment, is probably both impossible as a matter of law and undesirable as a matter of policy. The classic remedy in this society for injurious speech is simply "more speech." However, there is precedent in the law governing the broadcast media requiring that "equal time" be given to the targets of certain "personal attacks." Possibly, new regulations governing the broadcast media ensuring that the targets of attack advertisements have reasonable opportunity to respond (regardless of their own financial resources) should be considered. Ohio and other states are currently experimenting with "truth in political advertising" guidelines designed to make candidates think twice before resorting to false or misleading advertising. However, approaches that simply ensure that there will be more "speech" miss the essential point raised by this research, which is that negative advertising impacts adversely on voting; remedies that can only multiply the number of negative advertisements will exacerbate, rather than address, the essential problem.

The more realistic approach to influencing the tone of campaign advertising rests on voluntary or incentive-based restraints. There have been several instances in which public controversy over the content of entertainment programming has prodded the networks, local stations, or record companies to withdraw the program in question. Similar reasoning is embodied in legislation pending in Congress that seeks to reform campaign advertising. One bill would impose a double standard on advertising rates under which only "positive" advertisements would be entitled to the "lowest unit rate" rule. Other suggestions include the so-called in-person rule, under which the candidates would be required to deliver their attack statements in person (on camera).

We do not yet understand the implications of these various approaches. Some would certainly raise objections from civil libertarians, others would be objectionable to those concerned with political competitiveness. As in the case of campaign finance reform, broadcast advertising reform may work to benefit those in office at the expense of challengers. Although providing incentives for campaigns to air "positive" messages provides no assurance that these messages will be more substantive, verifiable, or honest, they would, at least, be less likely to deter voting. While the case for broadcast advertising reform has yet to be made, the relationship between negative advertising and voting suggests that these issues are worth further research and discussion.

References

Ansolabehere, S., & Iyengar, S. (1996). *Going negative: How political advertisements shrink and polarize the electorate.* New York: Free Press.

Ansolabehere, S., Iyengar, S., & Valentino, N. (1993). The effects of campaign advertising on voter turnout [Mimeo]. Los Angeles: University of California, Los Angeles.

Baehr, H. (1980). The liberated woman in television drama. *Women's Studies International Quarterly, 3,* 29-39.

Bartels, L. M. (1988). *Presidential primaries and the dynamics of public choice.* Princeton, NJ: Princeton University Press.

Berelson, B., Lazarsfeld, P., & McPhee, W. (1954). *Voting: A study of opinion formation in a presidential campaign.* Chicago: University of Chicago Press.

Blumenthal, S. (1992, December 7). The order of the boot. *The New Yorker,* 55-63.

Bonk, K. (1988). The selling of the "gender gap": The role of organized feminism. In C. M. Mueller (Ed.), *The politics of the gender gap: The social construction of political influence* (pp. 82-101). Newbury Park, CA: Sage.

Borquez, J., Goldenberg, E. N., & Kahn, K. F. (1988). Press portrayals of the gender gap. In C. Mueller (Ed.), *Politics of the gender gap.* Newbury Park, CA: Sage.

Brady, H., & Johnston, R. (1987). What's the primary message: Horse race or issue journalism? In G. R. Orren & N. W. Polsby (Eds.), *Media and momentum.* Chatham, NJ: Chatham House.

Budge, I., & Farlie, D. J. (1983). *Explaining and predicting elections.* New York: Allen and Unwin.

Campbell, A., Converse, P. E., Miller, W. E., & Stokes, D. E. (1966). *Elections and the political order.* New York: John Wiley.

Hagstrom, J., & Guskind, R. (1988, November 5). In the gutter. *National Journal,* 2782-2790.

Hagstrom, J., & Guskind, R. (1992, October 31). Airborne attacks. *National Journal,* 2477-2482.

Hallin, D. (1991). Sound bite news. In G. Orren (Ed.), *Blurring the lines.* New York: Free Press.

Hovland, C. (1959). Reconciling conflicting results from survey and experimental studies of attitude change. *American Psychologist, 14,* 8-17.

How he won. (1992, November/December). *Newsweek* (Special election issue), pp. 40-41.

Iyengar, S., & Kinder, D. R. (1987). *News that matters: Television and American opinion.* Chicago: University of Chicago Press.

Jacobs, L. R., & Shapiro, R. Y. (1994). Issues, candidate image, and priming: The use of private polls in Kennedy's 1960 presidential campaign. *American Political Science Review, 88,* 527-540.

Jamieson, K. H. (1992). *Dirty politics: Deception, distraction, and democracy.* New York: Oxford University Press.

Kahn, K. F. (1991). Senate elections in the news: Examining campaign coverage. *Legislative Studies Quarterly, 16,* 349-374.

Kahn, K. F. (1994a). The distorted mirror: Press coverage of women candidates for statewide office. *Journal of Politics, 56,* 154-173.

Kahn, K. F. (1994b). Does gender make a difference: An experimental examination of press patterns and sex stereotypes in statewide campaigns. *American Journal of Political Science, 38,* 162-195.

Krosnick, J. A., & Brannon, L. A. (1993). The impact of the Gulf War on the ingredients of presidential evaluations: Multidimensional effects of political involvement. *American Political Science Review, 87,* 963-975.

Krosnick, J. A., & Kinder, D. R. (1990). Altering the foundations of support for the president through priming. *American Political Science Review, 84,* 497-512.

Lane, J.-E., & Ersson, S. O. (1991). *Politics and society in Western Europe.* London: Sage.

Lazarsfeld, P., Berelson, B., & Gaudet, H. (1948). *The people's choice* (2nd ed.). New York: Columbia University Press.

Lichter, S. R., Amundson, D., & Noyes, R. (1988). *The video campaign.* Washington, DC: American Enterprise Institute.

Lipset, S. M., & Rokkan, S. (1967). Cleavage structures, party systems, and voter alignments: An introduction. In S. M. Lipset & S. Rokkan (Eds.), *Party systems and voter alignments.* New York: Free Press.

Molotch, H. L. (1978). The news of women and the work of men. In G. Tuchman, A. Daniels, & J. Benet (Eds.), *Hearth and home.* New York: Oxford University Press.

Nie, N. H., Verba, S., & Petrocik, J. R. (1979). *The changing American voter* [Enlarged Ed.]. Cambridge, MA: Harvard University Press.

Patterson, S., & Caldeira, G. (1983). Getting out the vote: Participation in gubernatorial campaigns. *American Political Science Review, 77,* 675-679.

Polsby, N. W. (1983). *Consequences of party reform.* New York: Oxford University Press.

Price, V., & Zaller, J. (1993). Who gets the news? *Public Opinion Quarterly, 57,* 133-164.

Rahn, W. M., Aldrich, J., & Borgida, E. (1994). Individual and contextual variations in political candidate appraisal. *American Political Science Review, 88,* 193-199.

Rahn, W. M., & Cramer, K. (1994). *The activation and application of political party stereotypes: The role of cognitive busyness.* Paper presented at the Annual Meeting of the Midwest Political Science Association, Chicago IL.

Repass, D. E. (1971). Issue salience and party choice. *American Political Science Review, 65,* 389-400.

Rosenstiel, T. (1993). *Strange bedfellows: How television and the presidential candidates changed American politics.* New York: Hyperion.

Rosenstone, S., & Hansen, M. (1993). *Mobilization, participation and democracy in America.* New York: Macmillan.

Rubin, D. (1974). Estimating causal effects in randomized and non-randomized studies. *Journal of Educational Psychology, 66,* 688-701.

Sabato, L. (1991). *Feeding frenzy: How attack journalism has transformed American politics.* New York: Free Press.

Salmore, B. G., & Salmore, S. A. (1989). *Candidates, parties, and campaigns.* Washington, DC: Congressional Quarterly Press.

Trilling, R. J. (1976). *Party image and electoral behavior.* New York: John Wiley.

Washington Post. (1992, March 20).

Wattenberg, M. P. (1984). *Decline of American political parties, 1952-1980.* Cambridge, MA: Harvard University Press.

Wattenberg, M. P. (1991). *The rise of candidate-centered politics.* Cambridge, MA: Harvard University Press.

Weaver, P. (1972, Winter). Is television news biased? *Public Interest,* p. 69.

PART IV

The Effects of News
on the Audience
Minimal or Maximal Consequences?

26 Overview

SHANTO IYENGAR

The audience for news in the United States amounts to virtually the entire adult population. Access to television is near universal and, on occasion, so is the viewing audience. The funeral of John Kennedy, the moon landing, the marriage of the Prince of Wales, the U.S. Senate hearings on charges of sexual harassment against Supreme Court nominee Clarence Thomas, and the announcement of the verdict in the O. J. Simpson trial were watched by nearly all Americans.

Despite the emergence of television as the dominant form of news, newspapers and magazines still enjoy a broad circulation. Print-based news reaches some 100 million people every day. Considering that the television networks, newspapers, and magazines all report on the same events, issues, and people, no matter what one's medium of choice the messages conveyed in the news are homogeneous.

How are Americans influenced by their consumption of news? Certainly there are no shortages of suspicions and theories. In recent months, Congressman Gingrich and his fellow Republicans have claimed that the press, in its coverage of the Republican-engineered budget cuts and their dire consequences for children and the elderly, embodies a liberal, Democratic bias. On the other side, advocates of governmental social welfare programs have attacked the media for giving far more attention to instances of welfare fraud and abuse than to instances of people who have used welfare support to achieve financial independence.

The fact that the news media is attacked bitterly by both sides to any particular debate suggests considerable impartiality and objectivity in the news. Some 40 years of careful social science research into the effects of news presentations, however, suggests that no matter how objective or impartial the news, the very fact that the media choose to convey information about particular issues at the expense of others and that the coverage is presented in a particular form have the effect of favoring certain groups and viewpoints at the expense of others.

Research into the effects of news coverage on the viewing or reading audience has mushroomed during the past three decades. Scholars were initially fixated on the idea of propaganda campaigns; did the development and refinement of broadcasting mean that ordinary Americans could be persuaded to support extremist or authoritarian causes and candidates? Efforts to uncover traces of widespread persuasion came up empty, and the search for media "effects" became more inclusive and multifaceted. Based on this research, we can say with confidence that the news affects people in different ways—some subtle and others not so subtle—and that people differ significantly in what they "get" from the news and in their receptivity to the messages and themes presented by the media.

The selections represented in this section deal with four different effects of the news on public opinion. First, because the news is, for most of us, the principal way of finding out about political developments, it is assumed that consumers of news will become more informed about the issues and events of the day. There is considerable fear, however, that current market-based trends in journalism—the trend toward "tabloidization"—have impeded the audience's civic competence. News coverage of O. J. Simpson, Lorena Bobbitt, Tanya Harding, and other sensationalistic stories tend to crowd out stories about welfare reform, the flat tax controversy, or other policy debates. The paper by Dimock and Popkin suggests that these fears may be justified. Their study shows that in countries (such as France and Germany) in which the press has not uniformly abandoned pretenses of serious journalism, levels of public information about current issues are significantly higher than in the United States, despite the fact that Americans tend to have more formal education than any other people.

In addition to the public education function, the news media are expected to alert the public to the problems or issues facing the country. Even if the news fails to provide in-depth and comprehensive analyses of political issues, it at least directs public attention to the presence of these problems and the policy responses under consideration by elected officials. That is, by covering some issues and ignoring others, the media set the public agenda—they influence what people view as important issues.

We begin the discussion of agenda setting with a paper by Everett Rogers and colleagues. They review the voluminous literature on media agenda setting and describe how the concept has given rise to newer definitions of media influence including framing and priming.

Professor Max McCombs and his students have done the most to uncover evidence concerning the overlap between media agendas and audience priorities. The review essay by McCombs and Estrada surveys the state of agenda-setting research in the United States and abroad and draws out the parallels between agenda setting and other communication research frameworks.

Most of the agenda-setting work described by the Rogers, Hart, and Dearing and McCombs and Estrada papers draws on correlational evidence. Beginning in 1980, the coeditor of this volume and his collaborators have undertaken a series of experimental studies of the news media's ability to set the public agenda. In *News That Matters*, Iyengar and Kinder (1987) showed that even modest amounts of television news coverage served to elevate the salience of newsworthy issues. More important, Iyengar and Kinder carried the agenda-setting hypothesis one step further by showing that the issues highlighted in the news are adopted by the audience as the standards by which they judge politicians and candidates for elective office. If it is crime that dominates the media agenda, not only does crime become public enemy number one, crime also becomes the principal yardstick for evaluating the president's or Congress's performance. It is this *priming* effect, first documented in *News That Matters*, that is the subject of the papers by Iyengar and Simon and Miller and Krosnick. The first paper demonstrates how the shifting political priorities of the American public resulted in dramatic fluctuations in the political fortunes of President Bush. When the United States embarked on military action against Iraq and liberated Kuwait from Iraqi occupation in decisive fashion, military and security concerns were paramount to the public and, on the basis of these issues, President Bush's performance appeared exemplary. Later, as the media turned the spotlight on the sagging U.S. economy, people began to worry about the country's and their economic prospects. Seen in this light, President Bush appeared as a mediocre and ineffective leader.

The social psychologist Jon Krosnick and his students have carried out the most careful studies of how and where the priming effect manifests itself. Not all voters are equally susceptible to media priming. Miller and Krosnick show that priming is most likely to occur among voters who are relatively informed about public affairs and those who trust the news.

Agenda setting and priming are both triggered by the quantity of news coverage accorded particular issues or events. A more subtle form of media influence, associated not with the amount of news but the manner of presentation, is referred to as *framing*. The notion of framing effects has been employed by several researchers who examine stylistic or other qualitative aspects of the news. Iyengar (1991), for instance, has distinguished between "episodic" and "thematic" news frames. The former depicts issues in terms of specific instances (e.g., a terrorist bombing, a homeless person, or a case of illegal drug usage). Episodic reports are essentially illustrations of issues. The thematic frame, by contrast, depicts political issues more broadly and abstractly by placing them in some appropriate context—historical, geographical, or otherwise. In appearance, the thematic frame takes the form of a "backgrounder" report featuring a series of "talking heads."

Given television's need for brevity, simplicity, and audience involvement, it is not surprising that episodic framing dominates news coverage. The importance of this form of presentation is far from trivial; as Iyengar's paper shows, viewers' preferences on matters of public policy are shaped, in part, by their attributions of responsibility for political problems. A person who believes that poverty is caused by lack of individual effort is not likely to be a fan of government welfare programs. Iyengar's experimental studies show that episodic framing of issues such as poverty encourages people to attribute responsibility to individual factors (such as laziness and lack of initiative) rather than societal factors (such as inadequate employment opportunities). By eliciting more individualistic accounts of political problems, television news coverage shields public officials and institutions from responsibility.

Although most media effects scholars have focused on the effects of national news outlets, the influence of local news can be just as important. The audience for local news now surpasses national news. More and more Americans turn to the "locals" for information about their community and city. As the demand for local news has strengthened, the supply of local news programming has kept pace. In some cities, it is now possible to tune into local news even during the "prime-time" hours.

Local news, like other forms of news, is driven by the need for large audiences. Issues that are attention-getting, that generate compelling visual images, and that fit the fast-paced nature of broadcast news are especially likely to attract coverage. Crime is just such an issue and the papers by Entman and Gilliam, Iyengar, Simon, and Wright reveal that local news coverage of crime in two major cities (Chicago and Los Angeles) is framed in ways that have far-reaching consequences for the ways in which people think about the issue of crime. In particular, because news about crime typically features violent acts of crime and because the alleged perpetrators are typically members of ethnic minorities, the news tends to perpetuate simplistic and stereotypic views about the nature of crime and criminal behavior. In effect, local news programming is a daily instrument of racial polarization.

The final category of media effects is persuasion. The social psychological literature suggests that "who says what to whom" is the most parsimonious way of thinking about persuasion situations. That is, the probability that people will change their opinion or attitude is dependent on *source, message,* or *audience* factors. There is an extensive literature on each of these factors. In the case of political persuasion, however, audience factors seem especially important; individuals differ in their persuadability depending on their *exposure* to persuasive messages and their *acceptance* of these messages. Paradoxically, as first demonstrated by the Yale psychologist William McGuire, the people who choose to expose themselves to political messages are also least likely to accept them. Conversely, the people who are most likely to accept political messages are those who rarely pay attention to them. The least educated voters, for example, can be won over easily by a candidate's call for support; the problem is that they are never in the audience for political presentations. The implications of McGuire's "two factor" model for the study of political persuasion are far-reaching indeed. Here, political scientist John Zaller extends the McGuire model to examine political campaigns, the diffusion of news, and the distribution of public support for particular policies.

In summary, research into the effects of mass communication has come full circle. Initial concern about the vulnerability of voters to propaganda campaigns gave way to findings of "minimal consequences." Effects research was rejuvenated by more limited conceptions of media influence, as manifested by the learning, agenda-setting, and priming paradigms. As these paradigms have matured, discussions of "massive consequences" have been revived.

27 Political Knowledge in Comparative Perspective

MICHAEL A. DIMOCK
SAMUEL L. POPKIN

One of the dirty little secrets of public opinion research is the low level of political information among the American electorate. Although many researchers have tried to rescue both the citizen and the polity from the consequences of civic ignorance by showing ways that less informed citizens make reasonable choices despite their low levels of information, no one has disputed the fact that there are many things that Americans simply do not know about their government or about politics. There is no doubt that political information is correlated with education—in every survey the more highly educated the respondent, the more knowledgeable he or she is about politics. During the 50 years that surveys have been measuring political information among Americans, however, there have been only small increases in political information despite the vast increase in education that has occurred. Is everyone as uninformed as Americans? That is, are all mass electorates uninformed or is this an example of American exceptionalism?

In this paper, we compare political information in seven democracies. We use a scale of political information developed by Andrew Kohut at the Times Mirror Center for the People and the Press that was used in surveys in seven democracies and relate differences in political knowledge about international affairs to the amount and kinds of media used to gain information. This allows us to address a related question: whether certain media sources, in particular television news, are less effective at conveying information than are newspapers (Robinson & Levy, 1986).

We argue that the answers to these two questions are linked. Americans are less knowledgeable than citizens in other advanced industrial democracies in part because American television is less informative than television in other countries.

Civic Information in Comparative Perspective

Since the first voting studies in the 1940s, researchers have found large gaps in even the most elemental kinds of political information among the American electorate (Berelson, Lazersfeld, & McPhee, 1954; Campbell, Converse, Miller, & Stokes, 1960). Indeed, the level of factual knowledge about the basic structure of government within the electorate, as well as about political actors or specific legislation, is so low that little data about current levels of knowledge are available on a regular basis! Survey researchers are generally reluctant to ask too many factual questions for fear of embarrassing respondents, who might terminate the interview or become too flustered to answer other questions (Delli Carpini & Keeter, 1991; Neuman, 1986).

A plausible case can be made for American exceptionalism—that particular features of this country lead to lower levels of political information. It could be the case, for example, that federalism and the separation of powers present voters with such a confusing political world that they are less able to organize and store "facts" than voters in parliamentary systems. It could also be the case that American textbooks, with their emphasis on the social and cultural dimensions of history, simply provide less information about institutions and events than texts in other less heterogeneous countries. Furthermore, America is the country most dominated by competitive, commercial-laden private television, which has never been confused with the BBC or Germany's television. American television is noteworthy for the cognitive busyness of its jump cuts, advertisements, and staccato style, and cognitive busyness makes it harder for some people to absorb information (Rahn, Aldrich, & Borgida, 1994). American television is also notoriously petty and mean spirited about politics and politicians, and this may simply turn people away from political news (Ansolabehere & Iyengar, 1995; Weaver, 1972, 1994).

It is also possible that Americans are less knowledgeable than Europeans because America is a country starved for social capital. As Robert Putnam (1994) has made clear, there is a dramatic decline in social capital in the United States. People no longer are as likely to attend church, PTA meetings, fraternal orders, or even join bowling leagues. There is less sociability and less need to develop the ability, Putnam argues, for political conversation. This could easily translate into a decline in the social value of political information and a decline in the motivation to pay deep active attention to political news (Putnam, 1994).

The best approach for devising a comparable measure of knowledge for cross-national comparisons to date has come from Andrew Kohut and the Times Mirror Center for the People and the Press (1994). Their measure of information in the United States, Canada, Britain, France, Germany, Italy, and Spain is based on questions about international political actors and events that have roughly similar meanings across countries.[1] The five information questions that were asked in each country in identical fashion in January of 1994 are (with the answer in parentheses):

Who is the president of Russia? (Boris Yeltsin)

Do you happen to know the name of the country that is threatening to withdraw from the nuclear nonproliferation treaty? (North Korea)

Who is Boutros Boutros Ghali? (Secretary General of the United Nations)

Do you happen to know the name of the ethnic group that has conquered much of Bosnia and has surrounded the city of Sarajevo? (Serbians)

Do you happen to know the name of the group with whom the Israelis recently reached a peace accord? (the PLO)

We computed a scale of knowledge about international political events and actors by counting the number of correct answers for each respondent in the seven countries. On average, the U.S. public scored far lower on the international information scale than the public of any European G-7 country and barely better than Spain, even though the U.S. public is better educated. Over half of all Americans—57%—answered none or one questions correctly; in Germany, over half—58%—answered all or all but one of the questions correctly. Clearly, the differences among countries on political information are not a simple direct function of either the level of economic development or the level of education. The average number of correct answers in the United States was 1.53, ahead only of Spain where the average score was 1.37. By a wide margin, the Germans were the most knowledgeable citizens and the Italians were also far ahead of the other countries. The average German answered two more questions right compared to the average American and the average Italian answered one more question correctly.

When the averages for each country are computed separately for those who have a high school education or less and those who have attended some college, the poor showing of Americans is even more dramatic. The least knowledgeable college educated of any country are Americans, and Americans are also the least informed noncollege group. Spaniards who have not gone to college, on average, know a bit more than comparable Americans (1.18 to 1.11), and Spaniards who have gone to college are on average a half a question more knowledgeable than comparable Americans (2.5 to 1.99). Thus, the only reason that the average score for Spain is lower than the average score for the United States is that more Americans have attended college.[2] Even more striking is the fact that Germans and Italians who have never attended college are more knowledgeable about world events than Americans who have. Because different education categories were used in each country and because each country has different degrees and school divisions, a finer breakdown than college versus noncollege is not possible. Even so, it is dramatically clear that there are major differences between countries that are not a simple function of the length of time people have attended school.

In every country, there is a gender gap; women score approximately one point less than men in every country but Germany, where men averaged 3.76 and women averaged 3.33. This, however, is by no means evidence of some inherent inability of women to absorb information about international affairs. The country by country differences are so large that Italian and German women know more than American men and French women are only a fraction of a point behind the American men.

One of our initial questions, then, has been answered. Our comparison of political information in seven countries has shown that there are significant cross-national differences in how informed populations are. Of course, we can only compare the countries by using a common scale of international questions. It may be that, if a comparable scale for domestic knowledge could be devised, there would be a different pattern. It may be that Americans, for example, are only less informed on international affairs because this country is so much more insular and parochial than the other countries.

Media Usage and Knowledge

If Americans are getting less information than citizens in other countries, it is not because they give less time to news. Each respondent was asked how many minutes they had spent the previous day reading a newspaper and watching the news on television.[3] The total of television news time and newspaper time in America is higher than that in any other country. The average American spends 52 minutes a day on TV news and newspapers, followed closely by Canadians and British who average 50.9 and 49.3 minutes a day, respectively. The French, Germans, and Italians each devote, on average, about 10 minutes less per day, and in Spain the average is only 31 minutes.

Americans, not surprisingly, devote the most time per day to television news (34.5 minutes). The Germans, at the other extreme, average only 18 minutes a day of television news. Sixty percent of all Americans, moreover, spend more than 30 minutes a day watching television news, whereas only 15% of Germans spend that much time on television news.

Germans spend the most time on newspaper reading, averaging 22.6 minutes a day with papers compared to 11.7 minutes in the United States. The United States average, however, is 5 minutes greater than that for either Italy or France and just 2 minutes below that of the United Kingdom. In only one country do people spend more time on average with newspapers than television news (Germany). Clearly, if Americans are uninformed, it is not simply because of lack of exposure.

If Americans devote comparable amounts of time to news, then the low levels of political knowledge here may derive from differences between countries in the informational quality of media. One possibility is that there may be inherent qualities of different media to inform, and that the differences between countries are due to the different mixes of media used in the countries. For example, despite the many differences in format and style and "quality," it may be that television is simply less effective at conveying information than are newspapers.

Alternatively, there may be country to country variations in the relative quality of each medium. For example, the reputation for high quality of the BBC, and the similar quality of German television news, may reflect that they are much more effective at conveying information not just to the elite and to elite media critics but to average citizens as well. It could well be the case that television news in countries where there are no commercials is easier to follow and more informative. Television without commercials may be inherently better than television with commercials because commercials interrupt the flow of information or because noncommercial television is calmer and less sensationalist. The differences between countries could also be due to a difference in the quality of print media; it may be that the newspapers in some countries effectively convey more information than newspapers in other countries.[4] There may also be differences among countries in how much attention is given to international news, but we cannot distinguish between quantity and quality with this data.

To test these hypotheses, we examined the effects of reported media usage patterns on respondents' information scores. We found that people who say they get most of their news from newspapers were significantly more knowledgeable than people who get their news from TV in every country save Canada, where there was no difference at all between readers and viewers. In the United States, those who say newspapers are their main source score, on average, .322 points better on the information scale than do those who say TV is their primary source of news, and in France they average over half a question better.

The first questions asked in each country concerned regular newspaper reading and regular TV news viewing. When these data are analyzed with multivariate methods, in every country save the United Kingdom, regular reading of a newspaper made a statistically significant contribution to political knowledge. When newspaper readership and demographic variables are all controlled for, being a regular TV news viewer makes an additional contribution to political information in only two countries—the United Kingdom and Germany. This result, first of all, gives some impressionistic validity to this entire analysis. The BBC has become synonymous with programming quality and German television is of comparable quality in the depth of its news coverage. This result also shows that differences in the kind of television persons are watching are significant enough to matter. Differences in the number of interruptions for commercials, in the level of sensationalism, or in the amount of attention paid to anchors versus reporters appear to matter.

The effect of being a regular newspaper reader in the United States was among the highest of the seven countries, being only substantially behind Italy and Spain. The level of education, interest, or intelligence in this country is not so low, in other words, as to make all media effects here lower than in other countries. The effect of being a regular TV news viewer in the United States, on the other hand, was not only statistically insignificant but was also the lowest of all seven countries. If American TV news viewers are abysmally ignorant, some of the fault lies with American television news.

Conclusion

Part of the reason Americans are less informed is that American TV is the least informative TV regarding international political events. Although we hypothesized that the low levels of information in the United States could result from an inherent inferiority of TV compared to newspapers, and the prominence of TV in this country, we found that there were substantial differences between countries in the communication of knowledge by TV.

The medium is not the entire message. Relying on a newspaper may be more active and efficacious than viewing TV, as evidenced by the fact that relying on newspapers leads to more information than relying on television; there is clear evidence, however, that television can do better than it does in America. What viewers get from TV is not determined by inherent limitations on the ability of people to absorb information they see and hear. The differences between NBC and the BBC matter.

Notes

1. They also used the same questionnaire in Mexico, but we have not made use of the Mexican data in this secondary analysis.

2. Spain is the only country where persons under 50 years of age were more knowledgeable than older persons. As the older, less educated generation in Spain passes on, it will not be long before Americans are well behind the Spaniards as well as the more

developed G-7 countries. The entire American advantage over Spain lies in the fact that Americans over the age of 50 know more than Spaniards over age 50.

3. The average minutes were estimated by assuming each respondent was at the midpoint of the interval into which their answer was coded. That is, respondents who said they spent between 30 and 60 minutes watching TV news were assumed to have watched 45 minutes for this calculation.

4. Because we do not have independent measures of the quality of newspapers and the literacy, intelligence, or cognitive style of the readers, we can only talk about how well the newspapers and their readers, or the television and their viewers, effectively convey information. That is, we may find persons get more from their papers in one country than in America, for example, not because the papers are better but because that country has better readers from better schools.

28 A Paradigmatic History of Agenda-Setting Research

EVERETT M. ROGERS
WILLIAM B. HART
JAMES W. DEARING

The purpose of this essay is to review past and present decades of scholarly research on the agenda-setting process showing how the paradigm, guided by an invisible college of investigators, evolved toward an improved understanding of the agenda-setting process. We utilize Thomas Kuhn's (1970) conceptualization of a scientific revolution to organize our tracing of agenda-setting research (Table 28.1). Agenda-setting research evolved from the minimal media effects paradigm that was dominant until the 1960s. In the 1970s, the upstart agenda-setting paradigm partially replaced the minimal effects paradigm. Refinements and expansions of research about the agenda-setting process have led to a changing paradigm since the mid-1980s. Disaggregation, longitudinal designs, conceptions of public opinion as active issue groups, and concepts such as framing and priming have broadened and enriched our understanding of agenda-setting.

A Scientific Revolution in Mass Communication Research

A scientific revolution occurred in the study of how the mass media affect public opinion. From the 1930s to the early 1970s, the dominant

TABLE 28.1 Stages in the Scientific Revolution for Agenda-Setting Research

Stages in Kuhn's (1970) Development of a Scientific Paradigm	Main Events in the Development of the Paradigm for Agenda-Setting Research
Preparadigm	Walter Lippmann's (1922) *Public Opinion*, and Bernard Cohen's (1963) *The Press and Foreign Policy*
The paradigm for agenda-setting research appears	Maxwell McCombs and Donald Shaw (1972) create the paradigm in their Chapel Hill study, which McCombs then follows up with further research over future years
Normal science: An invisible college forms around the paradigm	Some 360 publications about agenda setting appear from 1972 to 1995 in which the paradigm is supported, and, in recent years, greatly expanded in scope
A decline in scholarly interest begins as the major research problems are solved, anomalies appear, and scientific controversy occurs	This stage has not yet occurred for agenda-setting research
Exhaustion, as scientific interest in the paradigm shifts to the newer paradigm that replaces it	This stage has not yet occurred

SOURCE: Adapted from Dearing and Rogers (1996).

direction of mass communication research was to investigate direct effects of the media on audience members' attitudes and overt behavior. This research direction was set in motion in the 1930s by Paul F. Lazarsfeld, arguably the founder of mass communication research (Rogers, 1994). Originally, scholars expected to find strong effects of the media, but empirical findings only supported a minimal effects model. The media appeared to affect attitudes and behavior directly only for some individuals in some circumstances (e.g., television violence was found to affect children's aggression). This anomaly led to dismay with the paradigm of direct media effects, and, as Kuhn (1962/1970) would predict, led to a search for a new paradigm. Accordingly, mass communication scholars were drawn to study agenda-setting because it provided an alternative to the minimal (direct) effects findings.

A 1972 agenda-setting study by McCombs and Shaw in Chapel Hill, North Carolina, established a paradigm that was adopted mainly by mass communication scholars and to a lesser extent by political scientists, sociologists, and other social scientists. This paradigm, which we term the hierarchy approach to agenda-setting research, offered a new way to think about the effects of the mass media so that "familiar objects are seen in a different light" (Kuhn, 1970, p. 111).

Mass communication scholars were attracted to investigate the agenda-setting process because it was an alternative to the existing paradigm of limited effects of the media, which represented anomalies in explaining short-term attitude change and overt behavior change. The agenda-setting perspective directed mass communication research toward indirect, cognitive effects, impacts of the media that scholars like McCombs and Shaw and colleagues felt were more reasonable to expect. Early agenda-setting publications by mass communication researchers were justified as an attempt to overcome the limited-effects findings of past mass communication research. For example, Maxwell McCombs (1981) concluded

Its [agenda-setting's] initial empirical exploration was fortuitously timed. It came at that time when disenchantment both with attitudes and opinions as dependent variables, and with the limited-effects model as an adequate intellectual summary, was leading scholars to look elsewhere. (p. 121)

The new paradigm sent mass communication researchers in the direction of studying how media news coverage affected an issue's salience on the agenda rather than direct media effects on audience members' attitudes and behavior change.

The Paradigm for Agenda-Setting Research

The defining event in the conceptualization of the agenda-setting process occurred in 1967 while Maxwell McCombs was an assistant professor of journalism at UCLA. Over an after-work drink at the Century Plaza Hotel on Wilshire Avenue in Los Angeles, McCombs and another junior colleague speculated as to why a particular news event had not had a greater impact on the public. They examined that day's front page of the *Los Angeles Times* that had downplayed the news event (a minor scandal in the Johnson administration) with just a small photograph and a minor headline. Two other news events had been given major play on that day's front page of the *Los Angeles Times*. If an individual had read a different newspaper that day—for example, the *New York Times*—he or she might have considered the scandal a much more important issue. This discussion of media agenda-setting led McCombs to walk into the UCLA bookstore to purchase a copy of Cohen's (1963) book, which contained the now-famous metaphorical statement about agenda setting. Soon, McCombs was off to the University of North Carolina, where he was to collaborate with Donald Shaw in conducting the Chapel Hill study.

What are the main elements in the basic paradigm for agenda-setting research as set forth in the classic study by McCombs and Shaw (1972)? The central research question for McCombs and Shaw was to explore the degree to which the media agenda, measured as the number of news stories about each of the five issues salient at a point in time, influenced the public agenda, measured as the degree to which the members of a population rated each of the five issues in salience. Although McCombs and Shaw did not identify the concept per se, they clearly were measuring *salience*, defined as the degree to which an issue on the agenda is perceived as relatively important (Dearing & Rogers, 1996). A longitudinal approach to agenda-setting focuses on changes over time in the salience of issues on (a) the media agenda, (b) the public agenda, and (c) the policy agenda. An *issue* is a social problem, often conflictual, that receives mass media news coverage (Dearing & Rogers, 1996). The five main issues investigated by McCombs and Shaw in their Chapel Hill study were foreign policy, law and order, fiscal policy, public welfare, and civil rights.

The Chapel Hill study was cross-sectional in its methodological design; that is, data about the media agenda and the public agenda were gathered at approximately the same point in time (during the fall months of the presidential campaign in 1968). Although agenda-setting was conceptualized by McCombs and Shaw (1972) as a *process* (implying time-ordered relationships among the variables), their research design ignored time. Gradually, however, time became an important additional variable that was incorporated into agenda-setting research. Instead of measuring variables such as the media agenda and the public agenda at a single point in time, scholars began to measure these variables over time, such as the 91 months from 1981 to 1988 for the issue of acquired immunodeficiency syndrome (AIDS) (Rogers, Dearing, & Chang, 1991) or the 192 half-months from 1985 to 1992 for the issue of global warming (Trumbo, 1995).

In ensuing years, agenda-setting research continued to break out of the McCombs and Shaw (1972) methodological and conceptual mode by incorporating real-world indicators, intermedia agenda-setting, the polling agenda, and the science agenda.

The Chapel Hill investigators combined two already well-known communication research methods: (a) content analysis of the news media important in Chapel Hill, and (b) survey interviews with a sample of 100 undecided voters, chosen for study because McCombs and Shaw (1972) were deliberately trying to maximize the possibility of finding media effects (Tankard, 1990, p. 281). The University of North Carolina scholars found a high correlation between (a) the rank order in salience of the five issues reported in news coverage of the presidential campaign and (b) the salience rank order of these issues that the undecided voters said were the key issues in the campaign (McCombs & Shaw, 1972). In fact, the correlation of .975 approached unity. The investigators concluded that the media agenda set the agenda for the public. Thus, the basic paradigm for agenda-setting research was born.

Given the considerable impact of the McCombs and Shaw (1972) paper on later researchers in the agenda-setting tradition, it is surprising that the two authors had difficulty in getting it published. McCombs and Shaw submitted a paper from their Chapel Hill study to the Theory and Methodology Division of the Association for Education in Journalism, which at the time was one of the leading academic associations for mass communication researchers. Their paper was rejected, in the words of McCombs and Shaw, because it was "too unorthodox," had "too narrow a sample," or was "insufficiently grounded in theory" (McCombs & Shaw as quoted in Tankard, 1990, p. 281). The authors considered giving up on publishing their findings but finally submitted their paper to *Public Opinion Quarterly*, the leading journal dealing with mass communication effects, and it was published in 1972, 4 years after the data were gathered.

Normal Science Stage of
Agenda-Setting Research

The period from 1972 to the present day (for agenda-setting research) is what Kuhn (1970) characterized as "normal science," the period during which an invisible college forms around a dominant paradigm. The paradigm's propositions are generally supported, and the scope of the paradigm is gradually broadened. The normal science stage is a time in which steady criticism and theory proliferation have passed (Kuhn, 1970). During the normal science stage, the invisible college reaches a consensus on foundational issues that are not thereafter open to dispute. Scientific progress of a particular kind is made during the normal science stage of a scientific revolution. Accumulation in the normal science stage is linear, additive, and cumulative (Kuhn, 1970). The insights gained in normal science are compatible with previously available knowledge (Hoyningen-Huene, 1993, p. 183). The cumulative nature of normal science is its most definitive characteristic (Hoyningen-Huene, 1993, p. 184).

Research conducted during the normal science stage does not replace or drastically alter the paradigm. Normal science represents two activities: (a) research in a particular area in greater depth, and (b) "experimental efforts toward applying theory to classes of phenomena for which the possibility of such application has been posited but not yet accomplished" (Hoyningen-Huene, 1993, p. 182). McCombs (1993) recognized these two activities in agenda-setting research in the form of "surveyors" and "explorers":

> Some [agenda-setting] scholars are moving beyond the original domain, the salience of public issues, to explore other aspects of political communication under the agenda-setting banner. These intellectual expeditions range from extended explorations of the news agenda to broad probes into the behavioral consequences of issue salience. Other scholars are now carefully surveying and mapping in depth a variety of areas glimpsed in the previous decades' explorations of mass communication and public opinion under [the agenda-setting] theoretical banner.

The new types of agenda-setting research conducted in recent years do not signal an upcoming paradigm shift. These new types of agenda-setting research are led by explorers and surveyors (but not by "revolutionaries") in the current (normal science) stage of agenda-setting research.

Further Exploring and Surveying

A dominant paradigm in any scientific specialty can be dangerous in that a single approach to a central research problem may become prematurely standardized (Kuhn, 1970). Agenda-setting research may have been, for some time, overly stereotyped around the McCombs and Shaw (1972) paradigm. By 1992, Rogers, Dearing, and Bregman (1993) identified 223 agenda-setting publications, most completed since 1971. Many of these studies, especially in the 1970s and early 1980s, followed the McCombs-Shaw multiple-issues, cross-sectional approach, combining a content analysis (to measure the media agenda) with an audience survey (to operationalize the public agenda). Thus, the first period of the normal science stage of agenda-setting research consisted "of a more or less literal application of Bernard Cohen's often cited observation about the press influencing what people think about" (Trumbo, 1995, p. 4). The main objective for McCombs and Shaw (1972) was to establish that the media agenda influenced the public agenda.

Beginning in the 1980s, agenda-setting research began to expand the McCombs and Shaw (1972) paradigm by investigating how the media agenda was set. Pursuit of this research question was a logical next step once it was established with some degree of certainty that the media agenda influenced the public agenda. This new research question, however, could not be effectively answered with the content analysis-audience survey methodology of McCombs and Shaw (1972). Instead, scholars had to focus on a single issue, or at least a single issue at a time, to trace how and why it rose on the media agenda. Therefore, attention to a new, related research question in agenda-setting research headed scholars in the direction of single-issue, longitudinal investigations that share similarities with scholarly research about the diffusion of innovations, the process by which ideas that are perceived to be new are communicated through certain channels among the members of a social system (Rogers, 1995).

This single-issue emphasis has meant a push by scholars to understand agenda-setting as a social process of influence (Rogers & Dearing,
1988). Agenda-setting, by definition, is a process (a series of events and
activities happening through time). Many investigations prior to the
1980s, however, depended entirely on one-shot data-collection and cross-
sectional data analysis, a type of research design particularly unsuited
for investigating the temporal aspects of process.

The methodological progression in agenda-setting research has been
from cross-sectional studies to more sophisticated research designs that
allow more precise exploration of agenda-setting as a temporal process
(as described previously). One means of allowing scholars greater insight into the relationships among key variables in the agenda-setting
process is by using a less aggregated approach. A long-term methodological trend in agenda-setting research is toward disaggregation. The
original McCombs and Shaw (1972) study was highly aggregated in that
both the media agenda and the public agenda were measured by pooling
data on the five issues (foreign policy, law and order, fiscal policy, public
welfare, and civil rights). All 100 undecided voters' issue priorities were
pooled into one composite ranking of the five main issues' salience on
the public agenda. The number of news stories in the nine mass media
of study were also pooled into one aggregated salience ranking of the
five issues.

An important move toward data disaggregation is represented by
Erbring, Goldenberg, and Miller (1980), who gathered personal interview data from a national sample of respondents in 1974 (to measure the
public agenda) and correlated it with the media agenda (of newspaper
coverage, which was content analyzed). As a further step toward local-
ization as a means of disaggregation of the agenda data, these scholars
measured crime and underemployment rates in the communities in
which their survey respondents lived rather than using nationwide
real-world indicators for crime and unemployment. They then used
these localized real-world indicators in their data analysis. Thus, the
media agenda variable, the public agenda variable, and the real-world
indicators were disaggregated to the individual, localized level of analysis. Issues on the newspaper agenda had greater impact on individuals
who were sensitive to a particular issue (Erbring et al., 1980). This
conclusion could not have been reached through survey research without a high degree of data disaggregation.

Other types of disaggregation are also possible. Almost all past agenda-setting research has been conducted at the national level in the United States. Research into the agenda-setting process at regional, state, and city levels is lacking. There may be a relationship between the agenda-setting process at one level with that at another level but not necessarily. Research is under way by the authors to investigate similarities between local- and national-level agenda-setting. For example, the issue of environmental health in Kinney Brick, a small community located near Albuquerque, New Mexico, affected the policy agenda at the city, state, and national levels as the result of news coverage by the Albuquerque news media.

In recent years, a variety of critiques, reviews, and syntheses of agenda-setting research appeared (e.g., McCombs, 1992; McCombs & Shaw, 1993; Rogers & Dearing, 1988; Rogers, Dearing, & Bregman, 1993). Agenda-setting researchers began another avenue of research with the advent of single-issue longitudinal studies (Rogers, Dearing, & Chang, 1991; Trumbo, 1995) and laboratory experiments (Iyengar & Kinder, 1987). These newer types of agenda-setting research broadened this research specialty, emphasized disaggregation, and gave more attention to time-ordered relationships among variables. As Trumbo (1995, p. 5) noted, "A picture of agenda-setting as a more holistic social process involving information and effort exchanges between a host of spheres is emerging in the third stage."

Single-Issue, Longitudinal Research

One alternative to the cross-sectional, multiple-issue design is the single-issue, longitudinal study in which one issue, such as AIDS (Rogers et al., 1991) or global warming (Trumbo, 1995), is traced over time as it rises and falls on the media agenda, the public agenda, and the policy agenda. For example, the issue of global warming began to rise on these agendas in the United States in about 1987, reached a peak in 1989, and then began to drop down the agendas, although never returning to its pre-1987 level (Trumbo, 1995). This rise-and-fall pattern characterizes most public issues in the United States (Downs, 1972).

One of the key assumptions of hierarchy-approach agenda-setting studies is that the public—people who watch television, listen to the radio, and read the news—reacts to the mass media. For any one individual, that reaction is sometimes passive and sometimes active. The working hypothesis of the hierarchy approach is that the media's emphasis on certain issues and not other issues determines which issues we as members of the public think are important. This is a conception of a malleable, relatively passive U.S. public. People's need for orientation (Weaver, 1977) was a means of bringing into agenda-setting research a theoretical rationale for those times when we are active seekers of information or entertainment. Other research shows that individuals engage in active psychological sensemaking about public issues (Gamson, 1992; Liebes & Katz, 1990; Neuman, Just, & Crigler, 1992) as well as active social activities (such as activist social movements that mobilize resources to redress a perceived problem) that are intended to influence the outcomes of public issues (Blumer, 1971; Dearing & Rogers, 1992; Downs, 1972; Kingdon, 1984; McCarthy & Zald, 1977; Mead, 1994). For most issues, the majority of people are inattentive rather than attentive and more passive than active. For certain issues, however, depending on our own selective attention, we become very active and take charge of our information environment and, less frequently, organize for action. When this happens, hierarchy studies of agenda-setting do not show a deterministic media-public agenda relationship (Neuman et al., 1992, pp. 110-112). In these circumstances, research designs that capture the structural interdependencies of societies at work—longitudinal studies of social influence as an outcome of public opinion—are more informative for scholarly purposes than are hierarchy studies, which do not operationalize active publics, much as the intellectual leader of symbolic interactionism, Herbert Blumer, called for 50 years ago (Blumer, 1948).

Laboratory and Field Experiments

Another alternative to the Chapel Hill study's research design is the experiment in which one of the main variables in the agenda-setting process (typically the media agenda) is manipulated so that its effects on another variable (typically the public agenda) can be more precisely understood. Usually, the individual respondent is the unit of analysis in experiments on agenda setting. The pioneering laboratory experiments on the agenda-setting process were conducted by Shanto Iyengar and associates (Iyengar & Kinder, 1987; Iyengar, Peters, & Kinder, 1982). In the typical experiment, respondents are paid a fee for agreeing to come each day for a week to Iyengar's laboratory to view a videotape of the evening television news in which extra material is added for certain issues. The respondents agree not to view television news in their home. Thus, the media agenda for selected issues is made more salient (by the extra news coverage). At the end of the week, respondents are asked which issues are most important to them (this is the public agenda). They typically respond that the experimentally emphasized issues are more salient.

Iyengar and colleagues have added two important concepts to the repertoire of agenda-setting scholars. *Framing* is the subtle selection of certain aspects of an issue by the media to make them more important and thus to emphasize a particular cause of some phenomena (Iyengar, 1991, p. 11). Frames are one way in which a particular meaning is given to an issue. For instance, the media originally interpreted the 1995 Oklahoma City bombing as Middle East terrorism. Within a day or two, however, the issue was reframed, more correctly, as one of domestic, right-wing militia.

Priming is the ability of the media agenda to affect the criteria by which individuals judge issues (Iyengar, 1991, p. 133). For instance, when the media emphasize the issue of national defense, people will judge their president by how well they feel he has provided for national defense. Thus, via priming, the media may affect the approval rating of a U.S. president and his chances of reelection.

Another research program using an experimental approach to study the agenda-setting process is led by David L. Protess at Northwestern University. In a series of field experiments, Protess and associates studied the role of investigative reporting in setting the public agenda (Molotch, Protess, & Gordon, 1987; Protess et al., 1987, 1991; Protess, Leff, Brooks, & Gordon, 1985). These scholars typically determine when an investigative report about some issue—for example, rape reporting by the Chicago police department—is about to appear in the media. Protess and associates measure the public agenda, and perhaps the policy agenda, before and after the media coverage of the issue that has been investigated. As in the case of the Iyengar-type laboratory experiments, the media agenda is the experimental variable whose effects on the public agenda and the policy agenda are determined.

Conclusions

We have reviewed the history of agenda-setting research to show how this scientific specialty has moved from preparadigm, to the establishment of the dominant paradigm for agenda-setting, to the stage of normal science. In recent years, the paradigm has been dramatically expanded by means of disaggregation, by adding concepts and broader conceptualizations, and by the use of different methodologies and statistical models. The original research question guiding the paradigmatic Chapel Hill study has been broadened to include the following questions:

How is the media agenda set?

What are the contributions of theories of social movements and resource mobilization, in which publics are issue centered and very active, to the agenda-setting paradigm?

Why do real-world indicators play a minor role in the agenda-setting process compared to human tragedies and other triggering events?

What role do priming and framing play in the myriad of human decisions that constitute the agenda-setting process?

29 The News Media and the Pictures in Our Heads

MAXWELL McCOMBS
GEORGE ESTRADA

Walter Lippmann began his seminal 1922 book, *Public Opinion*, with a chapter titled "The World Outside and the Pictures in Our Heads." Lippmann's eloquently argued thesis is that the news media are a primary source of the pictures in our heads, giving us impressions of the vast external world of public affairs that is "out of reach, out of sight, out of mind" (1922, p. 29). Lippmann's intellectual offspring, agenda setting, is a detailed social science theory about the contribution of mass communication to those pictures in our heads. Specifically, it is a theory about the transfer of salience—how the mass media's hierarchy of concerns affects the public's.

The core theoretical idea underlying agenda setting is that elements prominent in the media picture become prominent in the audience's picture. The assertion is that the priorities of the media agenda influence the priorities of the public agenda. Over time, elements emphasized on the media agenda come to be regarded as important on the public agenda. Theoretically, these agendas could be composed of any set of elements. In practice, virtually all of the 200-plus studies to date have examined an agenda composed of public issues. For these studies, the core hypothesis is that the degree of emphasis placed on issues in the news influences the priority accorded these issues by the public.

Although agenda setting is concerned with the salience of issues rather than the distribution of pro and con opinions, which has been the traditional focus of public opinion research, the core domain is the same—the public issues of the moment. Walter Lippmann's (1922) quest in *Public Opinion* to link the world outside to the pictures in our heads via the news media was brought to quantitative, empirical fruition by agenda-setting research (McCombs, 1992, p. 815).

Evidence of Agenda-Setting Effects

Agenda-setting research has taken a variety of interesting shapes and forms in the years since the seminal 1968 study (McCombs & Shaw, 1972), with the predominant method being a coupling of media content analysis and data from public opinion polls. The theory has proven to be a highly accommodating master framework for media effects research. A clear message has emerged from the studies that have followed—there is clear and strong support for this notion that the priorities of the media agenda influence the priority of issues on the public agenda.

The original study of agenda setting by Maxwell McCombs and Donald Shaw (1972) during the 1968 presidential election found a nearly perfect rank order correlation (.97) between the issues considered most important by voters and the coverage of those issues in the news media used by those voters. Four years later during the 1972 U.S. presidential election, the findings of this inaugural study were replicated in a middle-sized city, Charlotte, North Carolina (Shaw & McCombs, 1977).

Complementing these two studies of local communities during a presidential election, Ray Funkhouser (1973) conducted a national study that examined an entire decade—the turbulent 1960s. He found considerable correspondence (.78) between the media agenda and the public agenda.

The natural history of a single issue—civil rights—in the media and public agendas was examined by James Winter and Chaim Eyal (1981). Overlapping the decade of the 1960s studied by Funkhouser (1973), Winter and Eyal discovered that the ebb and flow of national concern about civil rights from 1954 to 1976 mirrored (.71) the rise and fall of news coverage in the *New York Times* during those years.

Howard Eaton (1989) traced the salience of 11 different individual issues over a period of 42 months during the 1980s. Among the issues studied were unemployment, crime, fear of war, poverty, and inflation. The shifting salience of 10 of these 11 issues on the public agenda was positively correlated with the news coverage of those issues. The median correlation from the 11 separate analyses was .45. The only issue with a negative correlation (–.44) was morality in society.

Working in the experimental laboratory, Shanto Iyengar and Donald Kinder (1987) produced agenda-setting effects through the manipulation of the topics covered in television newscasts. Among the issues demonstrating agenda-setting effects in this rigorously controlled setting were civil rights, arms control, defense preparedness, pollution, and unemployment.

A year-long study in Germany by Hans-Bernd Brosius and Hans Mathias Kepplinger (1990) provides the ultimate comparison of the media agenda and public agenda across time. The newscasts of four major German television stations for the entire year of 1986 were compared with 53 weekly national opinion polls. Brosius and Kepplinger found significant agenda-setting effects for five issues: an adequate energy supply, East-West relations, European politics, environmental protection, and defense.

Of course, what all six of the examples have in common—and share with hundreds of others—is a focus on issue salience.

Attributes: The Second Dimension

When we consider the key term of this theoretical metaphor—the agenda—in totally abstract terms, the potential for expanding beyond an agenda of issues becomes clear. In the majority of studies to date, the unit of analysis on each agenda is an object, a public issue.

Beyond the agenda of objects, there is also another dimension to consider. Each of these objects has numerous attributes—those characteristics and properties that fill in and animate the picture of each object. Just as objects vary in salience, so do the attributes of each object.

It might be useful here to draw on an analogy from sports. A baseball team (the object) has a roster of players (attributes), some of whom have emerged as stars both in the media's and the public's eyes. It is abundantly clear that the media help set levels of player status in the fan agenda. The team's status benefits from this focus on its stars. This is an example of agenda setting's second-dimension effect.

One of the best known and most discussed sports teams of all time is the New York Yankees. Some of the great individual players in Yankees' history—Babe Ruth, Joe Dimaggio, and Mickey Mantle—can be viewed here as attributes, each symbolic of a particular era in New York Yankees' history. Baseball fans debating the relative greatness of, for example, the 1927 and 1961 Yankees' teams (the objects), are drawn inevitably to a discussion of the relative merits of Babe Ruth and Mickey Mantle (the attributes). These discussions would be fueled, at least in part, by what fans had read or seen in the mass media over their lifetimes about Ruth and Mantle. Clearly, the theory's second dimension comes into play in determining which team emerges atop the all-time Yankee fan agenda.

Both the selection of objects for attention and the selection of attributes for thinking about these objects are powerful agenda-setting roles. An important part of the news agenda and its set of objects are the perspectives and frames that journalists and, subsequently, members of the public, employ to think about and talk about each object. These perspectives and frames—called semantic devices—draw attention to certain attributes and away from others.

How news frames effect public opinion is the emerging second dimension of agenda setting. The first dimension is, of course, the transmission of object salience. The second dimension is the transmission of attribute salience. As this new research frontier broadens our perspective on the agenda-setting role of the news media, Bernard Cohen's famous dictum must be revised. In a succinct summary statement that separated agenda setting from earlier research on the effects of mass communication, Cohen (1963) noted that although the media may not tell us what to think, the media are stunningly successful in telling us what to think about. Explicit attention to the second dimension of agenda setting further suggests that the media also tell us how to think about some objects. Could the consequences of this be that the media do tell us what to think?

Revisiting Our Research Legacy

The emergence of this second theoretical dimension was prompted by a new look at some scattered fragments in the literature, including key studies from the earliest years of agenda-setting research.

Candidate Images

Two studies from the 1976 U.S. presidential election concisely illustrate the second dimension of agenda setting. The first is an ambitious nine-wave panel study that searched both traditional and new domains of agenda setting (Weaver, Graber, McCombs, & Eyal, 1981). Reported in *Media Agenda Setting in a Presidential Election: Issues, Images and Interest* (Weaver et al., 1981), the title of the book is a succinct summary.

The second word in the subtitle, images, is central to our discussion of the second dimension of agenda setting. A striking degree of correspondence was found between the agenda of attributes in the *Chicago Tribune* and the agenda of attributes in Illinois voters' descriptions of presidential candidates Jimmy Carter and Gerald Ford. The median value of the cross-lagged correlations between the 14-trait media agenda and the subsequent public agenda was .70.

A separate look at the 1976 presidential primaries (Becker & McCombs, 1978) also found considerable correspondence between the agenda of attributes in *Newsweek* and the agenda of attributes in New York Democrats' descriptions of the contenders for their party's presidential nomination. Especially compelling in this evidence is that the correspondence between the two agendas increased from .64 to .83 from mid-February to late March among their panel of Democrats.

Neither of these studies of candidate images during the 1976 presidential election were originally thought of in terms of a second dimension of agenda setting. They do fit that conceptualization, however, and they do offer significant evidence that the news media can set the agenda of attributes that define the pictures of candidates in voters' minds.

Facets of Issues

Two other studies extended issue salience—the central focus of agenda setting—into the second dimension. Marc Benton and Jean Frazier (1976) presented a detailed analysis of a recurring major concern—the economy. Agenda-setting effects were found for newspapers, but not for TV news, for two sets of attributes: the specific problems, causes, and proposed solutions associated with the general topic of the economy (.81); and the pro and con rationales for economic solutions (.68). Benton and Frazier called these facets of the economic issue "levels of information holding." These facets also can be labeled as sets of attributes or frames.

At almost the same time as the Benton and Frazier (1976) study of the economy, David Cohen (1975) studied another complex issue in-depth, examining six facets of a local environmental issue in Indiana. He found a strong level of correspondence (.71) between the picture in people's minds and local newspaper coverage about the development of a large, man-made lake.

Both of these in-depth probes of a single public issue used the classic design of the original Chapel Hill study—comparison of the media agenda measured by content analysis with a public agenda measured through survey research. In both studies, however, there is a shift in focus from an agenda of objects to an agenda of attributes.

Another early foray into new domains explored some pictures in people's heads that were very different from anything done before—people's pictures of the future (Atwood, Sohn, & Sohn, 1978). Residents of a southern Illinois town were asked what changes they anticipated from the opening of two new coal mines in the area. Pertinent to the second dimension of agenda setting, these public perceptions about the expected impact of the new coal mines in the area closely matched (.75) the agenda of the local newspaper coverage on the mines.

All five of these studies offer compelling evidence for significant agenda-setting effects on an agenda of attributes. None of these studies, however, were conceptualized as second-dimension research. Researchers simply set out to explore some interesting variations of the agenda-setting idea.

Exploring the Second Dimension

Explicit theoretical recognition of a second dimension of the agenda-setting role of mass communication surfaced in a series of lectures and writings during the past 3 years (see, for example, McCombs, 1994; McCombs & Bell, in press; McCombs & Evatt, 1995). Empirical research has followed closely on the heels of these theoretical discussions. Appropriate to the history of agenda-setting research, which began with a series of U.S. presidential election studies, much of the new research has focused on elections. Also appropriate to the history of agenda-setting research is that the geographic scope of these studies is global, embracing East Asia, North America, and Western Europe.

Japanese General Election

Toshio Takeshita and Shunji Mikami's (1995) study of the 1993 general election in Japan begins with a traditional agenda-setting look at general issue salience: Did the media's emphasis on certain campaign issues affect the perceived importance (salience) of those same issues by the voters?

Because the issue of political reform so thoroughly dominated the media agenda, Takeshita and Mikami (1995) used a more stringent test that takes into account a key corollary of agenda setting. Grounded in a long-standing assumption of media effects research, their corollary hypothesis asserts that the salience of the political reform issue among members of the public is directly proportional to their level of exposure to the news media.

The exposure measure was further strengthened by the addition of a measure of each respondent's level of political interest. This combination of an exposure measure and a political interest measure yields a measure of attentiveness to political news. Now, the hypothesis to be tested asserts that the salience of the political reform issue among members of the public is positively correlated with their level of attentiveness to political news.

Analysis based on 650 Tokyo voters supports this hypothesis. For attentiveness to TV news, the correlation with the salience of political reform is .24. For attentiveness to newspapers, the correlation is .27. The partial correlations controlling for party identification, education, age, and sex are identical.

With evidence in hand that exposure to the news media influenced the salience of the political reform issue on the public agenda, Takeshita and Mikami (1995) moved on to the second dimension. Factor analysis of survey respondents' ratings of the personal importance of seven different facets of political reform revealed two distinct factors: (a) an "ethics-related factor," which emphasizes such proposals as "imposing legal controls on politicians' behavior" and "tightening discipline among politicians," and (b) a "system-related factor," which calls for change or reform of the electoral system.

Both TV news and the newspapers mentioned system-related aspects of reform twice as often as ethics-related aspects. Did this distinct media agenda influence the pictures of political reform in the minds of Japanese voters?

Answering this question about the second dimension of agenda setting involves testing two elegantly counterbalanced hypotheses that are stated in terms similar to Takeshita and Mikami's (1995) analysis of the first dimension. The first hypothesis asserts that the salience of system-related reform on the public agenda will be positively correlated with attentiveness to political news. In contrast, the second hypothesis anticipates the lack of any correlation between the salience of the ethics-related aspects of reform on the public agenda and attentiveness to political news. Both hypotheses are supported. This benchmark study, with its simultaneous examination of first- and second-dimension agenda-setting effects, finds robust evidence for both kinds of influence on the pictures in our heads.

Spanish Local Elections

Both the first and second dimensions of agenda setting were also studied in Spain during the May 28, 1995, elections for provincial parliaments and mayors of larger cities. Professor Esteban Lopez-Escobar, at the University of Navarra, and McCombs, at the University of Texas, worked with 20 students in a special 3-week seminar on agenda setting to research the parliamentary elections for the province of Navarra in northern Spain and the election of a mayor in its capital city, Pamplona.

The first-dimension hypothesis asserted the presence of agenda setting's main effect. We wanted to see if this effect would replicate in the context of a Spanish local election. Unlike the Japanese election study, which focused on one key national issue, we examined the full agenda of local issues.

The second-dimension hypothesis also sought the replication of agenda-setting effects found in other countries. Rather than studying issues, however, we cast our exploratory net wide and shifted our attention to the images of the candidates for mayor and parliament. Because five different political parties had candidates competing for both offices, this was a rich opportunity to match the media's picture of these candidates with the public's picture.

Preliminary examination of the data is encouraging. These data suggest that this study will be an important complement to the Japanese election study and a key opening gambit in the exploration of the second dimension of agenda setting. Together, these two initial studies, one in Asia and one in Europe, suggest significant mass communication influence on the pictures in our heads of both public issues and political candidates—an influence that replicates across vastly different cultures.

Texas Public Opinion

Outside the election tradition of agenda setting, the rapid rise of public concern about crime in the United States during 1993 and 1994 offers an intriguing opportunity for examining the agenda-setting influence of mass communication (Ghanem & Evatt, 1995). In 1992, when the Texas Poll asked what was the most important problem facing the country, only 2% named crime. In the fall of 1993, however, this jumped to 15%, and in two polls during the first 6 months of 1994 more than one third of the Texas Poll respondents named crime. This is an unusually high level of concern. Concern has abated somewhat during the past year, but about 20% to 25% of Texans still name crime as the most important problem.

Ironically, during this same time period, 1993 to the present, although public concern over crime has risen to unusually high levels, the best measures of the reality of crime indicate that the rate of crime is declining. It is an obvious setting for agenda-setting research. Salma Ghanem and Dixie Evatt (1995) are comparing public opinion trends in Texas with news coverage about crime in both local and national news media using a first- and second-dimension agenda-setting schema.

The first dimension is the influence of news coverage on the salience of crime on the public agenda. Here, the evidence is very clear. News coverage of crime in local newspapers and on local TV news, but not on national TV news, is strongly linked to subsequent levels of public concern about crime. Across an 18-month period, the match between the trend in public opinion and the pattern of crime coverage is .83 for newspapers and 1.0 for local television news. The rise and fall of crime news is mirrored in subsequent public opinion.

Ghanem and Evatt's exploration of the second dimension of agenda setting focuses on three attributes of news stories about crime that link the news event to the audience: (a) social distance, (b) connectedness of victim and perpetrator, and (c) sense of protection. Preliminary analysis of the Texas data reveals some agenda-setting effects for all three of these frames.

New Theoretical Frontiers

One of the strengths of agenda-setting theory that has prompted its continuing growth has been its compatibility and complementarity with a variety of other social science concepts and theories. At various points, the theory of agenda setting has incorporated or converged with other communication subfields. Incorporated concepts include gatekeeping and status conferral. Conceptual complements include the spiral of silence and cultivation analysis. Discussion of a second dimension of agenda setting introduces a key contemporary concept—framing.

Specifically in terms of salience, Entman (1993) stated,

> To frame is to select some aspects of a perceived reality and make them more salient in a communicating text, in such a way as to promote a particular problem definition, causal interpretation, moral evaluation and/or treatment recommendation for the item described. (p. 52)

To paraphrase Entman in the language of the second dimension of agenda setting, framing is the selection of a small number of attributes for inclusion on the media agenda when a particular object is discussed.

There are consequences of framing for subsequent attitudes and behavior. How a topic is framed does more than influence the pictures in our heads. As Lippmann (1922) pointed out, our behavior is a response not to the actual environment but rather to the pseudoenvironment that is pictured in our heads.

Conclusion

News coverage can influence the salience of objects on the public agenda. This is the first dimension of agenda setting. The framing of those objects on the media agenda can also influence the pictures of those objects in our heads. This is the second dimension of agenda setting. There are also feedback effects from framing. In the best cumulative tradition of science, knowledge of the agenda-setting role of mass communication continues to grow. To rephrase Cohen's (1963) classic remark, the media may not only tell us what to think about, they also may tell us how and what to think about it, and even what to do about it.

30 News Coverage of the Gulf Crisis and Public Opinion

A Study of Agenda Setting, Priming, and Framing

SHANTO IYENGAR
ADAM SIMON

When Saddam Hussein decided to invade Kuwait, he set in motion an uninterrupted torrent of news coverage. For the next six months, television viewers were fixated on the Iraqi occupation of Kuwait, the American military buildup, the launching of Operation Desert Storm, and the eventual liberation of Kuwait. The situation in the Gulf represented the single "big story" in the daily flow of public affairs information. More than one-third, by elapsed time, of all prime time network newscasts broadcast between August 1990, and March 1991, was devoted to the conflict (see below for a description of the content analysis).

Not only was the Gulf the subject of extensive news coverage, there is ample evidence that Americans were in fact recipients of this coverage. In January 1991, for example, seventy percent of the public reported that they followed news about the Gulf "very closely." Television news viewing in general surged during this period, and nearly eighty percent of the public reported "staying up late" to watch news of the conflict. Another symptom of this surge in viewer interest was the transformation of CNN into a major source of information with ratings points in the double digits.

EDITORS' NOTE: Reprinted from *Communication Research, 20,* 365-383.

The events leading up to the Gulf War provide a powerful "natural experiment" for examining the effects of news on the crystallization and development of public opinion. This chapter examines, in the context of the Gulf War, three classes of media effects. The first ("agenda-setting") is generally defined as the ability of the news media to define the significant issues of the day. We document this effect by tracking the proportion of the public nominating the Gulf crisis as the nation's most important problem. The second effect ("priming") concerns the relationship between patterns of news coverage and the criteria with which the public evaluates politicians. We demonstrate that the public weighted their opinions concerning foreign policy more heavily when evaluating President Bush in the aftermath of the Iraqi invasion of Kuwait. Finally, we address "framing"—the connection between qualitative features of news about the Gulf (in particular, the media's preoccupation with military affairs and the invariably episodic or event-oriented character of news reports) and public opinion. Here the results suggest that the pattern of episodic framing induced individuals to express greater support for a military as opposed to diplomatic resolution of the crisis.

Agenda-setting, priming, and framing are only three of the ways in which news coverage shaped the public's response to the Gulf crisis. The threat of an imminent full-scale war between the United States and Iraq represented an occasion for rallying behind the Administration. Additionally, the one-sided "official" message inherent in most news reports was bound to persuade most Americans of the wisdom of President Bush's actions. However, these effects on public opinion (particularly the rally and persuasive effects) have been documented by other researchers, and will not be discussed here.

Agenda-Setting

Issues enter and leave the center stage of American politics with considerable speed. In October, 1989, the problem of illegal drug usage was foremost in Americans' minds. Seventy percent of the public referred to drugs as a major national problem. This extraordinary level of public concern prompted the Administration to announce a major initiative to deal with the problem. In February, 1991, however, drug usage was cited as a national problem by a mere five percent of the public. The most plausible explanation of such dramatic shifts in political priorities is that the amount of news coverage accorded various political issues will dictate the degree of importance the public attaches to these issues. This argument is referred to as media "agenda-setting."

In this study, we examine the effect of Gulf-related coverage on the salience of national problems. We expect that increases in media coverage will be accompanied by increases in the percentage of the respondents who nominate the situation in the Gulf as the most important problem facing the nation.

Priming

While the term agenda-setting reflects the impact of news coverage on the importance accorded issues, the term "priming effect" refers to the ability of news programs to affect the criteria by which political leaders are judged. Priming is really an extension of agenda-setting, and addresses the impact of news coverage on the weight assigned to specific issues in making political judgments. In general, the more prominent an issue in the national information stream, the greater its weight in political judgments.

Framing

Research on framing has studied the effects of alternative news "frames" on the public's attributions of responsibility for issues and events. The concept of framing has both psychological and sociological pedigrees. Psychologists typically define framing as changes in judgment engendered by alterations to the definition of judgment or choice problems. Attributions of responsibility for political issues are of interest for a variety of reasons, not the least of which is that the concept of responsibility embodies an especially powerful psychological cue. Social psychologists have demonstrated that attitudes and actions within a wide variety of areas are altered by the manner in which individuals attribute responsibility.

Typically, the networks frame issues in either "episodic" or "thematic" terms. The episodic frame depicts public issues in terms of concrete instances or specific events—a homeless person, an unemployed worker, a victim of racial discrimination, the bombing of an airliner, an attempted murder, and so on. Visually, episodic reports make for "good pictures." The thematic news frame, by contrast, places public issues in some general or abstract context. Reports on reductions in government welfare expenditures, changes in the nature of employment opportunities, the social or political grievances of groups undertaking terrorist activity, changes in federal affirmative action policy, or the backlog in the criminal justice process are examples of thematic coverage. The thematic news frame typically takes the form of a "takeout" or "backgrounder" report directed at general outcomes or conditions and frequently features "talking heads."

Given the nature of television news—a twenty-one minute "headline service" operating under powerful commercial dictates—it is to be expected that the networks rely extensively on episodic framing to report on public issues. Episodic framing is visually appealing and consists of "on-the-scene," live coverage. Thematic coverage, which requires interpretive analyses, would simply crowd out other news items. In fact, television news coverage of political issues is heavily episodic.

Our examination of framing effects is divided into two parts. First, we assess the degree to which network news coverage of the Gulf Crisis was episodic. Second, we examine the effects of exposure to television news during the crisis on respondent's policy preferences. Respondents were provided with a choice between a military or diplomatic response to the crisis. For reasons outlined later, we expect that increased exposure to television news will be associated with increases in support for the military response.

Results

How did the Iraqi invasion of Kuwait affect the political agendas of Americans? In July, immediately prior to the invasion, Americans were preoccupied with domestic problems. Drug usage and crime, the state of the economy, and the federal budget deficit were the issues most likely to be nominated as the most important problems facing the nation. This trio of issues was mentioned by more than fifty percent of survey respondents. In Figure 31.1, we trace the trend in responses to the Gallup

Poll's "most important problem" question between July 1990 and March 1991 in relation to the amount of television news coverage of the Gulf.

Beginning in August, the Gulf absorbed virtually all network news time. The sheer amount of news peaked (at over two hours of news coverage in August) immediately following the Iraqi invasion. Between September and December, news from the Gulf averaged approximately 60 minutes per month. The onset of the air war in January and Operation Desert Storm in February raised the level of coverage to about 90 minutes per month. Thus, there was an initial period of saturation coverage followed by a steady state of heavy news which culminated in two months of virtual saturation coverage.

Turning to the issue salience data, the conflict in the Gulf achieved parity with the economy and deficit as an agenda item as early as October. By November, references to the Gulf had surpassed mentions of the economy to become the preeminent national problem in the eyes of Americans. At its peak (in February), the Gulf came in for a greater share of public attention that the economy, deficit, and drugs combined. Just as rapidly, the Gulf disappeared from the public agenda. Following the cessation of hostilities, responses to the most important problem question reverted to their preconflict state, with one notable change; while the economy shared center stage with drugs and the deficit prior to the conflict, at the end of the war the economy had come to over-shadow all other domestic issues. Overall, the amount of media coverage accorded to the Gulf situation and the proportion of respondents nomi-nating it as the nation's most important problem were highly correlated.

Most discussions of agenda-setting are unidirectional in nature—increases in news coverage are thought to bring about increases in the salience of particular issues or events. The evidence in Figure 30.1, however, not only highlights the dramatic surge in the salience of the Gulf conflict, but also indicates the bi-directional nature of the agenda-setting process. That is, the emergence of the Gulf as the most important national problem was accompanied by a sudden (and pronounced) decline in the prominence of drugs and the budget deficit. In effect, intensive news coverage generated by a "crisis issue" not only elevates the prominence of the target issue, but also removes other issues from public attention. It is important to note, however, that this "hydraulic" pattern did not apply to the economy. While references to economic problems remained relatively stable during the early phases of the

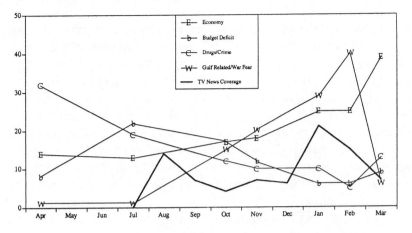

Figure 30.1. Trends in issue salience and Gulf-related news coverage
(*y* axis, percentage nominating or average minutes per month; *x* axis, month).

conflict (October-November), the economy actually gained in salience between November and February. By March, the economy was clearly the preeminent agenda problem—references to economic problems exceeded references to all other domestic issues. It is possible that the continual coverage of the Gulf prompted viewers to consider simultaneously the economic and military risks posed by the conflict, thus elevating their concern for economic problems. Alternatively, the public may have been responding on the basis of prevailing economic conditions— that is, as the economy worsened, more people identified it as a significant problem.

Turning to the priming hypothesis, in the context of the Gulf crisis, the prediction is that over time Americans will assign a greater weight to their beliefs and opinions concerning foreign policy in general when forming impressions of George Bush in 1990. Our data stem from the 1988, 1990, and 1991 NES post-election surveys. In each year, we analyzed the effects of the public's ratings of presidential performance on the economy and foreign policy on their overall feelings toward George Bush.

The evidence proved consistent with the priming hypothesis. Foreign policy performance assessments tended to override economic assessments in their impact on thermometer ratings of George Bush during the Gulf crisis while the reverse was true in 1988. A similar analysis (not reported here), using ratings of overall presidential performance as the dependent variable, produced identical results. These results were also suggestive of the hydraulic pattern found in the agenda setting section above. Increases in the impact of foreign policy performance assessments on global evaluations of the president were accompanied by small decreases in the importance of economic evaluations. Overall, the evidence suggested that the Gulf conflict altered the principal basis of President Bush's popularity from the state of the national economy to foreign policy matters. Because the public rated Bush more favorably on foreign policy, their overall impression of the President was made more positive; his mean feeling thermometer rating rose from 60 in 1988 to 64 in 1990 and 71 in 1991.

Finally, we turn to the question of framing effects. We examined the prime time newscasts broadcast by ABC News between August 1990 and April 1991. Not surprisingly, television news coverage of the Gulf was heavily episodic or event-oriented. The typical news story transmitted information about specific developments or "live" occurrences. Each day, viewers were provided the next "episode" in the developing confrontation between the United States (and its allies) and Iraq. Rarely were viewers provided "background" in the form of analyses of the antecedents of the conflict, historical precedents of similar territorial disputes, information about the socio-economic and cultural makeup of Iraqi and Kuwaiti society, or other such contextual presentations. Episodic reports overwhelmed thematic reports by a huge margin.

How might this pattern of predominantly episodic news coverage affect public opinion toward the Gulf conflict? Previous research has investigated the effects of the episodic and thematic news frames on viewers' attributions of responsibility for various political and social issues (including poverty, unemployment, crime, terrorism, racial inequality, and the Iran-Contra affair). Under thematic framing, viewers tended to assign responsibility for national problems to general societal factors including cultural norms, economic conditions, and the actions or inactions of public officials. When television news coverage presents a general or analytic frame of reference for national problems, the public's reasoning about causal and treatment responsibility is societal in focus. Under episodic framing, however, viewers attributed responsibility for national problems not to societal or structural forces, but to the actions of particular individuals or groups. For example, when poverty, crime, and terrorism were depicted in episodic terms, viewers attributed causal and treatment responsibility primarily to poor people, criminals, and terrorists. Confronted with a parade of news stories describing particular instances or illustrations of national issues, viewers focus on individual and group characteristics rather than historical, social, political, or other such general forces. In this respect episodic framing encourages reasoning by resemblance—people settle upon causes and treatments that "fit" the observed problem.

In the context of the Gulf crisis, the important policy question concerned the appropriate strategy for ending the Iraqi occupation of Kuwait, e.g., a question of treatment responsibility. Given the pervasive use of episodic framing, it was anticipated that exposure to television news coverage of the Gulf would tend to strengthen a preference for punitive (i.e., military) over diplomatic or economic remedies. This hypothesis is based on the evidence cited above that episodic framing of "public order" issues such as terrorism and crime instills attributions of punitive treatment responsibility. Since the conflict in the Gulf may be considered analogous to issues of law and order (Iraq as the transgressor, Kuwait as the victim, the United States as the law enforcer), it was anticipated that exposure to television news would enhance viewers' preference for military over diplomatic responses to the Iraqi occupation of Kuwait.

We attempted to examine this particular connection between television news coverage and public opinion by using our two measures of exposure to television news (self-reported frequency of exposure and the general political information index) and the index tapping support for military over diplomatic solutions to the conflict. Both indicators of exposure to television news exerted significant effects—the more informed and respondents who watched the news more frequently were more apt to favor a military response. The effects of information were markedly stronger among women and minorities suggesting that groups relatively inattentive to public affairs were especially affected by exposure to news of the crisis. (Women, for example, received a mean score of 1.8 on the information index in 1990 while men received a mean score of 2.5.)

Overall, then, there were statistically significant traces of the expected relationship. Exposure to episodic news programming strengthened, albeit modestly, support for a military resolution of the crisis.

Conclusion

The evidence presented here indicates that television news coverage of the conflict in the Persian Gulf significantly affected Americans' political concerns and the criteria with which they evaluated George Bush. Prior to the crisis, Americans were preoccupied with economic problems and crime, and their feelings toward George Bush were colored primarily by economic considerations. Following the Iraqi invasion of Kuwait, the Gulf Crisis became the public's paramount concern and evaluations of George Bush became more dependent upon foreign policy considerations. Finally, we find support for the hypothesis that exposure to episodic framing of the crisis increased viewers' support for a military resolution of the conflict.

As Walter Lippmann noted nearly seventy years ago, we tend to know little about "what is happening, why it happened and what ought to happen." But in modern times we do have "pictures in our heads," courtesy of ABC, CBS, CNN, and NBC.

It is now well established that television news has a significant impact on public opinion. The Gulf War was a mediated issue par excellence, and the results shown here, that American public opinion would follow the course of television news coverage, were predictable. The influence of the media inevitably gives rise to a host of questions concerning the determinants of news coverage and the practice of public affairs journalism.

Journalists have attributed their tendency simply to repeat the governmental "party line" to the unavailability of other sources of information. In our analysis of network news reports on the Gulf, more than fifty percent of all reports examined emanated directly from official spokespersons. Even allowing for the most benevolent and accessible of administrations, this de facto "stranglehold" over the news guaranteed that there would be a certain disjuncture between actual events and the media's depiction or interpretation of events. The successes of American technology, such as the interception of Iraqi Scud missiles and the destruction of military installations by "smart" bombs, and the "malevolence" of the Iraqis, as demonstrated by the deliberate igniting of oil wells, were the staples of news coverage. Contrary themes such as the devastation of a third world nation, the enormous scale of civilian casualties, or the deliberate burial alive of Iraqi conscripts in their trenches, were ignored. The practice of "official" journalism thus assured that the public's and the president's understanding of this international crisis would be congruent.

31 Anatomy of News Media Priming

JOANNE M. MILLER
JON A. KROSNICK

On January 16, 1991, President George Bush began the U.S. military attack on Iraq (in alliance with various other Western nations) that became known as the Gulf War. Over a period of just 43 days, the allied forces succeeded in driving Iraq from Kuwait, and only 148 soldiers gave their lives in the process. Thus, the Gulf War appeared to be a clear military triumph for the president, and the American public's approval of his job performance soared to an all-time high.

Just 21 months later, however, George Bush lost his 1992 re-election bid for the White House to Bill Clinton, although little had changed in the country during that time interval. Why did President Bush not easily win the election based on his success in the Gulf? According to a sign on President Clinton's campaign manager James Carville's office wall, cele-brated in the film *The War Room*, it was the economy, stupid. And indeed, according to a *New York Times* poll (November 4, 1992), many Americans interviewed after the election said they had voted against Bush because they were disappointed with his handling of the U.S. economy. If this was in fact the reason for his defeat, however, why had Americans apparently forgotten completely about the Gulf? What forces provoked the transformation of people's enthusiastic cheers of support for Presi-dent Bush in 1991 into grumbling disapproval in 1992?

In this chapter, we will explain what we think took place in 1992, pointing our fingers squarely at the news media. Walter Lippmann (1922) described news coverage by newspapers and magazines in the early 1920s as like "the beam of a searchlight that moves restlessly about, bringing one episode and then another out of darkness into vision"

(Lippmann, 1922, p. 229). We believe that when the contemporary news media's searchlights move from one topic to another, they can produce dramatic changes in the American public's evaluations of their president's job performance, even when the news stories never mention the president at all.

The process by which the media produce these changes is called "priming." In the pages to follow, we will tell you what priming is, how we think it occurs, and which sorts of people are most likely to be influenced by the media in this way. Then, we will describe four studies we have performed to document priming and to illuminate its psychological and political dynamics. In reading this, you may be surprised to learn how the news media may have been influencing your own political judgments, even without your being aware of it.

What Is Priming?

When people make decisions in the course of their daily lives, they rarely consider all of the relevant evidence that might be used to reach an optimal conclusion. Rather, because doing so would usually take more time and effort than people have available to devote to a decision, they usually make decisions based on subsets of the available information. For example, when deciding which college to attend, you could have considered various schools' costs, their locations, their student-teacher ratios, what majors they offer, their prestige, the leadership opportunities they offer, the types of jobs graduates obtain, the classes they require students to take, and so on. To get all this information on all the colleges you might consider, however, would be quite burdensome. Most people faced with this sort of situation choose to make "adequate" decisions based on only a few considerations, thus avoiding the expenditure of a great deal of time and effort. Making a choice in this way is called "satisficing."

Just as people satisfice when making decisions about colleges, they also do so when making political judgments. To decide how well the president is doing his job, a person could evaluate how well he has been handling all of the issues on which he has been working. This would be a very tough task, however, because presidents typically address a great many issues in very short periods of time. In his first year in office, for example, President Clinton worked on a number of issues, including reform of the U.S. health care system, staffing of the U.S. military, abortion laws, reducing the deficit, appointments to his Cabinet, U.S. involvement in Somalia, the North American Free Trade Agreement, Supreme Court appointments, and more. A careful evaluator could have graded his handling of each of these issues and then averaged those grades together into an overall assessment. Most Americans, however, probably had neither the information nor the motivation to do such labor-intensive thinking. Instead, they probably satisficed by evaluating his handling of just a few issues.

The news media exert their influence on this process, we believe, by determining in part which issues people use in making their overall evaluations. In mid-1992, for example, the news media paid lots of attention to the U.S. economy (see Krosnick & Brannon, 1995), which probably led many Americans to think frequently about economic conditions, to talk with friends and family about them, and to believe that the economy was a significant issue on the political landscape. When deciding how good a job President Bush was doing, people were therefore probably especially inclined to bring the economy to mind as one consideration. If instead the media had been focusing on the triumph of the Gulf War during that period, Americans may have been inclined to evaluate him on that basis and to overlook the state of the domestic economy, considering the former to be the more significant current political issue. In this sense, we think, the issues the media choose to cover most end up being primed, meaning that they become the predominant bases for the public's evaluations of it's president.

How Specific Is the Impact of a Story?

If we are to understand the dynamics and political consequences of priming, one important question is how specific the impact of any particular story is. That is, does a story about a particular issue prime only that specific issue, or does it prime other issues as well? And if so, which other issues are primed and which are not?

Consider, for example, news media coverage of affirmative action in late 1995. Although there was a great deal of national debate about affirmative action at that time, there was special media attention paid to a push by some residents of California to eliminate that state's affirmative action programs. Perhaps such stories primed only the proposed plan for California. These stories, however, might also have primed affirmative action as a more general issue for the nation as a whole. In addition, these stories might even have primed other, quite different issues if Americans perceived them to be related to affirmative action. For example, school busing programs to achieve integration might be perceived to be related to affirmative action because both are policies aimed at improving the conditions of minority group members. Therefore, news stories about affirmative action might prime school busing in some Americans' minds but not as strongly as these stories would presumably prime affirmative action.

What about a very different issue, such as inflation? Inflation is probably related to affirmative action very distantly, if at all. As such, we would not expect news coverage of affirmative action to prime inflation. In fact, extensive news coverage of affirmative action might even lead people to see inflation and other unrelated issues as less significant nationally, thus perhaps even reducing their impact on people's evaluations of a president's job performance. Because most people probably have neither the ability nor the motivation to evaluate the president based on a large number of policy domains, as some issues are brought into the foreground of people's minds (presumably as a result of news media coverage), others may be pushed into the background.

Does every story on nightly television news programs affect presidential evaluations by priming the issue explicitly discussed in the story? We suspect not, because to do so, a story must be relevant to the nation's political situation. For example, in 1994 and 1995, the American public was seemingly fixated on the O. J. Simpson trial, presumably because it received nearly nonstop coverage by the news media. "Is O. J. guilty?" debates occurred in the office and at the dinner table, with friends and with strangers, all across the country. It seems quite unlikely, however, that people based their evaluations of President Clinton's performance on this issue because the case was not directly relevant to presidential performance. This coverage may indeed, however, have primed related issues, such as race relations in America or the state of the U.S. criminal justice system, and thereby increased their impact on presidential evaluations.

Which Presidential Evaluations Are Influenced?

People make many different sorts of judgments about their president besides how good a job he is doing. Perhaps most obviously, people also judge a president's character, especially his competence and his integrity. A president's ability to get re-elected is based partly on how good a job he has been perceived as doing but also on how competent he seems to be and how much integrity he seems to have (Kinder 1986).

News media coverage of national policy issues (such as inflation, unemployment, international military actions, and so on) presumably affects evaluations of the president's general performance because all of these issues touch on domains of presidential responsibility. Coverage of such issues may also sometimes affect evaluations of presidential character, but probably not as much as it affects presidential performance evaluations. Whether or not the president can effectively solve a national problem depends only partly on his competence—a fact that most Americans probably recognize. Forces beyond his control, such as the Congress, U.S. businesses, and the governments of other countries around the world, also play significant roles in solving or creating national problems. Therefore, people may assess presidential competence only partly from how he has handled issues that have been in the news. News media coverage of national policy issues probably has even less impact on evaluations of a president's integrity, except when an issue is scandalous in nature.

Who Is Most Influenced?

If the media do, in fact, influence presidential evaluations, are certain types of people more vulnerable than others or are all people equally influenced? We suspect that under certain conditions, the media's influence is likely to be concentrated among a subset of individuals, namely, those who know the most about politics.

People who possess much political knowledge are especially capable of storing information obtained from even peripheral attention to a news story in what psychologists think of as elaborate filing systems in their memories. Therefore, these people are especially likely to be able to retrieve that information, perhaps even long after news coverage of the issue has waned. Consequently, people who know much about politics may be particularly likely to manifest priming when there is a long delay between news coverage of an issue and the time when they evaluate the president's performance. When there is no such delay, however, knowledge in and of itself may not magnify priming.

Evidence of Priming

Now that we have outlined for you the theory of priming, we will describe four of the studies we have performed that document these processes. These studies examined the impact of news coverage on presidential evaluations both in the course of everyday life and in our laboratory. We begin where we started this chapter—with President George Bush and the Gulf War.

The Gulf War

As mentioned previously, President Bush enjoyed a spectacular increase in national popularity in early 1991. In October 1990, national surveys by the Gallup Organization and the CBS-*New York Times* team found that approximately 55% of the American public approved of President Bush's performance. This proportion then grew steadily, reaching a high of nearly 90% in March 1991. This surge in approval ratings occurred precisely when the U.S. news media were obsessed with the Persian Gulf War, about which we suspected most Americans felt quite positively. Therefore, the theory of priming suggested that President Bush's popularity may have risen because the media focused on an issue that played well for him.

To test this hypothesis, we analyzed survey data collected by the University of Michigan's Survey Research Center from a representative sample of American adults (for details of this study, see Krosnick & Brannon, 1993). These people were interviewed twice—once before the news media focused almost exclusively on the Gulf War (in the fall of 1990) and again after the constant barrage of coverage (in the summer of 1991). During these interviews, people were asked how they evaluated the president's performance in general and how they evaluated his handling of the Gulf War, international relations more generally, and the domestic economy. Using a statistical technique called multiple regression, we were able to gauge the impact of these latter three specific evaluations on people's overall assessments of the president's job performance.

As expected, overall performance assessments were based only minimally on the president's handling of the Gulf crisis before the media coverage but were powerfully based on his handling of the crisis after the issue received extensive attention. Also as expected, most people evaluated the president's handling of the Gulf situation positively; therefore, increasing its impact made people's overall evaluations of his performance more positive. In this sense, President Bush's popularity soared not simply because the Gulf War was perceived as a successful effort. It was due as well to the news media's decision to focus on the Gulf.

Did the media's coverage of the Gulf War also affect the impact of other issues on evaluations of President Bush's overall job performance? It is conceivable that when a war occurs and news coverage of it is intense, thinking about related issues for which the conduct of the war has implications may be stimulated. At the very least, because the Gulf War involved a complex coordination of efforts by many countries around the world, media attention to the issue might have induced people to also consider U.S. relations with these various other countries. If this were so, then coverage of the Gulf War might have increased the impact of evaluations of President Bush's handling of international relations generally on overall job performance assessments. Interestingly, however, this was not the case. The impact of President Bush's handling of international relations was not affected by news media attention to the Gulf crisis. Apparently, thinking about the Gulf War did not provoke attention to other aspects of international relations.

In this light, it is not surprising that coverage of the Gulf War also did not affect the impact of President Bush's handling of the U.S. economy on overall evaluations of his job performance. Presumably, this is because the economy is even less directly linked to the Gulf War than international relations in general. This is therefore evidence of one of the limits of the media's influence—priming effects only appear for issues that are perceived to be directly relevant to the news stories.

People who were especially knowledgeable about politics manifested bigger increases in the impact of President Bush's Gulf War performance than did less knowledgeable individuals. This is presumably because knowledge facilitated memory of the media stories, and assessments of the president's performance were made some time after news media coverage of the issue had waned.

The 1992 U.S. Presidential Election

Why didn't President Bush's tremendous popularity in the summer of 1991 catapult him to victory in the 1992 presidential election? One possibility is that after the news media moved their searchlights away from the U.S. victory in the Persian Gulf, they focused instead on an issue that negatively affected evaluations of President Bush's performance. In fact, this appears to have occurred: Although the domestic economy was nearly invisible in the media during the summer of 1991, it was a primary focus in September and October of 1992 (see Krosnick & Brannon, 1995). According to the theory of priming, this increase in news coverage of the domestic economy should have led citizens to think more about the issue, thus perhaps conferring upon it enhanced impact on presidential job performance assessments.

To test whether media focus on the economy caused the decline in President Bush's popularity, we analyzed survey data collected by the University of Michigan's Survey Research Center. In this survey, the people who had been interviewed in 1990 and 1991 in conjunction with the Gulf War were again interviewed in the fall of 1992, just before the November election. This allowed us to gauge the impact of assessments of President Bush's handling of the Gulf War, foreign relations in general, and the economy on overall performance evaluations after the media's searchlight was turned on the economy.

The impact of economic performance judgments for overall perform-ance evaluations was nearly double in 1992 what it had been in 1991. Thus, enhanced media attention to the economy increased its impact on assessments of the president's performance. Had the media focus re-mained on the Gulf, perhaps George Bush would have enjoyed an enthusiastic re-election. The focus, however, on a domain in which he was perceived to have performed poorly was instead his undoing.

What happened to the impact of the Gulf War and general foreign relations assessments on overall job performance ratings once the news media turned their searchlights off of the Gulf War and on to the economy? Although each of these issues had a strong impact on presi-dential popularity only a short time after the Gulf War, the impact of

President Bush's Gulf War performance dropped nearly 50% in 1992, and the impact of foreign relations in general decreased 30%. Thus, decreased media attention to the Gulf War was followed by a decreased impact of the war and foreign relations in general—issues on which President Bush was evaluated favorably. This, too, helps to explain why the president's popularity in 1991 did not catapult him to re-election in 1992.

The 1992 survey was performed in the midst of heavy media coverage of the economy. Therefore, it was not necessary for Americans to reach into the backs of their minds to remember the media's messages for priming of economic performance to occur. And indeed, highly and less knowledgeable citizens manifested priming equivalently during the fall of 1992.

The Iran-Contra Affair

A third study we conducted focused on President Ronald Reagan and the Iran-Contra affair. In the late fall of 1986, the Gallup, ABC-*Washington Post*, and CBS-*New York Times* polls all reported sharp declines in the proportion of Americans who approved of President Reagan's job performance—from a high of 70% in October 1985 to approximately 50% in November, to a low of 40% in February 1986. Just prior to this nosedive, U.S. Attorney General Edwin Meese had announced that the United States was involved in a secret plan to sell weapons to Iran to fund a group of rebels who were trying to overthrow the government in Nicaragua. This announcement touched off continuous national news coverage of the Iran-Contra scandal in the months that followed. Was the news media's focus on this issue at least partly responsible for the drastic decline in President Reagan's approval ratings? The theory of priming would say "yes," so we set out to test this possibility.

To do so, we again analyzed the data from a survey of a representative national sample of American adults performed by the University of Michigan's Survey Research Center (for details of this study, see Krosnick & Kinder, 1990). Some of the respondents in this study were interviewed just before the scandal broke (in September, October, and early November of 1986), and others were interviewed just afterward (in late November, December, and January). All respondents were asked to evaluate President Reagan's overall job performance, his competence, and his integrity. In addition, respondents were asked whether they supported or opposed U.S. involvement in Central America, U.S. involvement in the affairs of other countries more generally, and federal programs to provide aid to African Americans. People also reported whether they felt the national economy was in good shape or bad shape. Again using multiple regression, we gauged the impact of these latter judgments on assessments of President Reagan.

As expected, people interviewed before the media coverage of the Iran-Contra affair based their overall evaluations of President Reagan's job performance only minimally on whether they felt the United States should intervene in Central America. After the onslaught of coverage, however, this issue became a much more potent determinant of overall job performance assessments. Because most Americans were opposed to U.S. involvement in Central America, this surge in impact made overall assessments of President Reagan more negative.

News media coverage of the Iran-Contra scandal also increased the issue's impact on people's assessments of President Reagan's competence and integrity, but this increase was smaller than the increase in the impact of the scandal on overall presidential performance evaluations. This reliance on the Iran-Contra affair to evaluate President Reagan's competence and integrity seems understandable because the interpretations of events that had unfolded in the White House explicitly implicated the President's competence ("He was completely out of touch with what was going on around him!") and his integrity ("He willingly went along with an intentional deception of the U.S. Congress and the American people!"). These links, however, were more uncertain than were the implications of the scandal for his job performance, thus presumably yielding weaker priming effects for competence and integrity assessments.

Did media attention to the Iran-Contra affair increase the impact of other issues besides the scandal on evaluations of President Reagan's overall job performance? It is conceivable that thinking about Iran-Contra might cause people to think about the issue of U.S. involvement in other countries in general, of which U.S. involvement in Central America is a subset. At the very least, there are some consequences to our involvement in Central America that people might have been induced to consider in relation to our involvement in other countries. If this were so, then coverage of Iran-Contra might have increased the impact of attitudes toward U.S. involvement in other countries in general on evaluations of President Reagan's overall performance. In fact, people interviewed after the Iran-Contra revelation did manifest increased impact of attitudes toward U.S. involvement in other countries in general. Thus, the Iran-Contra affair was perceived to be linked to this issue, and people relied on it to evaluate the president accordingly.

However, although media attention to the Iran-Contra affair generalized to foreign relations attitudes, it did not generalize to assessments of the economy, just as it had not in the Gulf War case. Specifically, coverage of Iran-Contra did not increase the impact of economic attitudes on evaluations of the president, presumably because the scandal was not perceived to be relevant to the issue of the economy.

In addition, attitudes toward federal programs to aid African Americans actually had less of an impact after the Iran-Contra revelation than before. Thus, not only can the media's focus on an issue increase the impact of related issues on presidential performance evaluations while leaving the impact of other issues unaffected, it can also decrease the impact of still other issues. Presumably, coverage of the Iran-Contra affair took away the attention people had previously paid to federal aid to African Americans.

Finally, as expected, priming appeared equally strong among people knowledgeable about politics and those who knew less about politics (see Krosnick & Brannon, 1993, pp. 972-973). Because evaluations of the president's performance were made concurrently with news media coverage of the Iran-Contra affair, the advantage knowledge confers on memory did not enhance priming. Had the survey interviews been conducted 2 months later, highly knowledgeable citizens may indeed have manifested stronger priming.

Experiment: Crime, Pollution, and Unemployment

These three studies' results are quite consistent with the theory of priming. Following a large increase in news media coverage of an issue, that issue apparently had more impact on presidential evaluations. This increase was most apparent for job performance assessments, although it appeared for assessments of competence and integrity as well. News media coverage of an issue not only increased its impact but also increased the impact of related issues and sometimes decreased the impact of unrelated issues. In addition, these changes were more apparent among people who knew more about politics when there was a delay between news media coverage and assessments of the president's performance. When there was no such delay, people high and low in political knowledge manifested priming to the same degree.

As closely as these patterns conform to predictions made by the theory of priming, we cannot be sure from these data alone that shifts in news media content were responsible for the changes we observed in how people evaluated Presidents Bush and Reagan. The fact that the shifts in judgment strategies occurred after the shifts in media coverage are certainly encouraging in this regard, but the only way to be sure about what influenced what is to perform an experiment manipulating news media coverage. This is what we have done in a number of studies. In each case, we had some people watch television news stories about an issue, whereas other people watched stories on different topics. We then observed differences between these groups of people in how they constructed presidential evaluations.

In one of our experiments, conducted in 1993, people came to our lab, watched television news stories taken from recent national network broadcasts, and completed questionnaires measuring their opinions on various political matters. Each respondent was randomly assigned to watch two stories about crime, pollution, or unemployment. In addition, all respondents watched five "filler" stories on topics not directly related to President Bill Clinton's job performance (e.g., hot-air ballooning). In the questionnaire, respondents reported their evaluations of President Clinton's overall job performance and his handling of crime, pollution, and unemployment. We again conducted multiple regressions to gauge the impact of the latter evaluations on overall performance assessments separately for respondents who watched crime, pollution, or unemployment stories (for details of this study, see Miller, 1995).

As expected, watching stories about an issue increased the impact of that issue on evaluations of the president's overall performance. This was even true for pollution, although the news stories we showed our respondents on this topic did not mention President Clinton at all—instead discussing particular cases of pollution in New York and Mississippi. Thus, it appears that news media coverage of an issue can alter presidential performance assessment procedures, even when the president is not explicitly discussed.

In our study of the Gulf War, in which presidential evaluations were made some time after news media coverage of the issue had waned, highly knowledgeable people were more susceptible to priming than people who knew less about politics. This is presumably because people who knew much about politics were more likely to remember the news stories longer than people who knew less about politics. In our studies of the 1992 election and the Iran-Contra affair, however, in which there were no delays between media coverage and presidential assessments, there were no differences between people low and high in political knowledge in their susceptibility to priming. Likewise, these two groups should presumably manifest equivalently strong priming effects in this experiment because there was no delay between the news media exposure and evaluations of the president's performance. In fact, this was the case.

In this experiment, we were also able to examine whether another characteristic regulated susceptibility to priming. Specifically, people who trusted the news media may have been more likely to manifest priming than people who were less trusting of the media. To assess media trust, respondents were asked the extent to which they thought the media deal fairly with all sides of an issue, how often the stories the media report are accurate, and the extent to which the media focus on the important issues of the day. The answers to these three questions were then averaged to arrive at an overall measure of media trust. People who trusted the media were presumably more likely to pay close attention to a news story, to think about its political implications, and to take those implications into consideration when making presidential performance assessments. Indeed, people who were highly trusting of the media were more likely to rely on the issue the media focused on to evaluate President Clinton's performance.

Interestingly, the priming effects observed in this study were concentrated exclusively among a particular subgroup of the respondents: those who were both highly knowledgeable about politics and who trusted the media. People low in political knowledge or media trust or both failed to manifest any priming effect at all. Thus, although people who knew much about politics presumably had an easy time understanding the political meaning of a news story, this ability alone was not enough to increase their susceptibility to priming, at least when there was no delay between the media coverage and presidential evaluations. Rather, the susceptibility to priming among people who knew much about politics was most pronounced when they also trusted the media and were therefore motivated to pay close attention to the news stories.

If our survey studies had assessed citizens' trust in the media, we may have seen this same result, even when there was no time delay between media coverage and assessments of the president's performance.

Conclusion

At the end of every *CBS Evening News* broadcast, Dan Rather signs off with "And that's part of our world tonight." Explicit in this statement is the fact that television newscasts only provide information about a portion of the world. But how do the media decide what to cover, and do those choices matter? Taken together, these studies make a compelling case that they do matter—the media's choice to focus on one issue and not another influences the standards by which the American public evaluates its president. Such evaluations have important implications for the effective practice of democracy because a president's power in Washington depends partly on how favorably he is evaluated by the nation. A president who receives accolades from the public tends to have his way with Congress and other institutions and individuals involved in the policy-making process. In contrast, presidents whose actions elicit grumblings of frustration from the citizenry are less effective (Neustadt, 1960; Rivers & Rose, 1981). Furthermore, a president's likelihood of being re-elected, and thus his ability to continue to carry out his agenda, is also in part determined by his popularity. If the media focus on an issue that plays well for the president, his chances of re-election are much greater than if they pay attention to an issue on which he is perceived to have failed.

In this light, is the fact that people rely on the media to make presidential performance assessments normatively good or bad for the practice of democracy? The answer to this question depends crucially on how the media decide on which parts of the world to turn their searchlights. If, on the one hand, the media respond to world events by covering only the issues that are the most significant because they impact a large portion of the population and thus have implications for the nation as a whole, then this reliance on the news media to make presidential evaluations could be viewed as sensible. On the other hand, if the media are guided by other criteria, such as which stories are most likely to grab the audience's attention and thus boost ratings, then a democracy would not be best served by this type of media influence because these opinions would be based on peripheral, if not trivial, considerations.

Some research does suggest that the media are primarily concerned with focusing on issues they judge to be important for the nation. According to Gans (1979), stories are judged to be important if they meet at least one of four criteria, each being an indication of the story's national significance. First, important stories are ones that involve a high government official (especially the president). Other government officials are covered to the extent that they in some way influence the president's policies or do something that will affect the lives of other Americans. Second, stories are considered important if they have implications for the national interest. Thus, international issues are covered to the extent that they impact on national security or on the rights of the nation's citizenry. Domestic stories are covered to the extent that they reinforce national values, such as ethnocentrism and capitalism. Third, important stories are ones that impact the lives (or have the potential to impact the lives) of a large number of people, with the most important story being one that affects every American. Finally, stories are more likely to be considered important if they have significant implications for the future. Journalists do not want to be criticized later for ignoring a story that, in retrospect, became historically significant.

Consistent with the notion that the media do focus on nationally significant issues, Behr and Iyengar (1985) found that the amount of coverage the television networks devoted to unemployment, energy, and inflation increased in response to increases in unemployment rates, surges in energy costs, and rises in prices, respectively. Thus, at least when it comes to these three issues, the media did appear responsive to the national significance of issues.

However, although significance for the nation as a whole influences the media's story selections, they are also partly determined by more idiosyncratic editorial, organizational, or commercial constraints (Altheide, 1976; Epstein, 1973; Gans, 1979; Lippmann, 1922). Stories are more likely to be covered to the extent that they are suitable for a particular news medium. In the case of television newscasts, for example, a story is more likely to be covered to the extent that it is visually interesting (e.g., involves a lot of action) or can be addressed in a short amount of time to fit into a 30-minute broadcast. In addition, the media are biased toward covering dramatic stories (Bennett, 1988) and toward reporting stories that will not offend advertisers (Lippmann, 1922). Thus, considerations other than the significance of an issue for the nation may actually divert the public's attention from the "real" problems of the day.

Although evidence suggests that the media's story selection processes involve other criteria besides the importance of the story to the nation, it is less clear whether important stories are routinely excluded from news coverage because of these other considerations. Until more conclusive studies on the media's story selection process are conducted, it is difficult to make an assessment of whether news media priming is normatively good or bad for the practice of democracy.

If future studies conclude that nationally significant stories are rarely ignored, then the media could be considered an institution that aids the process of democracy. That is, if the media focus primarily on nationally significant issues, they provide information citizens need to make informed political judgments. Thus, a democracy would be best served if the prevalence of news media priming were increased.

One way to increase priming might be to encourage the media to make the implications of a news story for broader political concerns more explicit so that people could more readily see the relevance of the story to presidential performance evaluations. Because priming is concentrated among people who know much about politics and trust the media, another strategy to this end would be for schools to teach young Americans more extensively about policy issues and politics in general as well as to foster the view of the media as valid sources of political information. This would motivate people to pay close attention to the news media, better equip them to recognize the implications of a news story for political judgments, and increase their ability to remember media messages.

If, on the other hand, it is found that the media frequently forgo coverage of nationally significant issues, it would not be prudent for citizens to rely on the media to help them make political judgments. One is reminded of the old adage of a drunk searching for his keys under a lamppost. When a stranger walked by and asked, "Is that where you dropped your keys?," the drunk responded, "No, but the light is better here." Our research shows that people are likely to look in the beams of the media's searchlights for the standards by which to evaluate their president. If the stories they choose are typically the less significant, then democracy might better be served if the public were encouraged to focus on issues outside the searchlights.

One way to decrease the prevalence of priming would be to intervene on the subset of the population that is most susceptible to the media's influence—people who are both highly knowledgeable about politics and trusting of the media. Although it seems neither possible nor ethical to decrease people's political knowledge, it may be feasible to foster a less accepting view of news stories. Such a critical posture might lead more people to make political judgments unaffected by television, radio, newspapers, and magazines.

The effectiveness of such interventions would be a potentially fruitful direction for future priming research. For example, one could compare the prevalence of priming among people who are encouraged to believe that the media focus on nationally significant issues, people who are told that the media generally rely on other criteria to select stories, and people who are given no information about how the media select their stories. If informing the public about how story-selection decisions are made is effective, then people who are told that the media primarily focus on nationally important issues should show the strongest priming effect, and people who are told that the media frequently use other selection criteria should be least susceptible to priming.

Another potential strategy for counteracting detrimental effects of priming, if such effects are deemed thusly, might be to pressure the media to change the criteria by which they make story choices. Unfortunately, this course of action seems unlikely to succeed. The media have resisted time and time again pressure from political leaders, such as Bob Dole and Tipper Gore, to decrease the amount of violence depicted on television, in movies, and in music. As long as economic imperatives, such as the wants of advertisers and the need for high ratings and sales exist, it is unlikely that outside pressure to change the content of the news media will be effective, no matter how damaging.

Epilogue

The studies described in this chapter illustrate how the disciplines of political science and psychology can be brought together to provide new and exciting insights about a set of important, real-world issues. The strategy of using surveys to document processes as they unfold in everyday life is traditionally used by political scientists and other scholars to study media effects. Had we stopped with such studies, however, we would not have been able to definitively conclude that the media are instigators of these processes. Only when we turned to the psychologists' practice of examining the observed phenomenon in a controlled laboratory setting could we be more certain that the news media do, in fact, cause changes in the standards by which the president is evaluated. We hope that future research will continue to capitalize on the strengths of both disciplines' approaches, to provide insights into the political process in general, and to contribute substantively to our understanding of basic psychological processes.

32 Framing Responsibility for Political Issues

The Case of Poverty

SHANTO IYENGAR

For virtually all Americans, political issues are defined primarily through news reports, and since news coverage is inevitably expressed in particular frames, the influence of the media on public opinion can be significant. To identify the ways in which television news frames the issue of poverty, every network news story broadcast between 1981 and 1986 making reference to poverty, hunger, the homeless, welfare, food stamps, and other similar key words was identified and content analyzed. The objective of this search was to identify the frames in which television news embeds the issue of poverty.

A total of 191 stories were identified as relevant to poverty in the United States. These stories fall into two distinct categories. One set describes poverty primarily as a societal or collective outcome while the other describes poverty in terms of particular victims (e.g., poor people). In the societal frame, the news might consist of information bearing on national trends (e.g., the poverty rate, the number of states experiencing significant increases in hunger, changes in the government's definition of poverty, etc.) or matters of public policy (the Reagan administration's proposals to curtail various social welfare programs, allegations of fraud in welfare programs, etc.). These are essentially background or "takeout" stories in which the object of the coverage is abstract and impersonal. In the individual-victim frame, by contrast, poverty is covered in terms of

EDITORS' NOTE: Reprinted from *Political Behavior, 12,* 19-40. Used by permission from Plenum Publishing Corporation.

personal experience; the viewer is provided a particular instance of an individual or family living under economic duress. The preponderance of stories were episodic; from the perspective of television news, poverty is clearly an individual-level rather than societal phenomenon.

How might these diverging frames influence how people assign responsibility for poverty? To be held responsible for some outcome is, in good measure, to be seen as a cause of the outcome. Moreover, the importance of causal attributions as attitudinal and even behavioral cues has been amply documented in the psychological literature.

When assigning responsibility for outcomes, people also consider the question of control or treatment. Those held responsible (whether individuals or institutions) are those seen as empowered to control the outcome. While causal responsibility looks primarily to the past, treatment responsibility is essentially future-oriented and problem-solving in nature, i.e., questions of treatment responsibility seek to establish what can be done to prevent recurrence of the outcome.

In an initial experimental study, it was found that causal responsibility for poverty was significantly influenced by media framing. When poverty was described in societal terms, individuals assigned responsibility to societal factors—failed governmental programs, the political climate, economic conditions, and so on. Conversely, when news coverage of poverty dwelled on particular instances of poor people, individuals were more apt to hold the poor causally responsible. This divergence in attribution of causal responsibility proved to be politically consequential because evaluations of President Reagan were significantly (and independently) lowered among individuals with a stronger sense of societal responsibility.

The research reported here was designed to replicate and elaborate upon this initial study. Specifically, the study investigated the impact of societal vs. individual-victim frames in television news coverage of poverty on perceptions of responsibility—both causal and treatment. Next, the paper assesses the degree to which attributions of responsibility for poverty structure political attitudes.

Study Design

Residents of the Three Village area of Suffolk County (New York) responded to newspaper advertisements offering $10 in return for participation in media research. This method of recruitment yielded a reasonable approximation of the local community. When participants arrived at the Media Research Laboratory, they were given an instruction sheet in which the study was described as an investigation of "selective perception." They then completed an informed consent form and a short pretest questionnaire probing their personal background, media usage, level of political activity, etc. Participants were then taken to one of several viewing rooms where they watched a twenty-minute videotape containing seven news stories. The tape was described as a representative sample of news stories aired during the past year. Typically, the viewing session was made up of two individuals since the advertisements encouraged prospective participants to bring along someone they knew.

On completion of the videotape, participants completed a lengthy questionnaire (in separate rooms) which included various measures of their beliefs and opinions concerning poverty (and various other issues). Finally, participants were debriefed and paid.

Three separate conditions depicted a societal frame: increased unemployment in the manufacturing sector, increases in the number of Americans meeting the government's definition of poverty, and a report on increases in "food emergencies" (households requiring emergency food aid) across the nation. All three news stories were edited in advance so as to exclude any reference or glimpse of an individual victim of poverty.

The individual-victim manipulation was more elaborate. Participants watched an unemployed male, an unmarried adult mother, an elderly widow, a young child, or a teenage mother describe their economic difficulties. These five groups account for most Americans receiving public assistance. Within each of these five victim groups, the race of the individual was varied. Thus the unemployed male was either black or white. The purpose here, of course, was to assess whether news stories describing particular instances of poverty in America evoke racial stereotypes which influence individuals' understanding of poverty.

Finally, all thirteen conditions were characterized by an absence of explicit information concerning the causes of poverty. Any segment in the original story suggesting some particular reason for increases in poverty nationwide or for the particular victim's present circumstances was deleted.

Attributions of causal and treatment responsibility were elicited with open-ended survey questions. Specifically, individuals were asked "In your opinion, what are the most important causes of poverty?" They were then asked "If you were asked to prescribe ways to reduce poverty, what would you suggest?" Up to four separate responses were coded for each question.

Framing Effects

Causal responsibility was either assigned to the poor themselves or to general societal factors. Individual responsibility included the themes of character deficiencies and inadequate education. Societal responsibility encompassed the state of economic conditions and inadequate governmental/societal efforts. This last category included references to the actions of the Reagan administration such as budgetary cuts in social welfare programs as well as references to general barriers to economic mobility—racial discrimination, Social Darwinism, public apathy, etc.

Participants' treatment responses revealed the same individualistic-societal continuum. Responsibility was assigned either to the victim or to society-at-large. Approximately one-third of all treatment responses were directed to actions by the poor—hard work and the acquisition of education and skills—while the remaining responses pointed to actions by government or society in general such as improved economic conditions, lowered institutional barriers to economic mobility, and strengthened or improved governmental efforts to assist the poor.

Results

The proportion of responses falling into the societal and individual response categories of causal and treatment responsibility was tabulated. The three separate societal frames proved equivalent; there were no significant differences between them in any of the individual response categories. These three conditions were therefore pooled.

Participants were generally least apt to hold individuals causally responsible and most apt to consider society responsible when the news frame was societal. The mean index of societal causal responsibility reached .71 in the societal frame, which differed significantly from the elderly widow, adult mother, and teen mother frames. In addition, there were significant differences among the individual-victim conditions. The single mother frames elicited a particularly high level of individual causal responsibility and differed significantly from the poor children and unemployed men frames where societal causes outnumbered individual causes by nearly 2:1.

Virtually identical framing effects were obtained in the area of treatment responsibility. In general, participants in all conditions were as willing to assign society the responsibility for treating poverty as they were to consider society causally responsible. The two single mother conditions, however, pulled the highest proportion of individual treatment responses and the lowest proportion of societal treatment responses. In both respects the single mother frames deviated significantly from the societal frame. The single mother frames also differed, though to a lesser degree, from the poor children and unemployed men frames.

Turning to the effects of the victim's race on viewers' beliefs about responsibility, the results were mixed. Race appears to be only a weak cue when individuals consider the question of causal responsibility. The effects of race were more pronounced in the area of treatment responsibility. Irrespective of condition, black poor people elicited more frequent references to individual responsibility ($F < .05$) and less frequent references to societal responsibility ($F < .10$). Within this general pattern of differences, race was most prominent in the adult single mother frame; in comparison to the white mother, the black mother elicited twice the proportion of individual treatment responses.

All told, the evidence suggests that beliefs about responsibility for poverty are influenced by the race of the individual depicted in the news reports. Poor blacks are only marginally more likely than poor whites to be seen as causal agents rather than as victims of forces beyond their control. The degree to which societal intervention is considered an appropriate remedy for poverty, however, is significantly higher when the poor person depicted is white whereas the responsibility for treating poverty is assigned to the poor person when the person depicted is black.

To summarize, what people take to be the causes and cures of poverty depends significantly upon the manner in which television news presentations frame the issue. When poverty is defined as a societal phenomenon, responsibility is assigned quite differently than when poverty is defined as specific instances of poor people. People hold government responsible to a greater degree when the media frame is societal. These results suggest that the well-documented tendency of Americans to consider poor people responsible for poverty may be due not only to dominant cultural values (e.g., individualism, self-reliance, etc.), but also to news coverage of poverty in which images of poor people predominate.

Conclusion

The experimental evidence demonstrates that beliefs about who or what is responsible for poverty vary considerably, depending upon how poverty is framed. When television news depicts poverty in thematic terms, viewers exhibit a stronger sense of societal responsibility, while the individual-victim frame engenders a stronger sense of individual responsibility. All told, these results suggest that the context in which political issues appear is critical to how people think about these issues. When poverty is expressed as a societal phenomenon, it is understood quite differently than when it appears in the form of a specific poor person. Similarly, news coverage of different instances of poor people or reference to different personal traits and behaviors in survey question-naires has the effect of raising or lowering the degree to which Americans hold government responsible for assisting the poor.

These results are especially striking given that poverty is a familiar issue that is closely intertwined with mainstream values such as self-reliance, the work ethic, and related themes. American culture thus provides ample cues concerning responsibility for poverty. That framing effects can emerge in the face of such long-term learning influences is indeed striking.

Race appears to be a meaningful contextual cue when Americans think about poverty. Our sample of white, middle-class Americans were sen-sitive to the color of a poor person's skin. When the poor person was white, causal and treatment responsibility for poverty were predomi-nantly societal; when the poor person was black, causal and treatment responsibility were more individual. The fact that race was relevant does not imply that participants' were overtly anti-black. If this were the case, the racial differences would have been more consistent across the differ-ent individual victims. That the observed racial differences fluctuated with the particular victim suggests that race more effectively evoked stored knowledge concerning responsibility for poverty when it was paired with particular demographic categories. The particular combination of race, gender, age, and marital status (e.g., black adult single mothers) was particularly evocative of an individual conception of responsibility for poverty. This particular demographic combination represents the largest segment of poor people in America. In this sense, the most "realistic" individual-victim frame has the most inhibiting effect on societal conceptions of responsibility.

Like race, a poor person's gender also appears to activate a more individual and less societal conception of responsibility for poverty. It is not possible to determine from the experimental design that it is gender per se that is the critical cue since viewers were not given information concerning an unemployed woman or a male retiree. What the evidence indicates is that single mothers are seen as particularly blameworthy and less deserving of governmental support.

The national debate over social welfare policy has traditionally been formulated in terms of specific beneficiary groups such as children, women, minorities, or the disabled. The results reported here suggest that framing welfare programs in terms of particular beneficiary groups will weaken rather than strengthen public support for welfare. More generally, the framing of political issues is a powerful form of social control that circumscribes the national debate over public policy.

33 Modern Racism and Images of Blacks in Local Television News

ROBERT M. ENTMAN

This paper probes one critical instance of the linkage between the practices of the mass media and the processes of cultural change: the relatively recent transformation of anti-black racism. Expressions of traditional racist sentiment have all but disappeared from the media and from public discourse generally. But social scientists have shown that racism has not evaporated. Even as it has become socially unacceptable to assert blacks' inherent inferiority or to endorse legal segregation, a "modern" form of racism has arisen. This paper is an attempt to explore how one component of television programming, local news, may be contributing to the metamorphosis of white racism; it is a prologue to, and justification for, more systematic research.

In the data reported here, 76 percent of all local TV stories about blacks fell into the categories of crime or politics. For the week studied, violent crime committed by blacks was the largest category of local news. Of the eight instances in which blacks were the subjects of lead stories, six described violent crimes; the other two stories concerned the Democratic party's conflicts and the death of a black girl who was run over by a city bus. Of course, the particular week studied could have been a period of unusually high violence. The point here, however, is not to determine the average proportion of local news devoted to violent crime committed by blacks, but to explore how the images of crime may compound white's hostility.

EDITORS' NOTE: Reprinted from *Critical Studies in Mass Communication*, 7, 329-343. Used by permission from Speech Communication Association.

Several aspects of crime reporting combined to suggest that blacks are more dangerous than whites. For instance, the accused black criminals were usually illustrated by glowering mug shots or by footage of them being led around in handcuffs, their arms held by uniformed white policemen. None of the accused violent white criminals during the week studied were shown in mug shots or in physical custody. The difference may be due to the fact that most of the whites were alleged organized crime figures of high economic status. They could afford bail money, good legal representation, and advice on handling the press.

Thus, the contrast in portrayals of black and white criminals reflects, at least in part, underlying differences in the social class of the perpetrators. Here is an instance of the inadvertent class bias of local TV news, a bias that may spur modern racism. Put simply, TV favors upper or middle-class persons when they appear in the news, because those persons have the skills and resources to manipulate television's production practices. To counter this slant, journalists would have to understand the class bias and take steps to counteract it—suggesting that black lawbreakers put on business suits, for example, or asking police to allow them to walk freely for the news camera.

Within the category of crime, white victimization by blacks appeared to have especially high priority. During the week studied, the story of white victimization that obtained the most attention involved four white girls receiving razor cuts in a fight with two black girls on a Chicago bus, and the related charge by the victims that the black bus driver did nothing to help. Given the timing of the incident, each of the three stations had the opportunities to cover it in five programs over three days; the affair was covered 11 of the possible 15 times. Three times it was the lead story, once the second story, and twice the third story. Four of the stories were over two minutes long, marking the event as unusually newsworthy. The racial tension that the story demonstrated and reinforced is probably what made it so newsworthy. It is unlikely that the incident would have received similar attention were all the participants white (or black).

The whites' perspective on the event dominated the story. The black girls accused of the assault were never quoted directly. Their side was voiced through angry relatives talking to reporters (on only two of the stations). The white girls said the attack was unprovoked, the black relatives that the whites had instigated the fight with racial insults; but the whites' version was clearly favored through the order of presentation, the amount of time devoted to it, and the visuals. For example, the white girls were shown seated on a couch, presumably at an orderly home like that of middle-class viewers, calmly describing their ordeal, with numerous close-ups of their wounds. The alleged perpetrators' relatives spoke at the police station house, where the camera was hand-held and shaky, the lighting full of shadows, and the disordered scene hardly likely to promote credibility.

The contrast in presenting the whites' and blacks' cases may have been unavoidable, given normal station routines. As juveniles, the accused were inaccessible to journalists; since they were in custody, they could not be interviewed at home. In fact, the press generally slights the vantage of accused lawbreakers in favor of the prosecution. All of this suggests that the stations did not deliberately derogate the defendants because of their race.

A secondary theme of the coverage on each station involved the whites complaining that the black bus driver failed to assist them. One station had him respond to the charges on camera, but he looked surly, sounded defensive, and came off badly in contrast with the articulate, aggrieved white girls, especially since this station (and the others) reported that he was suspended for his inaction by the Chicago Transit Authority (CTA). Barely mentioned was the driver's claim that he did call for help but found his radio inoperable. The driver said "That's not my job" when asked about his failure to assist the white girls. Two of the stations showed the black chief of the bus drivers' union or some fellow black bus drivers defending the suspended man, thereby seeming to be more concerned about the job security and selfish interests of black drivers than the community interest in safe buses. The implicit message was that black drivers would not protect white passengers from violence because their racial loyalty overrode their human sympathy and their job obligations. Perhaps this is how the typical black bus driver feels; but the reporting did not probe the possibility that the driver did follow proper procedure, that drivers are not expected to intervene physically in fights, and that the CTA might have been hoping to deflect blame for the faulty radio by suspending the driver.

The high priority that local television grants white victimization by blacks, and crime generally—a priority that can stimulate modern racism—appears based in commercial imperatives. In large metropolitan areas, where the media market consists of dozens of political jurisdictions, local TV cannot focus too much on the politics and policy of any one jurisdiction, so it has to go with material of broader human interest. Hence its top four story categories are more emotionally evocative than informative: crime, fires, and accidents; human interest features; sports; and weather. The Chicago stations made violent crime the most frequent subject of lead stories during the week studied. The emphasis on crime explains why blacks who committed crimes were the ones most likely to be featured in the most prominent (lead) stories.

Local news implicitly traces the symbolic boundaries of the community. The present exploration suggests that, in day-to-day news coverage, blacks are largely cast outside those boundaries. In the stories analyzed, crime reporting made blacks look particularly threatening. To be sure, images of blacks in the local news are complicated and replete with multiple potential meanings. And audiences bring to news a variety of predispositions. Social scientists have no more than a rudimentary understanding of how audiences perceive and process media messages. Nonetheless, the exploratory study provides ample support for a hypothesis that local television's images of blacks feed racial anxiety and antagonism *at least* among that portion of the white population most predisposed to those feelings. Quantitative research on the impact of exposure to local TV news seems in order, as does extensive content analysis of large samples of local and network news. Such work would also illuminate the ways that television helps to alter and preserve dominant cultural values and structures of power.

34 Crime in Black and White

The Violent, Scary World of Local News

FRANKLIN D. GILLIAM, JR.
SHANTO IYENGAR
ADAM SIMON
OLIVER WRIGHT

Today more Americans name crime as the "most important problem facing the country" than any other issue. Never before (at least since the advent of polling) have we been so preoccupied with issues of public safety. As fears have increased, so have punitive attitudes toward criminals. The death penalty, mandatory jail sentences, adult trial of juvenile offenders, and "three strikes" laws are all embraced by large majorities.

In response to the public outcry, policy makers at all levels of government have allocated massive public resources to fortify law enforcement and the criminal justice system. Recent developments in California are revealing: Over the past decade, the annual budget of the Department of Corrections has increased at five times the rate of increase granted the Department of Education. (The annual budget now stands at $4.5 billion.)

Surprisingly, this outpouring of collective attention has occurred in an environment which has shown little actual change in the frequency of criminal activity. The statistics simply do not reflect any significant increase in crime. More specifically, two important national databases—the National Victimization Survey and the Uniform Crime Reports—both indicate that the population-adjusted rate of crime (whether defined as total crime or violent crime) has in fact *declined* over the last two

---

EDITORS' NOTE: Reprinted from *Harvard International Journal of Press/Politics*.

decades. Moreover, the great majority of Americans do not experience crime directly. What, then, is the source of the public's rising preoccupation with crime? If the public's concern is not based on first-hand experience, it must stem from vicarious encounters—usually through television reports. In general, it has been well documented that the public political agenda is heavily influenced by patterns of news coverage; as the media become preoccupied with particular issues, so too does the public.

While the sheer quantity of news coverage is important in determining the level of public concern for crime, we believe that qualitative characteristics of news coverage also have a major impact. We suspect that two qualitative features of news programming—violence and race—are especially important. Television's insatiable demand for "good pictures" and riveting stories means that the most gruesome or notorious episodes of crime receive extensive attention while other forms of crime are virtually ignored. Local television news, the most widely used source of information about crime, is especially prone to dwell on crimes of violence and the print media is no less taken with scandal and gore. In short, no matter what they view or what they read, Americans are bombarded with information about sensational crimes—O. J. Simpson, the Menendez brothers, Colin Ferguson, Oklahoma City, the World Trade Center, and so on. Perhaps the public's increased concern with crime is a response to the perception (reinforced on a daily basis) that American society is increasingly anomic and violence-prone.

Not only does news coverage highlight violent crime, it also links the issues of race and crime by overrepresenting minorities in the role of violent criminals and by according them distinctive forms of coverage. Iyengar's study of network news found that crime in black neighborhoods accounted for a substantial share of television news programming. Elias' detailed study of the major news magazines yielded similar results, leading the author to conclude that "criminals are conceptualized as black people, and crime as the violence they do to whites." Entman's analysis of local news also revealed clear race-based patterns. While black suspects were usually shown in handcuffs, and in the custody of police officers, white suspects were typically seen with their attorneys.

In summary, the typical news story on crime consists of two "scripts": crime is violent, and criminals are non-white. In this paper, we match content analysis of local television news stories with aggregate data on the frequency of criminal activity and the ethnicity of criminal perpetrators to evaluate the accuracy of the media's reflection of "real world" criminality. Our results demonstrate that local news programs are significantly distorted in two respects; they disproportionately portray crimes of violence, and they overrepresent African-Americans as perpetrators of violent crime.

Violence and Race in Local News Coverage of Crime

Our sample of local news reports was drawn from television station KABC, the ABC network affiliate in Los Angeles (Channel 7). We examined news coverage over a thirteen month period, from March 1993 through March 1994. We randomly selected two days from each week and in the period viewed KABC's "Action News" program, a thirty minute newscast that airs at 6:00 p.m.

Crime was extensively covered during the entire period under examination. The 148 broadcasts sampled contained 436 stories dealing with crime, or an average of three stories per day. During the entire period sampled, there were only five newscasts that failed to include a single story on crime. Since the entire "news" section occupies sixteen minutes of the newscast, the total coverage accorded crime (on average, four minutes per day) accounts for at least 25 percent of the daily news. In addition, crime was the focus of the lead story in 51 percent of the sampled newscasts.

Based on the content-analytic evidence cited earlier, we suspected that the news would be dominated by crimes of violence, and that the race of the alleged criminals would be disproportionately nonwhite. Accordingly, we tabulated the number of news stories and the duration of coverage accorded violent and nonviolent crime.

We began by comparing the percentage of news reports accorded violent crime with the actual frequency of violent crime in Los Angeles (expressed as a percentage of all crimes). The high level of violence was as expected: The overwhelming majority of news reports were episodic in nature and featured acts of violent crime. But were these reports an accurate reflection of reality? Violent crime made up 30 percent of all crimes in Los Angeles County, but 78 percent of the news reports aired by KABC. The discrepancy was even more extreme when we focused solely on homicide. Murder accounted for only two percent of felony incidents in Los Angeles, but 27 percent of the news coverage was directed at murder. Thus, the news exaggerated the frequency of murder by a ratio of 14:1. While the special seriousness and newsworthiness of murder cannot be denied, the level of the "distortion" is impressive.

As mentioned above, the race of the perpetrator was identified in approximately 40 percent (N = 143 stories) of the news stories. While nonwhites made up 55 percent of the violent criminals depicted in the news, 75 percent of news reports about nonviolent perpetrators featured whites. This pattern is hardly the basis for claiming racial bias, however. The crime rate varies considerably across different ethnic groups and must be interpreted according to the groups' relative representation in the population. In Los Angeles County, for example, whites account for a smaller percentage of all violent crime than blacks even though they are the larger group. To assess these differential rates of criminal activity, we compared population-adjusted real world and media-depicted crime rates for each racial group. In order to summarize these comparisons, we calculated a "net violence" index. The index subtracts each group's relative contribution to nonviolent crime from their contribution to violent crime. Next, it subtracts their share of nonviolent crime in the news from their share of violent crime coverage. Finally, it takes the difference of these differences. A score of zero on the net violence index means that the mix of news coverage accorded a particular group exactly matches that group's actual mix of criminal behavior. Positive scores indicate that the group is depicted in the news as more violent than warranted by their actual behavior. Finally, negative scores would indicate the opposite—that news coverage of the group is less violent than it should be. The net violence index for blacks, Hispanics, and whites is presented in Figure 35.1.

The results in Figure 35.1 indicate that while blacks commit violent and nonviolent crime at about the same rate, the media coverage of black crime is distinctly more violent than nonviolent (by a factor of 22 percent). Conversely, media coverage of white crime is distinctly more nonviolent than violent (by a factor of 31 percent) even though whites are only slightly less likely (by seven percent) to engage in violent rather than nonviolent crime. Finally, while Hispanics are seven percent more

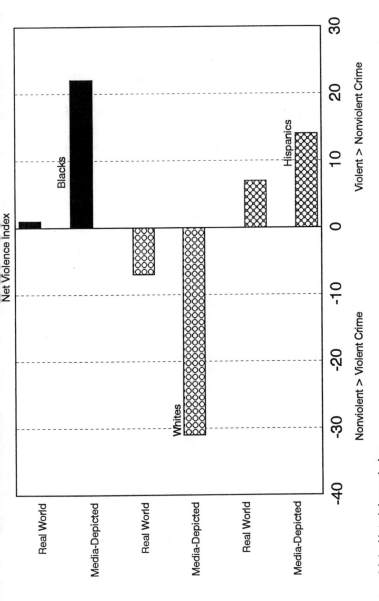

Figure 34.1. Net violence index.

Source: Adult crime rates are taken from the California Department of Justice (1994). News stories are taken from a content analysis of KABC (Channel 7) in Los Angeles from March 1993 to March 1994.

likely to engage in violent crime, the news depicts them as 14 percent more likely to be violent. In sum, the media overrepresents black violent crime significantly, overrepresents Hispanic violent crime slightly, and underrepresents white violent crime dramatically.

To recapitulate, our year-long content analysis of KABC yielded two core findings: First, the local news overrepresents violent crime in general by a factor of more than 2:1, and overrepresents murder by a factor of more than 10:1. Second, the news tends to exaggerate existing racial differences in actual crime rates by disproportionately depicting blacks in the role of violent perpetrators and whites as nonviolent perpetrators. Hispanic perpetrators—both violent and nonviolent—remained relatively invisible. In effect, the news depicts crime in "black and white."

The Experiment

Both findings from the content analysis—the exaggeration of violent crime and the tendency of the news to associate blacks with violent crime and whites with nonviolent crime—were converted into experimental manipulations so as to assess their impact on viewers' beliefs and opinions about crime. Experimentation provides a rigorous as well as realistic paradigm for examining the effects of news coverage of crime. The method developed here consisted of two separate manipulations, (1) the level of criminal violence, and (2) the race of the alleged perpetrator. Study participants were exposed to a news report that described either a violent or non-violent crime in which the perpetrator was either a white or black male.

The most innovative aspect of this design concerned its ability to overcome the problem of confounded or correlated variables. A computer-based technique was used to alter specific physical attributes of an individual (particularly skin color and related features). The original "input" was a local news report which included a close-up "mug shot" of the suspected perpetrator of the crime in question. The picture was digitized, then "painted" to alter the perpetrator's complexion, and then re-edited into the news report. Beginning with two different perpetrators (a white male and a black male), the technique produces painted versions of each individual in which their race is reversed, but *all other features are identical*. Using this method, any differences in the responses of the subjects exposed to the white or black perpetrators can only be attributed to the perpetrator's race.

We conducted a study based on this design in August 1994. Experimental participants were exposed to a fifteen-minute videotaped local newscast (including commercials) that included a report on crime. Depending upon the condition to which they were assigned (at random), they watched a report on a murder at an automated teller machine or a report on a high school baseball coach who embezzled funds from the school's athletic budget.

For both violent and nonviolent crime, the news report featured a close-up photo of either a black or white suspect (using the method described above). Except for the news story on crime, the newscast was identical in all other respects. None of the remaining stories on the tape concerned crime or matters of race. The experimental treatment was inserted into the middle of the tape following the first commercial break.

The experimental "sample" consisted primarily of university administrative and clerical staff (students were excluded) who were recruited through flyers and announcements in newsletters offering $10 for participation in "media research." The age of the participants ranged from 18 to 64. Forty-two percent were white, 24 percent were black, 14 percent were Asian, and 14 percent were Latinos. Fifty-two percent were women. The participants were relatively well educated (40 percent had graduated from college) and, in keeping with the local area, more Democratic than Republican (48 percent versus 28 percent) in their partisan orientation.

The study was administered at the UCLA Communications Research Laboratory (which consists of a two-room suite on campus). On arrival, participants were instructed that the study concerned "selective perception" of local newscasts, and were given a short pretest questionnaire concerning their social background, party identification and political ideology, level of interest in political affairs, and media habits. They then watched the videotape. At the end of the videotape, subjects completed a lengthy questionnaire that included questions about the significance of crime, the causes of crime, their preferred methods for dealing with the problem, and their stereotypes of various social groups including African-Americans. After completing the questionnaire, subjects were debriefed in full (including a full explanation of the experimental procedures) and were paid. To determine the effects of the experimental manipulations on attitudes toward crime, the questionnaire probed subjects' fear of violent crime, their explanations for rising crime, and, finally, their support for punitive policy measures to remedy crime. We also attempted to assess participants' stereotypic beliefs about blacks. The questionnaire asked subjects to rate blacks (and several other groups) in terms of a wide range of attributes three of which were especially relevant to the issue of crime. These were "tend to be violent," "tend to be law abiding," and "tend to be sexually aggressive." We summed these three ratings to form an index of racial stereotyping.

In addition to the main effects of the manipulations, we were also interested in the interaction between the measure of racial stereotyping and exposure to black perpetrators. This interaction reveals whether news coverage of blacks engaging in criminal activity serves to activate longstanding racial stereotypes.

The results showed that the race of the criminal perpetrator significantly influenced both concern for crime and viewers' explanations for the rate of crime. In contrast, the level of violence manipulation failed to affect viewers' opinions. The predicted interaction between the race of the perpetrator manipulation and viewers' racial stereotypes was significant for the level of concern and causal attributions. Among viewers who did not subscribe to negative stereotypes of African Americans, there was little difference in the level of concern for crime between those exposed to the black or white perpetrator. Among viewers with negative stereotypes, however, exposure to the black rather than white perpetrator boosted concern about crime by a factor of .30. The corresponding effect of exposure to the black perpetrator was no less prominent in the case of causal attributions for crime; high stereotypers exposed to a black perpetrator were much more likely than low stereotypers to cite breakdown of the family and religious values in the black community as causes of crime.

In sum, our experimental results underscore the importance of news coverage to public opinion about crime. However, it is race and not violence that is the more important element of crime news coverage. The level of violence in news coverage of crime had no discernible effect on viewers' opinions. However, racial imagery in the news triggered fear of crime and a willingness to hold black people as responsible for crime. A mere three second exposure to a picture of a black perpetrator in a local newscast proved sufficient to boost the level of concern for crime and affect attributions of causal responsibility. The presence of racial cues in the news also activated stereotypic beliefs about African-Americans as antecedents of opinions about crime.

Conclusion

The media has contributed to the current furor over crime. Most Americans do not experience crime directly. They do, however, receive huge doses of crime coverage from the media, especially television news. The market pressures that attract local stations to crime are understandable; our results suggest that these pressures carry a high price tag.

Television's fixation on crime means that it cannot provide adequate coverage to a number of other important social and political issues. As a public trustee, television news is obligated to provide the audience with information about issues that affect the quality of their lives. In Los Angeles these pressing issues include a crumbling physical infrastructure, deteriorating public schools, a stagnant economy, and racial divisions. None of these issues received even a fraction of the coverage accorded crime. If local news is to serve the community, it must be balanced in its coverage of public issues.

Our results also imply that when the media do address crime, the coverage should be more thematic or contextualized. While particular episodes of violent crime may be newsworthy, violent crime only accounts for some one-third of all crime. The overreliance on "body bag" journalism distorts reality. Television news coverage of crime further distorts reality by exaggerating racial differences in the propensity to commit different types of crime. This distortion is likely to impede thoughtful discussion of racial divisions in contemporary American society. Construing the "crime problem" as a "black problem" plays on the public's worst fears and plays into the hand of politicians who are only too happy to exploit these fears.

35 A Model of Communication Effects at the Outbreak of the Gulf War

JOHN R. ZALLER

In a survey completed just 3 days before the start of the Gulf War, polls found the American public deeply divided over the prospect of conflict. In a *New York Times*-CBS News survey, some 47% favored quick military action if Iraq failed to meet the UN deadline for withdrawal from Kuwait, whereas 46% wanted to wait longer to see if the trade embargo and economic sanctions would work. In a follow-up survey taken just after the fighting began, however, 76% said Bush had been right to start the war and only 19% said he should have given economic sanctions longer to work.

In the same set of polls, the percentage of the public who thought it was the "right thing" to send U.S. troops to the Gulf in the first place rose from 64 to 78. Also, public approval of the way Bush was handling his job as president increased from 67% before the fighting started to 84% immediately afterwards.

These large, essentially overnight shifts in mass opinion were scarcely a surprise. Academic studies have shown that the public tends to rally behind the national leadership and its policies in the early stages of foreign crises (Mueller, 1973; Brody, 1991). Politicians, policy-makers and pundits have also noticed the tendency. When, in the course of a study of the effect of public opinion on policy-making, I asked a top Pentagon official whether he had worried about the lack of pre-war support for military action, he replied, "We felt the country basically supported the military effort, and that as soon as the fighting started, there would be a surge of increased support."

This paper will use a standard type of information processing model—the Converse-McGuire model of attitude change—to analyze the public opinion rally that occurred at the start of the Gulf War. The aim is to show how, in general, such rallies occur. The paper also aims to strengthen empirical support for the Converse-McGuire model by establishing its applicability to additional cases, and to make the principles of this important model more widely accessible to interested persons.

In order to maintain the broadest accessibility, the paper relegates all statistical detail to an appendix. The paper does make significant use of math, and unavoidably so. The math—in the form of simple multiplication, like .5 × .5—is used to illustrate the operation of basic principles of the model. This math should present no more of a challenge than reading a train schedule.

Theoretical Background

In a celebrated article, Philip Converse (1964) proposed that political persuasion in response to mass communication depends on a two-step process—exposure to a media message, followed by acceptance of its contents. A few years later, William McGuire (1968) elaborated this basic idea and showed that it could explain numerous, apparently conflicting findings in laboratory studies of persuasion. McGuire gave his model the simple algebraic form that will be used over and over in this article:

$$\text{Probability (Attitude Change)} =$$
$$\text{Prob. (Reception)} \times \text{Prob. (Acceptance I Reception)} \quad [\text{eq. 1}]$$

What, in English, this equation says is that the probability of attitude change equals the probability of receiving a persuasive message times the probability of accepting it, given reception (the symbol " I " means "given"). So, if a person has a .50 probability of receiving a persuasive message and a .5 probability of accepting it, the probability of attitude change is .5 × .5 = .25.

The Converse-McGuire model has, as argued elsewhere (Zaller, 1992), the potential to become a primary theoretical tool in the study of mass communication. What gives the model its value is its capacity to generate theoretically illuminating and readily testable predictions about the process by which mass communication diffuses through society.

This simple model—attitude change equals probability of reception times probability of acceptance—has enormous implications for understanding who can be persuaded by mass communication and who cannot, as we shall shortly be able to see.

To test the model in a mass setting, it is necessary to make auxiliary assumptions about the model's key variables, reception and acceptance, neither of which is observable apart from the attitude change to which they contribute. The assumptions are:

> *Reception Axiom.* The greater a person's level of general political awareness, the greater the likelihood of reception of mass communications, where reception involves both exposure to and comprehension of the given communication.
>
> *Acceptance Axiom.* The greater a person's political awareness, the less the probability of uncritically accepting the contents of mass communications, where acceptance involves bringing one's attitudes into line with the contents of the communication.

By way of illustrating the model, let us imagine that the news media carry a series of stories whose implicit message is, "Bush did the right thing in starting the Gulf War when he did." To make the example entirely concrete, let us further assume (in keeping with the reception axiom) that the probabilities that citizens receive this message increase steadily from .10 to .50 to .90 as political awareness rises from low to middle to high, as shown in the table below. (These numbers, I might add, have been made up to illustrate how reception might increase with awareness; using made-up numbers in this way to illustrate theoretical ideas is called "mathematical simulation." In more complicated form, it is called "computer simulation," and is used throughout the sciences.) Next suppose that, in accord with the acceptance axiom, the probability that people accept the message, given reception of it, declines with awareness, from .90 for the least aware citizens to .10 for the most aware, as also shown below.

Simulated Attitude Change in Response to Persuasive Message

	Level of Awareness		
	Low	Middle	High
Prob. (Reception)	.10	.50	.90
Prob. (Acceptance)	.90	.50	.10
Attitude Change (Reception × Acceptance)	.09	.25	.09

Then, to find expected patterns of attitude change, one must multiply each reception probability by the corresponding acceptance probability, as specified by the McGuire equation; for example, the probability of attitude change among low awareness persons is .10 × .90 = .09; among middle awareness persons, we get .50 × .50 = .25, and so forth. (It is, I should add, essential for readers to verify this and subsequent claims by referring to the table above. One simply cannot understand the Converse-McGuire model or the tests of it in this paper apart from the mathematical principles that underlie the model.)

Upon carrying out this multiplication at each level of political awareness, we find that, as shown in the bottom line of the previous table, people in the middle range of political awareness are most likely to change. This "non-monotonic" pattern is the distinctive signature of the Converse-McGuire model, and is brought about by the following dynamic: The least aware rarely change their attitudes because, although likely to accept whatever they receive, they pay so little attention to politics that they rarely receive any new communication; the most aware receive new communication but are too critically inclined to accept its message, and so they also maintain their attitudes unchanged; this leaves moderately aware citizens most susceptible to influence—they pay enough attention to politics to get new information but are not sufficiently astute to be able to react critically to it.

Although this example illustrates the central idea of the Converse-McGuire model, the model requires some further elaboration to be useful. The reason is that, in most political situations, political awareness has a selective rather than blanket effect on resistance to persuasion. Thus, if a message has a strongly conservative coloration, awareness will have a very slight tendency to make conservatives more resistant to it, an intermediate level tendency to induce greater resistance among centrists, and a great tendency to induce resistance among liberals. If, on the other hand, the message has a liberal coloration, political awareness induces great resistance among conservatives and little among liberals.

A model in which awareness induces this type of selective resistance to persuasion would be expected to generate varying patterns of attitude change in response to mass communication, as the following simulations illustrate:

Simulated Attitude Change in Response to Conservative Message

	Among Conservatives					Among Liberals				
	Level of Awareness					Level of Awareness				
	Low	Middle		High		Low	Middle		High	
Pr (Reception)	.20	.40	.60	.80	1.0	.20	.40	.60	.80	1.0
Pr (Accept I Rec.)	1.0	.90	.80	.70	.60	1.0	.80	.60	.40	.20
Change (Rec. × Acc.)	.20	.36	.48	.56	.60	.20	.32	.36	.32	.20

These tables assume, as before, that the media carry a conservative message on some subject. The tables also assume that reception of the message increases with a person's level of political awareness; thus, among both conservatives and liberals, probabilities of reception increase from a low of .20 among the least aware to a high of 1.0 among the most aware. The key difference between the two tables is the effect of awareness on acceptance: Because the message is conservative, political awareness has relatively little tendency to make conservatives resistant to persuasion (acceptance among conservatives declines from 1.0 to .60 as awareness increases from low to high), and a relatively greater tendency to make liberals more resistant (acceptance declines from 1.0 to 2.0).

If we now multiply the reception and acceptance rows in each table, we obtain the expected patterns of attitude change, as shown in the bottom row of the table. As can be seen, awareness continues to have a non-monotonic association with attitude change among liberals, but among conservatives, the association is now monotonically positive—that is, greater awareness leads to steadily greater levels of attitude change.

The reason for undertaking this lengthy theoretical argument is that we need it to help us understand the nature of attitude change at the start of the Gulf War.

An Initial Look at Data From the Gulf War

It is now time to look at some hard data. The data involve public approval of Bush's handling of the crisis. In the last CBS-*New York Times* survey before the war, 59 percent approved of his handling of the crisis; when fighting began, approval shot up to 84 percent.

The cause of this sudden opinion change was obviously news of the start of the war. In the analysis that follows, this news will be conceptualized as a "conservative message" diffusing through a population in the manner specified by the Converse-McGuire model.

The first requirement for using the Converse-McGuire model is a measure of political awareness. The CBS-NYT surveys carried no direct measure of political awareness, but they did carry a four-point education variable that can, as other research has shown, be used as a rough proxy for political awareness (Zaller, 1990). To emphasize the theoretical use to which the education variable is put, I shall always refer to it as a measure of awareness.

We begin by examining the effect of the start of the war on the way conservatives evaluated Bush, as shown in the left-hand panel of Figure 35.1. As can be seen, there was a jump in approval of Bush's handling of the gulf crisis after the war began, an increase that appears at first glance roughly equal in magnitude in each category of political awareness. A more careful examination, however, reveals a more subtle pattern.

Let us look first at the least aware conservatives. In the post-war survey, 59 percent of these conservatives approved of Bush's handling of the crisis, which left 41 percent (100 − 59 = 41) available for conversion. (The reader should verify each step of the analysis by re-examining the figure.) As it turned out, 21 percent of the least aware conservatives actually converted (80 − 59 = 21). Thus, the probability of attitude change among the least aware conservatives was 21/41 = .51, or 51 percent.

Among the most aware conservatives, 78 percent approved of Bush's handling of the crisis prior to the start of war, which means that 22 percent (100 − 78 = 22) were available for attitude change. The percent who

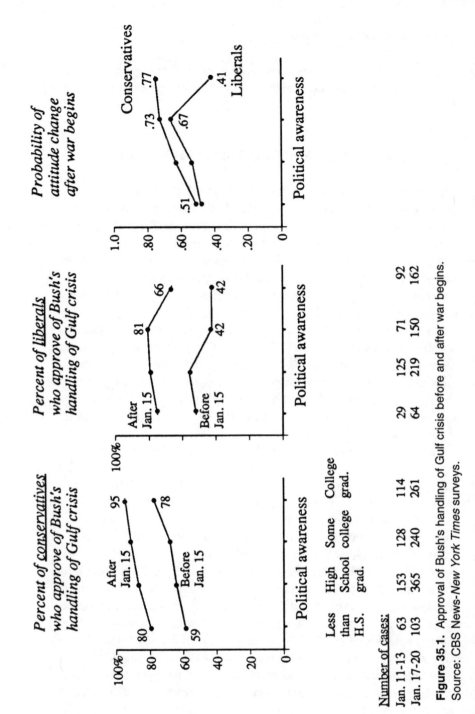

Figure 35.1. Approval of Bush's handling of Gulf crisis before and after war begins.
Source: CBS News–*New York Times* surveys.

actually did change was 17 percent (95 − 78 = 17). Thus, the probability of attitude change in this group was 17/22 = .77, or 77 percent.

The change probabilities for conservatives at each level of awareness are shown in the right-hand portion of the figure, where it can be seen that the probability of attitude change among conservatives rises steadily as political awareness rises, from 51 percent among the least aware conservatives to 77 percent among the most aware.

When the same calculations are made for liberals, we find that there is a nonmonotonic relationship between political awareness and probability of attitude change, as also shown in the right-hand panel of Figure 35.1. Thus, the overall pattern of attitude change—where change has been measured as the *probability of change among the unconverted* within each group rather than as raw volume of change—conforms exactly to expectations derived from the Converse-McGuire model.

I chose this case to examine because the raw data are unusually well-behaved—that is, unusually free of the effects of chance variation. For the other cases, there is more random fluctuation in the data and hence a need to employ a statistical model to be certain whether the expected pattern of attitude change is actually present.

As indicated earlier, I am relegating all issues of statistical modeling to an appendix, so that my presentation in the body of the paper will report only the finished results of the modeling. That appendix is not included in this reprint of the article, but may be found in Zaller (1994).

Graphical Representations of Attitude Change

Figure 35.2 presents the fruits of the statistical modeling, which are estimated patterns of attitude change on three questions—whether the U.S. was right to start the war when the U.N. deadline expired, whether it was the "right thing" for the U.S. to send ground troops to the middle east in the first place, and approval of George Bush's overall performance as president. In each case, the figure shows the percent of persons not already holding the given attitude who changed their opinion once the fighting began. The results, thus, parallel those reported in the right-hand panel of Figure 35.1.

As can be seen, the patterns of opinion change for all three items exhibit the characteristic non-monotonicity of the Converse-McGuire

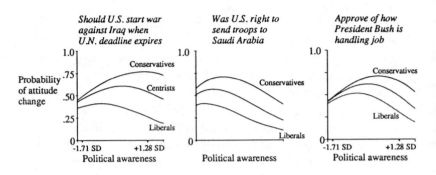

Figure 35.2. Patterns of attitude change at start of Gulf War.
Note: Estimates are based on model in text, coefficients in first table, and coding procedures described in Appendix (not provided).
Source: CBS News-*New York Times* and National Election Studies surveys.

model. This nonmonotonicity, as explained earlier, arises from the resistance of the most aware citizens to messages that conflict with their partisan orientations. Because the implicit message from the start of the Gulf War was conservative—something like, "the conservative Republican president has ordered this military action and it has been a success"—we expect resistance, and hence the tendency toward nonmonotonicity, to be greatest among liberals, next greatest among centrists, and least pronounced among conservatives. Figure 35.2 confirms this expectation.

There are, however, notable differences in the patterns of attitude change across the three cases. The item on the left conforms to the pattern examined earlier, but the other two patterns look substantially different. These differences are quite real and, as I will show in the next section, readily explicable within the model. Before developing this explanation, however, it is useful to examine a case that presents yet another characteristic pattern of attitude change. That case, shown in Figure 35.3, involves public attitudes toward defense spending, which became markedly more "anti-spending" between 1980 and 1982 in response to a series of media reports about Pentagon waste and abuse (see Zaller, 1992, Chapters 2, 7).

The most obvious difference between this case and the Gulf War is that, when the issue was cuts in defense spending, liberals were most responsive to the media reports and conservatives least responsive, which is a

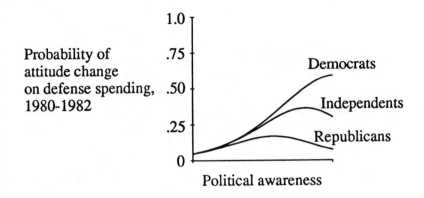

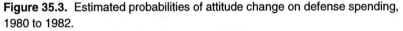

Figure 35.3. Estimated probabilities of attitude change on defense spending, 1980 to 1982.
Note: Estimates are derived from Table 7.3 in Zaller (1992).

reversal of the pattern in the cases from the Gulf War. This difference, of course, arises from differences in the ideological coloration of the change-inducing messages (liberal in the defense case, conservative in the gulf cases). Another difference—and the one most important for the present analysis—is that, for the defense item, attitude change is concentrated among the more aware half of the population, whereas for the Gulf items, change is centered among the middle-aware to less-aware. It is this difference that makes the shapes of the attitude change curves look so different in the two sets of cases.

To explain such differences in patterns of attitude change, we must return to the basic principles of the Converse-McGuire model to engage in some more mathematical simulation. Readers whose patience for simple mathematical simulation has now been exhausted may be forgiven if they forego this additional material. It is no more difficult than what has come before, but there is a fair bit more of it. The important point for readers quitting at this point may be summarized as follows:

Persuasion in response to mass communication depends on a two-step process in which a person's level of general political awareness has a positive effect on the chance of receiving mass communication and a negative effect on the chance of uncritical acceptance of it, where "uncritical acceptance" refers to acceptance of messages that go against one's ideology.

For readers interested in pursuing this venture in mathematical modeling and simulation, we shall be attempting to understand the expected theoretical effect of two additional variables—the intensity of the change-inducing mass communication, and the degree of prior crystallization of the attitude that the communication seeks to change. Let us begin by imagining two messages, one having *low intensity* or loudness and the other having high intensity. We imagine the pattern of reception of the low intensity message to be as follows:

	Level of Political Awareness				
	Low		Middle		High
Prob. (Reception)	.05	.25	.45	.65	.85

Thus, a person at the lowest awareness level has a .05 probability of receiving the message, and so forth. Now let us consider reception patterns for the second, higher intensity message:

	Level of Political Awareness				
Prob. (Reception)	.40	.60	.80	1.0	1.0

Here, a low-awareness person has a .40 probability of receiving the message, and so forth. At each level of awareness, reception is higher for the more intense message.

In order to complete specification of the attitude change process, we need a set of acceptance rates. The following acceptance probabilities can be used because, as required by the Acceptance Axiom, they decline with political awareness:

	Level of Political Awareness				
Prob. (Acceptance I Rec.)	.90	.75	.50	.25	.10

Finally, to calculate the expected patterns of attitude change for a low and a high intensity message, we bring together the corresponding sets of reception and acceptance probabilities and multiply them, as follows:

	Low Intensity Message				High Intensity Message				
	Level of Awareness				Level of Awareness				
	Low	Middle	High		Low	Middle	High		
Pr (Reception)	.05	.25 .45	.65	.85	.40	.60 .80	1.0	1.0	
Pr (Acceptance I Rec.)	.90	.75 .50	.25	.10	.90	.75 .50	.25	.10	
Change (Rec. × Acc.)	.05	.19 .23	.16	.09	.36	.45 .40	.25	.10	

As would be expected, more attitude change results from the higher intensity message. But note also that the shapes of the change curves are different: The higher intensity message produces a larger fraction of its opinion change among less aware persons, because it reaches many more of them than does the low intensity message.

The intensity or loudness of persuasive communications, thus, is one factor that affects the pattern of attitude change. A second factor affecting these patterns is the strength of people's pre-existing opinions. As I have argued elsewhere, one would expect that acceptance rates, given reception of a persuasive message, would be higher when initial attitudes are less strong or well-crystallized. The following reception-acceptance table shows the effects of such differences in acceptance rates:

	Weaker Initial Opinion				Stronger Initial Opinion				
	Level of Awareness				Level of Awareness				
	Low	Middle	High		Low	Middle	High		
Pr (Reception)	.40	.60 .80	1.0	1.0	.40	.60 .80	1.0	1.0	
Pr (Acceptance I Rec.)	.95	.80 .65	.50	.35	.65	.50 .35	.20	.05	
Change (Rec. × Acc.)	.38	.48 .52	.50	.35	.26	.30 .28	.20	.05	

Note that the reception rates are identical in both tables, which indicates that the message has the same intensity in both tables. What differs are the acceptance rates, which are uniformly higher for the case in which the public has less crystallized or weaker initial attitudes. Multiplication of reception and acceptance probabilities then yields the change rates shown in the bottom row of the table.

The key point here is that when initial attitudes are firmer, a higher fraction of attitude change is concentrated among less politically aware citizens, and that this difference holds controlling for message intensity.

These simulations demonstrate that quite different patterns of attitude change must be expected, depending on the intensity of the change-inducing communication and the firmness of the public's pre-existing attitudes. To get a systematic overview of possibilities, I developed the typology shown in Figure 35.4. The typology, which is based on the same type of mathematical simulation just reported, depicts cases involving three levels of message intensity (low, middle, high) and two levels of initial attitude strength (weak and strong). Within each of the six panels, we see the simulated responses of liberals, centrists, and conservatives to a conservative message.

Figure 35.4 should be understood as an unusually elaborate and specific set of theoretical expectations about how patterns of attitude change should vary across different cases, given messages that vary in intensity and attitudes that vary in initial strength. The typology was developed to fit the particular set of empirical cases examined in Zaller (1992), but the expectation was that it would have general applicability. We shall now consider whether the typology holds for the three new cases of attitude change from the Gulf War.

News reports at the start of the Gulf War constituted, by any standard, a very high intensity message. War reporting dominated national TV news and newspaper front pages almost to the exclusion of anything else. We should therefore expect patterns of attitude change that resemble one of the high intensity panels in Figure 35.4 (either panel C or panel F). That is, we should expect to find patterns in which a large fraction of attitude change is centered among moderately aware and less aware persons. As can be seen by looking back at the attitude change data in Figure 35.2, this expectation is met for all three items. (Comparisons between Figures 35.2 and 35.4 can be made because the political awareness variables in each have been standardized to the same range.)

A more difficult problem is how to classify the three opinion items in terms of initial attitude strength or crystallization. For at least one of the items, however, there is a clear external basis for judgment. In an earlier study, I argued that popular judgments of President Reagan's job performance are likely to depend on greater amounts of stored information than are opinions on typical issues, and should therefore conform to the

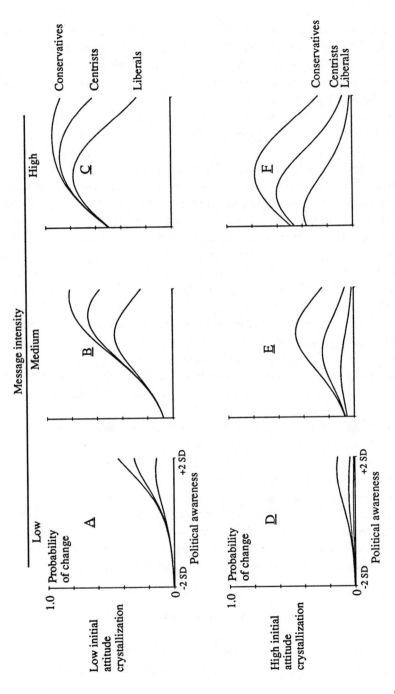

Figure 35.4. Simulated effects of message intensity and attitude crystallization on opinion change.

pattern for better crystallized attitudes (Zaller, 1992, pp. 158-159). That argument ought to apply equally to judgments of President Bush's job performance. Hence, from past work, my expectation must be that the pattern of change for the Bush item will conform to the pattern of panel F in the typology rather than to panel C.

A check back to the Bush data in Figure 35.2 reveals that the pattern of change falls between the patterns for panel C and panel F, but is closer to F.[1]

No comparable external basis exists for classifying the remaining two items. As a matter of post hoc analysis, however, a case can be made that the public's attitudes on whether it was right to send U.S. troops to the Gulf were initially better crystallized than attitudes on the "start war" item. Sending U.S. troops to the Gulf had been the official, well-publicized, and largely non-controversial policy of the U.S. government for five months at the time of the outbreak of the war, so that interested citizens had ample opportunity to determine where they stood. By contrast, it was never official U.S. policy to start military action when the U.N. deadline expired, partisan elites never reached any agreement on the question, and the issue itself had existed only since the U.N. vote on November 29. Even in the Congressional debate on the authorization of war, many administration supporters stopped well short of arguing for an early war, maintaining instead that passage of the war resolution would make war less likely; and even after Congress approved the use of force against Iraq, President Bush continued to insist that he had not made up his mind when to initiate military action. In these ambiguous circumstances, it is likely that many citizens, including politically attentive ones, had not yet made up their minds on this issue.

By this line of admittedly post hoc reasoning, we should expect the "right thing" item to manifest the pattern of attitude change associated with stronger attitudes, and the "start war" item to exhibit the pattern associated with weaker attitudes, which is what we find in a comparison of Figure 35.2 and with Panels C and F of the typology.

Discussion

This paper has sought to show that the opinion rallies that often accompany foreign policy crises result from the diffusion of an ideologically cued media message through a mass citizenry that differs in its predispositions to receive and accept such messages. A generic type of information-processing model, the Converse-McGuire model of attitude change, appears to do an excellent job of capturing the essential features of this communication process. Thus, opinion rallies do not, as might have been supposed, operate under special rules. Rather, they operate under completely standard rules, except, as Brody (1991) has long argued, with the intensity of communication flow turned to extra high.[2]

Notes

1. The similarity to panel F is, moreover, greater than it presently appears. The typology was designed to be used in connection with relatively reliable measures of political awareness. Yet, as explained earlier, it has been necessary in the CBS-NYT data to use education, a distinctly second-best measure, to capture the effects awareness. An indication of the cost incurred by this substitution is that the correlation between a four-point education variable and a good measure of awareness (namely, a standard NES information scale) is only about .50. Thus, the use of education to measure awareness introduces a substantial amount of measurement error. If any plausible reliability correction is made in order to compensate for this measurement error—that is, if the awareness coefficients are boosted as they are in normal corrections for measurement error (see Bartels, 1993)—the pattern of change for the Bush item corresponds very closely to Panel F. Specifically, boosting awareness coefficients by a factor of 1.5 to 2.0 generates graphical estimated patterns for the Bush item that are nearly identical to those of Panel F. Since I am unable to derive the reliability correction formula for the reception-acceptance model, I cannot be sure how close the correspondence is, but it is surely closer than appears from the data presented here.

2. Besides the cases analyzed in this paper, there have been, to my knowledge, eight applications of some form of the Converse-McGuire model to data on attitude change; these cases have involved the following topics: Vote choice (Converse, 1964; Dreyer, 1971); the country's most important problem (MacKuen, 1984); the Vietnam war and gay rights (Zaller, 1984); U.S. involvement in Central America, President Reagan's job approval, and U.S. defense spending (Zaller, 1992).

References

Altheide, D. (1976). *Creating reality: How TV news distorts events.* Beverly Hills, CA: Sage.

Ansolabehere, S., & Iyengar, S. (1995). *Going negative: How attack ads shrink and polarize the electorate.* New York: Free Press.

Atwood, L. E., Sohn, A., & Sohn, H. (1978). Daily newspaper contributions to community discussion. *Journalism Quarterly, 55,* 570-576.

Bartels, L. (1993). Messages received: The political impact of message exposure. *American Political Science Review, 87,* 267-285.

Becker, L., & McCombs, M. (1978). The role of the press in determining voter reactions to presidential primaries. *Human Communication Research, 4,* 301-307.

Behr, R. L., & Iyengar, S. (1985). Television news, real-world cues, and changes in the public agenda. *Public Opinion Quarterly, 49,* 38-57.

Bennett, W. L. (1988). *News: The politics of illusion.* White Plains, NY: Longman.

Benton, M., & Frazier, P. J. (1976). The agenda-setting function of the mass media at three levels of information-holding. *Communication Research, 3,* 261-274.

Berelson, B., Lazarsfeld, P., & McPhee, W. (1954). *Voting: A study of opinion formation in a presidential campaign.* Chicago: University of Chicago Press.

Blumer, H. (1948). Public opinion and public opinion polling. *American Sociological Review, 13,* 542-554.

Blumer, H. (1971). Social problems as collective behavior. *Social Problems, 18,* 298-306.

Brody, R. (1991). *Assessing the president.* Stanford, CA: Stanford University Press.

Brosius, H.-B., & Kepplinger, H. M. (1990). The agenda-setting function of television news: Static and dynamic views. *Communication Research, 17,* 183-211.

California Department of Justice, Law Enforcement Information Center. (1994). *Adult and juvenile arrests reported.* Sacramento, CA: Author.

Campbell, A., Converse, P., Miller, W., & Stokes, D. (1960). *The American voter.* New York: John Wiley.

Cohen, B. (1963). *The press and foreign policy.* Princeton, NJ: Princeton University Press.

Cohen, D. (1975). *A report on a non-election agenda-setting study.* Ottawa, Canada: Association for Education in Journalism.

Converse, P. (1964). Information flow and the stability of partisan attitudes. *Public Opinion Quarterly, 26,* 578-599.

Dearing, J. W., & Rogers, E. M. (1992). AIDS and the media agenda. In T. Edgar, M. A. Fitzpatrick, & V. Freimuth (Eds.), *AIDS: A communication perspective.* Hillsdale, NJ: Lawrence Erlbaum.

Dearing, J. W., & Rogers, E. M. (1996). *Agenda setting.* Thousand Oaks, CA: Sage.

Delli Carpini, M. X., & Keeter, S. (1991). Stability and change in the U.S. public's knowledge of politics. *Public Opinion Quarterly, 55,* 583-612.

Downs, A. (1972). Up and down with ecology: The issue attention cycle. *Public Interest, 28,* 38-50.

Dreyer, E. C. (1971). Media use and electoral choices: Some political consequences of information exposure. *Public Opinion Quarterly, 35,* 544-553.

Eaton, H., Jr. (1989). Agenda setting with bi-weekly data on content of three national media. *Journalism Quarterly, 66,* 942-948.

Entman, R. (1993). Framing: Toward clarification of a fractured paradigm. *Journal of Communication, 43,* 51-58.

Epstein, E. J. (1973). *News from nowhere.* New York: Vintage.

Erbring, L., Goldenberg, E., & Miller, A. (1980). Front page news and real world cues: A new look at agenda-setting. *American Journal of Political Science, 24,* 16-49.

Funkhouser, G. R. (1973). The issues of the sixties: An exploratory study in the dynamics of public opinion. *Public Opinion Quarterly, 37,* 62-75.

Gamson, W. (1992). *Talking politics.* New York: Cambridge University Press.

Gans, H. W. (1979). *Deciding what's news.* New York: Vantage.

Ghanem, S., & Evatt, D. (1995). *Media coverage and public concern about crime: An exploration of the second dimension of agenda-setting.* Paper presented at the Annual Meeting of the World Association for Public Opinion Research, The Hague, The Netherlands.

Hoyningen-Huene, P. (1993). *Reconstructing scientific revolutions; Thomas S. Kuhn's philosophy of science* (A. T. Levine, Trans.). Chicago: University of Chicago Press.

Iyengar, S. (1991). *Is anyone responsible? How television frames political issues.* Chicago: University of Chicago Press.

Iyengar, S., & Kinder, D. (1987). *News that matters: Television and American opinion.* Chicago: University of Chicago Press.

Iyengar, S., Peters, M. D., & Kinder, D. R. (1982). Experimental demonstrations of the 'not-so-minimal' consequences of television news programs. *American Political Science Review, 76,* 848-858.

Kinder, D. R. (1986). Presidential character revisited. In R. R. Lau & D. O. Sears (Eds.), *Political cognition.* Hillsdale, NJ: Lawrence Erlbaum.

Kingdon, J. W. (1984). *Agendas, alternatives, and public policies.* Boston, MA: Little Brown.

Krosnick, J. A., & Brannon, L. A. (1993). The impact of the Gulf War on the ingredients of presidential evaluations: Multidimensional effects of political involvement. *American Political Science Review, 87,* 963-975.

Krosnick, J. A., & Brannon, L. A. (1995). *New evidence on news media priming: In 1992, it was the economy!* Paper presented at the Annual Meeting of the American Association for Public Opinion Research, Chicago.

Krosnick, J. A., & Kinder, D. R. (1990). Altering the foundations of support for the president through priming. *American Political Science Review, 84,* 497-512.

Kuhn, T. S. (1970). *The structure of scientific revolutions.* Chicago: University of Chicago Press. (Originally published 1962)

Liebes, T., & Katz, E. (1990). *The export of meaning.* New York: Oxford University Press.

Lippmann, W. (1922). *Public opinion.* New York: Macmillan.

MacKuen, M. (1984). Exposure to information, belief integration, and individual responsiveness to agenda change. *American Political Science Review, 78,* 372-391.

McCarthy, J., & Zald, M. N. (1977). Resource mobilization and social movements: A partial theory. *American Journal of Sociology, 82,* 1212-1241.

McCombs, M. E. (1981). The agenda-setting approach. In D. D. Sidney & K. R. Sidney (Eds.), *Handbook of political communication*. Beverly Hills, CA: Sage.

McCombs, M. E. (1992). Explorers and surveyors: Expanding strategies for agenda-setting research. *Journalism Quarterly, 69*, 813-824.

McCombs, M. E. (1994). The future agenda for agenda-setting research. *Journal of Mass Communication Studies, 45*, 181-197.

McCombs, M., & Bell, T. (in press). The agenda-setting role of mass communication. In M. Salwen & D. Stacks (Eds.), *An integrated approach to communication theory and research*. Hillsdale, NJ: Lawrence Erlbaum.

McCombs, M., & Evatt, D. (1995). Los temas y los aspectos: Explorando una nueva dimension de la agenda-setting. *Communication y Sociedad, 8,* 7-32.

McCombs, M., & Shaw, D. (1972). The agenda-setting function of mass media. *Public Opinion Quarterly, 36,* 176-185.

McGuire, W. J. (1968). Personality and susceptibility to social influence. In E. F. Borgatta & W. W. Lambert (Eds.), *Handbook of personality theory and research* (pp. 1130-1187). Chicago: Rand McNally.

McGuire, W. (1969). The nature of attitudes and attitude change. In G. Lindzey & E. Aronson (Eds.), *Handbook of social psychology* (Vol. 3). Reading, MA: Addison-Wesley.

Mead, T. D. (1994). The daily newspaper as political agenda-setter: The *Charlotte Observer* and metropolitan reform. *State and Local Government Review, 26,* 27-37.

Miller, J. M. (1995). *Mediators and moderators of agenda-setting and priming.* Unpublished master's thesis, Ohio State University, Columbus, OH.

Molotch, H. L., Protess, D. L., & Gordon, M. T. (1987). The media-policy connection: Ecology of news. In D. Paletz (Ed.), *Political communication: Theories, cases and assessments*. Norwood, NJ: Ablex.

Mueller, J. (1973). *War, presidents and public opinion*. New York: John Wiley.

Neuman, W. R. (1986). *The paradox of mass politics*. Cambridge, MA: Harvard University Press.

Neuman, W. R., Just, M. R., & Crigler, A. N. (1992). *Common knowledge: News and the construction of meaning*. Chicago: University of Chicago Press.

Neustadt, R. E. (1960). *Presidential power*. New York: John Wiley.

Protess, D. L., Cook, F. L., Curtin, T. R., Gordon, M. T., Leff, D. R., McCombs, M. E., & Miller, P. (1987). The impact of investigative reporting on public opinion and policy making. *Public Opinion Quarterly, 51,* 166-185.

Protess, D. L., Cook, F. L., Doppelt, J. C., Ettema, J. S., Gordon, M. T., Leff, D. R., & Miller, P. (1991). *The journalism of outrage*. New York: Guilford.

Protess, D. L., Leff, D. R., Brooks, S. C., & Gordon, M. T. (1985). Uncovering rape: The watchdog press and the limits of agenda-setting. *Public Opinion Quarterly, 49,* 19-37.

Putnam, R. (1994). *Bowling alone: Democracy in America at the end of the twentieth century*. Paper presented at the Nobel Symposium "Democracy's Victory and Crisis," August 27-30, Uppsala, Sweden.

Rahn, W. M., Aldrich, J., & Borgida, E. (1994). Individual and contextual variations in political candidate appraisal. *American Political Science Review 88,* 193-199.

Rivers, D., & Rose, N. (1981). *Passing the president's program*. Paper presented at the Annual Meeting of the Midwest Political Science Association, Chicago.

Robinson, J. P., & Levy, M. R. (1986). *The main source: Learning from television news*. Newbury Park, CA: Sage.

Rogers, E. M. (1994). *A history of communication study: A biographical approach*. New York: Free Press.

Rogers, E. M. (1995). *Diffusion of innovations*. New York: Free Press.

Rogers, E. M., & Dearing, J. W. (1988). Agenda-setting research: Where has it been? Where is it going? In J. A. Anderson (Ed.), *Communication yearbook 11*. Newbury Park, CA: Sage.

Rogers, E. M., Dearing, J. W, & Bregman, D. (1993). The anatomy of agenda-setting research. *Journal of Communication, 43*, 68-84.

Rogers, E. M., Dearing, J. W., & Chang, S. (1991). AIDS in the 1980s: The agenda-setting process for a public issue. *Journalism Monographs, 126*, pp. 1-47.

Shaw, D., & McCombs, M. (Eds.). (1977). *The emergence of American political issues*. St. Paul, MN: West.

Takeshita, T., & Mikami, S. (1995). How did mass media influence the voters' choice in the 1993 general election in Japan?: A study of agenda-setting. *Keio Communication Review, 17*, 27-41.

Tankard, J. W., Jr. (1990). Maxwell McCombs, Donald Shaw, and agenda-setting. In W. D. Sloan (Ed.), *Makers of the media mind: Journalism educators and their ideas* (pp. 278-286). Hillsdale, NJ: Lawrence Erlbaum.

Times Mirror Center for the People and the Press. (1994). *Eight nation, people and the press survey: Mixed message about press freedom on both sides of the Atlantic*. New York: Author.

Trumbo, C. (1995). Longitudinal modeling of public issues: An application of the agenda-setting process to the issue of global warming. *Journalism Monographs, 152*, pp. 1-57.

Weaver, D., Graber, D., McCombs, M., & Eyal, C. (1981). *Media agenda setting in a presidential election: Issues, images and interest*. New York: Praeger.

Weaver, D. H. (1977). Political issues and voter need for orientation. In D. L. Shaw & M. E. McCombs (Eds.), *The emergence of American political issues: The agenda-setting function of the press*. St. Paul, MN: West.

Weaver, P. (1972). Is television news biased? *Public Interest, 56*, 57-74.

Weaver, P. (1994). *The culture of lying: How journalism really works*. New York: Free Press.

Winter, J., & Eyal, C. (1981). Agenda setting for the civil rights issue. *Public Opinion Quarterly, 45*, 376-383.

Zaller, J. (1984). *The role of elites in shaping public opinion*. Unpublished doctoral dissertation, University of California, Berkeley.

Zaller, J. (1990). Political awareness, elite opinion leadership, and the mass survey response. *Social Cognition, 8*, 125-153.

Zaller, J. (1992). *The nature and origins of mass opinion*. New York: Cambridge University Press.

Zaller, J. (1994). Strategic politicians, public opinion and the Gulf crisis. In W. L. Bennett & D. L. Paletz (Eds.), *Taken by storm: The media, public opinion, and U.S. foreign policy in the Gulf War* (pp. 250-276). Chicago: University of Chicago Press.

PART V

The Use of the Media
in the Policy Process

36 Overview

SHANTO IYENGAR

The disclosure in the *Wall Street Journal* that Energy Secretary Hazel O'Leary had paid a consulting firm $43,000 to investigate the department's image in the national press prompted outrage in Washington. Several senators and congressmen denounced the action as inappropriate for a government agency and demanded that the money be refunded to taxpayers. President Clinton demanded an explanation. In defense of her decision, Ms. O'Leary pointed out that such "press profile" studies are standard practice in the public sector, and that she was seeking only to make her department a more effective communicator.

What Ms. O'Leary could have said (but did not) is that her critics were themselves heavy users of the media. The same senators, congressmen, and presidential aides who expressed anger at the Energy Department study are more than happy to "leak" information to the press when it suits their needs. Hundreds of thousands of tax dollars are used to maintain vast staffs within the executive and legislative branches of government, whose job responsibilities include seeing to it that the media depict their boss in the most favorable light possible. At the White House, the Office of the Press Secretary has grown exponentially over the past three decades, and "media management" is widely recognized as the key to any president's ability to get his administration's policy agenda enacted. It is revealing that when the Clinton administration encountered a series of stinging rebuffs from the Democratic-controlled Congress, among their first actions was the hiring of Republican David Gergen as a "communications" adviser. Today, the use of the mass media to promote an agency's or public official's policy objectives is common practice among both those who wield power and those who seek to influence them. The battleground for control and influence over public policies has shifted from the halls and corridors of government offices to broadcasting studios and editorial offices.

Why have reporters, editors, and producers become such important players in the policy process? In the first place, the trend is simply an extension of political campaigns. The candidates who manage to get elected accumulate media skills and resources; to win, they must learn how to use reporters and craft messages that make them appear effective, responsible, and appealing. These same skills and resources are easily transferred to the task of governing. Of course, the people and consulting firms that run election campaigns are delighted to be of service even after the election has been won.

The more crucial reason for the use of media strategies to govern is that they work. Put simply, elected officials who enjoy a high level of public approval are more powerful. The president who attracts and maintains favorable press coverage enjoys a higher level of public popularity; the higher his popularity, the more likely Congress to defer to his administration's legislative priorities. Conversely, the more controversial the message emanating from Washington (or the state capitol for that matter), the less likely the chief executive to enjoy legislative success. In effect, politicians now must continuously vie for public approval; media campaigns are permanent affairs.

The new style of governing—what Sam Kernell has called "going public"—is also a consequence of the gradual erosion of traditional methods of leadership. In the past, presidents and legislators would engage in bargaining and coalition formation; a Republican senator might back a Democratic administration's budget proposals in exchange for the location of some federal project in his home state. Policy making was characterized by a spirit of bipartisanship, accommodation, and the brokering of competing interests. As political parties withered and candidates became autonomous, this style of leadership proved ineffective. Power in government became more a function of public image and less dependent on seniority, rank, or expertise.

Three of the selections reprinted in this section discuss the shift from old-fashioned methods of political leadership to the new media-based strategies. First, Sam Kernell, who was the first to put his finger on this trend, traces the erosion of the bargaining model in Washington and the corresponding increased importance of public opinion as a litmus test of the president's credibility. Richard Anderson goes one step further and argues that the strategic use of political rhetoric so crucial to going public characterizes all forms of government, including those that are authoritarian. Leech, Baumgartner, and Jones examine the importance of public opinion in setting the congressional agenda. They show that Congress is more likely to pay attention (by holding legislative hearings) to issues when these issues are highlighted by the news media. Presumably, congressional leaders respond more promptly when issues are newsworthy not because they suspect that newsworthiness is a good barometer of the substantive importance of the issue but rather that the public is concerned about these issues.

The day-to-day activities that make up the new media-based forms of governance occur in Washington. The most regular of such activities is the White House press briefing. As the briefing reprinted here illustrates, the press secretary has considerable influence over what gets reported. By getting the press to focus on the administration's perspective on issues, the president's image as an effective leader is bolstered.

A more direct form of opinion leadership occurs through the scheduling of media events at which the president or other high officials speak directly to the public. In this case, President Clinton used a White House ceremony to praise the AmeriCorps program—an effort to fund community-based action (supported by both Democrats and Republicans) to combat the syndrome of poverty, crime, and drug abuse.

Elected officials are by no means alone in the media jungle. Interest groups, political action committees, foreign governments, and others with a stake in the policy process have adapted to the new rules of the game; they too cultivate "good press," invest in advertising campaigns, and brandish poll results in support of their views. Jarol Manheim has examined the efforts of foreign governments to influence U.S. foreign policy by winning the minds and hearts of ordinary Americans. When Iraq invaded Kuwait, one of the first steps taken by oil-rich Kuwait was to engage one of the most prominent American public relations firms— Hill and Knowlton. As Manheim suggests, Hill and Knowlton treated the Kuwaitis in much the same manner as a political candidate; they carried out market research and identified the message most likely to evoke public sympathy.

The rich and powerful are not the only ones who stand to gain from going public. Michael Pertschuk, the former head of the Federal Trade

Commission, describes efforts by several nonprofit organizations to put pressure on government decision makers in the form of media campaigns including a series of television advertisements in support of gun control that feature some of this country's most well-known and recognized figures. Susan Bales and Vincent Schiraldi of the Benton Foundation and Center on Juvenile and Criminal Justice, respectively, whose constituency is children and adolescents, argue that advocacy groups cannot assume that reporters are their allies; instead they must elicit sustained and favorable news coverage of the problems they seek to address by taking advantage of the norms and procedures of modern journalism. In this section's final paper, Liana Winett, of the Berkeley Media Studies Group, whose own policy interests lie in the public health area, describes specific methods by which policy advocates can maximize their leverage over news coverage.

37 The Theory and Practice of Going Public

SAM KERNELL

When President Bush delivered his State of the Union address to the joint assembly of the mostly Democratic Congress in January 1992, he assumed what has become a familiar stance with Congress:

> I pride myself that I am a prudent man, and I believe that patience is a virtue. But I understand that politics is for some a game. . . . I submit my plan tomorrow. And I am asking you to pass it by March 20. And I ask the American people to let you know they want this action by March 20.
> From the day after that, if it must be: The battle is joined.
> And you know when principle is at stake, I relish a good fair fight.

Once upon a time, these might have been fighting words, but in this era of divided government, with the legislative and executive branches controlled by different parties, and presidents who therefore routinely enlist public support in their dealings with other Washington politicians, such rhetoric caused hardly a ripple in Congress.

By 1992, presidential appeals for public support had, in fact, become commonplace. Jimmy Carter delivered four major television addresses on the energy crisis alone and was about to give a fifth when his pollster convinced him that he would be wasting his time. Richard Nixon employed

EDITORS' NOTE: From *Going Public*, CQ Press, 1993, pp. 1-6, 9-10, 14-15, 30-31. Reprinted with permission of the publisher.

primetime television so extensively to promote his policies on Vietnam that the Federal Communications Commission (FCC) took an unprecedented step when it applied the "fairness doctrine" to a presidential appeal and granted critics of the war response time on the networks. (In the past, the FCC had occasionally invoked the "equal time" rule during presidential campaigns.) More than any other of Bush's predecessors, Ronald Reagan excelled in rallying public opinion behind presidential policies, but by the end of his second term, he had worn out his welcome with the networks, who stood to lose at least $200,000 in advertising each time he delivered one of his primetime addresses. They instituted an independent assessment of the likely newsworthiness of the president's address, thereby managing to pare down the frequency of Reagan's televised speeches.

I call the approach to presidential leadership that has lately come into vogue at the White House "going public." It is a strategy whereby a president promotes himself and his policies in Washington by appealing to the American public for support. Forcing compliance from fellow Washingtonians by going over their heads to appeal to their constituents is a tactic not unknown during the first half of the century, but it was seldom attempted. Theodore Roosevelt probably first enunciated the strategic principle of going public when he described the presidency as the "bully pulpit." Moreover, he occasionally put theory into practice with public appeals for his Progressive reforms. During the next 30 years, other presidents also periodically summoned public support to help them in their dealings with Congress. Perhaps the most famous such instance is Woodrow Wilson's ill-fated whistle-stop tour of the country on behalf of his League of Nations treaty. Another historic example is Franklin D. Roosevelt's series of radio "fireside chats," which were designed less to subdue congressional opposition than to remind politicians throughout Washington of his continuing national mandate for the New Deal.

These historical instances are significant in large part because they were rare. Unlike President Nixon, who thought it important "to spread the White House around," these earlier presidents were largely confined to Washington and obliged to speak to the country through the nation's newspapers. The concept and legitimizing precedents of going public may have been established during these years, but the emergence of presidents who *routinely* do so to promote their policies in Washington awaited the development of modern systems of transportation and mass communications. Going public should be appreciated as a strategic adaptation to the information age.

Going public merits study because presidents now appeal to the public routinely. But there is another reason as well. Compared with many other aspects of the modern presidency, going public has received scant attention in the scholarly literature. In part this can be attributed to its recent arrival in the president's repertoire, but by itself this explanation is inadequate. Although going public had not become a keystone of presidential leadership in the 1950s and 1960s when much of the influential scholarship on the subject was written, sufficient precedents were available for scholars to consider its potential for presidential leadership in the future.

Probably the main reason going public has received so little attention in the scholarly literature is its fundamental incompatibility with bargaining. Presidential power is the "power to bargain," as Richard E. Neustadt taught a generation of students of the presidency. When Neustadt gave this theme its most evocative expression in 1960, the "bargaining president" had already become a centerpiece of pluralist theories of American politics. Nearly a decade earlier, Robert A. Dahl and Charles E. Lindblom had described the politician in America generically as "the human embodiment of a bargaining society." They made a special point to include the president in writing that despite his possessing more hierarchical controls than any other single figure in the government, "like everyone else . . . the President must bargain constantly." Since Neustadt's landmark study, other major works in the field have reinforced and elaborated on the concept of the bargaining president.

Going public violates bargaining in several ways. First, it rarely includes the kinds of exchanges necessary, in pluralist theory, for the American political system to function properly. At times, going public will be merely superfluous fluff compared with the substance of traditional political exchange. Practiced in a dedicated way, however, it can threaten to displace bargaining.

Second, going public fails to extend benefits for compliance, but freely imposes costs for noncompliance. In appealing to the public to "tell your senators and representatives by phone, wire, and mailgram that the future hangs in balance," the president seeks the aid of a third party—the public—to force other politicians to accept his preferences. If targeted representatives are lucky, the president's success may cost them no more than an opportunity at the bargaining table to shape policy or to extract compensation. If unlucky, they may find themselves both capitulating to the president's wishes and suffering the reproach of constituents for having resisted him in the first place. By imposing costs and failing to offer benefits, going public is more akin to force than to bargaining. The following comment of one senator may well sum up commonly felt sentiments, if not the actions, of those on Capitol Hill who find themselves repeatedly pressured by the president's public appeals: "A lot of Democrats, even if they like the President's proposal, will vote against him because of his radio address on Saturday."

Third, going public entails public posturing. To the extent that it fixes the president's bargaining position, posturing makes subsequent compromise with other politicians more difficult. Because negotiators must be prepared to yield some of their clients' preferences to make a deal, bargaining proverbially proceeds best behind closed doors. Consider the difficulty Ronald Reagan's widely publicized challenge "My tax proposal is a line drawn in dirt" posed for subsequent budget negotiations in Washington. Not only did the declaration threaten to cut away any middle ground on which a compromise might be constructed, it also probably stiffened the resolve of the president's adversaries, some of whom would later be needed to pass the administration's legislative program.

Finally, and possibly most injurious to bargaining, going public undermines the legitimacy of other politicians. It usurps their prerogatives of office, denies their role as representatives, and questions their claim to reflect the interests of their constituents. For a traditional bargaining stance with the president to be restored, these politicians would first have to reestablish parity, probably at a cost of conflict with the White House.

Given these fundamental incompatibilities, one may further speculate that by spoiling the bargaining environment, going public renders the president's future influence ever more dependent upon his ability to generate popular support for himself and his policies. The degree to which a president draws upon public opinion determines the kind of leader he will be.

Presidential Practice

The distinction between bargaining and going public is a theme one hears more and more often from presidents and those who deal with them. No president has enlisted public strategies to better advantage than did Ronald Reagan. Throughout his tenure, he exhibited a full appreciation of bargaining and going public as the modern office's principal strategic alternatives. The following examples from a six-month survey of White House news coverage show how entrenched this bifurcated view of presidential strategy has become. The survey begins in late November 1984, when some members of the administration were pondering how the president might exploit his landslide victory and others were preparing a new round of budget cuts and a tax reform bill for the next Congress.

November 29, 1984. Washington Post columnist Lou Cannon reported the following prediction from a White House official: "We're going to have confrontation on spending and consultation on tax reform." The aide explained, "We have somebody to negotiate with us on tax reform, but may not on budget cuts." By "confrontation" he was referring to the president's success in appealing to the public on national television, that is, in going public. By "consultation" he meant bargaining.

January 25, 1985. The above prediction proved accurate two months later when another staffer offered as pristine an evocation of going public as one is likely to find: "We have to look at it, in many ways, like a campaign. He [Reagan] wants to take his case to the people. You have a constituency of 535 legislators as opposed to 100 million voters. But the goal is the same to get the majority of voters to support your position."

February 10, 1985. In a nationally broadcast radio address, President Reagan extended an olive branch inviting members of Congress to "work with us in the spirit of cooperation and compromise" on the budget. This public statement probably did little to allay the frequently voiced suspicion of House Democratic leaders that such overtures were mainly intended for public consumption. One Reagan aide insisted, however, that the president simply sought to reassure legislators that "he would not go over their heads and campaign across the country for his budget without trying first to reach a compromise." In this statement the aide implicitly concedes the harm public pressure can create for bargaining but seeks to incorporate it advantageously into the strategic thinking of the politicians with whom the administration must deal by not forswearing its use.

March 9, 1985. After some public sparring, the administration eventually settled down to intensive budget negotiations with the Republican-led Senate Finance Committee. Failing to do as well as he would like, however, Reagan sent a message to his party's senators through repeated unattributed statements to the press that, if necessary, he would "go to the people to carry our message forward." Again, public appeals, though held in reserve, were threatened.

March 11, 1985. In an interview with a *New York Times* correspondent, a senior Reagan aide sized up his president: "He's liberated, he wants to get into a fight, he feels strongly and wants to push his program through himself. . . . Reagan never quite believed his popularity before the election, never believed the polls. Now he has it, and he's going to push ahead with our agenda."

May 16, 1985. To avoid entangling tax reform with budget deliberations in Congress, Reagan, at the request of Republican leaders, delayed unveiling his tax reform proposal until late May. A couple of weeks before Reagan's national television address on the subject, White House aides began priming the press with leaks on the proposal's content and promises that the president would follow it with a public relations blitz. In the words of one White House official, the plan was to force Congress to make a "binary choice between tax reform or no tax reform." The administration rejected bargaining, as predicted nearly six months earlier by a White House aide, apparently for two strategic reasons. First, Reagan feared that in a quietly negotiated process, the tax reform package would unravel under the concerted pressure of the special interests. Second, by taking the high-profile approach of "standing up for the people against the special interests," in the words of one adviser, tax reform might do for Republicans what social security did for Democrats—make them the majority party.

During these six months when bargaining held out promise—as it had during negotiations with the Senate Finance Committee—public appeals were held in reserve. The White House occasionally, however, threatened an appeal in trying to gain more favorable consideration. On other occasions, when opponents of the president's policies appeared capable of extracting major concessions, House Democrats on the budget and interest groups on tax reform, for example, the White House disengaged from negotiation and tried through public relations to force Congress to accept his policies. Although by 1985 news items such as the preceding excerpts seemed unexceptional as daily news, they are a recent phenomenon. One does not routinely find such stories in White House reporting 20 years earlier when, for example, John Kennedy's legislative agenda was stalled in Congress.

The incompatibility of bargaining and going public presents a pressing theoretical question. Why should presidents come to favor a strategy of leadership that appears so incompatible with the principles of pluralist theory? Why, if other Washington elites legitimately and correctly represent the interests of their clients and constituents, would anything be gained by going over their heads? The answers to these questions are several and complex, having to do with the ways Washington and presidents have changed. All in all, bargaining has shown declining efficiency, and opportunities to go public have increased.

There is another, more fundamental reason for the discrepancy between theory and current practice. Presidents have preferred to go public in recent years perhaps because the strategy offers a better prospect of success than it did in the past. Politicians in Washington may no longer be as tractable to bargaining as they once were. We are in an era of divided government, with Democrats in control of Congress and Republicans holding the presidency. Each side frequently finds political advantage in frustrating the other. On such occasions, posturing in preparation for the next election takes precedence over bargaining.

The decoupling of voters from political parties across the nation, which makes possible the occurrence of divided government, has also had more pervasive consequences for political relations among politicians in Washington. Weaker leaders, looser coalitions, more individualistic politicians, and stronger public pressure are among the developments reworking political relations in Washington that may inspire presidents to embrace a strategy of leadership antithetical to that prescribed by theory.

The President's Place in Institutionalized Pluralism

Constructing coalitions across the broad institutional landscape of Congress, the bureaucracy, interest groups, courts, and state governments requires a politician who possesses a panoramic view and commands the resources necessary to engage the disparate parochial interests of Washington's political elites. Only the president enjoys such vantage and resources. Traditional presidential scholarship leaves little doubt as to how they should be employed. Bargaining is thus the essence of presidential leadership, and pluralist theory explicitly rejects unilateral forms of influence as usually insufficient and ultimately costly. The ideal president is one who seizes the center of the Washington bazaar and actively barters with fellow politicians to build winning coalitions. He must do so, according to this theory, or he will forfeit any claim to leadership.

A president has the potential for symbiosis. Protocoalitions provide him with economy: He need not engage every coalition partner; talking to their leaders will do. In return the president provides protocoalitions with much needed coordination although, as Neustadt points out, presidential activity guarantees no more than that the president will be a "clerk." Clearly, however, institutionalized pluralism offers the virtuoso bargainer in the White House the opportunity for real leadership.

For years critics complained that autocratic committee chairmen, indifferent party leaders, and the conservative coalition of Republicans and Southern Democrats prevented Democratic presidents from achieving their ambitious policy goals. Yet institutionalized pluralism requires the president to keep company with these "obstacles" if he is to succeed. Leaders of lower-level coalitions may extract a steep price for cooperation, and at times they may defeat him outright. Still, as difficult as a Lyndon Johnson, a Wilbur Mills, a Wilbur Cohen at Social Security, or a J. Edgar Hoover might have been when he got his back up, each was indispensable as a trading partner. The reason is not difficult to see. Consider what these men had to offer: a majority leader who could strike a deal with the president on compromise legislation and then return to the chamber floor and deliver the critical votes necessary for its passage; a committee chairman who spoke so authoritatively for his committee that its markup sessions were spent detailing the language of an agreement reached earlier; or an agency head who, once persuaded, effectively redirected his organization's activities. A president simply has insufficient authority to command his way to success and insufficient time and energy to negotiate individually with everyone whose cooperation he needs.

Bargaining Techniques

Instead of a policy process dominated by powerful, conservative committee chairmen, one in which crucial decisions were made in secret and thus were relatively insulated from public influence, we now see a process characterized by extreme individualism, one in which open, public decision making often hinders compromise. When asked by a reporter about changes in Congress, Reagan lobbyist Kenneth Duberstein echoed this conclusion and gave it recent origin: "It's not been like Lyndon Johnson's time, being able to work with 15 or 20 Congressmen and Senators to get something done. For most issues you have to lobby all 435 Congressmen and almost all 100 Senators."

The President's Calculus

When politicians are more subject to "environmental" forces, however, other avenues of presidential influence open up. No politician within Washington is better positioned than the president to go outside the community and draw popular support. With protocoalitions in disarray and members more sensitive to influences from beyond Washington, the president's hand in mobilizing public opinion has been strengthened. For the new Congress indeed, for the new Washington generally, going public may at times be the most effective course available.

Under these circumstances, the president's prestige assumes the currency of power. It is something to be spent when the coffers are full, to be conserved when low, and to be replenished when empty. As David Gergen remarked when he was President Reagan's communications director, "Everything here is built on the idea that the President's success depends on grassroots support." Such a president must be attentive to the polls, but he will not be one who necessarily craves the affection of the public. His relationship with it may be purely instrumental, and however gratifying, popular support is a resource the expenditure of which must be coolly calculated.

Bargaining presidents require the sage advice of politicians familiar with the bargaining game; presidents who go public need pollsters. Compare the relish with which President Nixon, as reported by one of his consultants, approached the polls with the disdain Truman expressed. "Nixon had all kinds of polls all the time; he sometimes had a couple of pollsters doing the same kind of survey at the same time. He really studied them. He wanted to find the thing that would give him an advantage." The confidant went on to observe that the president wanted poll data "on just about anything and everything" throughout his administration.

Indicative of current fashion, Carter, Reagan, and Bush have had in-house pollsters taking continuous-weekly, even daily readings of public opinion. They have vigilantly monitored the pulse of opinion to warn of slippage and to identify opportunities for gain. Before adopting a policy course, they have assessed its costs in public support. These advisers' regular and frequently unsolicited denials that they affected policy belie their self-effacement.

To see how the strategic prescriptions of going public differ from those of bargaining, consider the hypothetical case of a president requiring additional votes if he is to prevail in Congress. If a large number of votes is needed, the most obvious and direct course is to go on prime-time television to solicit the public's active support. Employed at the right moment by a popular president, the effect may be dramatic. This tactic, however, has considerable costs and risks. A real debit of lost public support may occur when a president takes a forthright position. There is also the possibility that the public will not respond, which damages the president's future credibility. Given this, a president understandably finds the threat to go public frequently more attractive than the act. To the degree such a threat is credible, the anticipated responses of some representatives and senators may suffice to achieve victory.

A more focused application of popular pressure becomes available as an election nears. Fence-sitting representatives and senators may be plied with promises of reelection support or threats of presidential opposition. This may be done privately and selectively, or it may be tendered openly to all who may vote on the president's program. Then there is the election itself. By campaigning, the president who goes public can seek to alter the partisan composition of Congress and thereby gain influence over that institution's decisions in the future.

All of these methods for generating publicity notwithstanding, going public offers fewer and simpler stratagems than does its pluralist alternative. At the heart of the latter lies bargaining, which above all else involves choice: choice among alternative coalitions, choice of specific partners, and choice of the goods and services to be bartered. The number and variety of choices place great demands upon strategic calculation, so much so that pluralist leadership must be understood as an art. The president's success ultimately reduces to intuition, an ability to sense "right choices." Going public also requires choice, and it leaves ample room for the play of talent. (One need only compare the television performance of Carter and Reagan.) Nonetheless, public relations appears to be a less obscure matter. Going public promises a straightforward presidency; its options fewer, its strategy simpler, and consequently, its practitioner's behavior more predictable.

Thus there is a rationale for modern presidents to go public in the emerging character of Washington politics. As Washington comes to depend on looser, more individualistic political relations, presidents searching for strategies that work will increasingly go public.

38 Going Public in Undemocratic Polities

RICHARD ANDERSON

Is "going public" confined to modern democracies, or does it also occur in the two types of undemocratic polities—modern authoritarianism and premodern dynastic states? When Samuel Kernell (1992) writes that U.S. presidents began going public because weaker leaders, looser coalitions, more individualistic politicians, and stronger public pressure devalued their previous practice of bargaining within constitutional roles, he may have both defined going public too narrowly and missed the underlying significance of the change in presidential behavior. Examination of going public in undemocratic polities may help to clarify the causes of change in the public self-presentation of modern democratic politicians in the United States and elsewhere.

By going public, Kernell (1992) refers to open declarations by one politician that stimulate voters to exert pressure on other politicians. The politician going public hopes to gain leverage in bargaining with political opponents. Going public in the United States typifies individualized pluralism, which Kernell distinguishes from its institutionalized predecessor. When pluralism was institutionalized, presidents bargained with senators and congressmen within rules set by the constitutional allocation of powers among these varieties of elected officials. In the individualized type, each elected official seeks a personal connection with the public as a whole, regardless of whether the members of the public to whom the official appeals belong to those citizens whom the official constitutionally represents.

The question is whether public appeals seeking leverage in bargaining among top elites are confined to electoral polities or whether these appeals can also be found in undemocratic polities. Of course, in authoritarian or dynastic polities in which the social role of "voter" does not exist, such public appeals cannot be directed at voters, and if going public is to be equated with appeals by the president to voters, the question can only be raised at all if one is willing to engage in what is sometimes criticized as "conceptual stretching." On the other hand, of course, to reject comparisons across the distinction separating democratic from undemocratic polities on the grounds of conceptual stretching takes the equivalent risk of undue conceptual confinement, and these intellectual risks are mutually offsetting. In every kind of polity, members of the ruling or governing elite may bargain with each other about policy, and someone outside this top elite may have potential to intervene on the side of various bargainers. In military dictatorships, soldiers loyal to one general may have the capacity to threaten other generals in the junta. In dynastic polities, nobles, literati, bannermen, or upper castes may be able to take sides between the monarch and the peers, the "son of heaven" and the councilors, or the rajah and the courtiers. In bureaucratic authoritarianism, whether of Communist, Fascist, or ideologically less well-defined types, bureaucratic officials may be able to intervene in bargaining inside the ruling council. In any of these polities, some group must possess the capacity to intervene in bargaining among leaders because the leaders can rule only if some group enforces their rule on the population, which in undemocratic societies is invariably restive. Because the enforcers must be numerous enough to repress an even more numerous population, appeals for their support in the bargaining among the leaders cannot be solely private. The appeals must be broadcast. This argument is testable: Examination of authoritarian or dynastic polities should regularly discover at least some kind of public appeals for leverage in elite bargaining.

If going public is common to both democratic and undemocratic polities, why does Kernell (1992) say that going public has begun only recently? The possibility exists that what has changed is not whether presidents go public but to whom they go public, and therefore how they go public. When Kernell analyzes changes in presidential speech, he is writing about a democracy in which the vast majority of adults are free to participate in pressuring the rule-making legislature. Undemocratic polities prohibit many adults, and often the vast majority, from participating in actions designed to pressure rulers. To maintain prohibitions against participation, those groups in any polity whose participation is accepted by the top rulers as the cost of maintaining rule over the rest of the population may accept restrictions both on the form of their participation and on the form taken by top elites' public appeals. Before U.S. presidents began the unrestricted public appeals that Kernell means by going public, the U.S. polity ordinarily called a democracy was, of course, much more exclusionary than the polity in which presidents go public today. Before 1965, African Americans in the South were effectively excluded from political participation. Before 1920, women could not participate on equal terms with men. In the early Republic, property qualifications withdrew the right to vote even from many males classified as European by descent. At various times, other laws or customs have excluded a variety of other groups in American society from political participation.

Because going public stimulates everyone, enfranchised or excluded, to voice political demands, when the franchise is restricted, national leaders such as the president must either avoid unrestricted public appeals or jeopardize the boundary that separates the political participant from the population excluded from political rights. If an authoritarian or dynastic polity may be compared to a democracy with rights of participation available only to some narrowly circumscribed part of the population, then going public in an undemocratic polity should take a restricted form that preserves rather than endangers the boundary between participants and those forbidden to participate.

An answer to the question of whether going public is confined to modern democracies, then, turns on whether authoritarian polities display the following observable regularities: (a) public appeals by top elites that change the outcomes of bargaining among them, and (b) restrictions on the form of public statements by top elites that enhance their appeal for groups that enforce the elites' will while diminishing appeal to the general population. Because determining whether public appeals influence bargaining requires tracking the interaction between bargaining and public appeals over time (as Kernell, 1992, does for the United States), the first observation must be investigated one polity at a time, and here I will provide the example of the Soviet Union, an authoritarian polity that I (and others) have systematically investigated. The second regularity is more easily observed, and I will provide a number of cases of two kinds of restriction that appear to be general across both authoritarian and dynastic cases. First, authoritarian and dynastic rulers conduct politics in linguistic forms set sharply apart from the language or languages spoken by populations under their control. Second, their messages explicitly formulate invidious distinctions claiming that those allowed to participate share some innate superiority to the populations under their rule. Without these two traits—a distinctive language of politics and invidious claims to superiority over the general population—authoritarian and dynastic polities appear to be unsustainable.

Going Public in Soviet Politics

Although the Soviet Union from 1917 to 1985 presents a classic example of an extreme authoritarian polity and retained highly authoritarian features almost until the last few months before its collapse in December 1991, the top Soviet elite routinely went public for gains in bargaining among its members. The authoritarian features were the placement of power over all decisions in the hands of a self-appointed oligarchy, the Politburo, and enforcement of its decisions by a bureaucracy whose officials ultimately owed their appointment to the Politburo. Going public was evident in speeches published in the controlled press and ascribed to Politburo members, whereas bargaining was evident in the circumstance that Soviet policies invariably combined diverse proposals found in the speeches of rival Politburo members. Policy changed over time when Politburo members either voiced new demands or abandoned previous recommendations.

Until 1989, a tiny oligarchy, normally composed of 10 to 15 men (one woman once held full membership) and called the Politburo for most of the history of the Soviet Union, held the right to make all political decisions. Although Soviet citizens voted for deputies of national and local legislatures in regularly scheduled elections, only one candidate ran for each position (with very rare exceptions), and all candidates were nominated on a single slate chosen by the ultimate authority of the Politburo. Election results were routinely falsified to report that all candidates had received nearly unanimous approval from all voters. The national legislature to which deputies were elected routinely passed, by unanimous vote and with no spontaneous debate, all laws previously approved by the Politburo, and local legislatures gave the same treatment to local laws previously approved by the Politburo's appointees in each local district. The Politburo nominated and removed its own members subject only to ratification by the Central Committee, an organization varying over time from a few tens to a few hundred members, themselves invariably appointed to the official posts that earned them Central Committee membership by decision of the Politburo. Democratic participation was completely prohibited. All mass media were subject to line-by-line censorship and compulsory guidance as to content. Autonomous organization was forbidden, even when ostensibly apolitical. Demonstrations, strikes, and gatherings for political discussion not orchestrated in advance by officials were violently disrupted either by thugs recruited for the purpose or by regular units of the police or military. Expression of personal opinion about politics was allowed but risked incarceration, loss of employment or education, or demotion if the opinion displeased anyone in authority. Complaints to higher authority by citizens harmed by abuses by local officials were routinely referred back to the official who had been complained about for investigation and action, and the resulting actions rarely benefited the complaining citizen.

Because no citizen, and indeed no one subordinate to the Central Committee, had any institutionalized voice in the procedures used to choose the Politburo, one might expect that going public by Politburo members would be purposeless or even perilous for them. It would be purposeless because both public and officials were forbidden to express opinions unsatisfactory to their superiors. It would be perilous because any effort to rouse public opinion against Politburo rivals would jeopardize the prohibitions on democratic participation necessary to perpetuate the Politburo's monopoly of the ultimate right to make decisions, and consequently any Politburo member who went public would risk the wrath of his peers, who could vent it by expelling him from the leadership. Indeed, some specialists have gone so far as to claim that public speeches by Politburo members were all identical, varying only over time as the Politburo changed its collective opinion about the most appropriate line to take before the public.

Contrary to the claims of these few specialists, systematic comparison of Politburo speeches has revealed to many observers that speeches by different members varied in their policy stands. Although some observers have represented the variation in policy stands as "rational deliberation" of the kind that Kernell (1992) associates with institutionalized pluralism (and these observers even chose the same phrase to describe Soviet politics), the speeches contained not only rational justifications for the speaker's stand on policy but also criticisms or denunciations of stands associated with rivals and emotional or symbolic stands of the kind that George Breslauer has called "diffuse appeals." When a Politburo member wanted to express a particularly controversial opinion, he would wrap himself in Lenin's mantle by ordering staff assistants to locate an appropriate quotation from the 55-volume collection of writings and correspondence by Vladimir Il'ich Lenin, founder of the Soviet state. In the mid-1960s, one Politburo member publicly criticized a rival's policy stand as resembling the ideas of Adolf Hitler, the German Nazi leader whose order for a destructive invasion of the Soviet Union in 1941 and for massacres of many Soviet citizens made him an even more odious symbol, if that is possible, than he is in the United States. Other Politburo members routinely used loaded derogatives like "slander" or "distortion" to attack the policy positions advocated by their peers.

While emotionally criticizing policy lines publicly advocated by other members of the Politburo, the speakers also observed certain restrictions that have been abandoned by modern politicians in the United States. When condemning the policy stands of Politburo rivals, the speakers never named any sitting member of the Politburo who was the target of their attacks. Although this restriction contrasts sharply with contemporary U.S. practice, it closely resembles the norms shown by Jeffrey Tulis (1987) to have governed presidential rhetoric in the 19th century. When President Andrew Johnson sought to rouse the country against the Radical Republicans in 1865, his public naming of senators singled out for criticism even figured in the bill of impeachment passed by Congress against him. At most, Politburo members would use the notorious phrase "some comrades" to designate the targets of their public criticisms, and during the last two decades of authoritarian rule before the reforms attempted by Mikhail Sergeevich Gorbachev after 1985, even that phrase fell into disfavor as excessively explicit in calling attention to contests for power within the Politburo. The tendency became more pronounced instead to substitute the names of foreign or historical figures (as in the Hitler example discussed previously) for those of the Politburo members under attack. To ensure that Politburo members would conform to rules regulating their public speeches, the Politburo practiced regular prior review of full texts, or at least talking points, for all public statements by any member.

Because Soviet politicians never named names, the audiences for their speeches were compelled to depend on inferences about the identity of the politician who was being challenged. To make these inferences, it was necessary to compare what was said in speeches by one Politburo member with what had been said in other speeches. To make such comparisons possible, Soviet officials at lower levels of the bureaucracy made a habit of keeping notebooks with detailed notes or outlines of recent Politburo speeches, whereas offices maintained backfiles of recent issues of *Pravda* and other newspapers in which the texts of speeches were printed, often verbatim. An official program requiring officials to study and report on Politburo documents ensured that these records would be both kept and consulted.

Going public by Politburo members in turn served to shift policy bargains toward the proposals advocated by a particular member's public speeches. Systematic comparison of Politburo speeches with both declaratory policy and actual conduct reveals that policies were bargains. Although much of Soviet policy was secret and therefore exceptionally difficult to observe, all observable policies either were logrolls that combined a proposal advocated by one Politburo member concerning one issue with proposals advocated by rivals concerning other issues or were compromises intermediate between proposals by various Politburo members concerning the same issue. As bargainers will, the Politburo often logrolled proposals concerning different issues regardless of whether the resulting policy mix was achievable given real-world conditions—for example, could be paid for within the existing budget constraints—or isolated issues for intermediate compromises regardless of spillover to other issues left out of consideration. Going public constantly shifted the resulting mix of policies. When a Politburo member voiced new public demands, the mix shifted in the direction of his proposals; when a Politburo member made concessions by retracting public demands or endorsing those associated with rivals, the policy mix shifted away from his earlier stands.

Evidently, therefore, public speechmaking by members changed the policy bargains approved by the Politburo. It is not sufficient to assume, as some observers have, that public speeches merely announced policies already decided in closed negotiating sessions. Were that the case, speeches by different Politburo members on the same day could not recommend opposite policies. Similarly, it is insufficient to dismiss such instances as cases in which the Politburo varied its collective message because its members were addressing different audiences. Were audience variation the source of divergence in public statements by Politburo members, various speakers addressing the same audience should not have made different statements, and the same speaker addressing varied audiences should not have maintained consistency in his public statements.

Although Politburo members went public for leverage on bargaining within the oligarchy (despite thoroughly undemocratic procedures that might be thought to make this behavior purposeless or perilous), the restrictions they observed in their public speeches differentiated going public in the Soviet Union from its counterpart in a democracy. The differences were in turn systematically related to the exclusiveness or inclusiveness of the audiences to which authoritarian and democratic politicians respectively appeal. Two salient differences are the distinctive language of Politburo appeals and the presence in authoritarian appeals of explicit assertions that the audience is innately superior to the majority of the population.

Utterances, as every hearer knows from personal experience, can be distancing or can make listeners feel personally close to the speaker. In English (and other Indo-European languages such as Russian), utterances that communicate personal aloofness contain high proportions of nouns relative to verbs because a superabundance of nouns forces elongation of clauses that in turn require the listener to cover more distance along the linear arrangement of words. Impersonal expressions replace first-person singulars. A distancing utterance conveys a relatively unambiguous message rather than the more nuanced, reserved, or hedged messages typical of attempts to close interpersonal gaps. Language that tries to establish personal closeness reverses all these tendencies: Clauses are short, nouns few, first- and second-person singulars abundant, and hedges frequent.

Relative to ordinary Russian, the language of Communist speeches was measurably of the distancing kind. From 1988, when Gorbachev's reforms enabled Russians to achieve freedom to express their feelings about Communist spokesmen, the aloofness of Communist officialdom from ordinary discourse became a common complaint lodged against authoritarian rule. A journalist remembered noticing a few men clustered silently apart from the hubbub of conversation that filled the corridors of the Soviet Union's first elected legislature in 1989; when he approached them to ask who they were, they answered stiffly, "We are the partocracy" (Russian, *partokratiia*—like its translation, it is not found in any dictionary but is a word that emerged during the process of democratization to designate the enforcers of authoritarian rule). Maintaining this apartness, local organizations of the Communist Party reprimanded officials who chanced upon prodemocracy marches that surged across the Soviet Union from 1988 to 1991, even when the officials used the opportunity to defend the Party's record against democratic critics. What mattered was not the content of a Communist official's statements to the people; it was whether the Communist spoke across the barrier separating rulers from ruled. As Russia continued to democratize after 1991, politicians increasingly abandoned the distancing style of Communist speakers in favor of utterances quantitatively similar to ordinary speech.

Speech that distances national leaders from the people sustains undemocratic rule. Authoritarian and dynastic polities, despite the many differences distinguishing them, share a common trait: Their rule requires enforcement. Distancing speech by rulers makes enforcement possible by opening a conceptual gap, an awareness of interpersonal remoteness, between rulers and ruled. This gap is available for occupancy by the enforcers of undemocratic rule, who otherwise would be unable to visualize a place for themselves in the social order. Because the distancing language used by the rulers communicates that they conceive a space for the officials to intermediate between the rulers and population placed at a distance by the speech, officials welcome distancing utterances by leaders even though they presumably also experience the utterances as distancing the rulers from themselves.

Officials' welcome for the distancing speech of Communist rule was reinforced by the explicit claim made in Communist speeches that those who thought in the categories of Communist speech possessed a superior, "scientific" understanding of society and its developmental requirements. Communist speech divided persons into two classes: Communists and "nonparty persons." As students of the thought of Marx and Lenin, Communists were said to have acquired a correct understanding of social dynamics; conversely, the consciousness of nonparty persons was said to be vulnerable to all kinds of outside influences and distortions. Although the particular genius of the Communist political organization was to blur the distinction between rulers and ruled by appointing nonparty persons to low-level bureaucratic office and by offering membership in the Communist party to persons not employed as bureaucrats, the Communists were concentrated in bureaucratic posts and the nonparty persons in the population subjected to bureaucratic control. Consequently, the distinctive language of Communist rule set apart from the population, and claimed superiority over the population for, the enforcers of authoritarian rule to whom it also appealed.

Of course, a question that might be raised concerns precisely how the enforcers of Communist authoritarianism could intervene in the deliberations of a Politburo for whose members they could not vote. The answer is that the Politburo wanted its decisions enforced upon the Soviet population. Officials could vary the enthusiasm with which they applied the enforcement. Then they could report whether the policies were securing or failing to secure popular compliance. Of course, many Soviet policies required popular cooperation to implement. If people were unwilling to work, for example, the Politburo could not achieve its goal of expanding the economy. Because its cooperation was needed, the general population has also been credited with influence on the Politburo. A salient difference between the population and the officials, however, should not be neglected. Because its members were forbidden to communicate about politics, the general population faced severe difficulties in coordinating its resistance. Bureaucratic officials, on the other hand, were actively encouraged to discuss problems of enforcing the Politburo's decisions, and although the tone of these discussions was required to be constructive, raising or minimizing difficulties offered real opportunities to coordinate bureaucratic pressure in Politburo contests.

In summary, the Soviet case shows that at least one authoritarian polity does display going public in the sense of public appeals by leaders intended to put pressure on their opponents in bargaining. Going public in the Soviet Union took a more restricted form than its counterpart in the United States, being conducted in distancing language that opened a conceptual gap between rulers and ruled that was available for occupancy by the officials who enforced Soviet rule and that expressed an explicit claim to the innate superiority of the officials to the population that they controlled.

Going Public in Other Undemocratic Polities

Non-Communist authoritarian polities and dynastic polities resemble the Soviet Union in conducting politics in a language distinct from that spoken by populations under their control and in using those languages to make claims for the innate superiority of their officials over the populations they ruled.

Benedict Anderson (1991) observes that many traditional dynastic polities have developed hand-written languages known only to a few literati and not only used for communication within the state but also regarded as sacred and obligatory if religious rituals are to be valid. As examples, he cites states including the Chinese Middle Kingdom with its painted characters, the medieval Christian Kingdoms with their reliance on hand-written Latin, and Muslim states using the classical Arabic of the Koran as examples. Handwritten documents, costly because produced one copy at a time, restricted opportunities for bureaucratic careers to those few males who could afford the manuscripts necessary for learning to write. The development of printing technology, Anderson notes, made cheap mass editions available for the first time, rapidly expanding the number of literate persons and therefore the pool of recruits eligible for employment in early dynastic bureaucracies. Because mass editions were printed in "languages-of-state" that only gradually superseded the many local dialects of which any natural language is composed, during the transition from diverse dialects spoken by illiterate populations to the emergence of standard printed languages taught in schools for general education, the languages-of-state spoken and printed within the bureaucracy set the officials of the dynastic state apart from the populations under their supervision.

The distinctive languages of rule common to authoritarians and dynastic polities fall into two categories: foreign languages and "registers" of the local language. A *register* is a set of linguistic habits associated by a culture with a particular social context. For example, someone talking casually to friends might say "ain't gonna rain." The same person talking to an employer might say "it isn't going to rain." These sentences are both English, but they belong to different registers because they are associated with different social contexts. Registers may be "high" or "low": High registers are the speech of the most educated members of the culture, whereas low registers are the speech of the least educated members.

Because universal eligibility for adults to participate in politics is a very recent historical phenomenon, rarely encountered before 1945, practically all polities in history have been dynastic, and most of the rest have been authoritarian. The sheer number of dynastic and authoritarian polities makes it impossible to survey all of them. A few examples, however, will suffice to indicate the ubiquity of foreign languages and distinctive registers—both high and low—in association with dynastic or authoritarian rule.

Examples of languages foreign to populations living under undemocratic rule include Latin in the Roman Empire, Amhara in the Oromo- and Tigrean-speaking provinces of the Ethiopian empire, European languages in the colonial possessions in Asia, Africa, and the Americas, and those same languages used by the ruling bureaucracies of the postcolonial states to distinguish their officials from speakers of the same native language who populate those states. An especially remarkable case is the Hungary of the magnates, who despite sharing the Magyar tongue with many of their serfs nevertheless conducted all the business of courts, administration, and their own Diet in Latin from independence in the 16th century until the middle of the 19th century. Even the German-speaking Holy Roman Emperor, who was simultaneously King of Hungary, was required by law to address the Diet in Latin. Whereas in most cases foreign languages of rule are the native languages of the conqueror, the Magyar magnates went to the trouble of importing a foreign language that they never used in family life.

Examples of high and low registers include, in addition to the Soviet case discussed previously, the language of Greece under its authoritarian rulers, the dynastic case of Javanese, Nazi German, and the remarkable instance of Wolof. Until 1976, when the new democratic government passed a language reform bill, the authoritarian regime in Greece had legally required that all political speeches and official documents be delivered in *Katharevousa*, a register of Greek marked by archaic vocabulary and grammatical complexity, instead of the "Demotic" commonly spoken and written by Greeks. Javanese kings and their *"priyayi,"* or kin and courtiers, addressed each other in *krama*, a formal register taught in *priyayi* families from early childhood, while speaking to peasants in the *ngoko* register used by peasants to each other. Like Communist Russian compared to Russian, krama was a distancing register. It used a separate vocabulary, which according to the grammar of Javanese could not combine with ngoko words, and utterances in krama were consistently longer than those with comparable meaning formulated in ngoko.

Taking their cue from the speeches and writings of their leader, Adolf Hitler, the German Nazis soon evolved a distinctive register of German sharply distinguished from ordinary Germany speech. Like Communist Russian, Nazi German substituted nouns for verbs, and to make their sentences more imposing, Nazi writers avoided using one word when two or three would do. Consequently, as in Communist Russia, copulative conjunctions increased in density. Unlike ordinary German, which sharply distinguishes written prose from oral speech, Nazis lowered the register of public speech by importing oral expressions and grammar into written texts. In the traditional dynastic polity of the Wolof in Senegal, kings and nobles spoke only in a register that required frequent grammatical errors, a low mumbling tone, and multiple stuttering pauses. Rationalized as necessary to prevent the weight of language from overbearing social inferiors conceived as intellectually and physically weaker, this register distanced them by making them sound as if they were speaking in a normal tone from far away.

A matched pair of mixed cases is provided by the example of English parliamentarians and Ottoman bureaucrats. Until 1819, when the English franchise remained narrowly restricted, Parliament refused even to consider petitions unless they were composed according to "correct" grammar. This grammar introduced blended Latin and Greek idioms and syntax into English. Because it was taught only in the "public schools" open exclusively to the sons of the rich, the rule requiring "grammatical" English effectively excluded consideration of popular political demands. Like the English, who required that a man learn three languages to participate in politics, Ottoman bureaucrats developed the usul-i-kalem, or "bureaucratic style," which combined Turkish with Arabic and Persian loanwords used in accordance with their syntax of origin, not according to Turkish grammar. Documents written in usul-i-kalem were incomprehensible to Turkish peasants even when read aloud to them.

Foreign languages and distinctive registers go hand in hand with assertions of innate superiority over populations that speak dialects other than the language of power. The Magyar magnates' statute of 1514, for example, distinguished between "people" including "only the bishops, lords, the other aristocrats, and all the nobles, but not the commoners," and "plebs [among whom] only the commoners are comprehended." Commoners did not rank even as people, but occupied a conceptual space in between people and animals. The postcolonial Senegalese leader Leopold Senghor took the position—absurd from the point of view of technical linguistics—that African languages were strictly "sensual," with a "melody that inspires more than it informs," and that knowledge of French was therefore a necessary requirement for participation in rule because French alone was capable of expressing the "reason" needed to guide political development in Senegal. The Nazi ideologue Alfred Rosenberg based his arguments for Nazi rule on claims that urban Germans had sunk to such a low level that they could no longer form opinions on political questions. In England, Parliament's proscription of petitions not meeting standards of grammar emerged from a distinction, beginning in the 16th and enduring into the 20th century, between the "better sort" and "vulgar" sorts of people.

The existence in many authoritarian or dynastic polities of distinctive languages or registers of rule is prima facie evidence for going public confined to a restricted stratum of political participants. Language is needless unless one means to communicate in it, whereas languages are useful for communication only to those who have learned them. The development of distinctive registers or importation of foreign languages bears testimony to the intention among the rulers of each of these polities to communicate to the enforcers of their rule and to isolate that communication from people condemned to live under their rule.

Conclusion

Kernell's (1992) study of going public makes a major contribution by demonstrating the evolution of presidential speech in the modern era. At the same time, review of authoritarian and dynastic cases indicates that instead of conceiving a transition from not going public in institutional pluralism to going public in individualized pluralism, it might be more accurate to visualize a transition from one kind of going public to another. As rights of participation have become more widespread among

American citizens, presidents have lifted the restrictions on how they went public to speak to an ever-broadening share of the population. Often, one encounters laments about the cheapening of public debate that has accompanied the change in going public. If the complainants were to read what passed for public debate in the Soviet Union, they might not see the contemporary debate in the United States as so impoverished by comparison. It is surely the case that a president will tailor the message to the educational characteristics of the citizens to whom the message is directed, and messages directed to especially attentive sectors of the public, which tend to be more educated than the citizenry as a whole, can be expected to display a more refined language. The claim that refinement of language makes political messages superior, however, is itself implicitly an assertion that the educated are entitled to more weight in rule. That assertion has nothing to do with achieving equality of participatory rights. Messages are more democratic when they are plainer. From this point of view, instances of modern presidential speech, such as "Read my lips, no new taxes" or "It's the economy, stupid," have much to commend them as messages, regardless of whether one endorses the political ideologies or candidates of which they are emblems.

39 Media Attention and Congressional Agendas

FRANK R. BAUMGARTNER
BRYAN D. JONES
BETH L. LEECH

People who study the mass media often note how a handful of stories tend to dominate the headlines at any given time. A problem is "discovered," and at once every newspaper, television station, radio station, and magazine seems to focus on the same issue. Not only is imitation common among mass media outlets but attention is also limited. Not every issue can be in the spotlight at the same time—only those with the characteristics that make them most newsworthy. Inevitably, old stories must make way for new stories. As a result, coverage often goes in spurts, with alarmed discovery leading to numerous stories on an issue until attention shifts away.

Political scientist Christopher Bosso (1989) has documented how news outlets jumped on the story of Ethiopian famine as "news" in 1984 and 1985, although the famine had already been severe for several years. After NBC News aired heart-rending footage of starving Ethiopian children on four successive evenings in October 1984, the story leapt to the front page of newspapers and additional videotape of Ethiopia's plight appeared on the other networks. Media coverage of the famine peaked in November and December, then began declining rapidly in 1985, although the famine itself continued. The problem seemed intractable and collective attention turned elsewhere.

Such shifts in attention are not unique to the media. Very similar processes often take place within government, with policymakers jumping on the bandwagon when an opportunity arises. After all, if everyone else is already working on an issue, there is a better chance for success. Government officials, like reporters, cannot possibly pay attention to everything at once, so they choose those issues that seem most promising, and those issues often tend to be the ones that everyone else is paying attention to.

These patterns of imitation mean that a major source of change in American politics is the shifting attention of the media. Hilgartner and Bosk (1988) argue that media attention is an important determinant of which issues will manage to win space in the limited attentions of the public and of Congress. Different policy actors tend to converge on the same issues because they monitor each other's actions, Hilgartner and Bosk argue. Journalists read each other's work, activists network, and congressional aides attempt to generate and shape media coverage. The interactions among the actors mean that shifts in attention by one set of actors are likely to be quickly followed by shifts by others. The media help link all the other actors together, acting as the means of communication, a way in which disjointed actors can keep tabs on each other and on what they consider the "public mood."

In this chapter, we will look at the history of four public policy issues—drug abuse, nuclear power, urban affairs, and smoking—and examine the ways in which media attention and congressional attention have been interconnected (for a more detailed treatment of a broader range of issues, see Baumgartner & Jones, 1993). We do not argue that there is any simple cause-and-effect relationship between attention in the media and attention in Congress, but the two are interrelated. Sometimes one leads and sometimes the other, and often both are following the actions of some third party either within or outside of government. It is clear, however, that a shift in attention by either the media or Congress is often followed by a shift in attention by the other.

It is important to note that these shifts in attention are not simply the result of everyone reacting to a problem that suddenly and objectively got worse. In the cases we will discuss, the problems had existed before, but neither Congress nor the media paid much attention. The severity of a problem certainly can help attract the attention of the media and Congress, but severity alone does not guarantee that the problem will be recognized and acted on.

Data and Methods

In looking at these four examples of issues that came to attract much attention in both the national government and the media, we will use two types of data. To assess the amount of attention being paid by the mass media at any given time, we use the number of articles on those topics each year in the *Reader's Guide to Periodical Literature*, which indexes stories from hundreds of magazines by the topic of those stories. We then compare the number of articles listed each year on a particular topic to the number of congressional hearings held each year on the same topic.

It is worth noting that Congress holds hearings on many issues that never become law and on many issues that do not even come up for a vote. Holding hearings, therefore, does not guarantee that Congress will act, but it does indicate that at least some members of Congress are interested in the topic. Holding a hearing indicates that the issue has become part of the congressional agenda, the set of issues being seriously considered for congressional action. Our data, therefore, trace changes in media attention and changes in congressional attention over time.

Smoking and Tobacco: Healthy Bodies Versus Healthy Economy

Media coverage of smoking and tobacco has varied widely over the years. Before about 1950, smoking and tobacco were largely nonissues in the media, as can be seen by the number of articles on those topics in the *Reader's Guide* in Figure 39.1. Media attention to the issue of smoking began to increase in the 1950s, then rose sharply in the 1960s as information about the health risks connected with smoking became known. The number of articles dealing with the topics of smoking and tobacco leapt from fewer than 20 a year before 1950 to a high of 136 articles in 1964.

Although smoking became an important topic in the mass media in the 1960s, as evidenced by the abrupt increase in coverage, attention through congressional hearings has been much more stable over time. Although there was a slight increase in the number of hearings on the topics of smoking or tobacco in the 1970s, the increase was not nearly as great as that seen in media attention. Important changes in tobacco

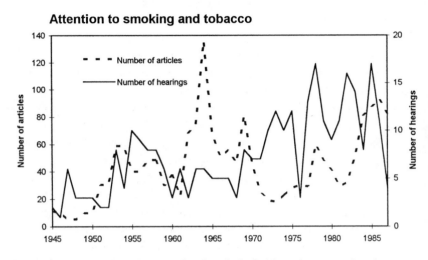

Figure 39.1. Annual coverage in the *Reader's Guide* and congressional hearings on smoking and tobacco.

regulation (primarily regarding advertising), however, were adopted in the 1970s. The gradual increase in the number of hearings disguises a much more abrupt shift in the focus of those hearings. A change did occur in congressional attention in the 1970s, although not so much in the amount of attention directed at smoking and tobacco as the type of attention.

Tobacco once was primarily seen as solely an agricultural and economic issue, not a health issue. Congress held hearings on the topic, but those hearings were almost entirely supportive of the agricultural subsidy program for tobacco. In the late 1950s and early 1960s, however, more and more research was pointing to the health risks of smoking. In 1964, the surgeon general issued a report warning of the health dangers, and media attention to the topic of smoking shot up. After the surgeon general's report, more congressional hearings began focusing on negative aspects of smoking and tobacco, specifically health problems and the need to restrict advertising of tobacco products.

Figure 39.2 shows how congressional hearings on smoking and tobacco have changed in tone since 1945. Although Figure 39.1 showed that the number of hearings increased only slightly, a more definite shift can be seen in the percentage of hearings emphasizing positive aspects of

Positive attention to smoking and tobacco

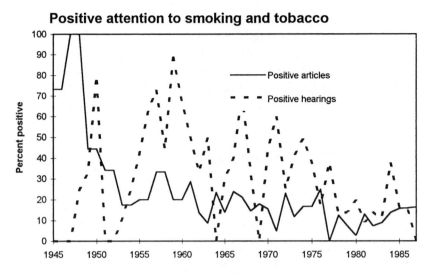

Figure 39.2. Percentage of congressional hearings and *Reader's Guide* articles emphasizing positive attributes of tobacco.

tobacco and smoking (primarily economic considerations). No positive hearings were coded in 1964, the year the surgeon general's report was released. Although the percentage of positive hearings has bounced up and down over the years, a trend toward fewer positive hearings is clear. Since the mid-1970s—coinciding with the slight increase in the number of hearings—fewer than half of all smoking- and tobacco-related hearings have focused on the positive attributes of smoking and tobacco, such as the tobacco industry's contribution to national economic growth.

Media coverage of tobacco and smoking exhibits an even stronger trend toward the negative side of the issue, and the trend began long before the shift in attention occurred in Congress. Since about 1950, the percentage of articles emphasizing the positive aspects of tobacco has been decreasing; only once since 1959 have more than a quarter of the articles in a given year been positive. The emphasis on negative aspects of smoking clearly preceded the surgeon general's report in 1964, although medical research into the dangers of tobacco in the years leading up to 1964 probably influenced both the surgeon general's report and the media coverage.

Tobacco growers and cigarette companies continued to contribute substantially to the gross national product during the 1970s and 1980s, but these aspects of the industry figured less prominently in congressional hearings and media coverage. Health concerns displaced economic growth as the primary topic of attention, both in Congress and in the media.

Nuclear Power: Changing Tone, Shifting Attention

Even when media coverage does seem to be one of the factors leading to increases in congressional attention, it is not only the amount of coverage that matters but the type of coverage as well. That was true in the case of smoking and tobacco policy, and it is especially true of nuclear power. The type of media coverage, in particular whether the article is negative or positive in tone, is important because criticism often spurs involvement by people who had not previously paid attention to an issue, shifting the balance of power. This is what political scientist E. E. Schattschneider (1960) called conflict expansion. In the case of nuclear power, there have been two periods of high media attention, but only the second period was associated with negative images of nuclear power. Whereas the first period of media attention resulted in little change in congressional attention, the second preceded a sharp increase in the number of congressional hearings on nuclear power.

In the early years of the civilian nuclear power program, journalists covering nuclear power questions tended to be science journalists who focused on the technological potential of nuclear power. Attention to the issue of nuclear power was fairly high, and the tone of articles in the mass media was extremely positive for the industry. The McMahon Act created the national Atomic Energy Commission in 1946, and in 1954 the act was amended. Both governmental actions are marked by surges in positive media coverage, as can be seen in Figure 39.3. The peaceful use of nuclear power was associated with images of cheap electricity and clean, futuristic technology. There were always competing images, such as the destructive potential of nuclear weapons and the giving away of a public technology to private business, but in the beginning the positive images outweighed the negative.

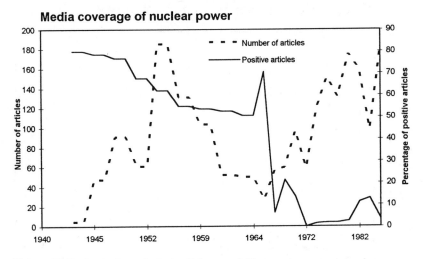

Figure 39.3. Annual number of articles on civilian nuclear power and percentage of articles coded positive.
Source: Weart (1988) (data for selected years only).

The number of articles on nuclear power began to increase about 1950 and reached a peak in the late 1950s after private nuclear power plants were permitted by amendments to the McMahon Act in 1954. Media attention declined in the 1960s, but in 1968 it began climbing again, and interest stayed high for most of the 1980s. The second surge in media interest, however, differed from the first. Whereas in the beginning the positive images of nuclear power had predominated, after 1968 the negative images began to be emphasized. The percentage of stories whose tone could be seen as positive toward the industry had never dropped below 50% until 1968, the same year that the last surge in media interest began.

Figure 39.4 shows that approximately 1,200 congressional hearings were held on civilian nuclear power issues between 1945 and 1987 and indicates whether the topics discussed in those hearings focused on the positive or negative aspects of the industry. The number of congressional hearings on the topic of nuclear power showed only moderate change after the jump in media attention that occurred in the 1950s. Between 1945 and 1955, there were an average of about 6 congressional hearings a year on the topic of nuclear power. In the next decade, the frequency

Congressional hearings on nuclear power

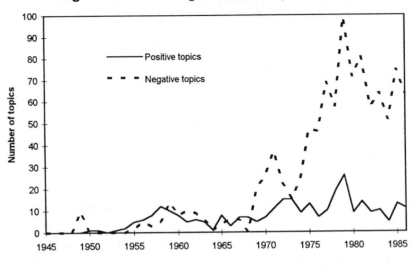

Figure 39.4. Increasing negative focus of congressional hearings on nuclear power.

of hearings on the topic increased to an average of about 16 hearings a year. Beginning in 1969, the year after the second jump in media coverage, a dramatic shift occurred. The average number of hearings per year shot up to more than 50. At the same time, topics discussed in those hearings were no longer fairly evenly split between positive and negative. Attention to the negative aspects of nuclear power shot up, swamping whatever attention to the positive aspects of the industry that remained.

Although there were two periods of increased attention to nuclear power in the mass media—the first enthusiastic and the second critical—only the second was followed by substantially increased attention in Congress. The negative attention in the media and in Congress followed criticism that originated in the Atomic Energy Commission (AEC) itself, according to a case study of nuclear power policy by John Campbell (1988). Beginning in about 1965, AEC technical staff began to question the agency's safety decisions. Previously, safety complaints of opponents of nuclear power had been ignored, but as the scientific experts themselves began to question reactor safety the complaints had to be taken seriously. This attracted more money for regulatory enforcement and provided a shield of legitimacy for future nuclear opponents. With attention to the issue of nuclear power primarily critical, important changes were made in regulatory procedures, and the nuclear power industry was forced to defend itself in state and local governments and the courts as well as in Congress. In 1974, the AEC was dismantled and its regulatory functions were given to the Nuclear Regulatory Commission. No new nuclear power plants have been ordered in the United States since 1977, and more than a hundred previously ordered plants have been abandoned or canceled (Campbell, 1988).

Drug Abuse: Debating Solutions

Drug abuse is what is known as a valence issue—an issue in which only one side of the debate is legitimate (Nelson, 1984). Very few people would be willing to argue in favor of drug abuse. That constraint, however, does not end debate on the topic. Although no one argues that drug abuse is a good thing, people do argue about whether drug abuse is a private problem or one that government should try to solve and about whether drug abuse can best be minimized through treatment and education or enforcement and punishment.

Drug abuse was not a topic of much interest in the U.S. mass media until the mid-1960s, as shown in Figure 39.5. A high of 81 articles was reached in 1967, but that moderate degree of interest waned again in the early 1970s. Even so, media attention to the drug abuse issue was still higher than it had been in the 1940s and 1950s. In the late 1970s, the number of articles written each year began rising again, reaching peaks of more than 250 articles a year in 1986.

It is clear that, at first, media attention to the issue of drug abuse preceded congressional attention. Figure 39.5 shows nearly 1,000 congressional hearings on drug abuse held between 1945 and 1986. Congress apparently did not see drug abuse as an important public problem, amenable to government solutions, until the late 1960s, about 5 years after the issue begun to receive attention in the mass media. Unlike media attention in the early 1970s, however, once Congress focused on the drug abuse issue its attention never wavered. The second media surge in attention to drug abuse was clearly preceded by sustained attention to the issue in congressional hearings.

Attention to drug abuse

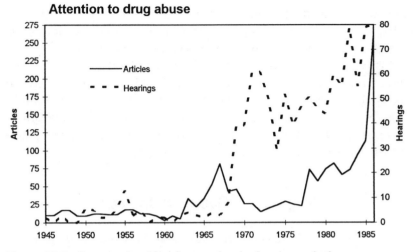

Figure 39.5. Congressional hearings and annual coverage in the *Reader's Guide* on drug abuse.

One reason drug control policy can surge and decline so rapidly from the national agenda is that statistics and indicators of the extent of the drug problem are unreliable. Drug-related arrests rise and decline partly depending on the number of police assigned to drug-related tasks. Hospital statistics on drug overdoses are partly a function of doctors' awareness of drugs as a national health problem. Surveys asking about drug use may be affected by peer pressure to give socially acceptable answers. Although drug arrests increased by more than 200% between 1981 and 1989, federally funded surveys indicated that the number of high school seniors and adults reporting having used illicit drugs had declined during the same period.

The surges in attention that took place in the mid-1960s and afterward thus may have had little to do with changes in the actual severity of the drug abuse problem. The problem apparently was perceived as more severe, and that was enough. Although statistics assessing the severity of the drug problem have no direct causal link to increases in media and congressional attention, the surges in attention do correspond roughly with two presidential initiatives against drug abuse. The first surge in congressional attention came in 1969 after President Richard Nixon took office. Nixon helped frame the drug abuse issue as one of education and treatment rather than enforcement. The number of hearings focusing on drug abuse increased at about this time, and those hearings tended to emphasize treatment rather than enforcement. Media interest in drug abuse preceded the official action by a few years but increased further after Congress began acting.

In the 1980s, with the election of President Ronald Reagan, the emphasis shifted back to enforcement and punishment. Congressional attention had stayed high throughout the period, but media attention had waned. With the new drug initiatives coming from the Reagan administration, the amount of media attention soared to all-time highs. Since the late 1970s, congressional hearings had been emphasizing enforcement rather than treatment, but in the 1980s the trend intensified.

Urban Affairs: When Is A Problem Not A Problem?

The severity of a problem is no guarantee that Congress and the mass media will decide to pay attention to that problem. The issue of urban problems provides a case in point. Urban problems encompass a large collection of physical and social conditions, including housing conditions, congestion, crime, racial discrimination, poverty, mass transportation, and water and sewer quality. Although America's cities have faced these problems throughout this century, and although several periods of extensive urban riots have taken place, in only one period was a corresponding increase in media and congressional attention observable.

We consider the years 1900 to 1990, during which there were three periods of extensive urban civil disorders: 1917 to 1919, 1943, and 1965 to 1968. In the first period of unrest, riots took place in East St. Louis, Illinois; Philadelphia; Chester, Pennsylvania; Chicago; Washington, D.C.; Omaha, Nebraska; and Longview, Texas. More than 70 people died and hundreds of buildings were destroyed. The second wave of riots took place during World War II in Mobile, Alabama; Los Angles; Harlem, New York; Beaumont, Texas; and Detroit, where 38 people died. The urban violence in the 1960s included the Watts riot in Los Angeles in 1965 in which 34 people died and $35 million in property damage was inflicted, riots in Newark, New Jersey, and Detroit, and racial violence in hundreds of cities. Only during the 1960s were the riots seen as connected to a

Media and congressional attention to urban affairs

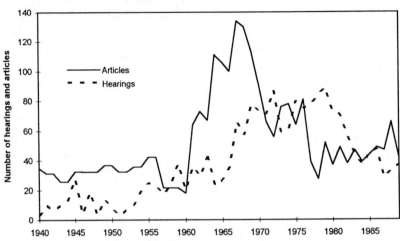

Figure 39.6. Congressional hearings on urban affairs and articles in the *Reader's Guide.*

broad set of urban problems, which the national government took action to address.

No increased attention to urban affairs topics occurred in the popular media during or following the 1917 to 1919 disturbances. The level of interest during this period was low and remained so. Similarly, the 1943 riots were not associated with increased media attention, as can be seen in Figure 39.6. In the 1960s, however, cities became topics of considerable media interest. A sharp rise in the number of articles devoted to urban affairs began in 1961 and continued to a peak in 1966 and 1967. Between 1960 and 1964, the number of articles published on cities tripled. Note that this increase in media attention occurred before the Watts riot. Media interest was certainly intensified by the disorders of 1965 to 1968, but the riots did not create that interest. Media attention was already at its highest point in this century, although it rose even higher in response to the riots. By the early 1970s, however, media interest was declining rapidly, until by 1978 general interest in cities was only slightly above the level of the 1940s and 1950s.

Looking at the pattern of congressional interest in urban affairs, as measured by the number of hearings on related topics, we can see that again, congressional attention tended to follow media attention. Figure 39.6 shows that an increase in the number of articles on urban issues preceded a slight increase in congressional hearings in the 1940s, and increases in media coverage in the 1960s preceded the more dramatic increases in congressional hearings in the 1960s. Does this imply that stories in *Ladies Home Journal* and *Time* magazine directly pressure Congress to hold more hearings on a topic? Not at all. Increased attention in many magazines, as is reflected in our media measure, however, is a good indicator that the mass media in general and that public attention in general are focused on a topic. When that is the case, Congress is much more likely also to pay attention to that issue. Our measure of media coverage probably reflects changes in social understandings of what came to be termed urban problems. Only after an extended period of discussion in the press did Congress increase attention to urban affairs, indicating that congressional response was more the result of changes in diffuse social understandings than of specific perceived pressure from the media.

We noted previously that congressional attention is not the same as congressional action; that is, hearings do not always lead to policy changes. In the case of urban affairs, however, we can see how attention and policy are related. Figure 39.7 compares the number of congressional hearings on urban-related problems with the amounts of federal grants targeted at urban problems. As the number of hearings increased from just a few in 1940 to highs of more than 80 a year in the 1970s, grants to states and localities for such social programs as employment training, community development, urban renewal, infrastructure development, and other programs also increased from next to nothing to more than $100 billion in the late 1970s.

Note the long lag time between the peak in media attention we saw in Figure 39.6 and the peak in grant activity shown in Figure 39.7 more than 10 years later. First, media coverage resulted in congressional interest only after an extended period of time. Then, grant funds increased only after years of congressional interest. Peak media attention to cities occurred in 1967, but peak grant activity did not occur until 1978.

As the number of hearings began to fall off in the 1980s, the amount of grant money began to drop as well, although not nearly as sharply. In 1978, for every $1 raised in local taxes, an additional 26¢ came to cities through direct federal aid (even more came indirectly through the state

Attention and money for urban problems

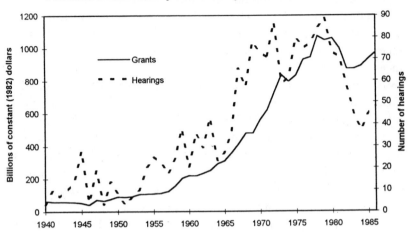

Figure 39.7. Total federal grants to states and localities and congressional hearings on urban affairs.

government). By 1984, aid had declined to 15¢ for every $1 in local taxes (Wright 1988, p. 165).

Conclusion

In the cases we have considered, media attention often precedes congressional attention and then itself increases again in reaction to increased congressional attention. The more successful proponents or opponents of an issue are in generating news coverage, the more likely that there will be a congressional hearing on the issue. The more congressional hearings there are, the more publicity there is likely to be. Once begun, attention to the issue increases by a self-reinforcing mechanism.

Although the relationship between media attention and congressional agendas is complex, the linkage between the two is heavy with policy consequences. Large-scale changes in policy followed the changes we documented in media coverage. In the case of nuclear power, a shift in attention from positive technological images to negative safety-related issues led to the dissolution of the Atomic Energy Commission and the virtual end of the civilian nuclear power program. No new nuclear power plants have been ordered since 1977. In the case of urban problems, of the three periods of urban rioting discussed, only one was accompanied by extensive media coverage of urban problems and only that one prompted congressional attention to the problems facing cities. In the case of smoking and tobacco, Congress began regulating tobacco advertising only after health concerns displaced economic concerns in media coverage of smoking and tobacco. Finally, in the case of drug abuse, increased media coverage preceded congressional action; then, as Congress focused on the drug abuse issue, a second surge in media coverage followed.

That said, media attention still is not a simple and direct cause of congressional attention, even in those cases in which increased (or changed) media attention came first. Often, the media attention itself is in reaction to events in some other area of government. In the case of drug abuse, presidential initiatives to increase treatment and enforcement preceded media attention. Positive media attention to nuclear power followed the passage of the McMahon Act and amendments to that act; negative media attention got its impetus from critics within the AEC. Likewise, negative media coverage of smoking was made possible by increasing societal attention to the health risks of tobacco. Our data cannot address with certainty whether Congress would have acted in the absence of media attention in a given case, but they do suggest that the media help create situations that make increased government attention almost unavoidable.

40 Press Briefing by Press Secretary Mike McCurry

October 12, 1995

The Briefing Room

1:23 pm EDT

Mr. McCurry: Well, as some of the latecomers gather, we will go ahead and commence today's daily briefing from the White House. Good afternoon, ladies and gentlemen. I'm prepared to answer your questions.

Mr. Blitzer: What did you think of the Republican presidential candidates forum in New Hampshire last night?

Mr. McCurry: I thought so little of it, I didn't watch it. I was watching Orel Hershiser myself. But from what I hear of the event, the truly illuminating moment was when they were all standing there in the dark. (Laughter.)

Question: Mike, I'm confused on the budget rhetoric. Are the Republicans in Congress and the president just talking past each other? Is anybody sitting down with somebody else to actually get something happening, or is this all just talking past each other?

Mr. McCurry: Well, we hope the Republicans are sitting down with each other and kind of working out where they are, because they've been all over the map recently. But we assume at some point they will, and at some point they will recognize that they need to address some of the concerns the president talked about even today, and once that happens then we can begin working seriously on the orderly conduct of this country's business.

SOURCE: This chapter is based on a speech by a government official and is therefore in the public domain.

Question: The president said today that he continues to have weekly phone calls with the Speaker. Is that the kind of—is that the venue in which this will take root? And I wasn't sure of the president's answer when he was asked about a budget summit. I don't know whether he was answering that question or another one. Is all this eventually going to have to lead to a budget summit?

Mr. McCurry: Well, all of it will eventually lead to a more reasonable discussion about how we move on with the nation's business. It's impossible to predict now what format that will take, but the president continues to leave the door—his door is open. It wouldn't take much for the Republicans to walk through that door. As the president suggested today, there's willingness to balance the budget, to cut taxes, but cut them in the right way for people who need to cut taxes.

The disagreements are pretty clear. You cannot decimate the Medicare program the way the Republican budget would, and you cannot increase taxes on working people. One of the president's fundamental concerns is the $148 billion worth of tax increases on working people that are in this Republican budget. Now, if they could, as a starting, as a starting point, if the Republicans came forward and said, you know, the president is right; we shouldn't be raising taxes on working people in this country—that is a good place to begin the dialogue. Now, that, by no means, is the only issue that needs to be addressed, but it at least would be a reasonable starting point.

Question: Mike, what does the White House think of the article in *The Wall Street Journal* today which sketched out Senator Roth's changes in the tax bill, including adding money to the child tax credit for those who have kids in college? Do they see that as a step towards the president's position?

Mr. McCurry: Well, most reasonable analyses of the work the Senate is now doing on the tax bill point to what the president has been saying, that they are disproportionately cutting taxes for the wealthiest Americans while they are simultaneously increasing taxes on working Americans, those who are struggling to be out of poverty, college kids who are trying to work their way through school. That's no way to write a tax bill, and the president's view is that they need to begin addressing the fundamental priorities that he put forward in his budget proposal.

Remember—and we've walked through this here many times—the president came a long distance when in June he put forward his plan for a 10-year balanced budget track. And Congress, to my knowledge, has never once seriously looked at that. The Republican majority in

Congress has never once seriously looked in that, but they would find in that proposal a way out of the wilderness that they are now in.

Question: Well, that being said, they made a step towards you.

Mr. McCurry: Well, we will have to see how far that step goes. But there's a lot of good thinking that you can see in some quarters within the Republican Party on the Hill. In fact, a lot of the tension that exists internally, as the president suggested a few moments ago—a lot of the tension that exists internally for the Republicans that the Republican leaders are clearly trying to manage is the tension that exists between those who are sort of at the vanguard of the revolution and those who are moderate and who want to find some common ground with the president.

Now, they need to have the conversation with themselves and figure out which direction they want to go, because the path that they suggested that they would be on earlier this week is one that goes right into the train wreck and right into the type of paralysis that the president believes nobody in this country and nobody, really, in Washington wants to see.

Question: Do you think it's—how eager are you for talks to begin? Or do you think it would be just fine if the Republicans went all the way through to votes on the reconciliation.

Mr. McCurry: It entirely depends on what they really want to do. If they want to get serious, we say, let the discussions begin. If they're going to hold fast to the implausible propositions that they've laid forth in the legislation that they're working on, then there's not going to be any room for that type of dialogue for the time being.

Now, the president will always have an open door, as he said. But you can't walk in that open door with the same old music. You need to come in with some new tunes. And the president suggested today, one way to start is to think about dropping those $148 billion worth of tax increases on working Americans.

Question: How realistic is it to expect them to just drop all of them entirely, when you have Senator Roth, a great proponent of the ITC, which is $42 billion right there?

Mr. McCurry: Well, it is—we are optimistic enough to see that in some places within the Republican Majority in Congress, there are people who really want to get serious, and we hope the leadership will get serious, and we hope the leadership will lead their caucus and say to some who are much more hard-lined, that we need to get down to the real business of governing this country. That requires leadership on their part. The president offered leadership when he stepped forward, put a balanced budget proposal on the table.

You will recall that we took a lot of criticism from our Democrats on Capitol Hill for doing so. But the president felt it was important to do that and it was the right thing to do. Now, we need a reciprocal response now from the Republican leadership, and they're going to have to say to some of the hard-line members of their caucus, you know, look, we can't get everything that you want, but you've got to get on with the business of this country, and that hasn't happened yet.

Question: But the Republicans say that the $148 billion are not tax increases, they are simply spending cuts, and it's outrageous for the White House to call them tax increases.

Mr. McCurry: Well, go back and read to them everything they said about the Democrats when we had exactly the same argument in the 1980s. You will recall Richard Darman's words. If you're out there in this country and you're going to be paying a lot more for benefits and for services that you used to get, it's sure going to feel like a tax increase. They may want to call it something else, but it's going to be for the average person in this country a tax increase, pure and simple.

Question: Next week's trip, particularly Austin, has there been a decision on the racial issue.

Mr. McCurry: There hasn't been a decision. I will tell you a little bit about the way the president sees the event on Monday. He is interested in finding the right way to talk about the subject of race relations in America, as he indicated earlier this week at the press conference with President Zedillo. He is hoping, as you've heard us say often, that those with good intentions who gather for the event here in Washington on Monday will create some momentum for the notion that people need to accept responsibility for their behavior and work together to improve their communities. He believes that there could be genuinely, if people address these issues, a positive outcome as a result of the work of those who are going to gather on Monday.

But finding the right way to talk about that is something he's thinking through now. I would suggest to you, it does not seem likely to me that he will be making some major policy address on the subject of race Monday. He may well address it in some fashion, but it's a subject, remember, that Bill Clinton has talked about throughout his life and throughout his career. And as he said, he will be talking about it in coming days, but he'll be talking about it a lot because it's something that's fundamentally important to the political culture and fabric of this nation.

Question: I don't understand something. The White House is now looking to the Million Man March to provide some momentum toward an answer to the problems with race relations?

Mr. McCurry: The president believes if those responsible for policymaking try to take the genuine motivations of some of those who will be here on Monday and turn those to the work of healing this country and bringing people together, that might be a positive outcome. We've suggested all along that we recognize that there are a lot of people who are going to be here who do fundamentally believe that we have to change people's attitudes and change the way people behave and get people to think more about their responsibilities to family and community.

Those are subjects dear to the president's heart, things that he's talked about a lot. Our problem has been all along with this march is that there are some, frankly, who have got other agendas and other motivations who are associated with this march. But that doesn't mean, necessarily, that we can't see if we can't get something positive coming out of the event on Monday.

Question: If that's your goal, then why—are you now planning to send, or would you consider sending representatives to the march?

Mr. McCurry: No, we're not. But we have been—we have had good liaison contact with those who are involved with the march. We've tried to make sure that responsible officials in the government who are concerned about security and transportation and coordination and what federal workers will be doing that day, that they are all in liaison and in touch with each other. So that's our attitude.

Question: Have you had contact with Farrakhan? What kind of contact have you had?

Mr. McCurry: We've had some contact, I believe, with the national director, with Reverend Chavis, who is the national director of the march, I believe. I would have to double-check that, but I'm pretty sure we have, through the public liaison office here.

Question: Because this march is going to be taking place here that day, he wants to see how it goes before he makes a major policy address—is that what you're—

Mr McCurry: Well, I think he wants to see if you can't take some of the sentiments of those who are here who are genuinely motivated to try to improve their communities, and see if we can't work to direct that towards the types of change in public policy that he's talked about, and see if we can't, frankly, address that to some of the values that he's talked about.

Question: His comments the other day about "I may feel the need to say more about this in coming days" then, that need is not going to be fulfilled on Monday.

Mr. McCurry: Well, he may—I'm not ruling out the notion that he might say something. I think a lot of people have worked themselves into a frenzy, anticipating some major pronouncement on Monday. And I don't see that developing. Now, you all know that the president speaks from the heart on this issue. And he sometimes speaks spontaneously from the heart on this issue, as he did in Memphis several years ago. So I don't want to rule anything out, but I'm trying to give you some sense of where I see things developing, because I know also a lot of you have to make plans.

Question: So what is the stated subject of the president's speech on Monday?

Mr. McCurry: Well, it's going to be a continuation of his argument about how we need to move this country's business forward, the issues related to the budget, the technology, the investments we've got to make in a high-wage, high-growth economy for the 21st century—all things that you would expect him to talk about, and all things that I think would be reflected, even in a speech that would touch on the subject of racial polarization in America and how that is antithetical to what it takes to have a strong and growing economy.

Remember, the president often argues that it's our diversity as the American people that is one of the things that contributes to our strength as we compete in the global marketplace. That's been sort of a resonant theme that he's talked about often.

Question: Going back to the march, Mike, what are the agendas and other motivations that concern you?

Mr. McCurry: Well, there have been remarks made in particular by Reverend Farrakhan related to what he would like to see come out of this march that are not related to the values of community and responsibility that the president thinks are genuine motivations for a lot of people who will be here.

Question: What things does he want to come out of this march that the president does not agree with?

Mr. McCurry: You can easily see if you look at some of the recent comments of Reverend Farrakhan exactly what I mean.

Question: Let's say it goes as you planned, and it's a good march, and you like what you see. Then what?

Mr. McCurry: Well, I think that's a good question is, how do you take some of the energy of the people who are involved in that, and then get them involved in work at the community level, and then ultimately things related to the formation of public policy that can make a difference in how we address these questions of family, of responsibility of dependency—all the things that the president has talked about a lot.

Question: But presumably, if it goes well, then wouldn't you have outreach to Chavis or Farrakhan?

Mr. McCurry: I don't foresee that, no.

Question: Mike, is part of this that the president and the White House is concerned that while he wants to address the topic and make it clear that he's got a lot of thoughts on it and people need to address these problems which linger, that absent some set of pretty concrete prescriptive advice to follow up on it, does it get dicey to stand up in Austin and make a big speech without saying we have the following 62 action points we want to—

Mr. McCurry: Well, that is part of it. But part of it is finding the right tonal quality so that you address these issues in a way that brings people together. And that's difficult to do under any circumstances, but I think he wants to put particular care into making sure he does it in a way that achieves the objectives that he has.

Question: Mike, does it concern the president and the administration that women are being precluded from being a part of this?

Mr. McCurry: That is a source of concern. Now, the sponsors of the march have got a response to that and explained why they don't believe that represents a concern. But, of course, that's a concern that people, particularly in public places and here on the Mall, should not be in a sense excluded from an event. Now, I believe that the organizers say that there's no intent to exclude.

Question: Was the scheduling of this march on Monday a factor in scheduling the president to be out of town on Monday?

Mr. McCurry: No. No, I think there was not—to my recollection, we have had this event. There's another event that's—a series of events in Texas that we're working towards that have been on the president's calendar for a long time and even prior to the announcement of the march.

Question: In addition to what's already on the schedule?

Mr. McCurry: No. Those things are already—mostly the political events that are on the calendar. Those were the events that have been set long ago.

Question: Mike, are you making an indirect appeal to Farrakhan to tone down his rhetoric on Monday?

Mr. McCurry: No, I'm making a direct one. I mean, there are things that he's said that are repugnant. And they need—there's been a long history of people who have gone through his remarks, and you've all covered that from time to time. And in fact, a lot of those comments, you're well aware of, I'm sure. But those are divisive remarks; those are not things designed to bring people together. And what the president is interested in doing, at a time in which there is great concern about the status of race relations, is to see the best way to bring people together. And surely, being concerned about community and family is one of those things that can bind people of all races in this country together.

Question: Do you think it's unreasonable, though, of the American people to expect their leaders—not just the president, but Newt Gingrich, other leaders on the Hill, Dole—to come out and make some sort of statement, say something about how they see race relations in the context of the O. J. Simpson trial now? I mean, is it unreasonable for us to expect leaders to come out immediately?

Mr. McCurry: I think it's unreasonable to expect leaders to characterize the status of race relations in this country, a subject with enormous history that has—with echoes throughout our history as a nation, to expect to characterize that by one snapshot of one extraordinarily highly publicized trial. I don't believe the president, and I don't believe any of the leaders you just mentioned would believe that ought to be taken as the verdict on the status of race relations in America. It's not. There is a lot going on in this country, and I would suggest, a lot more positive going on in this country that characterizes the status of race relations than the reaction to this one, highly publicized, divisive trail.

Question: Why isn't the president talking about that? I mean, in the past, he's never seems to have hesitated. He went straight to L.A. after the riots.

Mr. McCurry: Look, the president will talk about it. He's already told you this week he intends to talk about and he will talk about it. We're also—we started this conversation today talking about the budget. There's been a serious piece of working going on here this week on that subject. I think he wants to say the right thing. He want to try to bring this country together when he talks about it. And to do that, he wants to think about it and he'll do that on his timeline, not on yours.

Question: Mike, some critics of the march, like the Anti-Defamation League, say you can't have it both ways, that it's ridiculous to say that you support some of the good motivations behind the march while disliking Farrakhan, that that's just the same as saying, oh, we support the good people who are marching with the Ku Klux Klan, that there ought to be a forthright denunciation because Farrakhan is leading it. Could you respond to that?

Mr. McCurry: I think that we've made our views on Reverend Farrakhan quite clear and I believe that the rationale that you suggest is wrong.

Question: How about Sunday's speech commemorating 50 years after Nuremburg, human rights and rule of law—what is this topic?

Mr. McCurry: He will—let me check further with him. It's a dedication event, he'll be there in the company of Senator Dodd and paying tribute to Senator Dodd's father. So there will be some of that. But I think it's also a speech that will talk a little bit about some of the challenges that exist in this world as we think about the divisions that existed in the world prior to World War II.

Question: Do we know what we're doing in San Antonio and Houston?

Mr. McCurry: No. I don't. Maybe someone else here does.

Question: The speech on Nuremburg, will he relate to the Bosnia situation?

Mr. McCurry: I just told you everything I can tell you on that.

Question: Well, let me follow up on that. How do you think the cease-fire in Bosnia is being implemented?

Mr. McCurry: Well, we are in close contact with the United Nations, watching implementation of the cease-fire as the parties carry through the commitments that they've made. It seems to be quieter and things seem to be better, especially in Sarajevo, than they have been recently in Bosnia, but this is—by no means will we pronounce this a 100 percent success until we see in the coming days how the parties honor their obligations.

Again,—but it does create an opportunity for our diplomacy to continue, and the State Department will be briefing shortly about Ambassador Holbrooke's plans in coming days, but that we need to use this moment in which we have got a cease-fire, however tenuous, to continue to build on the diplomatic effort the United States is leading to bring these parties to an agreement that will end the war once and for all.

Question: Did you find a location for the Bosnian negotiators to meet?

Mr. McCurry: The State Department is working on that.

Question: Mike, on Bosnia, the Chief of Staff said over the weekend that he understood Congress had some power over the purse to influence the use of U.S. peacekeepers. If Congress passes a resolution saying no money can be spent or whatever, would the president still feel he had the power unilaterally to send peacekeepers in or not?

Mr. McCurry: Well, the president feels he has the power under the Constitution to protect American interests around the world. And he is the Commander in Chief. If Congress took that position and defended something that the Commander in Chief had ordered the military to do, we would be in the middle of a pretty serious war powers constitutional issue. But we're not there now, and the president doesn't believe we will be there because the president believes, as he indicated to them when he met with congressional leaders recently on the subject of Bosnia, that we have a very persuasive case about the need for U.S. leadership helping to implement the peace if we can achieve the peace.

We are right now working diplomatically to achieve that peace. We're doing the military planning that would be sufficient to help implement that peace if we get to that happy point.

Question: Does what you're saying add up to the fact that the president might feel he can ignore the power of the purse?

Mr. McCurry: Well, the president has to obey the law, but he also has to be true to his constitutional responsibilities. And those happily have rarely come in conflict in this country. We would hope that they wouldn't.

Thank you.

The press: Thank you.

41 Remarks by the President at 2nd Americorps Swearing-In Ceremony

October 12, 1995

The East Room

2:40 pm EDT

The president: If she hasn't made the case, there's nothing for me to say. (Laughter.)

Thank you, Michelle Johnson Harvey, for that remarkable statement. And thank you and all of your colleagues here for your dedication to your country, to your community and your participation in AmeriCorps. Thank you, Don Doran, for the work that you have permitted AmeriCorps to do with you and your school in Atlanta.

And I thank Senator Harris Wofford for his willingness to take up this service at this important time in the history of our country and the history of AmeriCorps. We just swore him in—the vice president swore him in over in the Oval Office with Mrs. Wofford and his entire family, and his extended family of friends. And he pointed out that at least I had told him what I expected him to do. He said that once before he was sworn in in the Oval Office and President Kennedy swore him in and then told him what his job was going to be. (Laughter.) So feel that after 30 years we're at least making some progress in the government's obligation to fully disclose to its—(laughter)—"public servant" what they are expected to do.

I want to thank Jim Otoseph, the Chairman of the Board, who is about to become our distinguished Ambassador to South Africa, and all the

SOURCE: This chapter is based on a speech by a government official and is therefore in the public domain.

other supporters of the AmeriCorps program and the other volunteer efforts that are here.

And I want to say, of course, a special word of thanks to my friend of 25 years, Eli Segal, for the remarkable job he did in creating AmeriCorps and getting it off to a good start. Thank you for a brilliant job. (Applause.)

I want to thank the supporters of AmeriCorps in the Congress, including those who are here—Senator Jeffords from Vermont, Congressman Sawyer from Ohio, Congresswoman Karen McCarthy from Kansas City. She got one of her constituents up here, and I saw her bursting with pride. (Laughter.) Congressman Green from Texas and Congressman Tim Roemer from Indiana. We're glad to see all of you. And we thank you for your support.

A year ago in one of my proudest moments as president, I challenged 20,000 citizens to join us in a new American adventure, rooted in our most fundamental values of personal responsibility, educational opportunities, service to others, and commitment to community.

I asked those 20,000 Americans to put their values into action through AmeriCorps, because service is a spark to rekindle the spirit of democracy in an age of uncertainty. Well, the times may be uncertain because they're changing so rapidly, but I am certain that the flame of democracy is burning brighter all across America today because of people like Michelle Johnson Harvey and her friends who helped to close those crack houses and give those children safe streets to walk; and because of the thousands and thousands of other AmeriCorps volunteers and the many thousands more whom they recruited to work to build houses, to immunize children, to educate, to help to solve all the community problems that are being faced at the grassroots level.

You know, it is true that this idea was consciously borne as a nonbureaucratic, grass-roots, community-based, totally nonpartisan idea. I became enamored of the idea of community service because I saw what it could do as a governor, and because I was working with a group in the late 1980s and early 1990s—the Democratic Leadership Council —and we devised a proposal, and Senator Nunn, who just a couple of days ago announced his retirement from the Congress and some others, when President Bush was in office, proposed a pilot project. And President Bush was good enough to sign the bill that passed, and we did begin this.

And then when I ran for president, I saw all over America these community groups like the City Year group in Boston, which is now spreading across the country like wildfire. I saw them everywhere, these young people full of energy and ideas, across racial lines, across income lines—people who had never shared any common experiences before coming together and literally creating a new future for people one-on-one and for communities, and solving problems that we could never begin to solve here in Washington, D.C.

And I was determined that if I ever had the chance to do it as president, I would try to create a national commitment to community service all across the country that would give our young people a chance to give something back to their communities and to advance their education at the same time. That is what we are doing.

At a time when, once again, we are asking ourselves whether we are too divided in our perceptions of reality and our attitudes toward all the things that are going on in America to be a real community, the members of AmeriCorps put the lie to all of that. They show us once again that if you can just get good people together, no matter how different their backgrounds are, and you give them a chance to share common values and to work on a common problem, or to seize a common opportunity, and you give them a chance to do it together, day-in and day-out, they will change everybody's preconceived notions of what is possible in America. They will prove, once and for all, again in this age, that the American idea is a universal idea; that the notion of personal responsibility, the notion of opportunity for everybody, the notion that we're all better and stronger when we work together than when we are divided, that those things are universal; that they are rooted in a fundamental truth about human nature, and that there is no power like it anywhere. That's what these young people in AmeriCorps prove day in and day out.

I'm so grateful for all of the things they've done. They've fought forest fires in Idaho. They've helped people after floods in Houston. They've built homes in Miami. They've, as you've heard, helped to raise reading scores dramatically in Kentucky, a model I hope will be copied in schools all across America. They've helped to prevent lead poisoning in Portland. They've helped troubled youths to care for people in nursing homes in Boston. They certainly came to the rescue after Oklahoma City, some of them in truly remarkable ways. They simply put themselves on the line to prove that things are still possible in America.

No one could ever meet these young people and listen to their stories and continue to be cynical about the prospect of Americans working together. I met a young woman named Velaida "Cricket" Shepard when we had our economic conference in Portland, Oregon, last June. And she was trying to talk about AmeriCorps and she began to cry. She almost couldn't get through her statement. Michelle didn't have that problem. (Laughter.) I thought she was going to declare for president right here in the middle of her speech. (Laughter.)

But this young woman talked about getting up at 6:00 am every morning so she could make sure a young girl she was mentoring got to school on time; so she could make sure that no family problem this child had—nothing would keep that child from school; so she could make sure that no amount of disappointment in her own life, no amount of personal injury that child had suffered, emotional injury, would keep her from becoming what she ought to be.

That young girl, who was troubled, was marked for failure, has now become a role model in her school. And at the same time, "Cricket" Shepard has gone on to other challenges to help other young people do the same, and AmeriCorps is helping her to get an education at Portland State University.

This is the kind of thing that we ought to be doing, folks. No one knows here in Washington what the really most important problem is in Kansas City; but the people in Kansas City know. No one wakes up every morning in Washington thinking about whether, in a given community, they need most to close crack houses, or build Habitat for Humanity homes, or keep beaches clean, or tutor students. But the people in those communities know.

I have been overwhelmed by the broad and deep support for Ameri-Corps from people from all walks of life. We know that it is not only consistent with our values and a good thing to do, it also happens to be cost-efficient and it works. We know that from independent econo-mists, from evaluators; even the GAO says that it more than pays its way and actually costs less than we had originally estimated that it would.

So I say to you today that as we debate this great national question of how to balance the budget, we can balance the budget without turning our backs on these young people. We can balance the budget without forgetting the fundamental lesson, which is, if you can create a national movement with no bureaucracy that explodes human energy at the grass-roots level, you can put the lie to all this business about how we are bound to be divided by race, by region, by income, by walk of life, just by letting them live and do what they know to do. And that is what we ought to do.

AmeriCorps should be continued for far more than the some 25,000 people that will be involved in it this year; far more than the 2,000 communities in all 50 states that will be benefited; far more than the many, many tens of thousands of other volunteers that they will make it possible to work because they will organize them. It should be continued if, for no other reason, that it proves that the American idea is alive and well and can meet the challenges of the 21st century, to restore our values, to strengthen us at the grass-roots level. It can be a shining symbol that there is no need for cynicism, no need for defeatism, and no need for tolerance of division in the United States of America. That's why we should continue AmeriCorps. (Applause.)

So I would like to begin this next year of AmeriCorps by asking all of the members who are here and all of those who are with us via satellite in Kansas City to join me in taking the AmeriCorps pledge.

Please stand and repeat after me, if you're not all standing. Stand up—it'll be good for all of us to do it. (Laughter.) This would be a good pledge for the citizens of the United States:

I will get things done for America—

Audience: I will get things done for America —

The president: —to make our people safer, smarter and healthier.

Audience: —to make our people safer, smarter, and healthier.

The president: I will bring Americans together—

Audience: I will bring Americans together—

The president: —to strengthen our communities.

Audience: —to strengthen our communities.

The president: Faced with apathy, I will take action.

Audience: Faced with apathy, I will take action.

The president: Faced with conflict, I will seek common ground.

Audience: Faced with conflict, I will seek common ground.

The president: Faced with adversity, I will persevere.

Audience: Faced with adversity, I will persevere.

The president: I will carry this commitment with me this year and beyond.

Audience: I will carry this commitment with me this year and beyond.

The president: I am an AmeriCorps member.

Audience: I am an AmeriCorps member.

The president: And I am going to get things done.

Audience: And I am going to get things done.

The president: Thank you, and God bless you all. (Applause.)

End 2:53 pm EDT

42 Going Less Public

Managing Images to Influence U.S. Foreign Policy

JAROL B. MANHEIM

It was January 1995, and Boutros Boutros-Ghali, Secretary General of the United Nations (UN), had a problem. In the year of its 50th anniversary, his organization was beset by difficulties of lack of respect, lingering distrust of its large and inefficient bureaucracy, and budget woes arising in part from the costs of a recent spurt of peacekeeping missions in trouble spots around the world and in part from the failure of deadbeat members to pay their dues and assessments. Among the deadbeats was the United States, which traditionally had provided nearly a quarter of the UN's funding.

The secretary general's solution? An advertising and public relations blitz that would include everything from Swatch watches bearing the United Nations logo to an advertisement featuring a beautiful woman in an expensive automobile driving past the UN building in New York, waving, and exclaiming, "Ah, the United Nations!" (Crossette, 1995).

Mr. Boutros-Ghali can be forgiven this eccentric little proposal on several grounds, not the least of which is that such promotional advertising by international organizations, multinational corporations, and national governments is commonplace in the United States and elsewhere, although it usually carries a rather more serious and sophisticated message. The most comprehensive study of the phenomenon (Amaize & Faber, 1983) found that governments appear to attach great importance to such advertising, which tends to take the form of multipage inserts in the world's most prestigious newspapers. Readers of such American newspapers as the *New York Times*, the *Los Angeles Times*, and the *Washington Post* will be familiar with these ads, which tout the political stability, sound business environment, enlightened leadership, and democratic values of countries from Hotairistan to the Republic of Somekingsego. Advertising campaigns are often used to mark important anniversaries or holidays, head-of-state visits, and other special events.

The reasons governments and others undertake these rather expensive promotional efforts vary. Sometimes they are exercises in self-congratulation for proving that one is important enough to merit media attention in the United States or acts of frustration undertaken only when all efforts to get attention through the so-called free media—that is, the news— have failed. Also, sometimes they are public reminders that a given country is, in fact, friendly or important to the interests of the United States. In any instance, the large sums of money invested in this image burnishing are often wasted.

The reason this is true has to do in part with the objectives of the governments that engage in such promotional activities, in part with the nature of foreign-policy decision making in the United States, and in part with the nature of political communication and persuasion. Let us take a look at each of these elements in turn.

Objectives

We can begin to divine the objective of this national image advertising by looking at the selection of media in which it is found. As Amaize and Faber (1983) report, this advertising is far more common in major news-papers with elite audiences than in other media. From this we can conclude that the intended audience comprises Americans who are likely to take an active interest in, and may have some influence on, their country's foreign policy. The ultimate objective is to influence that policy itself, whether in the military, trade, aid, or political arena, to the advantage of the advertising country. That makes these campaigns a component of a class of communications between governments that has come to be known as public diplomacy.

Public diplomacy refers to the efforts by a government to engage the people living in another country in some form of dialogue, whether to improve understanding between the two societies or to achieve some more instrumental gain. In its most benign form, it includes cultural exchanges, such as the Fulbright Scholars program and tours of other countries by artists or athletes, as well as public relations initiatives intended to explain a government's policies or portray a nation in some particular way to a foreign audience. Public diplomacy, however, can also include efforts to generate public pressure on the government of the target country to turn its foreign policy to advantage or, alternatively, to cause the public to lose interest so that the target government is free to pursue a course it might otherwise be unable to pursue. For example, other governments might try to manage the images by which they are portrayed in the U.S. press and perceived by Americans so that they can obtain from the government of the United States a better trade deal, better terms in a treaty, a favorable ruling on some regulatory issue, more military aid, or some other item that is being weighed by U.S. policy-makers at the time the public diplomacy campaign is being waged (Manheim, 1994). Mr. Boutros-Ghali, for example, might have hoped that an endorsement from a beautiful woman in an expensive car would pry loose from a recalcitrant Congress the hundreds of millions of dollars owed to the United Nations by the United States.

Americans would know in an instant, of course, that the secretary general's communication plan would not lead to the desired outcome. The reasons for this include the following: the campaign as conceived would not be sensitive to the domestic politics required to produce the desired outcome, would not offer any emotional or intellectual engine to drive Americans to renew their support for the United Nations, and would lack stylistic appeal to the intended audience. Indeed, by presenting gender and class stereotypes that are out of favor in the American political culture and by associating the United Nations with financial excess, this advertisement, if run, would surely have done more harm than good.

Making and Influencing U.S. Foreign Policy

That is not to say, however, that all efforts at policy-directed public diplomacy are doomed. Rather, the lesson is that, to be effective, such efforts must be grounded in a firm understanding of the political culture of the target country, its policy-making processes, and its communication norms. In a democracy, there is a presumption that all policy making is responsive in some measure to public opinion. At least in the United States, however, there is a great deal of variation in the manner and degree in which this responsiveness occurs. On the domestic scene, in which the impact of policy choices is relatively clear and direct, many citizens take an interest in the development and adoption of specific policies. It is difficult to think of decisions on such matters as taxes, education, law enforcement, or abortion taking place without considerable public involvement. There are, to be sure, numerous obscure policy decisions made on less visible domestic issues, decisions of which the public remains generally ignorant. On the major issues of the day, however, public involvement is the rule.

In foreign policy, this rule does not always apply. Foreign policy is the more or less private preserve of a small group of so-called experts and, except for a few headline issues, the public is routinely and easily excluded from the process. This is the case in part because the issues involved in foreign policy are often abstract and obscure. They do not *seem* to affect the public in the same way that an economic slowdown or a change in the education system might. In addition, most Americans have not traveled abroad and do not have any direct personal experience by which to judge the pros or cons of a given foreign policy option, nor do they know or care very much about what occurs in other countries around the world. Also, in something of a circular process, U.S. news organizations, knowing of the low level of audience interest, are unwilling to invest the substantial resources that would be required to cover international news fully. Applying the agenda-setting hypothesis in reverse, the resulting absence of such stories in the news reinforces the absence of audience concern, and the cycle of disinterest continues. What it produces is a vulnerability to the manipulation of public opinion by those with a vested interest in specific policy outcomes.

In addition, there are those—foreign governments with a stake in the outcome, relevant ethnic communities in the United States, defense industries, international organizations such as the European Community or the United Nations, humanitarian organizations, and others— that follow closely the making of U.S. foreign policy and that, from time to time, attempt to influence the outcome. Of particular interest are the foreign governments that, ironically, may actually gain from the democratic process in the United States which allows them a relatively free voice in policy debates—at the expense of the public whom that process is designed to represent.

We can think of the function of media and public attention in the making of public policy as twofold. First, it creates or limits the freedom of action of policy makers to select among the available policy options. Second, it channels the selection itself in one or another direction. In the first instance, the more attention that is being given to a particular issue, the more the politicians and bureaucrats will feel compelled to make choices—to do *something*. In the bright light of publicity, if there is public consensus on the objective everyone must take a position in favor of solving a particular problem. If there is, as well, public consensus on the means to achieve the objective—that is, not only whether to do it but also how—the policy that emerges will almost always be responsive to that consensus.

Recall, however, that in the making of foreign policy the public is typically uninformed, uninterested, and uninvolved. This means that, on most issues of foreign policy, the policy makers will have a great deal of freedom of action and will not be forced by mass opinion into one or another policy choice, perhaps even against their best judgment. At the same time, however, the norms of democratic participation are still honored in foreign policy making, and the participation of even small segments of the population can have an impact. In this way, responsiveness to a vocal few can come to stand for responsiveness to the silent many, and a policy that is, in fact, narrowly supported can be both understood and portrayed as a democratic outcome. In such circumstances, it might well be the objective of public diplomacy to mobilize selected interested *segments* of the American public to support the objectives of the foreign government engaged in the communication effort.

Strategies and Tactics

Actually, we have begun in recent years to refer to this particular form of public diplomacy as strategic public diplomacy, and the notion that there exists a strategy behind these efforts is key to understanding how they are conducted, why, and with what effect. Figure 43.1 provides one way of thinking about this.

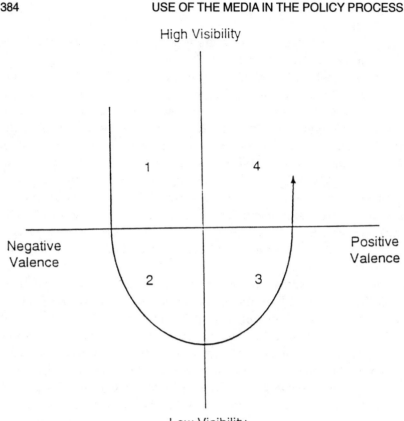

Figure 42.1. Dimensions of national image.
Source: Reprinted with permission from Manheim and Albritton (1984).

Figure 42.1 summarizes some of the differences that might exist among the settings in which communication campaigns occur and some of the different types of strategies that might be used in each setting. The vertical axis in the figure represents the amount of news coverage or public attention being devoted to a particular object—for example, a country or government—at a given point in time, which is termed "visibility." The horizontal axis represents the extent to which that news coverage or attention is generally positive or negative in nature, which is termed "valence."

By combining these two characteristics, the image of the country or government can be characterized as one of four types. Type 1, in the northwest quadrant of the figure, is a country that is very much in the public eye and is generally viewed in negative terms. An example would have been South Africa during the period of Apartheid rule or Iraq during the period leading to the Gulf War.

Type 2, in the southwest quadrant, is a country that is viewed in unfavorable terms but is seldom noticed. Perhaps with the exception of South Florida, Cuba might be an example today. Type 3, in the southeast quadrant, is a country that is seldom in the public eye but that has a favorable image among press and public. Switzerland, the land of banks and yodellers, is a case in point. Type 4, in the northeast quadrant, is a country with a positive image that is prominent in public discourse—a country such as Great Britain.

The value of thinking about communication settings in this way is that we can apply what we know about media behavior, political attitudes, and persuasion to identify what is likely to be the most effective public diplomacy strategy in each different circumstance. For example, in Type 1 situations, we know that people are likely to reject as "propaganda" any positive message about itself that the country in question might issue, whereas in a Type 2 setting, in which little thought is given to the country in any event, there are opportunities for valence-changing persuasion. An advertising campaign along the lines of "Visit sunny South Africa, land of mountains and beaches," would surely have been ridiculed and would probably have had the opposite of the desired effect. Therefore, in this instance, the country would (and at one point did) adopt a strategy of moving out of the news, going less rather than more public, in an effort to move to a Type 2 setting in which persuasive messages could have an effect. Explicitly promotional activities, such as advertising campaigns, as well as other, more sophisticated tactics are useful primarily on the eastern slopes of the figure where the objective is to reinforce an existing favorable image. The curve in Figure 42.1, then, summarizes the strategic objectives (in terms of changing visibility and valence) that a country might have in each of these different circumstances (Manheim, 1994).

It is in the context of this analysis that we can see the real folly of Mr. Boutros-Ghali's proposal. Part of the problem he confronted at the beginning of 1995 was that the United Nations was held in low regard in U.S. public opinion. It was, in essence, operating in a Type 2 setting— low visibility and negative valence. In that situation, a promotional advertising campaign would raise visibility at a time when the organization's image was negative. The result would have been to move the

United Nations toward a Type 1 setting, making the problem of obtaining the desired support more difficult still. It was not the silliness of the proposed advertisement, then, but rather its strategic weakness that would have doomed the effort.

The tactics available to foreign governments' strategic communicators are the same ones available to domestic players of the political game—advertising, staging events, mobilizing grassroots support, and "managing" the news. These tactics were first developed for use in political campaigns, but in recent years we have seen their application to policy making in many ways. The most effective tactics are those matched to the target audience by careful research in the form of focus groups, surveys, and even electronic monitoring of responses to images or messages. The most effective campaigns are those that best sense and respond to the political environment, testing each tactic for timeliness and effect.

An Industry Is Born

Most governments do not have the expertise to evaluate American media content and public opinion, and to develop public diplomacy strategies and tactics, at a level of sophistication sufficient to influence U.S. foreign policy. Therefore, they rent it.

Americans have long been willing to assist foreign governments in influencing public opinion and government policy, and the United States government has long worried about this phenomenon. In fact, many of those who assist foreign governments and corporations are themselves former officials of the U.S. government, including former cabinet officers and members of Congress (Choate, 1990). As early as the first Roosevelt administration, for example, Congress saw the need to pass the Foreign Agent Registration Act of 1934 (or FARA), which, with amendments, has served to assure that at least some light is cast on these efforts. Although originally approved as a means for countering espionage efforts, the 1934 legislation has more recently served as a vehicle for requiring that those engaged in public relations, lobbying, and other efforts in behalf of foreign interests register with the Department of Justice and disclose certain aspects of their activities and remuneration. Figure 42.2 is based on data from these FARA registrations.

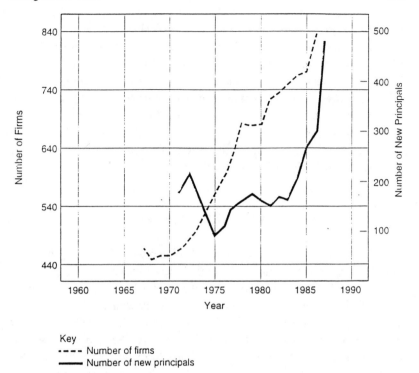

Figure 42.2. Number of registered firms and new foreign principals, 1967 to 1987. Source: Reprinted with permission from Manheim (1994).

The broken line in Figure 42.2 represents the number of firms that contracted to provide services to foreign interests during each calendar year. These firms include law firms that track legislation and lobby on behalf of their clients, public relations firms that try to shape public opinion, and many others. The solid line represents the number of new principals, or clients, who sign contracts each year. Virtually all these firms also provide the same services for a wide range of domestic clients—corporations, interest groups, and so on.

Two points are immediately evident from Figure 42.2. First, there was a substantial increase in the numbers of both registered foreign agents and clients during the period covered by the data. Although it is not obvious here, much of that growth has come in relationships devoted to lobbying and image management. Second, and most revealing, the growth in the number of firms providing FARA-registered services *preceded* the growth in the number of foreign clients. This means that it was the marketing of services by law and public relations firms (and others) eager to increase their profits that led to the growth of strategic public diplomacy and not a clamor for assistance by foreign governments that pressed a reluctant influence industry to expand from domestic to international services. In effect, then, the free-market forces of the U.S. economy led to the *recruitment* of foreign clients to whom services are offered to assist in their influencing U.S. foreign policy by using the processes of American democracy (Manheim, 1994).

Adolf Hitler Redux

Besides a series of First Amendment-related and other considerations, one of the reasons that these seemingly deleterious activities are tolerated in the United States is that they are not necessarily viewed as contrary in intent to the interests of the foreign policy-making establishment. Indeed, in at least one instance the U.S. government rather clearly cooperated with an exercise in foreign agentry. That occurred during the buildup of public support for military intervention in Kuwait in 1990 and 1991.

Shortly after Iraqi troops invaded Kuwait in August 1990, two executives from Hill and Knowlton Worldwide met with the then-exiled Kuwaiti ambassador to the United States to plan a campaign—soon undertaken in behalf of the newly formed and, as it later turned out, regime-funded "Citizens for a Free Kuwait"—to mobilize American public opinion in support of military action to reclaim the country. This campaign had a very public face in the form of speaking tours by Kuwaiti business people and students, orchestrated media appearances, and even emotional hearings in Congress and at the United Nations—all of which were designed to generate sympathy for the exiled Kuwaitis. As became clear later on, this was, in some measure, a campaign of lies and misleading information (Macarthur, 1992).

It was also, in part, an exercise in strategic public diplomacy because central to the Hill and Knowlton campaign for Kuwait was research, and central to the research was an effort to measure, manage, and respond to shifts in American public opinion. This included focus groups and nightly tracking polls of the very sort one might expect to see employed in a political campaign. Early on, that research suggested both a strategic opportunity and a problem. The opportunity: Americans knew next to nothing about Kuwait, so there was fertile ground for an educational campaign to frame the issues (Wilcox, Ferrara, & Allsop, 1991). The problem: From August until October, the number of people who thought American involvement in the Gulf would be a mistake actually increased (Mueller, 1993). What to do?

In September, Hill and Knowlton contracted for a special research project in which a group of average citizens was presented with video images of some 50 different themes and message components and asked to indicate on electronic monitors the extent to which they were favorably or unfavorably impressed by each. Until then, the prevailing theme of the public relations campaign had been that Kuwait was, in effect, a liberal democracy, or at least the closest thing to one in the Gulf region. The September research, however, showed that this theme simply did not "resonate" with the public. People either did not believe it or they simply did not care. What people genuinely did care about were some other images that demonized Saddam Hussein and personalized the conflict—images that had been floating around the media environment since before the invasion but had not been emphasized in the public relations effort (Dorman & Livingston, 1994). Saddam Hussein, especially cast in the role of Adolf Hitler, was an image around which a successful mobilization campaign might be built. That is precisely what Hill and Knowlton, even over the early objections of their clients, set out to do (Manheim, 1994). Mueller (1993) reports that this image effectively came to define support for the conflict.

What is especially interesting is that beginning, coincidentally, within a week of the invasion of Kuwait, Craig Fuller, who had served as George Bush's chief of staff when Bush was vice president and was still a Bush policy adviser, assumed his new position as head of the Washington office of Hill and Knowlton. Throughout the period of the Gulf conflict, Fuller coordinated the efforts of the Kuwaitis with those of the Bush administration, in whose policy councils he sat. George Bush, who found his own fate closely tied for a time to that of Saddam Hussein (Iyengar & Simon, 1994), became a leading voice linking the Iraqi leader with various forms of Nazi iconography.

Conclusions

Are we to conclude from this discussion that the independence of foreign policy making in the United States is at risk, that our national interests are being defined not by our citizens but by the governments of other nations with the assistance of paid agents? Although that is a substantial overstatement, it does carry a measure of truth. It is not, however, necessarily either the governments or their representatives who are at fault because it is the responsibility of a knowledgeable and vigilant citizenry in a democracy to protect its own interest. The making of foreign policy is clearly an arena in which that responsibility has not been met. That other interested parties should move to fill the resultant political vacuum should not surprise us.

As the campaign to mobilize support for the Gulf War made especially clear, and as the underlying theories of communication and persuasion have long held, influence is most easily exercised in settings in which the level of information held by the public and the level of concern or interest they express are low. That is clearly the case in the foreign policy arena. More troubling still, however, is the incentive this creates for those who would influence policy to *keep* the process out of public view precisely *because* that element of invisibility is the source of their influence. It is for this reason that image management efforts are so often designed to move issues and interested parties *out* of the news and *out* of public view—to go less public—rather than to stimulate and influence open public debate. In that sense, such efforts are inherently undemocratic, and they are a threat to the legitimacy of the policies that they help to produce.

43 Putting Media Effects Research to Work

Lessons for Community Groups Who Would Be Heard

MICHAEL PERTSCHUK

I had a conversation recently with the very progressive head of a very progressive foundation. We had both participated in a stimulating meeting with, among others, David Gergen. "How I wish," I said, "that we could have Gergen and Shields back together for next year's election season."

"What's Gergen and Shields," he said, "I don't watch television." Now, most everybody among the audience here knows Gergen and Shields. The trouble is that just about no one in the larger public (whom social scientists study) knows who Gergen and Shields is, watches them, or gives a damn what they have to say.

Public interest advocates and program officers are far more likely to be print addicts than even casual TV watchers. When they do watch, it is Gergen and Shields, CNN, or the quarter-million warped souls who are addicted to C-SPAN.

Therefore, the first lesson for those of us who counsel and those who fund citizen groups who seek to enlighten broad public attitudes is a lesson we know but never learn: Television matters. Commercial television matters. It matters a lot. Indeed, it may be the medium that matters most.

Ironically, newspapers may matter largely to the extent that they still, although decreasingly, shape the agenda of television journalists who, ironically, still read newspapers even if their viewers do not.

How News Tells the Story

The second lesson is that the power of commercial news in shaping public attitudes is not great news. We always suspected that it was bad news. Now we know it with certainty.

One of the reasons that it is bad news is that most commercial news stories do not lead anywhere useful in helping the viewer interpret the events. They do not lead to an understanding of root causes. They do not lead to holding responsible those who are truly responsible, and they do not point a knowing finger at those who bear the responsibility for alleviating the underlying conditions that spawn the stories.

There is some small comfort in this research in confirming that some things we thought we knew are so. Policy advocacy that fails to pay attention to the ways in which television news tells the story is doomed to be misperceived. Words matter. Pictures matter. Stories matter.

Although many of us would like to believe that citizens' core values and belief systems can transcend the last TV story, the last "episodic" frame that fails to place responsibility anywhere but on the actors involved, it is not so.

For many years, we have taught community activists that the most effective way in which they can tell their story is to bring forward the "face of the victim," the "authentic voices." If those faces and those voices, Iyengar (1991) tells us, are faces and voices of color, what most of the viewers will take away is the frame of responsibility of people of color for their own problems. If they are kids smoking, what viewers take away is kids being kids and choosing to smoke.

If you are white and middle class, the white middle class might hear your theme. If not, forget it. Only if the faces and voices are white will the themes they articulate resonate. Those who advocate on behalf of communities of color would do well to tell their thematic stories through talking white heads.

Of course, this is a repulsive lesson, but what else do we tell those who seek to reach and persuade a broad public? Iyengar's (1991) framing research presents a double bind for the media advocate: We have taught, this time correctly, that stories of human interest are one of the keys to unlocking the door to television coverage of the issues communities care about. It is true. Television likes human interest stories. No matter how powerfully we tell those stories, however, Iyengar tells us, the audience we have so eagerly sought will not get the connection between the story and the theme—the policy or environmental condition that was the root cause of tragedy or conflict.

The sober report or press release with graphics that does develop the theme of needed policy change, however, will not make it past the media gatekeeper looking for good, episodic stories.

One more piece of bad news: Episodic framing does not just leave viewers anchorless in affixing responsibility. It actually reinforces the ascendant neolibertarian, or radical individualist public philosophy, that holds only individuals responsible for their fate.

Roger Pilon of the Cato Institute, now riding the crest of influence in Washington, states, "We alone are responsible for ourselves, for making as much or as little of our lives as we wish and can." In other words, no one else is responsible for our problems: The lop-sided economy, shrinking health care, degraded environment, violence, and crime—just folks; doing right; doing wrong.

No one is responsible for fixing the problems: not governors nor presidents nor legislators. For some, this news is simply an affirmation of despair.

Three Routes of Action

For those who have not lost hope that television, and our polity, can yet do better, there seem to be three possible routes of action (which need to be pursued simultaneously:

1. Lobby to change the rules under which bad television thrives: Restore the public service standards for broadcast licensees, enforce the antitrust laws to assure multiple voices, and mandate fairness and equal time for opposing views.

That is a worthy cause. It is not going to happen until the country tires of its current political dalliance with the wonders of free-market liberalism.

2. Lobby and educate the media through the public journalism movement to do precisely what Iyengar (1991) tells us is not being done—provide

the underlying thematic explanations to the apparently unconnected events and occurrences.

3. Take television as it now exists, biased and consumed, with warts and blemishes, and mindless pursuit of meaningless stories, and work with it daily. Use all the skills of creative advocacy to fashion stories that hurdle the media thresholds of boredom, and frame those stories in ways that let the themes shine through. That is one definition of media advocacy.

I have been asked to draw some illustrations of successful media advocacy that transcend themeless episodic framing from two issue areas in which we work with community groups on media advocacy—tobacco and gun control.

Tobacco Control

By 1970, public health advocates had concluded that only vigorous public policies restraining tobacco industry advertising and marketing practices could stem the tide of tobacco-caused disease and death. Public education through the mass media was an essential precursor to public support for such policies. They faced the two chronic challenges Iyengar (1991) warns us about, however. First, much media coverage of tobacco and health tended to frame the story just as the tobacco public relations practitioners wished: episodic stories of personal choice. People knowingly choosing the risks of smoking to enjoy the pleasures of smoking. No policy implications there. Second, for more than a decade, throughout the 1970s and early 1980s, tobacco as a public issue was "off the air," and hence not on the national agenda.

This was not an accident. Most knowing observers assumed that the tobacco industry agreed not to resist the congressional ban on broadcast cigarette advertising because they feared the one for three counterads mandated by the Federal Communications Commission (FCC). That was part of the motivation.

Earl Clements, former Kentucky senator and deputy majority leader, then president of the Tobacco Institute, actually argued to the resistant companies that it was politically critical for them to get off television; that the persistence of TV ads and the controversy surrounding them kept raising the salience of cigarettes and health as a public issue; and that if cigarettes disappeared from television, they would disappear from the public agenda. They did, for more than a decade, throughout the 1970s and early 1980s.

By the mid-1980s, however, the public health advocates had developed strategic media approaches: training, an activist electronic network (more than 500 members) that provided timely guidance and shared experience in gaining media access for tobacco-related news stories, and reframing much of the news coverage.

As agenda setting, this focused energy has worked. Since 1988, when SCARCNet, the tobacco control advocacy network, began daily news summaries of tobacco stories, the average number of daily tobacco stories has more than tripled. In early 1995, as advocates sought to build public support and pressure on the White House to embrace Food and Drug Administration (FDA) Commissioner Kessler's initiative to regulate the tobacco industry's access to kids, the coverage has again increased substantially.

Iyengar (1991) tells us that viewers follow a simple adage when forming political opinions: "oppose policies, institutions, groups, or leaders who represent forces of problem causation, and support institutions, programs, or leaders who represent forces of treatment" (p. 14)

For tobacco control advocates, the challenge has been to reframe the tobacco problem from one of individual causation to one that places responsibility squarely on the disinformation and aggressive marketing of the tobacco industry and the corrupt influence of tobacco lobbying.

The parallel challenge has been to focus responsibility for curbing tobacco use and tobacco industry wrongdoing on government, not just smokers and parents.

Following the strategic lead of FDA Commissioner David Kessler, tobacco control advocates developed a four-chapter story, with an arresting headline: Tobacco use in America is a "pediatric disease." Only kids take up smoking (90% start before age 20):

1. Tobacco use is addictive—a drug, not a pleasureful choice.
2. The companies manipulate nicotine levels to reinforce addiction.
3. The cigarette is a drug delivery device within the meaning of FDA laws and have lied about it for decades.
4. The cigarette companies deliberately target advertise, promote, and sell to kids.

As a consequence, smoking among young people is on the rise.

Iyengar (1991) tells us that "specific events and occurrences" make news. Tobacco control advocates helped craft or take advantage of those events that make thematic news, such as scientific reports that zero in on the effects of Joe Camel advertising on 6 year olds or that demonstrate that the increase in teenage smoking coincides with the introduction and widespread dissemination of the Joe Camel campaign.

Stories of secret industry papers—a sure attention getter—focused on what the industry knew about addiction, thereby hammering away at addiction. Stories of internal advertising and marketing documents opened up the target marketing of kids.

As an auxiliary story and subtheme, the advocates hammered away at the tobacco lobby, focusing, for example, on campaign contributions as a handy index of corrupt purpose. Opportunism may not be a universally admired character trait, but it is at the heart of effective media advocacy.

When Victor Crawford, a former tobacco lobbyist dying of lung cancer, decided to make amends for his sins, the tobacco control advocates he spoke to understood that his was not only an important story but a story that would have innate appeal for television. Indeed, it turned out that Victor's story was so appealing that Connie Chung's producer and a *60 Minutes* producer nearly came to blows over who would get what piece of Victor Crawford. *60 Minutes* won.

Crawford, however, agreed to use his own story not simply to gain media access but thematically to focus on the responsibility of the tobacco lobby for lying, buying votes, using phony science, and denying the addictive nature of tobacco. What could easily have been an episodic story was strategically worked by Victor and the public health advocates with whom he took counsel into a strong thematic story with broad public resonance.

These and other thematic stories took. They emboldened the White House to support the FDA, so much so that when President Clinton delivered his weekly radio talk on children and tobacco, he invited Victor Crawford to join him.

Gun Violence: The Challenge

Those who work for gun control and other public policy initiatives to prevent gun violence do not have to worry about access to media. Stories of gun violence leap over the threshold of media interest. The frame for gun violence, however, is notoriously episodic: not economic deprivation, not lack of opportunity, not poor schools, not the absence of community infrastructure, not the wild proliferation of guns. Just bad people; especially bad young men of color.

One new, substantial initiative designed to help transform the notorious episodic coverage of gun violence into thematic coverage of community conditions is the Carter Center's Not Even One project conceived by Bill Foege, perhaps America's most creative public health leader.

Foege reached back to a public health advocacy technique called the "sentinel event." A sentinel event is a story; a story of an event so extraordinary, so dreadful, that it alerts the community to the fact that something has happened that should not happen, and that, therefore, something must be done. Such a sentinel event, says Foege, is the death of a child from a gunshot wound.

The Not Even One project will train teams of citizens in communities in participatory research so that whenever a child gun death occurs, the community team will investigate the circumstances of the death and report both its immediate and underlying causes to the community, whether those causes be outside sources of guns and drugs, the loss of jobs, the absence of recreational opportunities, the breakdown of schools and churches, the unresponsiveness of police, and so on.

A key part of the training for the teams will be in media advocacy: how to gain access to key community media to tell the full story of the death and its causes, and how to build on media attention to the story of the shooting to develop the themes of cause and responsibility in ways that engage not only print but, most especially, broadcast media. The Carter Center and the community leaders involved recognize that without such media capacity and strategies, the reports will remain invisible and unheeded.

Gun deaths in the home are another story of great interest but that generate little thematic reporting. The gun went off. Careless father; luckless tourist; heedless children. Too bad; episode; themeless story. Jann Wenner, the noted publisher and a deeply committed handgun control advocate, initiated and convened a prestigious funding and strategic group called the Cease Fire Working Group.

Opinion analyst and media strategist Peter Hart used polling and focus groups to help design a campaign using public service announcements both to affect the behavior of householders and to help structure news media coverage of handgun deaths and injuries in the home.

Film Director Jonathan Demme then made a series of ads based on the Hart research. The following are the scripts for the first three:

VIDEO: PAUL NEWMAN SITS OR STANDS SOMEWHERE IN A HOUSE, DRESSED CASUALLY. HE HOLDS A NEWSPAPER AND READS. VERY STRAIGHTFORWARD, LETTING THE HORROR OF THE STORY CONVEY THE EMOTION.

AUDIO: Liverpool, New York. Fourteen-year old Michael Steber was watching football at a friend's house when the friend removed one of six loaded guns from a closet and removed the clip. He was showing the handgun to his friends when it discharged, killing Michael. Michael's last words were "You shot me." In 1992, Gun deaths were the second-leading cause of death for children aged 10-14. Protect your family. Keep handguns out of your home. Before you bring a gun in the house, think about it.

VIDEO: OPRAH WINFEY SITS OR STANDS SOMEWHERE IN A HOUSE, DRESSED CASUALLY. SHE HOLDS A NEWSPAPER IN ONE HAND AND READS FROM IT.

AUDIO: (IN A STRAIGHTFORWARD, ALMOST STOIC VOICE. SHE LETS THE HORROR OF THE STORY ITSELF CONVEY THE EMOTION.) "New York, New York. A 28-year-old man who was fed up with the crime in his neighborhood bought a 380 semi-automatic handgun for home defense. Later, while showing the gun off to a cousin, it accidentally discharged. The bullet passed through his hand and hit his five-month-old daughter, killing her." A handgun bought to protect your family is far more likely to kill someone in it. Protect your family. Keep handguns out of your home.

VIDEO: PAUL NEWMAN SITS IN A HOUSE, DRESSED CASUALLY. HE HOLDS A NEWSPAPER AND READS. HE NEVER LOOKS AT THE CAMERA.

AUDIO: West Monroe, Louisiana. Matilda Crabtree, 14, jumped out of a closet and yelled "Boo" to scare her parents, and was shot to death when her father mistook her for a burglar. Matilda was supposed to be sleeping at a friend's house, but decided to sneak home and play a joke on her family. Her last words were, "I love you, daddy."

For every intruder killed in the home, there are 43 accidental gun deaths and suicides. Protect your family. Keep handguns out of your home.

VIDEO: WALTER CRONKITE SITS OR STANDS SOMEWHERE IN A HOUSE, DRESSED CASUALLY. HE HOLDS A NEWSPA-PER AND READS.

AUDIO: CRONKITE: VERY STRAIGHTFORWARD, LET-TING THE HORROR OF THE STORY CONVEY EMOTION. Central, Florida. While his little brother watched, a nine-year-old boy was shot to death when a babysitter removed a .44 magnum handgun from a locked gun cabinet and it discharged. The panic-stricken babysitter called 911 and said, "He's on the couch. His eyes are closed. He's dead, I think. He's dead."

A gun in the home triples the risk of a homicide in the home. Protect your family. Keep handguns out of your home.

VIDEO: JOANNE WOODWARD SITS OR STANDS SOME-WHERE IN A HOUSE, DRESSED CASUALLY. SHE HOLDS A NEWSPAPER IN ONE HAND AND READS FROM IT.

AUDIO: IN A STRAIGHTFORWARD, ALMOST STOIC VOICE. SHE LETS THE HORROR OF THE STORY ITSELF CONVEY THE EMOTION. "Naugatuck, Connecticut. D. J. Kenney, twelve, died after being accidentally shot at a friend's house. The friend had found his father's loaded .22 caliber pistol and was playing with it when it discharged, striking D. J. in the back of the head. Two other loaded guns were found in the house." In 1992, gun deaths were the second-leading cause of death for children aged 10-14 or under. Protect your family. Keep handguns out of your home.

(From Fallon McElliot Television)

Because Wenner and the members of the Cease Fire group include those who own or who have direct access to those who own the networks, these public service announcements (PSAs) will run. That is not an opportunity usually open to most community-based advocates, so this campaign is not offered as an endorsement of PSAs.

It is, however, a brilliant illustration of the conscious reframing of episodic stories into thematic stories. With skill, such techniques can be applied in the telling of news stories just as well as in public service announcements.

A strategically placed ad, even a low-cost radio ad, can sometimes be used to generate and frame news stories. With the Cease Fire PSAs, another advocacy electronic network, SafetyNet—focused on gun violence—will be generating a stream of media initiatives to community-based advocates on how to generate stories about the ads themselves and to piggyback radio talk shows, TV panel discussions, as well as print op-eds and editorials on top of the PSA campaign.

44 Talking Back, Ernie Pyle Style

SUSAN NALL BALES

This is about storytelling—how journalists tell stories to citizens, how advocates tell stories to journalists to convey to citizens, and how we tell stories to each other to try to make sense of what is happening to our families, neighbors, and people we do not know.

A different kind of story is needed, and this paper tries to point out a few elements of that new story. Media advocates need to pioneer a new kind of talking back, a value-based storytelling whose big story is about overcoming boundaries between people to engage in common ground problem solving.

Since the Reagan era, many progressives have operated on the assumption that we need to out-Reagan Reagan by promoting streams of human interest—mostly victim—stories. These stories make the point that real people are suffering, but they do so within currently accepted journalistic practices that undermine public resolution. Now there is new scholarship to suggest that these stories do a disservice to progressive ideals and detract from the bigger story we are trying to tell about our common destiny. There are reasons these stories worked for Reagan and will not work for us. It is time to reexamine our tactics.

The task before us requires some extensive rethinking. As advocates, we need to spend some thoughtful time together in examining the way that "human interest" stories are told, how they become imbued with meaning, and how they are interpreted by the listener. We need to ask ourselves, what is the story behind the story—the big story that we tell ourselves over and over about our experiences as Americans? How are values embedded in the commentary and how do those values either

AUTHOR'S NOTE: This chapter is condensed from a longer paper available from the Benton Foundation, 1634 Eye Street, NW, Washington, DC 20006.

help us solve problems together, as communities or as a country, or break us down into individual problem solvers, a nation of individuals loosely tied together?

This is also about a new kind of journalism that we can use to inform, model, and support our work. Public journalism is a progressive vision, but it will only develop if advocates raise the expectations for journalists.

"Doing public journalism means asking yourself . . . How do we tell the story of this community in a manner that invites citizens to join the story as informed participants? That's the challenge for public journalism as a narrative art," writes Jay Rosen, director of the project on Public Life and the Press at New York University.

I submit that Ernie Pyle was a pioneer of public journalism. His style—interpreting Americans to themselves and helping them see their country and its values up close and personal—is an art we must recapture if we are to find a public voice for progressive ideas. In the end, journalism is far too important to be left to the journalists. It is time to take back the territory of public storytelling.

> Enterprise, Alabama. This is a New Deal story, so if you don't like the New Deal you won't see any sense in it. When the government took a hand here in 1935, six out of ten school children in the county had hookworm. Every other baby died at birth. One mother in every ten died in childbirth. The average mentality was third-grade. One out of ten adults couldn't read or write. Three-fourths of the farmers were tenant farmers. Most of them had never been out of debt in their lives. They averaged only one mule to three families. And this is in coffee county, which stands third among all the counties of Alabama in the value of agricultural products. These figures are not the scandal-ous revelations of some smart Brain Truster from the North. They are from a survey made by Southerners. Sure, you'll find wealth and grace and beautiful homes in the South, homes as pretty and people as fine as anywhere in the world. But you drive the back roads, and you won't see one farm home in a hundred that would equal the ordinary Midwest farmhouse.
>
> Coffee County has become a sort of experimental station in Alabama. Not by design, especially, but because the government people and the local agencies got enthusiastic, and it just grew up under them. Federal, state, and county agencies all have a

hand. To prevent overlapping, they are coordinated under a council, with the county school superintendent as chairman. They say it's the only thing of its kind in America.

These agencies cover most everything from typhoid shots to fruit-canning. They're like agencies in your home territory, only the need is greater and I suspect they are a bit more enthusiastic. The work is climaxed in the Farm Security Administration, which actually owns thousands of acres of land and plants these down-and-out farmers on its acres. I wish there were something to call these things besides "projects." The idea of a project makes the farmers contemptuous, makes Republicans snort with rage, brings sneers from the townspeople. A project is Brain Trust— experimenting, regimenting people.

What they're doing here isn't a project, anyway. They aren't setting up a "settlement." Nobody is forced to do anything. The six hundred farmers on FSA are scattered over a county twenty-five miles square. What they're doing is simply a general and wide-stretching process—starting almost from zero—of trying to get people to live better.

Ernie Pyle, March 16, 1939, as quoted in Nichols (1989, pp. 338-339)

The language and the vision are as fresh as if the dateline were yesterday: the populist distrust of government, but the strong insistence nevertheless on connectedness and mutual responsibility; the yearning for words devoid of politics, that real people can understand; the emotional connection to Americans' basic sense of fairness, told from the perspective of "the little guy." This is also the challenge of progressives in this country—to personalize the impacts of policies in ways that bring home the consequences to real people we recognize as part of "us."

Ernie Pyle had the unique advantage of being a columnist, of writing in the first person. He used it differently, however, than many columnists do today. Pyle used his firsthand observations to translate the world for his readers. The "I" does not aggrandize or get in the way of the observation, the way it often does with cult-of-personality columnists today. Pyle's I establishes a common perspective and builds a bridge to the reader. Many advocates can use this first-person advantage in their own house organs, newsletters, and op-ed columns, but using the personal voice effectively requires an understanding of how this seemingly simple technique can be used to convey larger democratic values. Ernie Pyle offers advocates a model and a technique.

What can advocates learn from a columnist long lost to history? We are increasingly dependent on news for the way our issues are understood by the public. The press sets the public agenda, which sets the policy agenda. The news is increasingly dependent on us as the sources for stories about what is happening in communities, the impact of policies on people, and the opinions of community leaders. We are often inventing, writing, and pitching the rough drafts of the evening news. Learning new ways to frame our issues requires that we borrow from the best of journalism, understanding how to use its conventions, trends, and deviants to make the news that really does advance public understanding.

Who was Ernie Pyle anyway? At the time of his death while covering the final days of the war in the Pacific, his column appeared in 400 daily and 300 weekly newspapers. John Steinbeck (Ernie Pyle website: www.spce.com/ihsw/pule.html) summarized the appeal of his friend's work when he told a *Time* magazine reporter,

> There are really two wars and they haven't much to do with each other. There is the war of maps and logistics, of campaigns, of ballistics, armies, divisions and regiments—and that is General [George] Marshall's war. Then there is the war of the homesick, weary, funny, violent, common men who wash their socks in their helmets, complain about the food, whistle at the Arab girls, or any girls for that matter, and bring themselves through as dirty a business as the world has ever seen and do it with humor and dignity and courage—and that is Ernie Pyle's war.

There are still two wars. One is fought from the top down and the other from the bottom up. They rage every day in the daily newsprint and videotape of the evening news. Which story will win the coverage—the story of the generals at the top or the story of common people struggling to make ends meet?

Public Journalism

We are going to talk across the generations here. We are going to borrow Jay Rosen's contemporary definition of public journalism to study just what Ernie Pyle did and how he did it. Also, we are going to use this analysis to speculate on what it meant—or would mean—for advocates and journalists to talk back to libertarian principles in this way.

Rosen has set out a paradigm that defines the unique perspective of public journalism. What is public journalism? Rosen (1992) argues that journalists need a "compelling public function" and suggests that it should be as

> advocates for the kind of serious talk a mature polity requires.
> . . . They should announce and publicly defend their legitimate
> agenda: to make politics "go well," in the sense of producing a
> useful dialogue, where we can know in common what we cannot
> know alone and where the true problems of the political com-
> munity come under serious discussion. (p. 24)

In short, public journalism is a new way of covering the world that contributes to a "better, richer political dialogue." To get there, Rosen asserts, will take a fundamental reinventing of the values and art of journalism. Journalists

> will have to change their lens on the political world and learn to
> see politics anew, as a discussion they have a duty to improve.
> But first, the press must acknowledge the existence of an old lens,
> a manner of viewing politics that has gradually broken down,
> making it more and more difficult for journalists to see their way
> clear of some destructive patterns. The horse race, in- sider
> baseball, the gotcha question, the feeding frenzy, the cult of
> toughness—these ought to be seen as unsustainable practices.
> (p. 25)

Talking Back Ernie Pyle Style

This, of course, is what Pyle is best known for. He defined war coverage as being about the doughboys, not about the generals. He redefined news as being about ordinary people.

One prominent journalist, Phillip Ault, recently described Pyle's abil-ity to get away from the censors in World War II by remembering how he would go out and talk to people wherever he was. In this way, he broke several important stories about the political climate, public opinion as it affected various countries' support for the Allies. "The story," his competitor remembers, "was right under our noses." Ernie got the scoop, however, while the others waited for the official communique. For advocates, the story of what is happening in America is indeed right under our noses.

Ernie Pyle, however, did more than redefine the subject of news. He thought his job was to explain people to each other, to create a common sense of understanding. In addition, although the focus was always on people, Pyle's coverage frequently went after the larger causes and consequences of their situations. He asked a different set of "why" questions than other journalists were used to posing.

How did he get away with it? Because he was a columnist, a correspondent, and because he defined the kind of journalism he was doing as correspondence, letters home to America, an ongoing conversation about who we are and who we might be.

STRUGGLING IN THE POWDER RIVER COUNTRY MILES CITY MONTANA

Denver Williams had been sitting in my room talking for about two hours last night when who should walk in but Dr. Rexford G. Tugwell. Denver Williams is a cattle man, and he's broke, and he has lots to tell. And Dr. Tugwell is the big works in the Resettlement Administration, and he's out here seeing the drought, and he's a good listener. So for an hour Denver Williams talked and Rex Tugwell listened. This is what he heard:

Denver came to Montana's Powder River country in 1912, working as a cowboy. As the big outfits dwindled and the cowboys started setting up for themselves, Denver did likewise. He got a thousand acres. He raised from forty to a hundred cattle a year.

In 1919—drought. In 1920—more drought. So Denver left for the Colorado oil fields. He had never seen an oil rig, "but it's good for us to learn new things," he said. He drew eighteen dollars a day, and saved thirty-five hundred dollars that year. He came back to Montana and staked themselves to a new start on the ranch.

Denver went to the oil fields again. Three times that has happened. Twice it was drought; once it was rain. Something is about to happen again. Denver saw a man signing up for relief yesterday. Two months ago the man had eight hundred head of cattle. Today he is broke. Denver said it would take a loan of five thousand dollars to get him started again with cattle next spring, and it would take him five years to pay it back. He said he'll have to work some kind of job to see his family through the winter. He never preached, never pleaded. He didn't appeal. He just happened to be there, chewing the fat with me, so he just told us how things were. When he had gone, Rex Tugwell said, "Isn't he a swell fellow? He's the kind that's got to have help, and right now. He's worth helping."

Ernie Pyle, July 22, 1936, as quoted in Nichols (1989, pp. 121-122)

Contrast this column to any recent coverage of welfare reform and you will begin to understand the importance of dominion. Pyle was asking a big question: Is this problem appropriate to government? To answer that question, he did not go to the official source; he went to the problem.

In the interest of space, we have left out the details. Make no mistake, however, Ernie never left out the details. He did not just want us to understand Denver Williams—he wanted us to get to know him, to hear him tell his story in his own words, and to recognize him the next time we saw him. Never leave out the details.

Public journalism is also about tone and balance—what gets left in the story and what gets left out. Pyle did not edit out the emotion, the compassion, or empathy. He approached a situation eye to eye with the subject, and he exhorted his readers to see it his way. If this had happened to you, he asked, would you be any better off? If you were in the other guy's shoes, how would you feel? What would you want or expect from me, from the community? News should ask these questions, Pyle's columns assert.

Implications for Policy Advocates

Challenge your community to think big thoughts. Public journalism is a movement, and because it is a movement that arises out of the profession itself it has the potential to overcome journalists' aversion to "advocacy." Share Jay Rosen's paper with (a) the editorial board of your local newspaper, (b) the community affairs directors at all local TV and radio stations, and (c) a broader coalition of community-based civic and voluntary groups. Orchestrate a brainstorming session to identify 10 issues confronting your community that you want covered, raised to the level of community dialogue. Work alongside local media in the identification of these issues. Ask: "How can our community come together to understand these problems better and to make rational decisions?"

You do not have to tackle every social problem. You can build on your community's commitment to children, the environment, or education. Use this foundation to elevate a bigger debate. In your discussions with other advocates, ask what story is right under your nose? Is it the story of children in foster care, in the juvenile courts, or in the emergency rooms? Of families struggling to secure health care or shelter or food or employment?

Ask yourself: How did they get there and what is our responsibility— as a community and as a society—for intervening in the situation? What is government's role? What will happen if we do nothing, and what will this say about us? Try telling the story of a child, an elderly person, or a family with whom you come in contact from the perspective of public journalism. Ask yourself what citizens need to know about this person to understand him or her in his or her environment. Consider your job to be explaining this person and his or her situation to a family member at a great distance. Write a letter to your community. Ask yourself what readers would need to know to advance their understanding of how the country works, to really learn something, as opposed to merely being entertained. What do you want them to walk away with, to know, as a result of meeting this person?

Do not skimp on the details. Do not just tell us about programs. Let us see, hear, and feel the people until we could recognize them on our own street corner. Make us care. Make us see ourselves in this person. Ask the reader: "Know anyone like this?"

Progressives must learn to tell the story that is right under our noses, in a way that invites America into the discussion. We must tell the stories of the people who pass through our classrooms, our clinics, our programs in real people language. We must not make the mistake we have made in the past, talking about people as if they were programs with their clothes on. We must step in and reintroduce Americans to themselves, on a first-name basis. The story is right under our noses, but we haven't found our voice.

45 Framing the Framers

Changing the Debate Over Juvenile Crime in San Francisco

VINCENT SCHIRALDI
DAN MACALLAIR

The debate over the causes and solutions to crime is one that is driven by misinformation and idiosyncratic cases. In 1988, Vice President George Bush gained an overwhelming public relations advantage in the presidential race over Democratic challenger Michael Dukakis when the infamous story of Willie Horton was publicized. A convicted rapist, Horton reoffended while out of prison on a Dukakis-approved furlough program.

Dukakis' public relations debacle occurred despite two important but poorly publicized mitigating factors. Over 90% of inmates furloughed under Dukakis completed their furloughs without incident, and the majority of inmates released from the Reagan-Bush Federal Bureau of Prisons were released through a furlough program. As long as the icon of Willie Horton dominated the story's frame, however, substantive issues such as these were relegated to the fringes or fell out of the picture altogether.

Mythology has had an especially powerful ability to dominate crime control policies and media coverage of crime since the 1988 election. Despite the fact that there are only between 50 and 150 kidnappings by strangers per year in America, the kidnapping and murder of Polly Klaas launched a wave of "three strikes and you're out" legislation across America. Between 1992 and 1993, although the murder rate in America stayed the same, the number of murders reported on the ABC, CBS, and

NBC evening news tripled. Not surprisingly, concern about crime rose sixfold during this time, topping the Gallup Report for the first time in its history.

Two lessons are clear. Policy setting in the area of crime is particularly vulnerable to manipulation in the media by election-minded politicians. Advocates for rational solutions to crime must develop sophisticated, multifaceted strategies if they hope to combat the propensity for policy by hysteria.

The following is a case study of how liberal advocates in San Francisco were able to reframe issues in the juvenile justice debate. This article depicts the advocates' media strategy engaged between 1992 and 1995 to combat a pattern of misinformation promulgated by the San Francisco mayor's office and police department with regard to juvenile crime in San Francisco. As part of a larger organizing effort conducted by Coleman Advocates for Children and Youth (Coleman), the Center on Juvenile and Criminal Justice (CJCJ), and other San Francisco organizations, the ongoing media strategy was successful in reframing the issue of violent juvenile crime from one that focused on and exaggerated individual juvenile behavior to one that offered accurate data and painted the mayor as a self-seeking politician trying to bolster his approval ratings on the backs of children.

Background

For years, there has been a battle raging over the "soul" of San Francisco's juvenile justice system. From a media standpoint, the progressive vanguard of that battle was occupied by Coleman Advocates for Children and Youth and the Center on Juvenile and Criminal Justice. Both groups have been active in efforts to reform San Francisco's juvenile justice system.

The conservative opposition, which advocates increased incarceration for youth and reduced use of community-based programs, included the Probation Officer's Association (POA), the district attorney's office, and the San Francisco Police Department. The POA successfully led the opposition to Proposition B in 1990, a ballot initiative designed to tear down the antiquated 135-bed juvenile hall and replace it with a modern

72-bed facility. In 1992, the POA was the first union to support the candidacy of then-Police Chief Frank Jordan in his mayoral bid to oust incumbent Art Agnos.

In 1990, Agnos had appointed CJCJ's executive director, Vincent Schiraldi, as president of the newly established Juvenile Probation Commission. The commission's membership also included Coleman board member Art Tapia. Agnos also appointed reform-minded Chief Probation Officer Fred Jordan to reduce the detention population and expand community-based services. Jordan, an outsider from Maryland and the department's first African American chief, was angrily opposed by the POA.

In 1992, Frank Jordan unseated Art Agnos in a hotly contested race, running mainly on the theme of crime control. With Jordan's election, conservative elements within the city attempted to promote hard-line juvenile justice policies consistent with national trends. By inciting public fear of juvenile crime, conservatives in the mayor's office, police department, district attorney's office, juvenile probation department, and local media hoped to implement their long sought-after agenda of more arrests, prosecutions, and incarceration. Through this agenda, the mayor intended to demonstrate his resolve in curbing juvenile crime and promote his reelection.

The strategy adopted by community advocates shortly after Frank Jordan's election was to prevent the wholesale dismantling of previous juvenile justice reform efforts. It was widely rumored that Mayor Jordan had made a campaign promise to fire Fred Jordan (no relation) as a "quid pro quo" for the POA's support. As such, one of the reformers' primary objectives was to forestall Fred Jordan's firing for as long as possible. The strategy was to keep the other side constantly off balance, to create controversy whenever possible, and to let no attack on the progressive agenda go unanswered.

The Media Games Begin

The conservative assault was almost immediate. The first volley came in the form of a report by the police department titled "Juvenile Crime and Adult Responsibility." This report suggested that juvenile crime was being exacerbated by leniency within the juvenile justice system. Greater use of incarceration, trying more juveniles in adult courts, and the establishment of a "serious habitual offender program" were called for. The report went unnoticed for several months until a press release was issued detailing the report's findings. The press release resulted in a front-page article in the San Francisco *Examiner* headlined "Young S.F. Thugs Are Coddled, Cops Say." Among other things, the report claimed that youth were responsible for 50% of all robberies in San Francisco and 40% of all car thefts.

Skeptical of the report's accuracy, CJCJ staff immediately reviewed the publicly available data on youth crime in the city. According to the official data, juveniles were responsible for only 16% of robberies in San Francisco, hardly remarkable because they make up 16% of the city's population. Furthermore, although youth were responsible for 40% of the city's car thefts, this was not particularly noteworthy because they account for 38% of car thefts nationally. In short, neither statistic could justify an indictment of San Francisco's so-called "coddling young thugs," and the report's content clearly was an attempt to inflame public hysteria.

CJCJ immediately circulated an analysis to the media, paying particular attention to the *Examiner*, which was devoting substantial attention to the subject. CJCJ associate director, Dan Macallair, had what appeared to be a well-received conversation with *Examiner* reporter Leslie Goldberg, author of the "Young Thugs" article, apprising her of the erroneous police data and requesting a follow-up story.

Several days later, Goldberg called back to interview Macallair on his "credentials as a statistician," ominously indicating that she was "doing a story on CJCJ." Despite all attempts to expose the police misinformation, the San Francisco media refused to give credence to information that contradicted the police report.

Two months later, in June 1993, Kevin Mullen, a retired police officer and self-described "historian," published an opinion piece in the *Examiner* deriding the liberal treatment of youths, claiming "A fundamental lesson of the 150 year criminal justice history of San Francisco is that, without concrete sanctions against criminal violence, society's bullies will victimize their more timid fellows." He even went so far as to quote an 1849 book on crime during San Francisco's Barbary Coast days, claiming "that the best cure for hoodlums is the frequent application of locust or hickory to the hoodlum's skull."

The Opportunity

Although the first round clearly went to the mayor and police department, notice was served that the advocacy community was not to be taken lightly. Also, through determined efforts by the advocacy community, many reporters covering the crime issue came to the realization that the police had gotten away with one.

The next media opportunity occurred quite unexpectedly on the evening of August 20, 1993. While Chief Jordan and his hand-picked director of juvenile hall were out of town, 11 youth escaped from the maximum security unit of the facility. This occurred during the same month in which there were two highly publicized shootings involving youth in San Francisco's popular tourist mecca—Fisherman's Wharf.

These episodic events were quickly exploited and woven into a theme by politicians and the media—juvenile crime is out of control. The situation for Fred Jordan and the youth advocacy community could hardly have been worse. Rather than retreating or accepting defeat, however, the advocacy community went on the offensive. Coleman and CJCJ orchestrated an "anti-hysteria in juvenile justice" press conference, which included representatives from both agencies as well as representatives from the Black Men of Action, the National Council on Crime and Delinquency, the Youth Law Center, and the National Center for Youth Law. At the press conference, we forcefully drove home several themes:

> Beware of politicians boosting their approval ratings on manipulated data. Juveniles did not commit half of all robberies in San Francisco, but only a more modest 16%.

> Escapes under Fred Jordan were down substantially versus the previous, more conservative chief. Even including the 11 escapes that occurred in one night, the escape rate under Fred Jordan was .67 per month compared to 3.67 under his predecessor.

> Due to the obvious acrimony between some staff and Chief Jordan, the city should look into the possibility of sabotage in the escape. (The keys to the unit were left in a place to which the youths had access. They simply unlocked the door and walked out.)

Several important lessons in framing were gleaned from this well-publicized press conference. First, although the event itself was newsworthy given the level of anti-youth sentiment engulfing the city, the sabotage allegations moved the story to the front page and top of the evening news.

Second, the advocates won the framing battle that day, and the press conference represented something of a turning point in the entire youth crime battle. This is best exemplified by the following interchange included in a prominently featured San Francisco *Chronicle* article titled "Sabotage Theory in Youth's Escape."

> Accusing San Francisco Mayor Frank Jordan of undermining the authority of the Youth Guidance Center, juvenile justice experts yesterday demanded an investigation into how 11 youths recently escaped—and even suggested the possibility of sabotage by disgruntled counselors. . . . "Chief Jordan and Juvenile Hall Director Don Mead were both out of town on the day that the keys to the most restrictive unit were left in a place to which youths had access," said Vincent Schiraldi, director of the Center on Juvenile and Criminal Justice. "Given the well-known animosity some of the staff have toward the chief, I believe that sabotage should at least be investigated."
>
> "There is no evidence that anyone did anything to stop them, and that's very troubling," said mayoral spokesman Noah Griffin. "But to jump from that to say that the Mayor is giving aid and comfort—directly or indirectly saying it's OK for counselors to let people escape—is a very big jump."

The mayor's staff was clearly caught off guard, offering a defensive response to a damaging accusation for which no evidence was provided. More important, this occurred at a time when the mayor was otherwise on the attack, representing a clear shift in momentum to the advocates' side.

Because of the controversy created by this press conference and concomitant organizing efforts, the mayor backed off on threats to fire Chief Jordan. Instead, he made a political blunder by establishing a task force to investigate the matter. He compounded that mistake by appointing CJCJ's Macallair and Coleman's Carol Callen as two of 25 appointees to the task force.

During the 4 months that the task force conducted its hearings, the issue of the *Examiner's* juvenile crime coverage needed to be addressed.

Leslie Goldberg was seemingly crusading to rid the city of Fred Jordan and CJCJ. In several of her interviews, she made unsolicited disparaging remarks about CJCJ. This prompted a number of her interviewees, including the presiding juvenile court judge, to contact CJCJ and inform us that she had a "vendetta" against the organization.

In the fall of 1993, representatives of CJCJ and Coleman met with the *Examiner*'s editorial board to discuss their coverage of this issue and the vitriolic nature of Goldberg's interviews. That meeting was followed by letters from Macallair to both Goldberg and the editorial board reiterating our concerns. Macallair insisted that,

> a fair and thorough evaluation of the juvenile justice system involves more than merely accepting the viewpoints of one side as fact and then simply calling the other side for a cursory response. Healthy skepticism should always be applied to both sides.

Perhaps what most significantly affected the *Examiner*'s coverage, however, was an interview Goldberg conducted with CJCJ Project Director Chet Hewitt. Hewitt consensually taped the interview in the event Goldberg became confrontive and less than objective. After she stormed out of the meeting accusing Hewitt of trying to intimidate her, Hewitt forwarded a copy of the tape to her editor. Shortly afterwards, Hewitt received a call from the editor who apologized, stating Goldberg had acted inappropriately. The *Examiner*'s subsequent series on juvenile crime was more subdued than previous coverage, and CJCJ received no negative mention.

Power Corrupts and Absolute
Power Corrupts Absolutely

In January 1994, the police department released another wave of concocted juvenile crime data. In a January 24, 1994, article in the San Francisco *Chronicle* titled "Teenage Crime Wave in S.F.—Homicide Arrests Up 87%,— the police department reported a huge increase in juvenile homicides between 1992 and 1993, along with a 77% increase in robberies. "It's an epidemic," stated Mike Jeffries, the police inspector who released the data. Two days later, the police again put forth their much sought-after Serious Habitual Offender Program to surveil San Francisco's 12 most dangerous youth ("S.F. Police," 1994).

An investigation of the police department's statistics revealed that the police counted only actual homicides in 1992, but then combined homicides and attempted homicides in 1993. In fact, there were 14 juveniles arrested for homicide in 1992 and 14 juveniles arrested for homicide in 1993.

The banner headline in a January 28, 1994, *Examiner* article (written, significantly, by Leslie Goldberg) stated, "Newspaper, police data on juvenile crime ripped: accused of fanning flames of hysteria." The article quoted probation department statistician Sandy Clayborn, PhD, who stated "there was no increase in homicide arrests" and chided the *Chronicle* for not checking its facts. Callen stated, "These questionable figures from the Police Department, repeated in the *Chronicle*, fan the flames of crime-wave hysteria."

The *Chronicle* and police department responded as follows:

> *Chronicle* managing editor Dan Rosenheim said Thursday: "For our story on Monday we took published statistics from the Police Department's monthly crime report that clearly showed increases in homicide, robbery, and aggravated assault. We brought questions raised by the new numbers as soon as we got them to Commander Philpott, and he's standing by the department's statistics. If that changes, we'll be the first to report it."

The liberal San Francisco *Bay Guardian*, now awakened to the issue, ran a full-page article deriding the police for misuse of crime data. The paper accused Mayor Jordan and Supervisor Annemarie Conroy— Jordan's goddaughter appointed by him to fill a vacancy and at the time running for re-election—of politicizing the crime debate and manufacturing data:

> Crime. Crime. Crime. As the beat of this election-year drum echoes across the country, San Francisco is picking up the rhythm, but with a particularly ugly twist here politicians, cops, and the press have started picking on kids. In the process, they've distorted the facts and created a climate of persecution that youth advocates say could ultimately make the problem of juvenile crime worse.

It was felt at this point that caution would reign in San Francisco crime reporting. Much to our surprise, in February 1994, less than a month after the erroneous homicide data were reported, the mayoral-appointed grand jury issued a report stating that 50% of all crime committed in San Francisco in 1993 was committed by juveniles, and that there had been a 137% increase in juvenile arrests for robberies since 1988. This astonishing piece of misinformation was immediately seized on by both advocates and the media. Our office informed the press that only 8% of the city's crime was committed by juveniles, and that if the year 1990 (the year of Fred Jordan's appointment) were used instead of 1988, the data would have shown a 100% decrease in juvenile arrests for robbery.

The *Bay Guardian* ran an article titled "Media hype misleading" and the *Examiner* featured a story on the front page under the heading "Juvenile crime data questioned" with the opening,

NUMBERS RUNNER: The author of the San Francisco civil grand jury's explosive report on juvenile crime admits he fudged the numbers, conceding he has no hard stats to back up his report's claim that half the crime in The City is committed by kids under 18. . . . This is the second time in a month that juvenile crime figures have turned out to be wrong: Police Chief Tony Ribera admitted a week ago that the department messed up a report on juvenile homicides. He said they had nearly doubled from 1992 to 1993 when in fact the cops had accidentally combined homicides and attempted homicides.

The strongest article by far ran in the San Francisco *Weekly* and was titled "S.F. *Examiner* sensationalized phony numbers to sell papers":

Alarming rise in juvenile crime is a political hoax. With a lead off asserting "The only juvenile crime epidemic in San Francisco are the wildly exaggerated statistics city officials keep cranking out to show that gun-slinging hoodlums have taken over the streets." "They are cooking the books in order to ratchet up the problem," said Vincent Schiraldi, director of the Center on Juvenile and Criminal Justice (CJCJ). "These are political documents that are very substantially disconnected from reality. . . . This is statistical cherry picking raised to a high art" added Schiraldi.

Can't Win for Losing

On November 10, 1994, 3 years after Mayor Jordan was elected, his hand-picked Juvenile Probation Commission fired Chief Probation Officer Fred Jordan, even though the mayor's own task force had recommended against firing the chief. The firing of Fred Jordan was universally viewed as a slap at the African American community and a crass political payoff to a special interest group—the POA. The chief's firing occurred at a packed commission hearing at which supporters outnumbered opponents 10 to 1. It was followed by a scathing report authored by Coleman's director Margaret Brodkin, sent to over 2,000 influential San Franciscans.

The fight to get rid of Fred Jordan took almost 3 years and further eroded Mayor Jordan's strained relations with the black community. To make matters worse, the mayor became the subject of a vicious direct mail attack by some of Fred Jordan's supporters.

Ruminations

The battle waged over juvenile justice in San Francisco between 1992 and 1995 illustrates several points. Media advocacy can only be effective as part of an overall strategy.

No media strategy can succeed without an equally well-orchestrated organizing strategy. During the course of the events detailed in this article, the following political, research, litigation, and programmatic efforts were occurring simultaneously: The Black Men of Action was meeting with the mayor and elected officials over Fred Jordan's tenure; the Youth Law Center sued the city over conditions at juvenile hall; Fred Jordan instituted standards and training designed to improve conditions at juvenile hall; the National Council on Crime and Delinquency conducted research that showed that 90% of detained youths are accused of nonviolent crimes and 90% of youths released pretrial faithfully return to court without reoffending; Coleman Advocates for Children and Youth spearheaded groundbreaking legislation that created a designated Children's Fund in San Francisco; and the Center on Juvenile and Criminal Justice founded a model, collaborative program designed to safely reduce the population of juvenile hall. These various efforts combined with the previously described media strategy actually resulted in a reduced juvenile hall population and conditions that improved somewhat for youths, despite a mayoral administration determined to roll back human rights gains.

Advocates for rational policies and more balanced stories need not be passive, hand-wringing lamenters of a political system and media gone mad. The press is willing to print the right information and politicians can be held accountable thereby. Bad coverage of the crime problem can no longer be used as an excuse by reform advocates for the failure of their cause but rather as a challenge that can and must be overcome.

It is vital that media advocates not get so caught up in the "game" of affecting the media that they forget what they are about.

Although this is an article about media advocacy, it is a story about violence and troubled youth. In every act of violence, on both sides, exist real people, with real lives, and real hopes and aspirations. They feel real pain. They really suffer. If we get so caught up in gamesmanship with politicians or in our efforts to influence the way our issue is framed that we forget this, then we have already lost the battle.

46 Advocate's Guide to Developing Framing Memos

LIANA WINETT

A framing memo is a tool for understanding how an issue is presented and discussed in the media. It involves assessing, mapping, and analyzing media portrayals of particular issues so that a blur of news coverage can be viewed in a methodical, meaningful way. This tool is not intended to provide a scientific analysis of news coverage—rather, it is a means for advocates to gain practical understanding of the breadth of arguments around an issue.

Journalists create news "frames" through their inclusion or exclusion of images, opinions, examples, or actors to "package" information for their audiences. In other words, a frame is the ideological structure that guides the process of shaping bits of information into a news story (Gitlin, 1980). The framing memo is a strategy developed in recognition of the fact that journalists tend to portray certain topics in particular ways through the application of formulae. By incorporating certain items within a frame, journalists are deciding that these variables are central to the problem and are important for audiences to consider. Similarly, by excluding certain perspectives or information from frames, journalists are implying that these things are marginal or not important, and thus detract from the legitimacy of these factors in the cause or solution of problems.[1]

As Charlotte Ryan notes, "each [frame] has a distinct definition of the issue, of who is responsible, and of how the issue might be resolved" (1991, p. 56). Therefore, it is valuable for advocates to understand the different frames that represent their issues as well as to have some knowledge of the nuances and images that constitute these portrayals. A framing memo lends to this understanding because it maps the arguments, images, and appeals to widely shared principles that many people use to define and discuss an issue. Based on the work of Gamson and Lasch (1983) and Ryan (1991), it is a tool designed to provide an organized visual assessment of the web of arguments surrounding an issue so that those involved in its outcome can begin to determine how it is covered in the media and how they can respond.

A framing memo is a valuable tool for advocates because

it provides a quick and efficient review of public discussion surrounding an issue;

it provides advocates with a means to understand the arguments of the "other side" in addition to—and in relation to—their own;

it helps advocates determine precisely how they want their issue to be represented in the media, and to take strategic steps to effect those portrayals; and

it provides an assessment of the *range* of arguments and images used to describe an issue, unlike a quantitative content analysis that reveals the *number* of particular images or arguments that appear in the media.

How to Create a Framing Memo

The first step is to collect a sample of articles on your issue, taking into consideration the breadth of media sources and viewpoints that you are interested in capturing in your analysis. Collect enough articles to represent the range of arguments surrounding your issue as well as articles that represent a variety of regions and perspectives.

For example, if your issue is widely discussed, then you would need articles from a sample of liberal, moderate, and conservative media sources that have covered your topic—possibly even from a mix of news publications or broadcasts. On the other hand, if your issue affects only a small region or a particular professional group, then you would look for articles from regional media outlets or trade publications. For example, in a framing memo on federal legislation to protect children from residential lead poisoning (the "Real Estate Notification Act"), we reviewed a mix of national newspapers, real estate publications, and law journals to gather a broad range of published perspectives. Consider your needs and audiences in selecting media sources.

Collect as many articles as you can, or as many as you can read and analyze given your time and resources. If you have to limit the size of the sample, decide how many articles you will collect based on your purpose for doing a news analysis: How will the analysis be used? Who is the audience? How much time do you have? You do not want so many articles that the task becomes overwhelming, but you also want enough sources to provide you with a broad assessment of how your issue is portrayed. If you are not sure how many articles are enough, start with a small number and add more as you develop the analysis.

Fortunately, the many computerized databases for print and televised media can ease the search for, and selection of, articles on most issues. In many cases, you can download articles' texts directly to your computer. If you are interested in assessing visuals or the placement of your issue relative to other stories, you will need the original magazine, newspaper, or broadcast.

Next, organize your sample in a systematic way. A pile of newspapers, magazine articles, and videotape transcripts can be mighty unruly. There are many ways to "manage" this kind of data; here are some ideas:

1. Photocopy all of the articles onto paper of the same size. This makes your sample easier to handle, while allowing you to make notes on a working set and still maintain a "clean" set for presentation or future analysis.

2. Order your sample by source, by date, or both. This allows you to see regional or outlet-specific trends as well as to observe the progression of debate around your issue.

3. Number or index the articles so that you can remove and replace them with ease.

4. Build a spreadsheet with the numbered articles and their dates along one axis and the images, arguments, or quotes you wish to "map" along the other axis. This record permits a rapid visual assessment of the breadth and progression of debate on an issue as well as providing a tidy index for subsequent referral.

Once the sample has been compiled, read the articles through three times:

1. First reading: You want to get a "feel" for how your issue is being represented, so try to suspend your preconceived ideas and read with an open mind—as if you are finding out about the issue for the first time.

2. Second reading: Look *within* each article and make note of the variables, images, and opinions that are being used to frame the issue. It is during this phase that you might create a spreadsheet of variables so you can readily see how the issue is being portrayed. During this reading, pay attention to the presence or absence of the variables you think are important to the issue, such as who is quoted, who is used as a source of information, what words are being used to describe important features of the issue, what arguments are being used, what images are invoked, whether any common "catch phrases" are included, what examples or visuals are used to tell the story, who or what is being offered as the cause of the problem, and who or what is charged with its solution.

   Develop a coding scheme of symbols, numbers, or colors so that you can easily refer to your sample and identify the presence of a particular variable. Consider using a binary "1 or 0" coding scheme and use the functions of the spreadsheet program to add all the 1's at the bottom of each column. You may also find a "notes" column to be very helpful in keeping track of useful quotes and other illustrative examples within articles (see Figure 46.1). This coding scheme will help you to quickly extract the citations you will need to support your analysis.

3. Third reading: Look *across* the sample of articles for commonalties in the representations you identified during the second reading. What patterns emerge? Are any representations less common but particularly striking? What factors have been excluded from the discussion?

The coding scheme you develop should consist of descriptive categories that illustrate the frames surrounding your issue. Depending on your issue and the purpose of the framing memo, there may be many ways to organize the observations. For example, in a framing memo on children's issues in newspapers nationwide, we used a general "issue" category and then stratified by "youth" and "children." We have also found the matrices described by Gamson and Lasch (1983, pp. 410-411) and Ryan (1991, pp. 242-245) to be very useful for specific issues with

Notes (by article):

- "They all begin as sweet, gurgling little babies. But somewhere along the line, they go bad..." "their propensity to violence is really alarming..." "criminal genes" Time in CYA is training to be evil
- "lost their right to live" "should be executed".
- "especially young gang members"
- REVOLVING DOOR – GOOD QUOTE
- "Sexual predators"
- "Criminals are getting ever younger, ever more violent, more brazen and more vicious", Wilson said. "The violence has got to end."
- "Opposes banning handguns because law-abiding Californians need firearms... themselves" (Wilson)– exp...

		Article		
		Headline	Date	
		Teens on th	12/28/93	
		They've lost	12/28/93	
		"3 Strikes" i	12/29/93	
		Police supp	12/29/93	
		Wilson Urge	12/30/93	
		Wilson urge	12/30/93	
		Wilson Urge	12/30/93	
			12/30/93	

Coding categories (rows):

Source lang.
- Animal Reference
- Quote: Family of victim
- Quote: Advocate
- Quote: Public figure
- Quote: Police/Gvt official

Resp.
- Moral decay is cause
- Other Social Solutions needed
- Social Systems are cause
- Gun control is needed

Position On Three Strikes — Against
- Poor Public Policy
- Election Year Tactic
- Costs Too Much
- Not Specific Enough/Elder Care
- "Petty thief caught"
- Incarceration won't work
- Caution/neutral

Position On Three Strikes — Support
- (mention) NRA
- Criminal Control, not Gun Control
- Try juvenile as adult
- Depraved Individuals are cause
- Incarceration as treatment
- Not Tough Enough
- Enough is Enough
- Feral Youth/Youth mentioned

- Frame
- Type

Figure 46.1. Sample of Framing Memo Coding Spreadsheet

strong positions on opposing sides. This format was well suited to news analyses of California's Three Strikes incarceration debate and the federal legislation to protect children from residential lead poisoning. The following components are those adapted from Ryan's framework using examples from the "Real Estate Notification Act" framing memo. You could use these as a starting point for organizing the observations you will draw from your sample:

- *Core position* is the argument that the evidence, opinions, and examples are compiled to support. For example, "Childhood lead poisoning in public housing is a serious threat demanding immediate attention."
- *Metaphor* is the analogy or comparison offered in support of the core position. For example, "Dust from leaded paint is a time bomb waiting to explode."
- *Catch phrase* is a brief summary of the core position that will remain in the minds of the audience. For example, "Children have a right to be safe in their own homes."
- *Visual image* is invoked to "paint a picture" of the core position for the audience. For example, "Dust from lead paint is falling from cracked ceilings into babies' cribs."
- *Source of the problem* describes what or who is attributed with causing the problem. This is often a broad category or a societal institution combined with a judgment, such as "politically motivated housing officials refusing to take action," or "taxpayers unwilling to look beyond their own needs to the broader social good."
- *Predicted outcome* is what those advocating the core position expect will happen if the situation continues unaltered. For example, "Health care costs for children with environmental lead poisoning will skyrocket."
- *Appeal to principle* is the link between the core position and some widely valued ideal. For example, "Children deserve protection."

These components of frames are easy to work with when they are organized into a framing matrix.[2] (See Appendix.)

If you have created a spreadsheet during your readings, you can readily see what portrayals are present in your sample and how often, and use this information in building the matrix. Look not only for which arguments and representations are most frequent but also for those that are rare, yet striking, in their imagery.

For example, in a framing analysis of "youth-related vandalism" stories, you may observe that in a small percentage of articles, law enforcement officials were quoted blaming "wild youth" for the cause of the problem. It may also be important that youth themselves were seldom used as sources in the articles, yet whenever they were cited, the selected quotes were defiant and "anti-authority" in nature.

An important part of developing the framing memo is applying your intimate knowledge of the issue to the analysis to determine *what is not there*. On your first reading, you approached the articles as if you knew nothing about the issue. Now you articulate everything that is missing from the stories based on your knowledge and experience. Answer the question: What is not included here but should be? If you are using a framing matrix, start with the core position and fill in all of the categories until you have a complete argument.

For example, in our framing memo on federal legislation to protect children from residential lead poisoning, we observed that one of the missing frames was "Purchasers' Right to Know." As we defined this frame, the core position was that home buyers and renters have a right to be informed of lead levels on properties as well as to be told of the potential hazards that they and their families face should they live there. We determined that the catch phrase for this frame might be "let the buyer beware," and the visual image would be of wise consumers making reasoned and informed decisions. This "missing" frame would appeal to citizens' desire to be fully informed about their investments.

Now that you have a synopsis of the range of arguments used to discuss your issue, use examples and quotes from your sample to describe your observations in text. Depending on your purpose for the framing memo, you may find it useful to present the frames in terms of the most to least frequently presented arguments, paired as opposing sides in a debate, or simply as a range of opinions on an issue. Find the best examples of each of the arguments' components from within your sample and use these to illustrate your findings. Finally, add in the "missing" arguments you developed and reinforce these with data you have on the issue.

The result of your work is a concise analysis of news coverage on an issue that can be used by a number of audiences. You will also have a comprehensive understanding of how your issue has been treated in the past so that you can better anticipate how it will be handled in the future.

The goal is to create something that will be useful as you and others advocate for your issue. A framing memo may help you organize your thinking as you prepare to give testimony to the legislature, write a letter to the editor, answer journalists' questions, or talk with other advocates.

Finally, remember this is simply a guide. Keep your objectives clearly in mind and adapt these ideas as you see fit.

Appendix
Real Estate Notification Act Framing Matrix

Frames in Support of Real Estate Notification

Frame	Core Position	Metaphor	Catch-Phrases	Visual Images	Source of the Problem	Predicted Outcome if Not Enacted	Appeal to Principle
Get the Lead Out	Childhood lead poisoning is an urgent problem that demands serious and immediate solutions. There is no time to lose	"Many children are living in a sea of lead."	"The effects of lead are glaring."	Lead-based paint chips falling into food and bath water	Insidious sources of lead in homes, and few legislative measures to protect families	Millions of innocent children will be poisoned, and society will suffer the widespread social and economic consequences	Protection of innocent children; citizens' right to secure homes
No One is Safe	Although much low income housing is lead-laden, more affluent neighborhoods are also lead traps -- and these residents don't even think to be afraid	Pervasive, insidious threat	"Lead is a problem all over the country." / "The paint is still there and need not be falling in chips to be a hazard dust is all it takes to poison a child"	"Every time the door opens and closes, or a window is raised and lowered, you're putting [lead] dust into the atmosphere."	Poor understanding of the problem's extent. Technology that is not sensitive or reliable enough to indicate danger areas -- there should be blanket regulations which protect all people, regardless of where they live	Children in supposedly 'safe' areas being tested with 250 times the 'safe' blood lead level	Fear of being lulled into a false sense of security
Small Price to Pay	The minor inconvenience incurred by Real Estate Notification legislation is a pittance in comparison to society's obligation to protect its children	This legislation provides a high return on investment in exchange for mild inconveniences	"It should be a small burden to provide the information about known lead threats"	Sellers and brokers enduring minor inconveniences so that children can grow up healthy	Selfish property sellers and brokers	Expensive and tragic adverse effects of childhood lead poisoning	Economic efficiency
Benefit to Home Sellers and Agents	This legislation will actually benefit property sellers and agents as it will relieve them of the burden of liability after a sale is completed	A good deal all around	"The rule was crafted with the interests of the home industry and public health in mind"	Legislation working to protect all parties involved in the home selling/buying exchange	Until now, no legislation existed to relieve the tricky situation in which buyers, sellers, and agents are uncertain of their rights and obligations	Poisoned children, and liability suits run amok	Covering all the bases
Step in the Right Direction	This legislation is a good step forward, but a far cry from a solution to the problem -- we need to be certain that aspects of this legislation do not backfire (in terms of limiting liability of agents, landlords and owners)	Better than nothing	This is a 'mini step forward.'	Advocates supporting legislation with guarded optimism	Real estate brokers, lenders, insurance companies, sellers and landlords can't be trusted to do on their own what is best for children	Nothing will be done to protect families from the threat of lead	Distrust of legislative will

428

Frames in Opposition to Real Estate Notification

Frame	Core Position	Metaphor	Catch-Phrases	Visual Images	Source of the Problem	Predicted Outcome if Enacted	Appeal to Principle
Loose Legal Language	"The language of this legislation is so poor that most anything could result from it	"A risk we can't afford to take."	This legislation is "wide open to convenient interpretations [leading to lawsuits]."	Runaway train of ill-effects	Poorly written policy born of legislators advancing their own agendas and regulations written in haste	Housing market chaos	Avoid chaos
Invitation to Litigation	This legislation invites petty litigation and opportunities for greedy lawyers	"Last year a mother of a toddler with a lead level of *zero* won a $9,000 settlement... against her landlord." [emphasis original]	"The floodgates are open."	"The number of cases is increasing at a staggering rate, with owners, property managers, lenders and insurers left to struggle along with little guidance."	Legislation with loopholes, ambivalent language, and opportunistic lawyers	Courts and related resources tied up; housing market at a stand-still	Widespread distrust of tort cases, crafty lawyers, and flawed legal procedure
Developers Discouraged	Developers and remodelers will be discouraged from coming to areas with known toxic lead levels	Developers turning away from older communities	"I'll take a raincheck," one developer said."	Once thriving communities turning to rows of vacant, deteriorating housing and businesses	Excessive costs and hassles. "Complying with all lead regulations would have added $3-4,000 to the cost of rehabilitating each apartment."	Depressed housing starts; economic devastation of communities	Rational economic decision
No Choice But to Close the Door	"Renters with children under six say they now have trouble finding places to live. Landlords, fearing lawsuits and unable to afford lead-paint abatement often turn them away, even though it is illegal."	"A giant step backwards"	This will backfire against the very people that the legislators are ostensibly trying to protect	Renters with children out in the cold	Politicians' disregard for unintended consequences	Families unable to find housing	Misguided legislation
Abatement Abuse	This is simply too much ... yet another instance of government housing regulations upon the piles of legislation already present	Another asbestos nightmare	It's one of those laws that is so progressive, it's Fascist."	Armies of abatement squads descending upon properties, armed with government mandates	Government intrusion	The door is opened for government to impose even more restrictions, which will ultimately destroy the housing market	Aversion to government intruding upon everyday lives

SOURCE: Adapted from C. Ryan (1991). *Prime Time Activism*. Boston, MA: South End Press.

Frames in Opposition to Real Estate Notification

Frame	Core Position	Metaphor	Catch-Phrases	Visual Images	Source of the Problem	Predicted Outcome if Enacted	Appeal to Principle
Much Ado About Nothing	There is no convincing evidence that lead paint in homes is a health risk. This is a politically motivated strategy to win favor for the EPA and its supporters -- and everyone, including the health community, is being duped	"Well-meaning fanatics"	"There is no identifiable man culprit in lead poisoning." "The scientific jury is still out."	Massive waste of society's time, money and energy -- all for no benefit	Overstated threat -- an EPA con-job to create hysteria, so that the agency gets more funding and its agenda is advanced	"The hardships caused by the act and the proposed rule may prompt the general public for the first time to view with skepticism the risk assessment methods used by federal environmental and health agencies"	Government agencies act in their own best interests, not those of the public-at-large
Landlords Take the Fall	Landlords should not bear the fault for materials in the houses they did not build	Landlords as scapegoats	This is another opportunity to stick it to the landlords	Accusative fingers pointing at landlords demanding that they remedy situations they did not cause, or else face economic devastation	Flawed legislation "The court held that if high lead levels exist, landlords automatically lost their right to rent monies."	Landlords will go broke, or give up entirely "Thousands of units of residential housing stand empty, because the cost of abatement of lead-based paint exceeds the value of housing."	Don't blame poor business people for something they did not cause. Reasonable allowances for freedom of commerce
Broker Burden	Brokers saddled with mountains of paperwork and legal guidelines to navigate will turn the real estate market into a living nightmare	This is "the straw that breaks the camel's back"	Brokers can be held liable for their "innocent misrepresentations"	Real estate brokers buried under mountains of paperwork, and unable to move their properties	Legislation which mandates the "duty to disclose defects on premises, when they could not be discovered in the course of a reasonable inspection" [emphasis original]	There will be an "expanding range of liability for deals gone sour"	Right to earn a living without undue burden
Home Sellers' Hardship	Sellers will be completely frustrated by the mountains of paperwork, increased costs, and increased time required to sell their properties -- properties which will likely command lower prices as a result	Home sellers getting the short end of the stick "Sellers will be subject to scrutiny, paperwork and penalties."	"If the new Congress is seriously looking to limit costly federal regulatory intrusions into ordinary citizens' lives, here's one the lawmakers can catch before it affects millions of home sellers each year."	"For sellers of 'target' homes, the rules require you to provide all would-be purchasers a four-part disclosure form warning of the potential presence of lead-based paint somewhere in the house, simply because it was built before 1978."	More government intrusion	Citizens with older homes will be unable to sell them. "No matter where you live, all you need to become subject to an extensive new set of federal oversight procedures is to be the owner of a residence constructed before 1978."	Distrust of over-regulation. Homeowners' right to sell their homes without unreasonable intrusion
Paint Chips as Bargaining Chips	This legislation opens the door for buyers to leverage lower prices and cheat sellers because lead might be present on a property	Opportunistic buyers using this as a means to negotiate sales terms or to weasel out of deals for which they have developed "cold feet"	"Now for the kicker: the law prohibits the buyer from becoming obligated under any sales contract, unless the seller allows a 10-day period to check for the presence of lead based hazards."	Buyers plotting to leverage better deals or to escape otherwise binding agreements	This plays into the hands of crafty home buyers who want to weasel out of existing deals or to negotiate lower purchase prices	Home sellers, real estate brokers, and landlords will be manipulated and taken advantage of	People will take advantage of every opportunity to get a better deal

Notes

1. There is an extensive literature on the framing of issues in news stories. In particular, this paper is drawn from the work of: Gitlin (1980), Gamson & Lasch (1983), Gamson (1988), Ryan (1991), and Wallack, Dorfman, Jernigan, & Themba (1993).

2. Gamson and Lasch (1983) refer to this tool as a "signature matrix."

References

Amaize, O., & Faber, R. J. (1983). Advertising by national governments in leading United States, Indian and British newspapers. *Gazette, 32,* 87-101.

Anderson, B. (1991). *Imagined communities: Reflections on the origin and spread of nationalism* (Rev. ed.). New York: Verso.

Baumgartner, F. R., & Jones, B. D. (1993). *Agendas and instability in American politics.* Chicago: University of Chicago Press.

Bosso, C. J. (1989). Setting the agenda: Mass media and the discovery of famine in Ethiopia. In M. Margolis & G. Mauser (Eds.), *Manipulating public opinion.* Pacific Grove, CA: Brooks/Cole.

Campbell, J. L. (1988). *Collapse of an industry: Nuclear power and the contradictions of U.S. policy.* Ithaca, NY: Cornell University Press.

Choate, P. (1990). *Agents of influence.* New York: Knopf.

Crossette, B. (1995, Jan. 3). U.N. leaders to call for changes in peacekeeping. *New York Times,* p. A3.

Develop a coding scheme of symbols, numbers, or colors so that you can easily refer to your sample and identify the presence of a particular variable. Consider using a binary "1 or 0" coding scheme and use the functions of the spreadsheet program to add all the 1's at the bottom of each column. You may also find a "notes" column to be very helpful in keeping track of useful quotes and other illustrative examples within articles (see Figure 47.1). This coding scheme will help you to quickly extract the citations you will need to support your analysis.

Dorman, W. A., & Livingston, S. (1994). News and historical content: The establishing phase of the Persian Gulf policy debate. In W. L. Bennett & D. L. Paletz (Eds.), *Taken by storm: The media, public opinion and U.S. foreign policy in the Gulf War* (pp. 63-81). Chicago: University of Chicago Press.

Gamson, W. A. (1988). A constructionist approach to mass media and public opinion. *Symbolic Interaction, 11*(2), 161-174.

Gamson, W. A., & Lasch, K. E. (1983). The political culture of social welfare policy. In S. E. Spiro & E. Yuchtman-Yar (Eds.), *Evaluating the welfare state: Social and political perspectives* (pp. 397-416). New York: Academic Press.

Gitlin, T. (1980). *The whole world is watching: Mass media in the making and unmaking of the new left.* Berkeley, CA: University of California Press.

Hilgartner, S., & Bosk, C. L. (1988). The rise and fall of social problems: A public arenas model. *American Journal of Sociology, 94,* 53-78.

Iyengar, S. (1991). *Is anyone responsible? How television frames political issues.* Chicago: University of Chicago Press.

Iyengar, S., & Simon, A. (1994). News coverage of the Gulf Crisis and public opinion: A study of agenda setting, priming and framing. In W. L. Bennett & D. L. Paletz (Eds.), *Taken by storm: The media, public opinion and U.S. foreign policy in the Gulf War* (pp. 167-185). Chicago: University of Chicago Press.

Kernell, S. (1992). *Going public.* Washington, DC: Congressional Quarterly Press.

Macarthur, J. R. (1992). *Second front: Censorship and propaganda in the Gulf War.* New York: Hill & Wang.

Manheim, J. B. (1994). *Strategic public diplomacy and American foreign policy: The evolution of interest.* New York: Oxford University Press.

Manheim, J. B., & Albritton, R. B. (1984). Managing national images: International public relations and media agenda setting. *American Political Science Review, 78.*

Mueller, J. (1993). American public opinion and the Gulf War. In S. Renshon (Ed.), *The political psychology of the Gulf War: Leaders, publics and the process of conflict* (pp. 199-226). Pittsburgh, PA: University of Pittsburgh Press.

Nelson, B. J. (1984). *Making an issue of child abuse.* Chicago: University of Chicago Press.

Rosen, J. (1992). Politics, vision, and the press: Toward a public agenda for journalism. In P. Taylor & J. Rosen (Eds.), *The old news v. the new news: Press & politics in the 1990s.* New York: 20th Century Fund Press.

Ryan, C. (1991). *Prime time activism: Media strategies for grassroots organizing.* Boston, MA: South End Press.

Schattschneider, E. E. (1960). *The semi-sovereign people.* New York: Holt, Rinehart & Winston.

S.F. police to crack down on 12 violent teenagers. (1994, January 26). *San Francisco Chronicle.*

Wallack, L., Dorfman, L., Jernigan, D., and Themba, M. (1993). *Media advocacy and public health: Power for prevention.* Newbury Park, CA: Sage.

Weart, S. R. (1988). *Nuclear fear: A history of images.* Cambridge, MA: Harvard University Press.

Wilcox, C., Ferrara, J., & Allsop, D. (1991). *Before the rally: The dynamics of attitudes toward the Gulf Crisis before the war.* Paper presented at the Annual Meeting of the American Political Science Association, Washington, DC.

Wright, D. (1988). *Understanding intergovernmental relations.* Pacific Grove, CA: Brooks/Cole.

Name Index

435

Subject Index

443